PORNOGRAPHY IN AMERICA

A Reference Handbook

Other Titles in ABC-CLIO's
CONTEMPORARY
WORLD ISSUES
Series

Affirmative Action, Lynne Eisaguirre
AIDS Crisis in America, Second Edition, Eric K. Lerner and Mary Ellen Hombs
Censorship, Mary E. Hull
Children's Rights, Beverly C. Edmonds and William R. Fernekes
Domestic Violence, Margi Laird McCue
Feminism, Judith Harlan
Gay and Lesbian Rights, David E. Newton
Hate Crimes, Donald Altschiller
Human Rights, Second Edition, Nina Redman and Lucille Whalen
New Slavery, Kevin Bales
Prisons in America, Debra L. Stanley and Nicole Hahn Rafter
Privacy Rights in America, Leigh Glenn
Sexual Harassment, Second Edition, Lynne Eisaguirre

Books in the Contemporary World Issues series address vital issues in today's society such as terrorism, sexual harassment, homelessness, AIDS, gambling, animal rights, and air pollution. Written by professional writers, scholars, and nonacademic experts, these books are authoritative, clearly written, up-to-date, and objective. They provide a good starting point for research by high school and college students, scholars, and general readers, as well as by legislators, businesspeople, activists, and others.

Each book, carefully organized and easy to use, contains an overview of the subject; a detailed chronology; biographical sketches; facts and data and/or documents and other primary-source material; a directory of organizations and agencies; annotated lists of print and nonprint resources; a glossary; and an index.

Readers of books in the Contemporary World Issues series will find the information they need in order to better understand the social, political, environmental, and economic issues facing the world today.

PORNOGRAPHY IN AMERICA

A Reference Handbook

Joseph W. Slade

CONTEMPORARY WORLD ISSUES

ABC-CLIO

Santa Barbara, California
Denver, Colorado
Oxford, England

Library of Congress Cataloging-in-Publication Data

Slade, Joseph W.
    Pornography in America : a reference handbook / Joseph W. Slade.
        p.   cm. — (ABC-CLIO's contemporary world issues series)
    ISBN 1-57607-085-9 (alk. paper)
    1. Pornography. I. Title. II. Contemporary world issues.

    HQ471.S59 2000
    363.4'7—dc21   00-035548

06 05 04 03 02 01 00   10 9 8 7 6 5 4 3 2 1

ABC-CLIO, Inc.
130 Cremona Drive, P.O. Box 1911
Santa Barbara, California 93116-1911

This book is printed on acid-free paper ∞
Manufactured in the United States of America

For
Joseph W. Slade, IV

Contents

Laws and Legislation, 228

Reports, 231

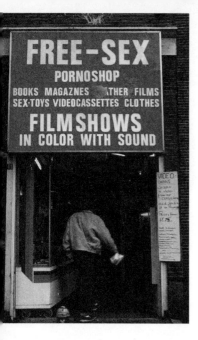

Preface

In this volume I have tried to present aspects of pornography as dispassionately as an old-fashioned liberal can. The subject does not lack for moralists and does not need another. By any standard, a great deal of pornography is garbage: distasteful, mean-spirited, ugly. There is probably no image so vile that some pornographer will not make use of it, just as there is probably no response so stupid that some censor will not embrace it. Nevertheless, as the new millennium drifts in on a sea of messages, I am conscious that the controversies once spawned by pornography seem to be losing their force. The Information Era has domesticated sexual representation as it has almost every other kind of expression.

It seems useful nonetheless to examine opinions. The commentary on pornography is almost as vast as the sexual expression produced by pornographers themselves, and most of it has approximately the same merit. Too often critics have other agendas in mind, and in speaking of pornography many really wish to establish their views on art or politics or gender issues. I have tried to select materials that actually confront sexual expression rather than pontificate about it.

Joseph W. Slade

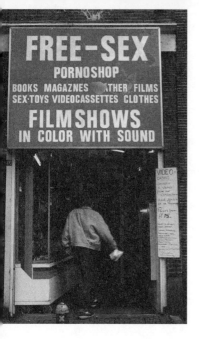

Introduction

1

The Cultural Dynamics of Sexual Expression

In March 1999, a month chosen randomly, several events illustrated the accelerating influence of graphic sexual representation on contemporary American cultural life. On Broadway, *Closer*, a British play starring Natasha Richardson, opened at the Music Box Theater. Just before the opening, *Vanity Fair* said that the drama "epitomizes a burgeoning genre—the X-rated sexual duel, fought without romance or illusion—that has injected the spirit of pornography straight into the cultural mainstream."[1] That same month the *New York Times* respectfully reviewed Catherine Breillat's new film, *Romance*, as it moved into limited American distribution. The review quoted the French director as believing that men and women vibrate between extremes of morality in motion best depicted through sexual images— "what is most trivial, most obscene, most debased and most beautiful in human beings." During the film, its protagonist, played by mainstream actress Caroline Ducey, has actual intercourse with Rocco Siffredi, star of dozens of hard-core features in Europe and America.[2] In its March 8 issue, the *New Yorker* carried an upscale household lighting retailer's advertisement for lamps. The ad's text (in its entirety) quoted Gloria Leonard, a celebrated performer in hardcore films: "The difference between pornography and erotica is lighting."[3] Two weeks later, the same magazine printed James Atlas's survey of academics who study pornography as a key to gender and sexual roles in America.[4] Galleries in Manhattan mounted shows of explicit photos, sculpture, and paintings by various international and American artists during the month. Bloomingdale's stores featured fashions inspired by Tom of Finland, perhaps the most notorious of all gay pornographic artists. These examples—and they could be multiplied beyond counting—mark the phases of a dynamic by which previously taboo sexual representations routinely energize artistic and intellectual endeavors.

Considered dispassionately, pornography's value may lie in its ability to serve as a fresh source of ideas and images in a culture whose mainstream relentlessly co-opts its edges. The issue then may become whether pornography can retain its marginality—continue to be outrageous—in an Information Age that commodifies everything. After tracking phases of a similar dynamic, the *Economist* predicted future equilibrium, a state in which pornography within a few years will devolve into a commonplace entertainment component of a global information economy, subject to the same imperatives of production, distribution, and consumption as television sitcoms, gardening texts, or computer games.[5]

Not everyone agrees that such a dynamic is in operation, let alone that it is healthy. Even among those who concede that pornography continuously sexualizes culture, Americans of various political persuasions regard the results as deleterious, ugly, and perhaps dangerous—hardly positive and enriching. Moderate Americans may well recoil from a popular culture that treasures the phrase "it sucks," Monica Lewinsky's thong underwear, telephone sex, tawdry romance novels, steamy soap operas, Internet smut, the *Jerry Springer Show*, and Bob Dole's ads for Viagra. Sexual expression, its critics charge, degrades experience, demeans women, affronts religious sensibilities, and generally trashes social structures already fragile to begin with.

However one thinks of pornography, social tolerance has elevated sexual expression to new levels. If reporters on radio and television seem giddy with post-Clinton freedom to say the word "penis" on air, if mainstream movie actors glibly murmur obscenities as they pull off each other's clothes, then perplexed journalists also labor to translate these vulgarities *and* Freudian, Marxist, poststructuralist, and feminist reflections on sexual expression into a middle-class language that enables Americans to think about pornography in ways they never have before. Although few Americans publicly endorse pornography, consumers spend somewhere between $8 billion and $10 billion a year on sexual representations of a fairly explicit sort. Comparing that figure to the more than $36 billion that Americans annually spend on hamburgers from such emporia as Burger King and McDonald's[6] puts this number in perspective, but it is still pretty impressive. In any case, disputes have moved beyond familiar accusations of hypocrisy and ignorance and the usual counter-charges of tastelessness and false sophistication.

Cautious Definitions

Pornography (or "porn") usually refers to representations designed to arouse and give sexual pleasure to those who read, see, hear, or handle them. Although sexual stimulation would seem to be a splendid goal, it is not always so regarded in a society still characterized as puritanical. Opponents often avoid dealing with the benefits of arousal in favor of attributing unflattering motives to makers of pornography, whereas producers of pornography themselves may cloud matters by insisting that their materials are educational rather than deliberately stimulating. Because arguments over sexual expression mask issues of politics, religion, gender, race, class and (above all) sexuality, irrelevant claims and assertions are not merely typical but seemingly essential to any discussion of pornography. At times, the confusion seems a deliberate means of demonizing enemies, achieving political advantage, or making a profit.

In a more general sense, the meaning of the term *pornographic* constantly shifts along a vast continuum moving between two equally slippery concepts, the *erotic* and the *obscene*. An erotic representation is usually considered socially acceptable. Associated with upper-class sensibilities, eroticism is primarily esthetic; erotic materials, say many critics, begin by stimulating physical responses, then transcend them, leaving a mildly sexual glow that one can speak of in polite company. Gloria Steinem, among others, claims that the differences between pornographic and erotic are always obvious.[7] Al Goldstein, among others, maintains that such descriptions are biased by gender, class, and factors such as personal preference: "Eroticism," says Goldstein, "is what turns me on. Pornography is what turns *you* on."[8]

At the other end of the scale are obscene representations, which are considered to be not socially acceptable. In a legal sense, obscenity denotes criminality, and its cultural connotation is lower-class vulgarity. In the United States, obscene material can be prosecuted because of its nastiness, its demeaning "prurience," or its sheer inhumanness. By contrast, pornography is entirely legal. Sexual expression is free to arouse, but only within limits, and those limits, which are set by concepts of obscenity, erode only over time. "I know it when I see it," Supreme Court Justice Potter Stewart once said of obscenity. Because Stewart was virtually blind, his comment illustrates the difficulty of deciding what is obscene rather than pornographic. Stewart's remark is also as close as the American judicial system has come to a definitive statement on the issue. If a representation transgresses against sexual norms (that themselves change), courts may judge it obscene; if it does not push against boundaries, however, it may not arouse. In contrast, when a representation once called obscene becomes so widespread that taboos against it weaken, it moves first into the category of the pornographic, then of the erotic. From the domain of the erotic, the representation (a public kiss, for example) can pass into the realm of the commonplace.

The problem, of course, is that not everyone uses the same measurements. Some Americans believe that sex is a necessary evil, sanctioned only by marriage for purposes of reproduction, and condemn sexual representations under any circumstances. At the other extreme, those who concede that sex can and should be recreational may nonetheless find some types of representation disturbing. A reader comfortable with a sexual scene in a novel, for example, may be repelled by the same scene in a movie or on stage. Others attempt to distinguish between degrees of explicitness—how much flesh is visible, say, or how vulgar a spoken word, or what kind of sexual act is depicted. For most Americans, pornography means peep shows, striptease, live sex acts, hardcore videos, adult cable programming, sexual aids and devices, explicit telephone and computer messages, adult magazines, and raunchy fiction. Conservatives might add prime-time television programming, soap operas, Music Television (MTV) and rock music, romance novels, fashion magazines, and all R-rated movies. Conflating sexuality and violence leads some critics to think of sexual representations as inherently aggressive. Others, noticing that most sexual representations contain no violence, condemn only those examples that mix the two. As Walter Kendrick has pointed out, pornography is not a thing but an argument.[9]

To avoid contentiousness, some theorists prefer a neutral term such as sexual materials over the charged word *pornography*. In any case, only a few things seem clear. First, what seems pornographic to one person will not necessarily seem so to another. Second, pornography is not monolithic: representation occurs in many media, and it adopts many forms and genres. Third, no group, gendered or otherwise, has a monopoly on sexual expression or representation. Fourth, our social, esthetic, political, legal, and economic attitudes toward pornography both affect and draw on complex responses to gender and sexuality. Fifth, pornography, an attempt at communication, conveys a host of messages, many of them contradictory. Some of those messages, in fact, are ancient.

Pornography as Folklore, or Why Pornography Is Important

Pornography *and* the debate that it occasions enshrine the sexual folklore of the species—the myths, legends, beliefs, customs, and mores that work both for and against establishing norms of behavior. Pornographic representations often contain archetypal stories of women and men in heterosexual and homosexual acts, often-told narratives of smutty humor and sexual anxiety, and endlessly recurrent motifs of desire, frustration, and satisfaction. Traditional folklore embodies and stores obscenity, the (originally) oral sources of "low," vulgar, even scabrous forms of expression. Modern media transmit archetypal pornographic images: males with enormous penises, women with dangerous vaginas, tales of ingenious seduction and gender trespass. Today's pornographers take filthy jokes, transparent stereotypes, hoary motifs, nasty themes, and quaint sexual notions directly from folklore.

Modern hard-core videos, for example, exhibit a fascination for male ejaculation. Although there are many plausible explanations for the fetish, one recurrent motif alleges the homeopathic properties of semen. Mae West, America's first porn diva, herself a legend, was convinced that sperm kept her skin and bosom healthy, insisted well into old age on daily oral sex with her lovers in order to ensure a fresh supply, and promoted the application of sperm along with her equally fervent trust in high colonics.[10] The prescription was already an old wives' tale even in the time of the Roman Empress Messalina (died A.D. 48), another celebrated partisan of semen. Despite high protein content, semen has no therapeutic or cosmetic value—but that is beside the point. Whether the myth is the result of a male conspiracy or an outgrowth of ancient worship of generative powers or simply a "just so" story, some people find it exciting—and have for thousands of years. Others find these scenes repellent. Class, of course, can affect reception. Vulgar images and vulgar stories—the kind born in folklore—often conflict with more refined, upper-class revisions of sexuality—the nice kind called erotic—especially since the latter types deny the sweaty physicality of intercourse that dirty jokes and stories insist upon.

Telling tales enables people to attribute meaning to subjects such as sexuality and gender even when the meaning is "wrong." One way for Americans to think about sexual representation is to construct stories about pornographers. Stereotypes enable people to deal with aberrations from the norm. The preferred narrative will characterize a mad person, say, as a shaman, a fool, a deviant, a patient, or a criminal. Once the story has been chosen—or more properly, repeated approvingly over time—then the genre's conventions determine the content and structure of experience. So it is with the "pornographer," who may seem to different audiences a romantic like Henry Miller, a misogynist like Larry Flynt, an artist like Eric Fischel, an adolescent like Hugh Hefner, a holy fool like Lenny Bruce, or just a criminal like Reuben Sturman. Each story appeals to specific prejudices.

Variations of folklore also "explain" pornography as a concept. For Americans who define it negatively, *pornography* usually means the sexual expression of "others." For Anthony Comstock, whose name became synonymous with censorship in the United States in the late nineteenth century, pornography was the voice of salacious East European immigrants he thought were poisoning American culture. For the Soviets in the depths of the Cold War, it was the decadence of a capitalism bent on sabotaging socialism (American politicians in turn denounced pornography as a tool of the international communist conspiracy). For radical feminists, pornography is violence against women, the everyday speech of a male society determined to subordinate females. For fundamentalists, pornography is the spearhead of secularization. Afro-Americans object to a racist sexual folklore that stereotypes them as sexually hyperactive, labor advocates resent assumptions that the underclass is promiscuous, and homosexuals complain that *all* of their expression has been denounced as pornographic for decades.

Misconceptions can be laid at many doors. Each generation "reinvents" sexuality and gender, using evidence from laboratories but also documents from popular culture. For all their public assurance, scientists and doctors understand relatively little about the biological basis of human sexuality, still less about gender, and even less about psychological triggers of arousal. Is sexual attraction biologically determined, or is it socially constructed? Does pornography mimic "natural" desire, or fabricate it? It is here, at the juncture of uncertainty and ignorance, that pornography seems most menacing and most entertaining.

In short, "folklore" is a term that we can apply to the understanding of sexuality and gender—if only because their mysteries are so compounded by ignorance—and *also* to our understanding of representations that address sexuality and gender. Legends such as "women prefer men with large penises" can be traced to ancient texts, but newer myths such as "pornography causes rape" spring from equally questionable beliefs. Legends of movie stars making stag films in order to break into Hollywood serve the American impulse to debunk celebrity. Urban myths of "snuff films" function as campfire stories. We uncritically accept stories about alleged harm from opponents of sexual materials, just as we leave unexamined coarse versions of sex promoted by pornographers. To anyone who has looked closely, there are lies—or folklore—on both sides.

Pornography as Technology: Learning Control

Sexual technologies can free people from the burden of unwanted children; alter sex roles; undermine power relationships among classes, races, and genders; sharpen sensitivity to stimuli; and enhance sensation through lubricants, pharmaceuticals, and appliances. Technologies can also dehumanize and oppress by standardizing experience, by emphasizing the unreal, and by intruding on intimate areas of life. Georges Bataille has observed that by divorcing sex from reproduction, technology has made the artificial itself erotic. Paradoxically, desire may be strongest when it is stimulated and gratified by nonhuman means; technology can reduce sex to an erotic calculus.[11] If we think of technology as any means by which a species alters itself or its environment, then pornography is a technology of pleasure. Andrew Ross, an astute critic, dismisses theories of pornography that do not recognize pleasure as the rational basis of sexual representation. Millions of Americans consume pornography not because they are psychologically flawed, criminally inclined, or personally inadequate, Ross believes, but because it makes them feel good, perhaps even human.[12]

At another level, pornography can function as a user's manual for desire. Many sexual representations are "about" control—control not as domination but as expertise, usually rendered as skilled performance. Earlier generations learned through pornography to use birth control technologies. Today pornography teaches Americans about sexual appliances, climax, genital muscular control, oral sex techniques, seduction, positions of intercourse, performance, intimate photography, and the construction of fantasies.

Though only a few forms endorse extreme body modification (as in videos about transsexuals and transgenders), most pornographic genres promote modest sexual engineering within reach of the ordinary citizen. Tens of thousands of Americans now silicone their breasts; inflate their penises; depilate their pubic hair; pierce their nipples, labia, and scrota; and tattoo themselves in intimate places, alterations made popular by pornographic media. Aficionados of pornographic genres may or may not imitate what they see or hear. Watching a performance, appreciating its nuances, as Roland Barthes has observed about wrestling,[13] can be satisfying enough. Fans of pornography may learn to stage-manage their own fantasies, and as a consequence develop a confident sexual consciousness. Or perhaps not. Issues of reproduction aside, sex without love goes against most civilized traditions. Representations make for poor partners and collectively are thin, unsatisfying, and alien. Opponents of pornography may think of sexual technologies as misdirected if not downright sick, and even those otherwise neutral on the subject of sexual representation can usually find plenty of repellent images.

In any case, the reciprocity of sexual representations and communication technologies is complex. On the one hand, technologies transform pornography into esthetic and social issues by mass-producing and then widely distributing sexual expression. Pornography worries people only when it can be reproduced for large audiences and thus can reach "vulnerable" citizens, that is, the young and impressionable, the weak-minded, those prone to antisocial behavior, or just the twit next door. On the other hand, the appeal of pornography—the need to represent and to enjoy those representations—quite literally drives the development of new media. In previous ages, cave painting led to pictures of vaginas and penises, clay tablets to sexy cuneiform, printing to steamy typographies. During the past two decades, erotic applications fueled the evolution of VCRs and computers.[14]

To an extent, any innovation can illustrate Slade's Law: whenever one person invents a technology, another person will invent a sexual use for it. The vulcanization of rubber in 1839 led immediately to the first effective condoms. The bicycle liberated women by providing cheap and efficient transportation; the bicycle seat, seemingly designed to rub against the clitoris, taught them another way to masturbate, much to the consternation of social critics.[15] For other guardians of morality, the backseat of the automobile was a platform for intercourse too easily removed from community surveillance. Conservatives condemned early telephones because they ferried the voices of seducers directly into the homes of vulnerable young women.[16]

Two aspects of communication technologies can be especially disquieting: increased access and ease of decoding. Television commands audiences of millions, rich and poor, young and old, male and female. Virtually every American now has access to the small screen. Moreover, everyone can decipher its messages. The printing press both fostered and demanded literacy, but learning to read still requires years of schooling. By contrast, children easily decode televised images. A self-reflexive medium, television in a sense comes with its own instruction manual. (Newer virtual reality technologies will be still more user friendly in their instant comprehensibility.) Although they have not always thought so, Americans now assume that the training essential to processing written messages arms the reader against seduction by printed erotica, whereas televised sexual messages menace viewers because processing them requires no tutoring. The Attorney General's Commission on Pornography declined to investigate printed pornography on the grounds that it is less a threat to the young than are electronic messages.[17]

Over time, according to the late feminist historian of technology Sally Hacker, patriarchal cultures have gendered technologies by reserving large-scale organization of labor for males. Lesser technologies—"clothing, scents, postures, or numerous social and physical accoutrements"—train women to be attractive, while "sex manuals" train them to be receptive and compliant. Hacker did believe, however, that technology in the form of sexual representations can "degender" social roles; a newer style of eroticism "legitimates a pouting, 'feminine' style for men, and a tougher, teasing, 'masculine' stance for women."[18] Given the widespread assumption that pornography serves only males, Hacker's observation is important.

Scholars agree that pornographic materials carry contradictory messages. Hard-core videos depict behavior that subordinates women yet at the same time urge women to seize sexual autonomy.[19] Romance novels aimed principally at women prize "sensitivity" in men but also delight in depicting males as powerful, aggressive, and protective. Inspected closely, nearly all pornographic genres depict gender instabilities that wobble between gay and straight, between women with masculine characteristics and men with feminine traits, as if to project warring impulses that men and women do not themselves fully understand. Factoring in tastes complicates matters further. Some men enjoy only soft-core scenarios whereas others insist upon gonzo hard-core sequences. And, as Susie Bright has noticed, "Some women want the stars, some the sleaze."[20] Common sense suggests that pornography is first and foremost communication; pornographers want to establish at least a semblance of community centered on a common folklore.

Americans doubtless learn—that is, are programmed by—pornographic messages (and by all other messages they encounter). Some of these are probably "good," such as the assertion of sex as a splendid source of exercise, joy, and spiritual well-being. Some are probably "bad," such as the primacy given to male pleasure or depictions of homosexuality as deviant. Even so, pornographers are hardly obliged to give equal time to clitorises or differently gendered penises. Besides, politically correct sex—a properly multicultural coupling of equals—would doubtless be boring, as in this tongue-in-cheek scenario: "Some people think that eroticism in a feminist utopia would be androgynous, non-violent, soft and fuzzy, and perfectly symmetrical, with both partners doing exactly the same thing for the same amount of time at precisely the same time. You know the myth: two happy significant others of no particular gender meet, like each other, talk, quietly kiss, and disappear between the sheets as the light fades. No lust; no sweat; no power struggle."[21]

While it is easy to lampoon such notions, how pornography "programs" a culture is very much a matter of dispute.

Pornography, Communication, and Politics: Three Views

Sociopolitical theories—as conceptual frameworks mutating over time—govern commentary on pornography. Scholars have recourse to any number of theories, but three models define the spectrum of opinion.

Pornography as Supporter of the Status Quo

Poststructuralist critical and cultural theorists assume that class, ethnicity, and gender stratify society. All forms of communication, including pornography, reinforce such divisions. For poststructuralists, representation is reality. People do not apprehend "reality" directly; all they can know are the languages and images used to describe and represent. Languages are key. Words, for example, are arbitrary; they can be decoupled from the things they represent. Linguistic and visual narratives—the stories we tell—shape interpretations of people, things, and events; those symbol systems, in short, construct meaning. When pornographic representation subordinates women, labels gays and lesbians deviant, and elevates impossible standards of beauty, these "meanings" reflect the arbitrary values dominant in society.

Critical and cultural schools differ chiefly in their estimates of degrees of dominance. All of them attempt to answer a long-standing riddle. It is this: proletariats rarely revolt, despite decades of Marxist and other political experiments. Given the exploitation of one class or one gender by another, why have the oppressed not risen up to throw off their masters? Leaving aside what are sometimes called social transfer payments—social security, unemployment benefits, and access to higher education—the kinds of sops that upper classes throw to lower to buy off resentment—theorists on the left believe that pornographic messages defuse rebellion. In *Eros and Civilization*, for example, Herbert Marcuse insists that a corporate state sells erotic expression as entertainment in order to control fantasies and ensure obedience. Far from fostering rebellion, Marcuse thinks, sexual representations reverse Freudian theories of sublimation: they encourage masturbation instead of action.[22]

Michel Foucault, founder of a poststructuralist school of behaviorism, argues that languages create the framework for thought; it is impossible to think outside states of mind constructed by a culture's symbol systems. Cultures categorize and condemn certain forms of behavior (homosexuality, for example) in order to program and "discipline" sexuality and gender. Foucault, a devotee of sadomasochism, a narrow, quasi-Christian obsession with exaltation and degradation, envisions a society modeled on that branch of pornography. Because citizens internalize "rules," the grammar and syntax of dominance and submission, they do not even require surveillance; without an enormous act of will they cannot think or act independently. Pornography thus perpetuates male superiority, homophobia, racism, and other inequities.

Variations on this theory emphasize hegemony. Representation is hegemonic because it establishes subtle control at a distance.[23] All messages express the will and preferences of dominant classes; expression thus compels assent through language and images that make certain practices and relationships seem reasonable, natural, and desirable. Hegemony is the "other" side of communication: what seems most liberating is actually most restrictive. No one has to enforce interpretations of sex and gender, because audiences willingly endorse them. From that perspective, pornography is simply an instrument of social engineering. Feminists often use the concept of hegemony to explain pornography as the province of males. Sexual expressions compel assent to sexual and gender stereotypes, to standards of beauty and behavior, and to ideals of pleasure and satisfaction. Feminists point out that media distribute messages besotted with metaphors drawn from war, sports, and masculine pursuits, and with language and images that favor powerful men at the same time that they subordinate women. In the face of this onslaught, women grow silent and retreat into "muted" groups, victimized by representation.

According to some poststructuralists, gender is socially constructed; sexuality resides between the legs whereas gender resides between the ears. The debate, of course, recalls older squabbles over nature and nurture. Are people biologically programmed to desire certain objects rather than others, or is desire culturally conditioned, taught, and learned? Is homosexuality genetically determined, for instance, or is it a matter of preference shaped by other factors? Does social control of sexuality—condemning some forms and thereby making them more attractive—really add more than mild zest to a biological urge? Is such control intended to regulate population—or merely state power—through suppressing or encouraging reproduction? Does the state permit expression that encourages masturbation in order to defuse challenges to its authority, as the Frankfurt School maintains? Does the control of erotic expression really bolster religious and other authoritarian institutions? Does eroticization of bodies and consumer goods ensure the triumph of capitalism? Is pornography really equal to all these tasks?

Not surprisingly, sociobiologists and evolutionary psychologists challenge aspects of social construction. Such scientists hold that people follow biological drives toward reproduction and argue that representations in many ways mimic natural behavior. (Many other scientists hold that nature and nurture both operate.) Some feminists condemn science (a "masculine" pursuit) for suggesting that genetics determines gender, or for ascribing evolutionary significance to features such as breasts and buttocks. Radical antipornography feminists in general ignore biology except as a source of inequity that is accentuated and directed by pornography.

One need not agree with poststructuralist analyses to appreciate that the value of such theories is their insistence that *different groups interpret pornography differently*. Women, ethnic groups, and homosexuals will find themes and motifs invisible to European American heterosexual males (and vice versa). Truth is not the issue, since truth—by poststructuralist definition—is simply the interpretation of whatever group holds the stage. In such a universe there can be few revolutionary ideas, since the idea of revolution itself is defined by whatever class is in power, and pornography is the last place that subordinates would expect to find insurgency. Nonetheless, when cultural critics "interrogate" pornography, they keep it at arm's length, shy away from discussing specific sexual acts, rarely admit to being aroused by representations, and avoid the precision of vernacular languages. Their theories sometimes resemble the protective clothing donned by those who handle radioactive isotopes, an implicit acknowledgment of pornography's dangerous power.

Pornography as Revolutionary

If poststructuralist cultural theorists adopt a top-down model of political power, historians who link pornography to the rise of democracy prefer a bottom-up orientation. In their version of events, a middle class struggling to establish itself wielded lower-class vulgarity to destroy pretense and humble feudal aristocrats.

For three hundred years, beginning in 1500, writers and artists used explicit sexual expression to undermine religious and political authoritarianism. By subverting standards of "decency" (a marker of class), radicals opened avenues of freedom. Pornography thus joined forces with evolving technology and industrialization, secularism and science, urbanization and law, realism and individualism to invent modernity. Most historians who link liberty and licentiousness[24] think that pornography shaped the political rebelliousness and liberal consciousness of the Enlightenment until commercialization blunted its political edge at the end of the eighteenth century.[25] As the intellectual ferment of the eighteenth century gave way to the capitalism of the nineteenth, a strengthened middle class began to cloak itself in respectability and abandon its vulgar lower-class tools. When artists adopted formal standards, they outlawed erotic materials.[26]

At this point scholars part company. One group says that as literacy spread to the masses, middle-class males tried to keep privileged information (e. g., sexual expertise) from falling into the hands of women and the less-educated.[27] Suppressing sexual expression cloaked sex itself in mystery that made it exciting, and reserving pornography for himself bolstered the middle-class male's sense of entitlement. A second group says that pornography retained its democratic power precisely because it was forced underground. Blasphemous and obscene speech helped secure democratic rights well into the nineteenth century,[28] and even into the twentieth. Today pornographic genres still teach Americans that spheres of privacy where sexuality can flourish must be kept distinct from realms of public life where tyrants trivialize the sexuality of citizens. Middle-class advertising and cultural messages relentlessly infantilize Americans; pornography has at least the merit of trying to get beyond such messages and thus helps to shape a more rational community.[29]

Pornography still draws language and themes from the economic underclass.[30] When the audio industry first released recordings of rap music, which originated in ghettos, outraged critics condemned lyrics as pornographic or obscene, especially those songs that denigrated women or called for "offing" police. Now, although notoriety still tinges performers and lyrics, rap music energizes hybrid forms of music. The question is, Does the process reflect the infusion of revolutionary ideas into the larger culture or, given the speed with which the culture has assimilated it, does the process illustrate the power of the establishment to defuse such messages, co-opt them through commerce, and use the process to support the status quo? Are rappers merely themselves exploited?

Again, common sense suggests that communication is complicated. "Pornographic" lyrics, books, or videos may carry traces of class and gender prejudices and simultaneously carry messages that subvert the culture in other ways. Pornographic genres have often satirized established ideas, often by parodying middle-class icons. "Tijuana bibles" debunked dominant ideas and assumptions during the 1920s and 1930s. One of the very first stag films, *El Satario* (Argentina, 1912/13), lampooned Nijinsky's Ballet Russe in general and his adaptation of Stravinsky's *Afternoon of a Faun* in particular.[31] Today pornography sniggers at hypocritical politicians, ministers, and bureaucrats; E-mail delivers a thousand dirty jokes the morning after some authority figure makes a fool of himself. Pornographic performers parody celebrity itself as a dominant ethos of American culture. For a pornographer, a diamond is just a rhinestone; to think otherwise is vanity. Pornographers are Kenneth Starrs, certain that in prurience there lurks truth.

But overuse blunts pornography's political edge. After special prosecutor Kenneth Starr detailed the sex between President Bill Clinton and White House intern Monica Lewinsky, a writer for the *New York Times* condemned Starr's report as a version of the *Malleus Maleficarum*, the witch-hunting text of the Inquisition.[32] A better comparison, however, would be the anonymous *The Amorous Intrigues of Aaron Burr* (1848?), one of endless attacks on prominent Americans.[33] When Larry Flynt retaliated against Starr by publishing exposés of Republican leaders in *Hustler* magazine, he was merely continuing an American tradition. Jeffersonian Democrats and Hamiltonian Federalists argued over whose candidates were the most sexually dissolute, just as did Jacksonians and Whigs. Dust thrown up by these battles obscures paradoxes. For example, during the 1840s, radical Democrats wrote pornographic books accusing the privileged of sexual degeneracy. But because publishers charged a lot for books with obvious sex appeal, only the wealthy could afford them. Then reformers sneered at the affluent for reading pornography. Aristocrats in their turn used explicit images to lambast the Democrats for writing filth for its own sake, and so on. Today, radical feminists attack males as sexual swine; outraged males attack radical feminists as sexual perverts. It would be convenient if pornography were the property of insurgents, but it seems to have devolved into a weapon for almost any group choosing to wield it, the more trivially the better. For the politically inclined, a dirty mind will doubtless remain a joy forever. To the degree that pornography retains a political dimension, however, it has been submerged in the flow of "infotainment." Pornography may be important only for so long as someone tries to suppress it.

Pornography as Market-driven Commodity

Still a third political model is the free market of ideas. In a capitalist system, especially the postindustrial type called an information economy, culture is synonymous with commerce. Whether one speaks of public or intimate information, ideas circulate to the degree that they can be packaged and sold. In an information economy, pornography competes with the full range of data delivered by books, newspapers, magazines, and electronic media. More specifically, fantasies of sexual satisfaction compete with fantasies of celebrity, power, success, and money—which in some ways are far more pornographic.[34] Advocates suggest that the market is an efficient if not equitable means of distributing information. Since a market economy makes little distinction between data and entertainment, neither merit nor intellectual coherence determine value. The market does not care if the message is subversive or merely coarse or unwholesome; it is focused on consumption. Alan M. Dershowitz, a First Amendment attorney, says flatly that pornography has triumphed in the marketplace of ideas as well as in the marketplace of commerce.[35]

A market history of pornography would note that American colonists at first imported pornography, then, as technologies of mass reproduction appeared, gradually capitalized domestic production. Jay Gertzman observes that early entrepreneurs functioned as "pariah capitalists," that is, agents who provided a desirable service (like drug dealers today) but who were despised for it. Because ordinary businesses were closed to them, some East European immigrants and other marginal groups moved into the production of pornography as a way of making a living.[36] From the entrepreneurial point of view, the problems were distribution and demand. Legal restrictions hampered distribution; authorities arrested sellers and interdicted supply lines. Well into the twentieth century, American distributors peddled dirty comic books, photos, novels, and movies mostly by hand to small clusters of customers, or were forced to use organized crime families as brokers. Although sexual representations sold well when they could be delivered, creating and shaping demand on a large scale was difficult, again because of legal and moral objections. The advertising open to merchandisers of most commercial products, for example, was not available to pornographers. Their ads for decades had to be written in code.

Increased affluence and increased leisure led to increased consumption of entertainment, which in turn spurred pornography by increasing the need for more products and by opening legitimate channels for distribution. By the 1960s, American producers were exporting their surpluses. In 1964, Great Britain's Home Secretary filed a protest against more than a million American erotic paperback books flooding the English market.[37] During the 1970s, France raised protective tariffs against American features such as *Deep Throat* (1972) in order to ensure that its homegrown pornography could compete,[38] although French audiences to this day prefer American triple-X videos. In the 1990s, rapid growth of television in Western Europe has quadrupled demand for American hard-core programming (European stations show pornography after midnight), especially since the world's stock of soft-core erotic movies has been exhausted.[39] American pornography dominates the global market today.

Competition in a free market requires product differentiation. Soft-core publishers condemn hard-core books and magazines in order to position their own products as socially desirable. Soft-core magazines, for example, sanitize images to make them appeal to large middle-class audiences with disposable incomes. Producers of mild erotica not only have learned to operate within a political system that has the power to censor but actually support the system because it favors them economically.[40] Hard-core producers in their turn distance themselves from upscale erotica. By claiming that their products are "the real thing," they assert the purity of their ingredients. When the controversial entertainer Madonna published *Sex*, a book of photos of herself having sex with friends, it was roundly condemned for "giv[ing] pornography a bad name."[41] David Aaron Clark, an editor for *Screw*, observed that when real pornographers watch ersatz material like *Sex* succeed they see "not only our art form (pornography, 'erotica' whatever name sells) but, for some of us, our very lifestyles co-opted, drained of all privacy and meaning, and offered up like so much marbleized meat on a butcher's block of straight world consumption."[42]

Product differentiation helps shape demand. Saying that pornography creates a desire for "deviant," trashy sex is like saying that McDonald's creates a desire for salty, greasy meat. Hugh Hefner did not invent the American fetish for women with large breasts; his Playmate of the Month merely exploited a taste already well-established. Increased availability and relentless promotion can nonetheless increase consumption. Catering to fetishes and tastes, which are largely psychological and esthetic, leads to lucrative niche marketing and greater control over consumption. Video customers, for instance, learn to look for brand names (Evil Angel, Sin City) for assurances of quality and consistent representations of favorite sex acts.

Free-market imperatives also alter technologies. The videocassette industry closed most adult cinemas and may itself be overtaken by DVD formats and, eventually, by videostreaming on the Internet. By providing images on demand, the Internet has already damaged the hard-core magazine industry. As pornographic industries mature, moreover, they replicate patterns of consolidation among conventional corporations. In the 1970s, more than fifty adult book publishers controlled three-quarters of the market for erotic paperbacks; now only seven firms control roughly the same percentage.[43] Five or six porn video companies divide the lion's share of the market; their lock on shelf space in rental stores means that Americans never see more than a fraction of the 10,000 tapes produced annually.[44] The majority of images to be found at erotic Web sites are furnished by only two or three companies.[45] Such statistics indicate that consumers of erotica may someday make complaints about lack of diversity just as consumers of television do now.

Or perhaps not. Pornography depends on the appearance of novelty to attract audiences jaded by scenes of plain-vanilla sex. Fortunately, a free market model assumes that every group of people needs representation if only for the sake of trade—though it values different groups most unevenly. That assumption, say those who put their faith in postmodern economics, offers opportunities to those who believe that pornography can empower. Gays, lesbians, straight women, African Americans—any group with a discernible erotic identity—can exploit the market's haphazardness in order to redress neglect.

Public Decorum versus Private Fantasy: The Trashing of Manners

Conservatives and liberals may agree that marketing sexual expression like any other product leads to deplorable consequences.

Political conservatives and religious fundamentalists decry pornography's tawdriness, besmirching of idealism, and affronts to propriety. Liberals add pornography to soft political campaign funds, unregulated health management organizations (HMOs), and rapacious corporate mergers as toxic fallout from a market-driven economy. Measured against a capitalist system of values in which public schools routinely sell children as unwitting subjects for market research[46] and in which digital editors can surreptitiously place products in televised programs,[47] pornography doesn't seem so insidious. Sociologists have long maintained that capitalism itself weakens social bonds, undermines family structures, exploits workers, soils the landscape, replaces personal relationships with commercial ones, corrupts politics, coarsens values, and stains spiritual experience.[48]

Calculating the social cost of pornography, however, is as difficult as measuring the downside of capitalism. The social cost of the automobile for example, includes the 30,000 to 40,000 Americans who annually die in accidents, the many thousands more who are hurt or maimed—plus magnified pollution, increased population densities, aggravated wear and tear on streets and structures, depletion of natural resources, and damage to peace of mind. Most Americans believe that these costs are outweighed by the car's benefits. Except for the real costs of urban blight and pornography's connection to organized crime (though both are diminishing), the ledger sheet for pornography is ambiguous. Few Americans agree on whether attitudinal changes associated with tolerance of sexual representation are healthy or unhealthy; whether the safe masturbation promoted by pornography offsets the HIV-dangers of actual promiscuity; whether the educational value of sexual candor exceeds pornography's recapitulation of stereotypes, ignorance, and inequity; or whether economic rewards exceed exploitation of pornographic workers. On such a scale, pornography would probably be more of a social threat than theme parks and televangelists but less a threat than nicotine or alcohol.

Rampant vulgarity is nonetheless difficult to ignore. Pornography, goes one argument, is the coinage that Gresham's Law warns about—a debased discourse that drives out ideas more deserving of respect. The same, however, can be said of most forms of popular expression, not simply the sexual; Rush Limbaugh is as crass as Howard Stern. Systemic voyeurism may be at fault. During the 1960s, flower children employed shocking expression to destabilize society. In theory, ridding the culture of tight controls on sexual expression should have set the stage for more significant intellectual advances. In practice, says Sandra Levinson, the media marketed "an appeal to the morbid envy with which an up-tight, dissatisfied middle class view[ed] the youth culture." Levinson points out that Americans are mere "voyeurs of freedom." She uses as one example the nudist movement, which aims at personal and social liberation but which is endlessly recycled by movies and other media as a vehicle for exploitation and prurience. Average Americans long for sexual freedom, can never achieve it, and consume its images vindictively, transforming them into something dirty.[49]

That may explain why feminists have less frequently attacked lower-class obscenity. Instead they condemn the artifacts of high and middle culture, from paintings by René Magritte[50] to *Playboy* magazine, on the grounds that the eroticism of everyday middle-class life poses a greater threat. Housewives celebrate their birthdays by piercing their labia, couples rent triple-X videos, college students dance naked instead of waiting tables to pay their tuition, and middle-level managers schedule a session with a dominatrix after a game of racquetball—activities that have become ordinary. The problem with pornography may not be that the experience it offers is too thin, but that the experience offered by the culture at large is thinner yet.

Class assumptions profoundly affect esthetic judgments. Although several authorities have insisted that pornographic genres can be held to artistic standards,[51] critics rarely apply such standards until the passage of time has sanitized outstanding artifacts. Just as critics can now appreciate nuances of theme in, say, Henry Miller's novel *Tropic of Cancer*, so cinema critics will doubtless in future weigh motifs and images in well-constructed hard-core movies. Pornography both challenges and affirms the power of art; it is the bottom line, the ultimate proof that representation has the power to disturb, to ravish, to arouse, to console. As erotic artist Mark Chester has remarked: "The pain of living is so beastly and so great that it is unbearable. But then the joy of sex, sexuality and eroticism is so beautiful and so powerful that it almost makes life bearable."[52]

Because Americans publicly condemn the sexual materials they privately consume, Europeans charge them with hypocrisy. The problem is the poor fit between public need for community and private need for fantasy, a dichotomy similar to traditional divisions between society and individual. Individuals may dream of wild, unfettered sex, but they also must subordinate themselves to structures whose purpose is social stability and security. Questions about the morality of pornography are nonetheless complicated by two related deceptions: Social etiquette requires that humans deny that fantasy is an essential component of arousal and deny also that they can be stimulated by a particular fantasy. Americans are suspicious of substitutes for authentic experience, and never more so than when representation mimics sex. Charges that pornography fakes sex are familiar and convincing. Romantic traditions exalt notions of spontaneous, inexplicable, and irresistible animal attraction: no artifice, no simulation, no mediation. In contrast, fantasy in pornography, like fantasy in any other context, is its own justification. Although it may well be true that sexual fantasies dodge responsibility, objectify bodies, mock mores, and sneer at reality, it seems unfair to hold pornography to a higher standard than, say, ballet, which asserts against evidence to the contrary that love, beauty, and grace reign supreme—and which ignores sensible shoes to boot. In any case, say psychologists, fantasy is crucial as an aphrodisiac. Some fantasies enable sexuality by furnishing its setting, not necessarily its object.[53] In other instances fantasy provides objects of desire, "a stock of visual repertoires constructed out of elements of the everyday."[54]

Ethnographers understand that humans actively search out fantasies rather than simply respond passively. Arousal may be constructed, but "it is not learned in the sense of acquiring new roles. Boys do not look at *Playboy* and learn to like big breasts and view sex objects any more than girls look at *Vogue* and learn to become anorexic and passive."[55] Because some fantasies may seem bizarre, people will not admit to stimulation even when doing so may be therapeutic. Both the female executive who daydreams of being ravished by an anonymous male and the teenaged boy who struggles with eight-hour-a-day erections can find relief in fantasies that are clearly shared by others. Many psychologists believe that pornography can help people who are sexually dysfunctional by teaching them to take charge of their erotic lives.[56] Medical evidence suggests that favorite sexual fantasies can be stronger pain-relievers than aspirin.[57]

When fantasies are obsessive, they are called fetishes. The fourth edition of the *Diagnostic and Statistical Manual of Mental Disorders* of the American Psychiatric Association defines fetishes as fixations on "nonliving objects (e. g., female undergarments)."[58] According to Freudian psychologists, fetishes are exclusively masculine because they function as penis substitutes. Less formally, "a fetish is a story masquerading as an object."[59]

That is, the fetish inscribes or recapitulates the psychosexual history of a man fixated on, say, a mother's garter belt, or on a leather garment associated with some early sexual experience. Some feminists have argued that women are subject to fetishes also,[60] others that they merely react to conventional tropes. Some not-very-scientific studies have distinguished different gender preferences for pornographic fantasies. According to some students, women gravitate toward soft romantic renditions of sexuality whereas males turn to graphic scenarios uncontextualized by emotional involvement. Others suggest that males are more voyeuristic, more fetishistic, and more likely to respond to visual genres than are women.[61] It is difficult to know whether these are merely categories socially constructed by political correctness; women may be indifferent to graphic visual materials because they have been socially conditioned to be.[62]

Fetishistic or not, preferences are powerful. Ethnographers observing patrons of adult bookstores quickly learn that most are in search of extremely narrow ranges of fantasy: pictures of women with blonde pubic hair, say, or short transvestites, or males with large penises. "Even within the extreme monotony of pornography," says one social scientist, "there was a marked specialization of fetishes and fantasies that kept the users separate and isolated in their antisocial pleasures."[63] For many people, specific fantasies are default drives. Men with narrow hips or dark hair, for instance, may be essential to fantasy for a given heterosexual woman. Libidos landscaped by experience are remarkably idiosyncratic. Sexual representation, fortunately, is not monolithic. Critics may construe pornography as a forest, but those who enjoy it seek out particular trees.

Condemning all sexual representations on the basis of specific examples that the critic finds disgusting or incomprehensible is thus misleading. Despite myths that sexual representations of any kind turn males on, sexual arousal is so quirky as to make prediction impossible. Surveys of sexual habits and preferences, by now virtually a genre of erotica themselves, are not much help; Americans lie about what they find sexually exciting.[64] The same representation may repel one person and attract another, but neither can logically elevate personal preferences into obligations for others. Much of what passes for criticism of porn thus falls into the category of *de gustibus non disputandem est*—there is no arguing with taste.

When conservatives worry that pornography destroys social structures, they often confuse ethics and tastes. Morality is not the same as manners.[65] Although tolerance of pornography may coarsen public decorum, so that rudeness seems to overwhelm manners, it need not have the same effect on private standards of right and wrong. Even so, disquiet can run deep. The language, the images, and the behavior embraced by pornography can keep one esthetically off-balance and emotionally queasy. Porn can be offensive in its mean-spiritedness and aggression, its downright nastiness—the elements that court decisions lump under the label "prurience." People can fear their own receptiveness to an aphrodisiac that seems cheap and tawdry. Those exposed to ersatz sex can be exalted by the sheer redemptive power of sex or ravished by the beauty of the bodies, but they can also feel shame at their own arousal and guilt at the thought that others might see such images.

As one critic has put it, "without sexual constraint, there would be no frustration. Without frustration, there would be no fantasy. Without fantasy, there would be no pornography."[66] Pornographic examples can make normally sensitive "liberal" viewers feel unclean, and knowing that taste is really at issue does not help much.[67] Public consumption of sexual materials can miscue social response, as is obvious to anyone who has watched packs of uncouth males at a strip club. Hearing a string of coarse words that someone thinks is an appropriate response to a mildly erotic image can make one feel kindly toward social restraints that ordinarily repress such language. Some people apparently need shame to process sexual representations—need a sense of transgression, guilt sharpened by taboo. Just how violations of propriety can heighten arousal is unclear, but it is very clear that such mechanisms do not operate for everyone. Differences become acute, for instance, when people decide that certain acts or postures are humiliating.

The Feminist Critique

Perceptions of humiliation launched the radical feminist critique of pornography. Among opponents of sexual representation, feminists can make the best case. Shabby treatment of women in many pornographic genres gave force to outrage. Antipornography feminists of the 1970s complained that the sexist words and images of pornography functioned as a blueprint of oppression: "Pornography is the theory, rape the practice."[68] To explain just how entrenched injustice was, the film critic Laura Mulvey advanced the concept of the "male gaze."[69] That theory holds that dominant males have so conditioned a culture to see things in masculine terms that audiences can "see" and interpret images *only* in those terms; there is no other kind of vision. The "male gaze," in short, was lethal, and language itself enslaved women. Given those premises, it is not surprising that indignation flowered into theories of global conspiracy.[70] Nor is it surprising that moderate feminists disputed such theories from the outset.[71]

Controversy erupted when the Minneapolis and Indianapolis antipornography ordinances defined degradation as penetration. Writers such as Joanna Russ, bewildered by insistence that penetration is humiliating, wondered how else intercourse could take place. Russ wondered also why the antiporn activists did not give examples of erotica they thought legitimately exciting.[72] Veronica Monet, a sex worker, has pointed out that calling penetration and "submissive" postures degrading simply reinforces patriarchy. Women should reject the contention that they are degraded by biology or anatomy. To believe that bending over or spreading one's legs is degrading, says Monet, is to acquiesce in masculine myths that women are inferior: "Our cultural stance seems to be that the person who moves and/or penetrates is powerful and the person who holds still and/or is penetrated is degraded. How convenient for the male power structure." Monet says that intent rather than posture counts, and that women should make pornography that declines to endorse patriarchy.[73]

Because of its fixation on penetration, the feminist antiporn position seems to have been fueled by an ancient, familiar sense of shame at bodies and their functions. Shame in turn interprets intercourse as coarse and animalistic rather than as pleasant and affectionate. That impression was strengthened when Andrea Dworkin, one author of the Minneapolis ordinance, wrote *Intercourse* to assert that intercourse should be repugnant to women and to urge development of technologies that would obviate its necessity.[74] Antiporn factions appeared to be equating sex with sexism.

Also, they equated sex with violence, a conflation that bewildered feminists who thought most pornography less violent than mainstream messages. Attorneys tried to outline the radical antiporn argument: Given society's attitude toward sexual candor, a male character kissing a woman's nipple would earn a movie an R-rating. Given society's preference for representations of aggression over depictions of sex, the character could cut off the nipple so that the movie would receive a PG rating. For

Catharine MacKinnon, however, there would be no difference.[75] The analogy seemed far-fetched until MacKinnon wrote *Only Words*, in which she appeared to be saying exactly that.[76]

Moderate feminists objected that making women "the sole arbiters of social morality and architects of social decency" is reactionary thought-control.[77] Others noticed that the antiporn position denigrated homosexuals,[78] lower-classes[79] and races other than white.[80] Critics noticed as well that both traditional pornographic expression and strident antiporn rhetoric promoted stereotypes, the one of females, the other of males, and could not decide which reading was the more simple-minded or sexist. Extremists on the left, like Camille Paglia, lashed out at the extremism of MacKinnon and Dworkin, but generally feminists quietly moved away from equations of sex and sexism to thoughtful reexaminations of pornography.

That images of sexualized women are everywhere is obvious. To charges that representations make women into objects, several feminists respond that objectification works in two directions, reducing and commodifying in one direction, humanizing and liberating in the other. Pornography is but one element of an economy that objectifies all humans. Objectification is reprehensible only when women are not allowed to be anything other than objects.[81] Other feminists asserted that criminalizing pornography would deny *women* the right to explore their own sexualities through representation, and would in effect reduce women to wards of a state that would decide what pleasures were permissible.[82]

Although pornography may humiliate women, says Ann Garry, doing so is not its purpose, which is "to arouse the audience." That distinction explains why males do not *experience* porn as humiliating to women, any more than women experience romances and soap operas as pornographic. Different recipients draw different meanings from the same messages.[83] Agreeing, Ellen Willis notes that the feminist antiporn position

> endorses the portrayal of sex as we might like it to be and condemns the portrayal of sex as it too often is, whether in action or only in fantasy. But if pornography is to arouse, it must appeal to the feelings we have, not those that by some utopian standard we ought to have. Sex in this culture has been so deeply politicized that it is impossible to make clear-cut distinctions between 'authentic' sexual impulses and those conditioned by patriarchy. Between, say, *Ulysses* at one end and *Snuff* at the other,

erotica/pornography conveys all sorts of mixed messages that elicit complicated and private responses.[84]

Despite contradictory claims, the feminist critique addressed
sexual representation as had no intellectual force before. Moreover, antiporn assertions carried emotional conviction for many
women. Saying that pornography denigrates women can *feel*
right to women who have encountered sexual discrimination and
outright abuse. Veteran performer Nina Hartley agrees with antiporn feminists up to a point. Hartley believes that a lot of contemporary pornography is both misogynistic and misanthropic.
Porn producers, she says, are Republicans, not "sex radicals";
they have been warped by a culture that has twisted and shamed
sex, and their products speak for that culture. According to Hartley, more—and more equitable—porn made by women and radical men is the answer.[85] If antiporn critiques continue to resonate
among women, however, attempts to legislate on the basis of
what were essentially bumper-sticker slogans have been disas-
trous. The Marxist charge that "religion is the opiate of the
masses" has a good deal of merit; eradicating churches on the
basis of that insight does not. The charge that pornography discriminates against women also has merit, but legally prohibiting
vast sectors of speech and imagery can never be just.

It is noteworthy that most of the truly illuminating essays on
pornography have been written by women—and virtually all of
them reject antiporn positions. A quick sampling might include
Susan Sontag's "The Pornographic Imagination"; Joan Nestle's
"My Mother Liked to Fuck"; Ellen Willis's "Feminism, Moralism,
and Pornography"; Constance Penley's "Feminism, Psychoanalysis, and the Study of Popular Culture"; Carole Vance's
"Pleasure and Danger: Toward a Politics of Sexuality"; and
Audre Lorde's "Uses of the Erotic: The Erotic as Power."

Censors

Americans often laugh at censors because they appear to strive
against the inevitable, because their zealousness leads to hyper-
bole, and because they often seem hypocritical. One of the first
professional smut-hunters was the Reverend John McDowall of
New York, who in 1833 began to print exposés in his *McDowall's
Journal.* A year later, he exhibited obscene items he had collected

with such prurience that other preachers denounced him. A grand jury charged McDowall with obscenity for publishing his journal, and members of his church, suspecting that he had misused some of the money set aside for his crusade, forced him to resign.[86]

According to his enemies, Anthony Comstock in 1881 paid three prostitutes $14.50 to strip and fondle each other for him privately for an hour and twenty minutes *before* arresting them.[87] John S. Sumner, Comstock's successor as the head of the New York Society for the Suppression of Vice, may well have taken bribes to leave certain publishers alone, and he may actually have resold some of the books he seized.[88] Courtney Riley Cooper, a New York judge enraged by attorneys who persuaded juries that a book could not be judged obscene on the basis of short passages, attacked publishers and popular entertainers in *Designs in Scarlet* (1939). So unseemly was the text that a decade later, Pyramid Books changed Cooper's title to *Teen-Age Vice!* (1952) and sold it as a dirty book.

More recently, members of the Attorney General's Commission on Pornography fell into disgrace: Father Bruce Ritter, charged with molesting children, was rusticated by the Catholic Church; Charles Keating, tried for defrauding investors in Lincoln National, went to prison; and Attorney General Edwin Meese himself, accused of financial irregularities, resigned under a cloud.[89] Famously hypocritical antiporn crusaders such as Jimmy Swaggart and Jim Bakker may have suffered from sexual and psychological illnesses. Censors such as Will Hays may have themselves been victims of a profound sexual ignorance; in seeking a divorce in 1952, Hays's wife told the court that her husband could not tell her navel from her clitoris.[90] As Calvin Tompkins has unkindly put it, the nation's censors, "from Anthony Comstock to Jesse Helms, have had the disadvantage of being morons."[91] Despite such examples, the legend that censors are always hypocritical or ignorant has about the same validity as anecdotes that pornography causes violence. Both stories are part of the nation's sexual folklore.

Comstock built the New York Society for the Suppression of Vice by enlisting the support of shrewd politicians and canny bureaucrats, hiring well-connected investigators, and trading favors with the powerful. In the 1870s the New England Watch and Ward Society (Boston), the Western Society for the Suppression of Vice (St. Louis, Missouri), the International Reform Federation (Washington, D.C.), and the Illinois Vigilance Association (Chicago) vied for supreme zealousness.[92] H. L. Mencken successfully sued both the New England Watch and Ward Society and its head, the Rev. J. Frank Chase, for attempting to suppress the April 1926 issue of his magazine *American Mercury*, which contained a story by Herbert Asbury about a prostitute. The society lost most of its influence by 1945, when Boston judge Elijah Adlow ruled that the group's argument that young women would be harmed by Erskine Caldwell's description of a bare male chest was "idiotic." About the same time, the New York Society for the Suppression of Vice, having lost public support, became the New York Police Athletic League.

By then, new censors had arisen. The most powerful of these was Frank Walker, virtually an agent of the National Organization for Decent Literature (NODL), who became Postmaster General in 1940. In 1934, prominent Catholics incensed by actress Mae West's performance in *She Done Him Wrong* (1933) formed the Legion of Decency. The legion pressured the Motion Picture Producers and Distributors of America (MPPDA) to rewrite the 1930 Production Code in order to ban virtually all references to sex, and to police the industry rigorously by refusing a seal of approval to any film not in compliance with the code's strict moral standards. The legion threatened to boycott or picket any theater showing a film without a seal. John Noll, bishop of Fort Wayne, Indiana, had founded NODL in 1930 to clean up books and magazines. Using its own Code for Clean Reading, it proscribed hundreds of books and magazines. Depending on one's perspective, these two Catholic censorship organizations were either authentic outpourings of a grassroots movement or the clever manipulation of docile parishioners by strong bishops. As Jeffrey Weeks points out, all religions regulate the degree of pleasure they permit their adherents; imposing their restrictions on others is a very different matter.[93] In 1938, the NODL prosecuted *Life* magazine for publishing "The Birth of a Baby" on the grounds that in one illustration the mother's labia were visible. The power of the NODL was so great that the American Civil Liberties Union (ACLU) published a book warning of its excesses.[94]

After becoming Postmaster General, Walker banned dozens of magazines from the mails and curtailed the second-class mailing privileges of dozens of others. In 1941, Walker revoked the second-class postage rate of *Esquire* (which would have cost the magazine's publisher vast sums) on the grounds that the magazine's words and pinups were obscene. *Esquire* went to court, won, and in 1946, in *Hannegan, Postmaster General v. Esquire, Inc.* (Walker having been replaced), the Supreme Court rejected the Post Office's appeal. Postal officials jealously guarded their roles as chief censors, often staking out ground that belonged to the U.S. Customs Office and the Department of Justice. The agency tried to ignore the *Esquire* decision[95] well into the 1960s. In 1966, Postmaster General J. Edward Day angered censorship groups by refusing to provide them with free samples of pornography, by firing "smut" consultants, and by closing the Post Office's obscenity museum (which catalogued confiscated materials by "perversion" for delighted tourists).[96] In 1970, the Post Office received 284,000 complaints about obscenity in the mails, the highest number for any year; by 1982, there were only 5,000.[97]

Few religious groups today have the clout of the NODL, although fundamentalist Protestant groups led by Jerry Falwell and Donald Wildmon have launched economic boycotts against various media for alleged offenses against Christian values. Moderate Christians who reject censorship as unconstitutional merely ask that sexual representations be limited to those who want them.[98] Common sense, however, rarely competes against fundamentalist charges that pornography promotes Satanism, child sacrifice, rape, and assorted lurid evils. Studies of such groups indicate that fear of change leads to political action.[99]

One of the stranger alliances evolved during the 1980s, when radical antiporn feminists joined forces with fundamentalists to oppose sexual expression. Shared reactionary philosophies aside, the most plausible explanation is "moral panic," a media-driven perception of crisis. Moral panics periodically recur in the United States and are often signaled by calls for censorship of vaguely defined "pornography." Moral panics feed on folklore transmitted by journalists and urban rumor. Reports of child abuse in day care centers triggered witch-hunts around the nation during the 1990s; in some cases the innocent accused spent years in prison until their convictions could be overturned. Historians have listed recent furors over explicit music, computer games, violent movies, and overly permissive media as spurs to moral panic;[100] these outcries resemble the public anxieties about the effects of popular amusements on the lower classes in the nineteenth century,[101] or the exaggerated reports of the traffic in pornography and the alleged devastating consequences to America's youth that led to the postwar Kefauver Commission. According to the National Coalition Against Censorship, recent hysteria over pornography qualifies as moral panic.[102]

The ruling that the radical feminist Indianapolis ordinance was unconstitutional triggered rancor that escalated. Radical antiporn feminists accused moderates of treason with a recklessness unheard since the ideological battles between Trotskyites and Stalinists during the 1930s. As moderates gradually began to marginalize the radicals, the latter sought receptive ears among conservatives and fundamentalists. As panic rises in such circumstances, says Lisa Duggan, "words assume the reverse of their common meaning: liberation becomes chaos, desire becomes deviance, and dissent becomes the work of the devil."[103]

The ultimate weakness of censorship movements has been demonstrated over the years most notably by the American Civil Liberties Union. By organizing coalitions of constitutional defenders, the ACLU has managed to check the worst national attacks on free speech, though it has been less effective on a local level, where ad hoc censorship of textbooks and libraries goes on apace. Every now and then someone triggers a panic, as was the case in Oklahoma City, when authorities declared without a hearing that *The Tin Drum*, which won an Academy Award for Best Foreign Film in 1979, was child pornography. Police raided Oklahoma City Blockbuster Video stores, demanded the names of everyone who had rented copies of the video, and started pounding on doors. One of the homes was that of the local head of the ACLU.

By focusing on sex, smut-hunters help eroticize a society by establishing boundaries to be transgressed. Censors share with pornographers an exaggerated sense of the importance of sex; in their different ways, both endorse Woody Allen's often-quoted witticism: "Sex is not dirty [pause] unless it's done right." Neither group will grant moral and intellectual motivation to the other side. Pornographers and censors can be sincerely indignant (the one about guilt and repression, the other about excessive freedom and license), can be driven by obsessions, can feel the need to bear witness to deeply held beliefs; both can feel that they are saving others.

Research on Pornography

Few topics have been subjected to such massive research as pornography. In addition to its completed *Report*, the President's Commission on Obscenity and Pornography (1970) released nine volumes of research studies, many of them specifically designed for the commission. The evidence did not point toward significant links between pornography and antisocial behavior. Two decades later, the Attorney General's Commission on Pornography, a group politically at the other extreme from the earlier body, marshaled all the evidence it could find to try to reverse the conclusions of the President's Commission. The second commission could not establish significant causal relationships, either.

Research into sexual representation generally falls into two categories: qualitative studies based on historical, cultural, critical, and ethnographic investigation; and quantitative studies based on laboratory experiments, field surveys, and statistical analyses of population samples. The quantitative side has dominated until quite recently, when the lack of clear conclusions began to shift the emphasis to qualitative studies. As qualitative specialists point out, even quantitative studies are socially constructed activities shaped by socially constructed theories. Thelma McCormack, one of the most authoritative students of pornography, maintains that most research is biased, especially that conducted between 1969 and 1972. During that period, sex seemed progressive and violence regressive, so liberal assumptions privileged sex, a bias that might have affected findings from that period; more recently, when radical feminists redefined sex itself as violence, that bias manifested itself in research agendas.[104] Given the culture's inability to establish norms of sexuality or gender, it is unlikely that researchers will agree on definitions, let alone measure the same things.

To sum up: no reputable study has established a credible link between adult exposure to garden-variety pornography (defined as nudity, scenes of intercourse, or lascivious discourse) and psychological or sociological damage. Reports to the contrary, including compendia assembled by conservatives and radical feminists, are a species of folklore, in particular the notion so beloved of novelists that pornography creates serial murderers. The lack of evidence does not exonerate plain-vanilla pornography; it simply means that so far standard methodologies and measurements have not demonstrated significant harm.

The jury is still out on (1) possible harm from combinations of sex and aggression that occur far more often in mainstream representations not usually called pornographic; (2) possible harm to children from inappropriate exposure; (3) possible harm to individuals from performing in pornographic media; and (4) possible long-term (and difficult to detect) harm to individuals, social institutions, and specific groups from aggregated sexual representation. Psychologists have noticed statistically significant (though far from overwhelming) correlations between early exposure to sexual materials and certain types of criminal sexual behavior in prison populations, though again without being able to isolate pornography as a variable, let alone demonstrate causality. Sociologists and political scientists *can* demonstrate that concentrations of sex-related businesses lower property values and community cohesion in specific areas. Investigators have also detailed connections between pornographic industries and organized crime.

Law and Sexual Representation

Americans often assume that the intricacies of major Supreme Court cases (summarized in Chapter 5) constitute a precise legal history of pornography. But for almost two hundred years police in countless towns, cities, and counties have arrested and convicted hundreds for distributing or possessing sexual materials. Until the 1950s, local authorities assumed that they had the right to regulate what citizens read and saw. For local magistrates, pornography was not an issue of free speech; it was just filth. It would never have occurred to an Iowa local sheriff that he did not have the authority to confiscate a dirty book.

Usually the sheriff would tell the town druggist that since Mrs. Jenkins had complained about the paperbacks on display, it would be better to just get rid of them. Outsiders were another matter. In a typical story of the 1950s, the sheriff in a small Indiana town arrested a man and his wife for selling pornographic photos. To get money to work their way west, the two had posed for the pictures. Rather than pay them, the photographer kept the negatives but gave them a stack of prints to peddle themselves. The case was handled quietly. There was no trial, no defense attorney, just a magistrate and a hearing. The man got two weeks in the local jail for "disorderly conduct." Typical sexist injustice of the time sent his wife to the county jail for six months for prostitution, though she had no previous record. The sheriff and the judge, of course, kept the photos to show to friends whose moral rectitude made them impervious to harm. Eventually the sheriff passed his on to the Kinsey Institute for Research in Sex, Gender, and Reproduction.[105] There is no reason to sentimentalize the plight of the couple. The point is that nobody remembers their names.

But colorful personalities decided the famous legal battles. Anthony Comstock carried opponents before him by dint of indignation, self-rectitude, and political savvy, as have counterparts in the present such as Rudolph Guiliani and Jesse Helms. But liberals had their powerful champions also in attorney Morris Ernst, who learned to delay trials until he got the judge he wanted, and in Justice John M. Woolsey, who actually read James Joyce's novel *Ulysses* before issuing his opinion. Personal assessments almost certainly weighted the obscenity sentences of Samuel Roth, whose piracy earned him no friends; of Ralph Ginzburg, whose tactics sneered at taste; and of Marvin Miller, whose criminal connections made him a poor symbol of free speech. Hindsight redeems other transgressors. Mary Ware Dennett now seems a benefactor of humanity; Mae West now seems a visionary; Walt Whitman and Henry Miller now seem literary giants.

Other forces were also at work. Despite the U.S. Constitution's First Amendment, which unequivocally endorses free speech, successive decisions have not affirmed protected areas but merely narrowed overly broad definitions of obscenity. Case law appears to have translated the language of the framers—"Congress shall make no laws abridging freedom of speech"—into a reversed negative—"That which is not prohibited is permitted." The law has nonetheless evolved. Colonists associated obscenity with trespass against religion and with dissent against authority,[106] circumstances that led American jurists to adopt the Hicklin test, based on *Regina v. Hicklin* (1868), a decision governing "obscene libel" made by English courts. (American law derives from English Common Law.) The Hicklin test was: Did the work, even in isolated passages, tend to "deprave and corrupt" those whose minds might be open to immoral influences? Those in danger of corruption were the "weak minds" of society: children, women, the underclasses, the ethnically different.

As journalists defused the concept of libel and secular Americans discarded the concept of sacrilege, sexual expression required a new label. The word *pornographer* first appeared in English in 1850; seven years later, *pornography* appeared as a noun.[107] Meaning gradually emerged from its etymology ("writing about prostitutes"): representation intended to arouse. Jurists still conflated pornography with obscenity, however, and *Hicklin* still applied. Defenders of speech have long insisted that protection offered by the First Amendment is content neutral whereas in practice the courts have always tended to judge expression on the content itself.[108]

The most recent significant challenge to the First Amendment was that advanced by radical feminists in the 1980s. Their legal premise was that the rights of groups are shielded by the Fourteenth Amendment, a protection that could be seen as conflicting with the rights guaranteed by the First Amendment. A shakier second premise was that pornography violated the rights of women as a group or class by denigrating them, and that women could ask for sanctions against pornography. In 1984, the Minneapolis City Council passed an ordinance embodying those premises written by Catharine MacKinnon and Andrea Dworkin. When Mayor Fraser vetoed it as unconstitutional, other radical feminists wrote a similar ordinance for Indianapolis, which led to immediate court challenges.

For some the ordinance echoed the Rushdie Affair, in which the Iranian Ayatollah Khomeni condemned the writer Salman Rushdie to death for having written *The Satanic Verses*, a work the Muslim leader insisted injured all Muslims as a group. (The Indianapolis ordinance provided for civil penalties, not death.) If upheld, the principles behind the ordinance would allow any group—or, more precisely, those *claiming* to speak for such a group—to sue for injury, and thus open the door to continual social warfare. To other critics, the ordinance's definition of pornography seemed bizarre and untenable. By posing one group against another, said still other critics, radical feminists were transforming pornography into a species of political discourse, which would guarantee its protection under the Constitution.[109] The framers of the ordinance insisted that they were attacking pornography not as speech but as harm. Since the harm could not be demonstrated, Federal Judge Sarah Evans Barker of the Seventh District Court in 1985 rejected the claim that speech was not involved as a transparent fiction; the Supreme Court the following year refused the appeal and thus let Barker's ruling stand.

In recent years, American law has been much more effective in dealing with *demonstrable* rather than *alleged* effects. Antidisplay and zoning ordinances, which are civil rather than criminal statutes, can forbid the display of explicit materials where they might be seen by children, and can move adult businesses to special zones to prevent their lowering property values, attracting unsavory elements, offending churchgoers, encroaching on school neighborhoods, or creating community nuisances. Courts must keep an eye on overzealous politicians who try to use zoning laws to eradicate rather than regulate sex businesses. In late 1999, for example, the New York State Court of Appeals ruled that New York City must take into account efforts to comply with regulations rather than drive sex shops out of business entirely.[110]

The limits to free speech caused by such ordinances have been offset by electronic technologies that deliver sexual materials to adults who have a right to view or read them in their homes.

In fact, electronic media have rendered most restrictions largely moot by separating expression from both time and place. Americans can rent videotapes from local stores that carefully segregate adult materials from family cassettes, just as newsstands take care not to display magazine covers that might offend. Consumers can access pornography on the Internet from sites that exist in cyberspace, or exchange fantasies with others by erotic E-mail. Soon Americans will be able to download full-length, full-motion videos at will, or exchange programs on the Net. Credit card access restrictions, age-geared rating systems, and net filters, all of them as yet imperfect, but all of them ways of avoiding censorship, are evolving to shield minors from material more appropriate to adults. Despite the Supreme Court's refusal to interdict speech for adults on the Internet, it has upheld the strictest of laws against child pornography.

The Court struck down the Communications Decency Act to protect the communication technology most likely to define American prosperity in the future, a reminder that most legal decisions governing sexual expression in this century have been economic at base. Literary censorship ended when mainstream publishers, realizing that only candor would enable them to survive, insisted on publication of forbidden works. Movie censorship ended when Hollywood studios, realizing that only sex would enable them to compete with television, abandoned the Production Code. During the 1920s, burlesque impresarios hired strippers to reclaim audiences lost to the movies. New York City's mayor Fiorello La Guardia later drove burlesque out of the city at the behest of property owners concerned about the value of their real estate. Contemporary social critics point out that New York City's current zoning campaign against adult businesses, far from tapping citizens' moral outrage, has simply delivered valuable opportunities to midtown commercial developers, realtors, and property owners.[111] "Cleaning up" Times Square has already led to unintended consequences. As corporations have transformed the area into a Disneyfied entertainment center, serious Broadway drama has fled to other parts of the city.[112]

Before long, censorship may concern itself principally with intellectual property, the currency of the Information Age. Safeguarding copyright through commodity (rather than political or sexual) censorship stabilizes markets by ensuring proprietary interests in information and entertainment.[113] U.S. trade missions are just as concerned with the foreign pirating of porn videos as they are with the pirating of mainstream films and music recordings; all contribute to balances of trade. Interestingly, two decades ago conservatives tried to deny copyright to pornographic books and magazines as a way of driving them out of the market but were not successful because only courts, not the Library of Congress, can determine obscenity.[114] Other critics have observed that today the First Amendment chiefly favors commercial interests, and often monopoly, especially where media are concerned. New commercial realities rather than individual freedoms collapse distinctions between high forms of discourse (art) and low (pornography).[115]

Criminal Aspects of Pornography

Connections with Organized Crime

One real threat posed by pornography, the involvement of organized crime, has diminished markedly. Because pornographic representations were small potatoes for most of this century, organized crime generally ignored such materials until the 1960s. The murky legalities of suddenly popular magazines and films encouraged the Mafia to take control of the distribution (and in some cases the production) of such materials. The Mob also moved aggressively into peep parlors, arcades, and adult movie houses where porn could be exhibited and sold, and rival factions fought, cheated, and killed each other for turf. In New York, for example, organized crime figures leased or purchased real estate in seedy neighborhoods, then subleased the premises to sex businesses at exorbitant rents, or operated protection rackets, in effect taking profits from adult arcades and shops.[116]

The Attorney General's Commission on Pornography reproduced Justice Department charts of criminal organizations and major crime involvement in pornography during the 1970s (including reports that over fifty pornographers had been murdered).[117] Organized crime thrives, of course, on providing goods and services that are forbidden but in high demand. Until gays revolted against police persecution at the Stonewall Bar (operated by the Mafia) in New York City in 1969, for example, organized crime owned or controlled virtually all homosexual meeting places in municipalities.[118] Once homosexuals began to enjoy the rights of other citizens, the Mafia's profits fell. Similarly, as the distribution of sexual materials was decriminalized (de facto if not de jure), organized crime began to retreat from adult enterprises.

Nonetheless, well into the 1980s organized crime still controlled some channels of distribution of pornographic magazines, films, videotapes, and sexual accessories, still owned some pornographic book distributorships, still financed topless and striptease joints, and still laundered money through adult entertainment centèrs (because they were large cash-flow enterprises like the pizza parlors and dry cleaners that the Mafia has traditionally used for the same purposes). Courts continue to convict pornographers with ties to organized crime, most recently Ken Guardino, head of Metro Video (the first porn video company to go public on a stock exchange), in 1997.[119] But Mob influence seems to be weakening. The reasons are fairly clear. Relentless prosecutions by the Justice Department have seriously weakened crime families. Competition has reduced profit margins. Zoning regulations and VCRs have put most porn arcades and theaters out of business. The Internet, a technology impossible for the Mob to control, now distributes pornography on massive scales. Public tolerance for most forms of sexual expression has eroded the rationale for criminal involvement.

Organized crime still pirates pornographic videotapes (though there is far more money in pirating blockbuster legitimate films), but it is less likely to run video rental stores. Prostitution aside, of various erotic enterprises only the connection between organized crime and nude dance clubs remains as strong as it once was. Some experts believe that strip clubs and bars may be the only sexually oriented venues in which organized crime still has a large financial interest, and the connection probably has more to do with opportunities for skimming profits and laundering currency than with erotic activities per se.[120] Pornographic businesses are hardly free of criminal taint, but many of them have acquired quasilegitimacy.

Child Pornography

Child pornography, that is, sexual material depicting or involving minors, is a small, constantly prosecuted syndrome about whose psychological dynamics little is known, save that it is a domain avoided carefully by most American consumers and even more religiously by commercial producers of pornography. Few Americans debate the need to protect children from exploitation. Even so, the perception of that need is of relatively recent origin. Only modern economies aware of the importance of information insist on universal education, let alone insist that children remain children—that is, forbidden to join the labor force—long enough for them to undergo a period of intense programming as future producers and consumers. Allowing children to grow up too quickly overpopulates economic underclasses and damages a complex society dependent on information processing skills. Once these rationales were established, child abuse became reprehensible. Sexual abuse is especially problematic because Americans believe that children are incapable of informed consent, so that forcing or cajoling a child into sexual acts or sexual representations victimizes the minor.

Ironically, pornographers in the nineteenth century helped construct, sentimentalize, and eroticize childhood.[121] The Reverend Charles Dodgson, better known as Lewis Carroll, invested childhood with sensual innocence by writing about a character named Alice and by shooting hundreds of nude photographs of prepubescent girls.[122] Any number of classic pornographic novels have mimicked mainstream literary models by tracing the effects of sexual experience on underage protagonists, but using actual children in clearly pornographic visual media did not often occur until after World War II. Prewar stag film audiences recoiled from seeing minors in intercourse. Pedophiles of the same period were often satisfied with photographs of fully clothed boys and girls.[123]

Juanita Slusher, better known as the striptease artist Candy Barr, appeared in the stag film *Smart Alec* (1951/52) when she was only sixteen. Given her physical precociousness, few viewers could have known that she was a minor. The first American pornographic film to present minors *as* minors was *The Sexy Sexteens* (1962/63), shot by a pedophile whose Long Island house caught fire. When firemen found the undamaged master reels in the ashes, police arrested Ivan Jerome, inventor of the remarkable film stock used to record the first explosion of an atomic bomb, who skipped bail on the charge and has never been heard of since. Somehow the masters were duplicated, and copies went on the market.[124] Decades later, two actresses, Traci Lords and Alexandra Quinn, were discovered to have been underage when they made porn film features. Under Section 2257 of the U.S. Code (Sexual Exploitation and Other Abuse of Children, "Record

Keeping Provisions"), a law passed in 1995, producers of all photographic sexual materials must ascertain the correct ages of performers and provide evidence.

During the 1960s and early 1970s "chicken" magazines (photos of nude children) circulated in major cities, and some Scandi-
navian hard-core movies included performers as young as
sixteen (the age of consent in Denmark). During the Vietnam war,
reports that photos and movies depicting Southeast Asian children in intercourse with American servicemen were circulating
in the United States led to several investigations. Those reports,
augmented by rumors of huge rings of American pedophiles, led
to moral panic.[125] The most meticulous investigation, a three-
year (1977–1980) study by a commission impaneled by the Illinois legislature, concluded that rumors had been inflated, that
the alleged profits made by child pornographers were mythical,
and that public reaction was disproportionate to the evidence.[126]
By contrast, a committee of the U.S. Senate held its own hasty
hearings to assert that traffic in child pornography was large and
lucrative.[127] Despite challenges to these poorly supported findings, Congress that year (1977) passed Federal Law 95–225 forbidding the use of children in sexually explicit materials.

Since then, misinformation has fed urban myth.[128] Claims
often beggar credulity; no illegal enterprise could absorb the hundreds of thousands of minors that panic-mongers allege. Fortunately, a 1985 report by the Senate Permanent Subcommittee on
Investigations pointed out that the Justice Department could identify no more than 2,000 domestic pedophiles engaged in small-
scale exchange of such materials.[129] When the Attorney General's
Commission on Pornography found little evidence that sexual materials lead to antisocial behavior, it devoted half of its recommendations to child pornography instead. Considering the number of
state and federal laws already on the books, this portion of the
commission's *Final Report* was redundant.[130] The commission also
encouraged prosecutors to entrap pedophiles. By some accounts,
special units of the Post Office, U. S. Customs, and the Justice Department conducting "sting operations" are the largest advertisers
and distributors of child pornography in the United States.[131] Sensational media coverage of arrests for child pornography generally
obscures the fact that small numbers are involved and that exist-
ing laws are quite sufficient to convict. The key to combating exploitation of minors is accurate information, not folklore.

Continuing moral panic fueled the Communications Decency Act (CDA) of 1996. When the Supreme Court struck down

its provisions because they infringed on the rights of adults, Congress passed the 1998 Child Online Protection Act, still moving through court challenges. Its stipulations—requiring Web sites to ascertain the ages of users, for example—are likely to become moot as sites require credit card information prior to access. Mindful of the threat of such legislation, many commercial sex sites already try to block access by minors. The *New York Times* has argued that American children surfing the Internet are far more at risk from advertising assaults from unbridled but "legitimate" marketers than from depredations of child pornographers.[132]

Notes

1. James Wolcott, "Act 1, Obscene Too," *Vanity Fair* 463 (March 1999): 108, 112–113; quotation, p. 108.

2. Leslie Camhi, "Baring the Intricacies of Desire and Shame," *New York Times*, 14 March 1999, pp. 13, 44 of Arts section; the film is a Rezo Films/Trimark Pictures release of 1999.

3. Advertisement for Rejuvenation Lamp and Fixture Company, *New Yorker*, 8 March 1999, p. 73.

4. James Atlas, "The Loose Canon: Why Higher Learning Has Embraced Pornography," *New Yorker*, 29 March 1999, pp. 60–65.

5. "The Sex Industry," *Economist* 346 (14–20 February 1998): 21–23.

6. Arthur Lubow, "Steal This Burger," *New York Times Magazine*, 19 April 1998 , pp. 38–43.

7. Gloria Steinem, "Erotica and Pornography: A Clear and Present Difference," in *Take Back the Night: Women on Pornography*, Laura Lederer, ed. (New York: William Morrow, 1980), pp. 35–39.

8. "Pornography: A Roundtable Discussion." *Harper's* 269 (November 1984): 31–39, 42–45.

9. Walter Kendrick, *The Secret Museum: Pornography in Modern Culture* (New York: Viking, 1987), p. 178.

10. The obituary of Paul Novak, West's companion, in the London *Guardian* reported that he dutifully supplied her with her favorite salve every day. See "The Playboy Advisor," *Playboy* 47, 1 (January 2000): 51.

11. Georges Bataille, *Eroticism: Death and Sensuality*, Mary Dalwood, trans. (San Francisco: City Lights Books, 1986); see also Bernard Arcand, *The Jaguar and the Anteater: Pornography Degree Zero*, Wayne Grady, trans. (New York: Verso, 1993).

12. Andrew Ross, "The Popularity of Pornography," *No Respect: Intellectuals and Popular Culture* (New York: Routledge, 1989), pp. 171–208.

13. Roland Barthes, "The World of Wrestling," *Mythologies*, Annette Lavers, trans. (New York: Hill and Wang, 1972), pp. 15–25.

14. See John Tierney, "Porn, the Low-Slung Engine of Progress," *New York Times*, 9 January 1994, sec. 2, pp. 1, 18.

15. See John S. and Robin M. Haller, *The Physician and Sexuality in Victorian America* (New York: Norton, 1977), p. 185.

16. Carolyn Marvin, *When Old Technologies Were New: Thinking about Electric Communication in the Late Nineteenth Century* (New York: Oxford University Press, 1987), p. 70.

17. Attorney General's Commission on Pornography, *Final Report* (Washington, D.C.: U. S. Government Printing Office, 1986), I, p. 383.

18. Sally Hacker, "The Eye of the Beholder: An Essay on Technology and Eroticism," in *"Doing It the Hard Way": Investigations of Gender and Technology*, Dorothy E. Smith and Susan M. Turner, eds. (Boston: Unwin Hyman, 1990), pp. 205–223.

19. Alison Hume, "Fear of Porn: What's Really behind It? An Interview with Carol S. Vance," *Vogue* 175 (September 1985), p. 679; see also Laura Kipnis, *Bound and Gagged: Pornography and the Politics of Fantasy in America* (New York: Grove Press, 1996).

20. Susie Bright, "Introduction," in *Herotica: A Collection of Women's Erotic Fiction*, Susie Bright, ed. (Burlingame, Calif.: Down There Press, 1988), p. 3.

21. Mariana Valverde, "Lesbiantics: The True Joy of Sex," *Rites for Lesbian and Gay Liberation* 1 (June 1984): 17.

22. Herbert Marcuse, *Eros and Civilization: A Philosophical Inquiry into Freud* (Boston: Beacon, 1955).

23. Hegemony, said Antonio Gramsci, the Marxist originator of the concept, compels assent to ideas because they seem reasonable and just. Gramsci also maintained that hegemonic dominance can be altered, that revolutionary movements can and must establish *their* ideas by educating a culture to their value; see Antonio Gramsci, *Selections from Cultural Writings*, William Boelhower, trans., David Forgacs and Geoffrey Nowell-Smith, eds. (Cambridge, Mass.: Harvard University Press, 1985), pp. 41–43, 275. Stuart Hall is the chief modern theorist of hegemony, but he does not address pornography directly.

24. Robert Darnton, *Forbidden Best-Sellers of Pre-Revolutionary France* (London: HarperCollins, 1996).

25. Lynn Hunt, "Introduction," in *The Invention of Pornography: Obscen-*

ity and the Origins of Modernity, 1500–1800, Lynn Hunt, ed. (Cambridge, Mass.: MIT Zone, 1993), p. 44.

26. Jean Marie Goulemot, *Forbidden Texts: Erotic Literature and Its Readers in Eighteenth-Century France* (Philadelphia: University of Pennsylvania Press, 1995).

27. Walter Kendrick, *The Secret Museum*, pp. 174–177.

28. Joss Marsh, *Word Crimes: Blasphemy, Culture, and Literature in Nineteenth Century England* (Chicago: University of Chicago Press, 1998).

29. Lauren Berlant, *The Queen of America Goes to Washington City: Essays on Sex and Citizenship* (Durham, N.C.: Duke University Press, 1997).

30. Joseph W. Slade, "Inventing a Sexual Discourse: A Rhetorical Analysis of Adult Video Box Covers," in *Sexual Rhetoric: Media Perspectives on Sexuality, Gender, and Identity*, Meta G. Carstarphen and Susan Zavoina, eds. (Westport, CT: Greenwood Press, 1999), pp. 239–254.

31. Joseph W. Slade, "Violence in the Hard-Core Pornographic Film: A Historical Survey," *Journal of Communication* 34 (Summer 1984): 148–150.

32. Stephen Greenblatt, "America's Raciest Read," *New York Times*, 22 September 1998, p. A31.

33. Wayland Young, *Eros Denied: Sex in Western Society* (New York: Grove Press, 1964), p. 324.

34. See, for example, Austin Bunn, "Money Porn," *Village Voice*, 30 November 1999, pp. 58–59.

35. Alan M. Dershowitz, "Justice," *Penthouse* (August 1999): 128.

36. Jay A. Gertzman, *Bookleggers and Smuthounds: The Trade in Erotica, 1920–1940* (Philadelphia: University of Pennsylvania Press, 1999).

37. "U. S. Pornography Irks British," *New York Times*, 13 April 1964, p. 58.

38. Sophie Bordes and Daniel Serceau, "L'irrésistible marginalisation du cinéma pornographique," *Érotisme et cinéma: Themes et variations*, Daniel Serceau, ed. (Paris: Atlas L'Herminier, 1986), pp. 155–172.

39. Joseph W. Slade, "Pornography in the Nineties," *Wide Angle* 19, 3 (1997): 3–4.

40. Arabella Melville, "The Dirty Doctor: A (Brief) Career in Porno," *Tales from the Clit: A Female Experience of Pornography*, Cherie Matrix, ed. (San Francisco: AK Press, 1996), pp. 1–11.

41. Calvin Tomkins, "Madonna's Anticlimax," *New Yorker*, 26 October 1992, p. 39.

42. David Aaron Clark, "Madonna Exposed," *Gauntlet* 5 (1993): 20.

43. "Ticker," *Brill's Content* 2, 1 (February 1999): 128.

44. Joseph W. Slade, "Inventing a Sexual Discourse," p. 242.

45. Steve Silberman, "The Golden Age of Porn Online," *Wired News* (October 1998), available Internet: www.wired.com/news/news/culture/story/16175.html.

46. Mary B. W. Tabor, "Schools Profit from Offering Pupils for Market Research," *New York Times*, 5 April 1999, pp. A1, 16.

47. David Bauder, "New Technology Inserts Ads in TV Show with Product Placement" [AP Story], *The Columbus* [Ohio] *Dispatch*, 2 April 1999, p. 7G.

48. Max Weber, *The Protestant Ethic and the Spirit of Capitalism*, Talcott Parsons, trans. (1905; reprint, New York: Scribner's, 1958).

49. Sandra Levinson, "Sexploitation in the Underground Press," in *Conversations with the New Reality*, Editors of *Ramparts*, eds. (San Francisco: Canfield Colophon, 1971), pp. 142–143.

50. See, for example, Susan Gubar and Joan Hoff, eds., *For Adult Users Only: The Dilemma of Violent Pornography* (Bloomington, Ind.: Indiana University Press, 1989).

51. Morse Peckham, *Art and Pornography: An Experiment in Explanation* (New York: Basic Books, 1969).

52. Statements by Erotic Writers, Photographers, Poets, and Artists, "On Eros and Erotic Art," in *The Erotic Impulse: Honoring the Sensual Self*, David Steinberg, ed. (New York: Tarcher/Perigee, 1992), pp. 101–106.

53. Jean Laplanche and J. B. Pontalis, "Fantasy and the Origins of Sexuality," *International Journal of Pyscho-Analysis* 49, 1 (1968): 1–18.

54. Beverley Brown, "A Feminist Interest in Pornography—Some Modest Proposals," *m/f* 5–6 (1981): 11.

55. Valerie Steele, *Fetish: Fashion, Sex and Power* (New York: Oxford University Press, 1995), p. 167.

56. Patricia Gilland, "Therapeutic Use of Obscenity," in *Censorship and Obscenity*, Rajeev Dhavan and Christie Davies, eds. (London: Martin Robertson, 1978), pp. 127–147; Maurice Yaffé, "Therapeutic Uses of Sexually Explicit Material," in *The Influence of Pornography on Behavior*, Maurice Yaffé and Edward C. Nelson, eds. (London: Academic Press, 1982), pp. 119–150.

57. John O'Neil, "Vital Signs: When Fantasies Outperform Aspirin," *New York Times*, 28 December 1999, p. D7.

58. American Psychiatric Association, *Diagnostic and Statistical Manual of Mental Disorders*, 4th ed. rev. (Washington, D.C.: APA, 1994), p. 526.

59. Robert J. Stoller, *Observing the Erotic Imagination* (New Haven, Conn.: Yale University Press, 1985), p. 155.

60. Elizabeth Grosz, "Lesbian Fetishism?" in *Fetishism as Cultural Discourse*, Emily Apter and William Pietz, eds. (Ithaca: Cornell University Press, 1993), pp. 101–115.

61. B. Ellis and D. Symons, "Sex Differences in Sexual Fantasy," *Journal of Sex Research* 27 (1989): 527–555; Glenn Wilson, *The Great Sex Divide: A Study of Male-Female Differences* (London: Peter Owen, 1989).

62. Christine Pickard, "A Perspective on Female Response to Sexual Material," in *The Influence of Pornography on Behaviour*, Maurice Yaffé and Edward C. Nelson, eds. (New York: Academic Press, 1982), pp. 91–118.

63. Jack Weatherford, *Porn Row* (New York: Arbor House, 1986), p. 45.

64. See Joseph W. Slade, "Inventing a Sexual Discourse," p. 239.

65. Mark Caldwell, *A Short History of Rudeness: Manners, Morals, and Misbehavior in Modern America* (New York: Picador USA, 1999).

66. Christopher Lehmann-Haupt, "Books of the Times," *New York Times*, 11 December 1980, p. C25.

67. Edward Sagarin, "On Obscenity and Pornography," *The New Sexual Revolution*, Lester A. Kirkendall and Robert N. Whitehurst, eds. (New York: Donald W. Brown, 1971), pp. 105–113.

68. Robin Morgan, "Theory and Practice: Pornography and Rape," in *Going Too Far: The Personal Chronicle of a Feminist* (New York: Vintage, 1978), pp. 163–169.

69. Laura Mulvey, "Visual Pleasure and Narrative Cinema," *Screen* 16, 3 (1975): 6–18; reprinted in *Visual and Other Pleasures* (Bloomington, Ind.: Indiana University Press, 1989).

70. See, for example, Kathleen Barry, *The Prostitution of Sexuality* (New York: New York University Press, 1994).

71. See, as just some examples, the essays in Eileen Phillips, ed., *The Left and the Erotic* (London: Lawrence and Wishart, 1983); Alison Assiter and Avedon Carol, eds., *Bad Girls and Dirty Pictures: The Challenge to Reclaim Feminism* (Boulder, Colo.: Pluto Press, 1993); and Lynne Segal and Mary McIntosh, eds., *Sex Exposed: Sexuality and the Pornography Debate* (New Brunswick, N.J.: Rutgers University Press, 1993).

72. Joanna Russ, *Magic Mommas, Trembling Sisters, Puritans and Perverts: Feminist Essays* (Trumansburg, N.Y.: Crossing Press, 1985), pp. 59–61.

73. Veronica Monet, "What Is Feminist Porn?" in *Porn 101: Eroticism, Pornography, and the First Amendment*, James Elias et al., eds. (Amherst, N.Y.: Prometheus Books, 1999), pp. 207–210.

74. Andrea Dworkin, *Intercourse* (New York: Free Press, 1987).

75. James R. Petersen, "Catharine MacKinnon Again," *Playboy* 39, 8 (August 1992): 37–39.

76. Catharine A. MacKinnon, *Only Words* (Cambridge, Mass.: Harvard University Press, 1994).

77. Jean Bethke Elshtain, "The Victim Syndrome: A Troubling Turn in Feminism," *Progressive* 46 (June 1982): 45.

78. Pat Califia, "A Personal View of the History of the Lesbian S/M Community and Movement in San Francisco," *Coming to Power: Writings and Graphics on Lesbian S/M*, Samois, ed. (Boston: Alyson Pubs, 1982), pp. 243–281.

79. Constance Penley, "Crackers and Whackers: The White Trashing of Porn," in *White Trash: Race and Class in America*, Matt Wray and Annalee Newitz, eds. (New York: Routledge, 1997), pp. 89–112.

80. Audre Lorde, "Uses of the Erotic: The Erotic as Power," in *Sister Outsider: Essays and Speeches by Audre Lorde* (Trumansburg, N.Y.: Crossing Press, 1984), pp. 53–59; bell hooks, *Outlaw Culture: Resisting Representations* (New York: Routledge, 1994); Tracey A. Gardner, "Racism in Pornography and the Women's Movement," in Lederer, *Take Back the Night*, pp. 105–114.

81. Lisa Steele, "A Capital Idea: Gendering in the Mass Media," *Women against Censorship*, Varda Burstyn, ed. (Vancouver: Douglas and McIntyre, 1985), p. 59.

82. Dany Lacombe, *Ideology and Public Policy: The Case against Pornography* (Toronto: Garamond Press, 1988), p. 102.

83. Ann Garry, "Pornography and Respect for Women," in *Philosophy and Sex*, rev. ed., Robert Baker and Frederick Elliston, eds. (Amherst, N.Y.: Prometheus Books, 1984), p. 325.

84. Ellen Willis, "Feminism, Moralism, and Pornography," in *Powers of Desire: The Politics of Sexuality*, Ann Snitow, Christine Stansell, and Sharon Thompson, eds. (New York: Monthly Review Press, 1983), p 463.

85. Quoted by Eric Schlosser, "The Business of Pornography," *U.S. News and World Report*, 10 February 1997, p. 47; see also Nina Hartley, "Pornography at the Millenium," *Gauntlet* 14 (1997): 20–24.

86. Milton Rugoff, *Prudery and Passion: Sexuality in Victorian America* (New York: Putnam, 1971), pp. 120–123.

87. Hal D. Sears, *The Sex Radicals: Free Love in Victorian America* (Lawrence, Kan.: Regents Press, 1977), p. 73.

88. Jay Gertzman, *Bookleggers and Smuthounds*, pp. 160–163.

89. Joe Domanick, "Maybe There Is a God," *Playboy* 37, 8 (August 1990): 110–111.

90. Gérard Lenne, *Sex on the Screen: Eroticism on the Screen*, trans. D. Jacobs (New York: St. Martin's, 1989), p. xi.

91. Calvin Tomkins, "Madonna's Anticlimax," p. 38.

92. Henry F. Pringle, *Big Frogs* (New York: Macy-Masius/Vanguard, 1928).

93. Jeffrey Weeks, *Against Nature: Essays on History, Sexuality and Identity* (London: Rivers Oram Press, 1991), p. 71.

94. American Civil Liberties Union, *Private Group Censorship and the NODL*, rev. ed. (New York: American Civil Liberties Union, 1958).

95. Edward de Grazia, "Obscenity, Censorship and the Mails I," *New Republic*, 23 January 1956, p. 16.

96. J. Edward Day, "Mailing Lists and Pornography," *American Bar Association Journal* 52, 12 (December 1966): 1103–1109.

97. Georgette Bennett, "Purveying Prurience," in *Crime Warps: The Future of Crime in America* (Garden City, NY: Anchor Press/Doubleday, 1987), p. 190.

98. See, for example, Tom W. Williams, *See No Evil: Christian Attitudes toward Sex in Art and Entertainment* (Grand Rapids, Mich.: Zondervan, 1976).

99. Louis A. Zurcher and R. George Kirkpatrick, *Citizens for Decency: Antipornography Crusades as Status Defense* (Austin: University of Texas Press, 1976); R. G. Kirkpatrick and Louis A. Zurcher, "Women against Pornography: Feminist Anti-Pornography Crusades in American Society," *International Journal of Sociology and Social Policy* 3 (1983): 1–30.

100. John Springhall, *Youth, Popular Culture and Moral Panics: Penny Gaffs to Gangsta Rap, 1830–1996* (New York: St. Martin's, 1999).

101. David J. Pivar, *Purity Crusade: Sexual Morality and Social Control, 1868–1900* (Westport, Conn.: Greenwood Press, 1973).

102. National Coalition Against Censorship, *The Sex Panic: Women, Censorship, and "Pornography"* (New York: National Coalition Against Censorship, 1993).

103. Lisa Duggan, "Sex Panics," in *Sex Wars: Sexual Dissent and Political Culture*, Lisa Duggan and Nan D. Hunter (New York: Routledge, 1995), pp. 74–78.

104. Thelma McCormack, "Machismo in Media Research: A Critical Review of Research on Violence and Pornography," *Social Problems* 25, 5 (1977–78): 544–555.

105. Interview with George Huntington, former investigator for the Kinsey Institute and former police chief of Bloomington, Indiana, 5 August 1977.

106. Martha Alshuler, "Origins of the Law of Obscenity," in *Technical Report of the Commission on Obscenity and Pornography*, 9 vols. (Washington, D.C.: Government Printing Office, 1971–72), II, pp. 65–71; Karin Dovring, "Troubles with Mass Communication and Semantic Differentials in 1744 and Today," *American Behavioral Scientist* 8, 1 (1965): 9–14.

107. Peter Wagner, "Eros Goes West: European and 'Homespun' Erotica in Eighteenth-Century America," in T*he Transit of Civilization from Europe to America: Essays in Honor of Hans Galinsky*, Winfried Herget and Karl Ortseifen, eds. (Tübingen: G. Narr, 1986), pp. 145–146.

108. Stanley Fish, *There's No Such Thing as Free Speech, and It's a Good Thing, Too* (New York: Oxford University Press, 1993).

109. Wendy Kaminer, "Pornography and the First Amendment: Prior Restraint and Private Action," in Lederer, *Take Back the Night*, pp. 241–247; see especially 247.

110. Richard Pérez-Peña, "Albany Court Says New York City Too Zealous in Closing Sex Shops," *New York Times*, 21 December 1999, p. A29.

111. Richard Goldstein, "Porn Free," *Village Voice*, 1 September 1998, pp. 28, 30, 33–34.

112. Robin Pogrebin, "Nary a Drama on Broadway," *New York Times*, 28 December 1999, pp. B1, B5.

113. See Sue Curry Jansen, *Censorship: The Knot That Binds Power and Knowledge* (New York: Oxford University Press, 1988).

114. Dan W. Schneder, "Authority of the Register of Copyrights to Deny Registration of a Claim to Copyright on the Ground of Obscenity," *Chicago-Kent Law Review* 51 (1975): 691–724.

115. Ronald K. L. Collins and David M. Skover, *The Death of Discourse* (Boulder, Colo.: Westview Press, 1996).

116. "Neighborhood Porn Wars," *Newsweek*, 18 April 1993, p. 39.

117. *Final Report*, II, pp. 1039–1238; any number of sources document organized crime's reach into pornographic industries during the 1960s and 1970s, but see Luke Ford, *The History of X: 100 Years of Sex in Film* (Amherst, N.Y.: Prometheus Books, 1999), pp. 111–146, for a quick overview.

118. John Cummings and Ernest Volkman, *Goombata: The Improbable Rise and Fall of John Gotti and His Gang* (Boston: Little, Brown and Co., 1990), pp. 60–61.

119. Ford, *The History of X*, p. 141.

120. Jeffrey Goldberg, "The Don Is Done," *New York Times Magazine*, 31 January 1999, p. 71.

121. See James R. Kincaid, *Child-Loving: The Erotic Child and Victorian Culture* (New York: Routledge, 1993; 2nd ed. 1994); and James R. Kincaid, *Erotic Innocence: The Culture of Child Molesting* (Durham, N.C.: Duke University Press, 1998).

122. See Morton N. Cohen, *Lewis Carroll's Photographs of Nude Children* (Philadelphia: Rosenbach Foundation, 1978).

123. Eugene Slabaugh and George Huntington, "Producers of and Nature of Stag Films," audio recording (1966) in the Erotic Film Archives, Kinsey Institute for Research in Sex, Gender, and Reproduction, Indiana University, Bloomington, Ind.

124. See Robert Weddle, "The Pied Piper of Sex and His Wild L. I. Orgies," *New York Post*, 14 August 1980, p. 9.

125. See Philip Jenkins, *Intimate Enemies: Moral Panics in Contemporary Great Britain* (Hawthorne, N.Y.: Aldine de Gruyter, 1992) for a comparison of public responses in America and Great Britain during the 1970s.

126. Legislative Investigating Commission of the Illinois General Assembly, *Sexual Exploitation of Children: A Report to the Illinois General Assembly by the Illinois Legislative Investigating Commission* (Champaign, Ill.: State of Illinois Printing Office, 1980).

127. Senate Committee on the Judiciary (95th Congress), *Protection of Children against Sexual Exploitation Act of 1977: Report on S 1585* (Washington, D.C.: Government Printing Office, 1977).

128. Lawrence A. Stanley, "The Child-Pornography Myth," *Playboy* 35, 9 (September 1988): 41–44.

129. Senate Permanent Subcommittee on Investigations of the Committee on Governmental Affairs (98th Congress, Second Session, Part I), *Child Pornography and Paedophilia* (Washington, D.C.: Government Printing Office, 1985).

130. Attorney General's Commission, *Attorney General's Commission on Pornography: Final Report.*

131. Lawrence A. Stanley, "The Child-Porn Myth," *Cardozo Arts and Entertainment Law Journal* 7, 2 (1989): 21–38.

132. Ian Austen, "But First, Another Word from Our Sponsor," *New York Times*, 18 February 1999, pp. A1, D1, D8.

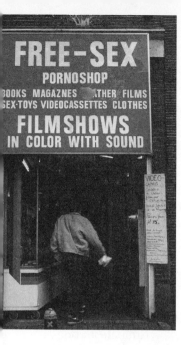

History and Genres of Pornography 2

S tyles of beauty, degrees of explicitness, types of representation, and receding taboos all shorten the appeal of particular artifacts. As a consequence, pornographic documents are difficult to trace. Also, a good deal of pornography has always circulated clandestinely, suffered seizure and destruction, or simply disappeared. When "secret" archives of books, paintings, and other items are discovered when their collectors die, heirs often disperse the contents. Dealers quickly buy the pieces that can be attributed to famous masters, leaving the rest to a capricious market. The anonymous and missing pieces, of course, would stitch together what so far are only fragments of a history of sexual representation. Such a history could never be monolithic in any case. Because sexual expression takes many forms and energizes many sectors of culture, dealing with representation by categories of communication technologies is the best way to chronicle genres.

Sexual Speech and Folklore

The most primal of human technologies is speech, which has always lent itself to sexual representation. Oral examples survive chiefly as folklore. "All folklore is erotic," says Gershon Legman[1]; it "is the voice of those who have no other voice, and would not be listened to if they did. Of no part of folklore is this more true— folk songs and ballads, folklife, language, artifacts, dances and games, superstitions and all the rest—than of the sexual parts."[2] Obscene folklore—the demotic rendering of human sexual imagination—serves as the fountainhead of pornography, a collective cultural id. Its impulses remain very much alive in jokes and stories, songs and legends.[3]

Students can choose from any number of theories of the obscene, from standard Freudian formulations to invocations of sexual magic and religious transgressions of taboo. As the psychologist Bruno Bettelheim points out, obscenity is essential to rites of passage in almost every culture.[4] Other scholars insist that a sense of obscenity enables humans to discriminate among ideas and to process information intellectually.[5] Obscenity can hurt and demean, but it can also mark territory, bond members of a group, entertain an audience, arouse a lover, or deconstruct the meaning of the universe. At base, erotic folklore assumes that there is a sexual explanation for every phenomenon.

Classic handbooks such as the *Bilderlexicon der Erotik* include sections on oral expression.[6] Once oral representations are printed, of course, they lose the ephemerality that is their protection and, having been fixed, become targets of the censorious. Other ironies are also apparent. Cultural critics assume that printed and visual technologies have allowed upper classes to impose their sexual preferences on society over the past several hundred years. The obscenity that fuels sexual expression, however, wells up from lower strata of society, and it has done so for thousands of years. Ancient dirty stories, songs, rhymes, and jokes have mutated across nationalities and ethnic groups in profusion and, when properly studied, reveal cross-cultural racial, gender, and sexual diversities.

For example, seventeenth century Native Americans adored sexual representations. Smutty stories, carved objects such as phalluses and vulvas, and paintings of human copulation were normal elements of a tribal life lived close to nature.[7] To the colonists, this rich sexual folklore made Native Americans seem uncivilized. Even so, historians have also discovered that Puritans were not quite the prudes that the nineteenth century envisioned; the early settlers engaged in sexual experimentation and spoke of such matters with bawdy glee.[8] Though publicly they enforced stern morality, the protocols of community life merely shunted sexual expression to taverns and stables, fields and forests. Nathaniel Hawthorne demonized the deep woods as frighteningly sexual in stories such as "Young Goodman Brown" (1846), as did oral and published Indian captivity narratives, which titillated colonists with allusions to the sexual prowess of Native Americans who carried off female settlers.[9] Orality eroticized frontiers.

The erotic residue of oral cultures is recoverable one expression at a time. American scholars long refused to investigate erotic oral materials; anthropologists still debate the propriety of doing so.[10] Folklorists and ethnographers who collected sexual songs, poems, and stories were the first academics to study erotica. Far more courageous than scholars who dabble in sexual materials today, they pursued research that took them afoul of the law, and when they published their work, they usually had to release it *as* pornography. Probably the most notorious scholar was John S. Farmer, lexicographer, linguist, philologist, folklorist—and the author of pornographic works. Farmer and his fellow compiler William Earnest Henley privately published their masterwork, the seven-volume *Slang and Its Analogues*, the etymologically brilliant exploration of those parts of the English language omitted by the *Oxford English Dictionary*, whose editors only grudgingly acknowledged the noun *pornography*.[11] They trace the derivation of the word "cunt," for example, to its probable origin as the name of a London street frequented by prostitutes in the thirteenth century, noting that it became legally obscene by 1700.

Lexicographers, philologists, and folklorists build on each other's work. The sexologist Adolph Niemoller's *American Encyclopedia of Sex* (1935)[12] borrows heavily from Farmer and Henley, as do a great many other dictionaries and encyclopedias published since. Allen Walker Read's *Lexical Evidence from Folk Epigraphy in Western North America: A Glossarial Study of the Low Element in the English Vocabulary* (1935),[13] another scholarly work that had to be published privately, deals with graffiti. The volume also contains Read's famous essay, "The Nature of Obscenity," a comment on the utility of violating taboo in order to puncture social reticence, superciliousness, class pretense, and false modesty aggravated by authorities such as Noah Webster, who bowdlerized classic texts from Shakespeare to the Bible. During the 1900s Webster anticipated the political correctness of the next century by purifying language of offense; "broadcloth secession" became the substitute for "hole" in one's trousers, for example.[14] Such delicacy acts as a red flag on ordinary Americans, not to mention the pornographically inclined.

Although oral traditions enshrine the sexual languages of all genders and groups, scholars have only recently begun to categorize them. Every sexual subculture cherishes its own vocabulary, nuanced by and for degrees of pleasure and complicity.[15] Gay and lesbian vocabularies evolve in opposition to straight discourse, use pronouns differently, devise neologisms for sexual behavior, reconfigure power relationships, and foreground verbal cues so that homosexuals can recognize each other.[16] Some poststructuralists believe that language "constructs" gender, taking to extremes the argument that whereas sex is a fact, gender is an idea in search of expression.[17] The most extreme linguistic position is that of Catharine MacKinnon, who in *Only Words* rejects distinctions between words and sticks and stones. According to MacKinnon, language and deeds are equivalent; to create a sexual fantasy about a woman is virtually to rape her.[18] In response, Judith Butler argues that language is secondary to the "performance" of desire, sexuality, and gender. Acts count far more than words,[19] according to her and others.

Phallocentric language has been parsed by numerous American and European feminists. Some scholarship indicts the sexism of males whereas some explores the rich potential of women's sexual expression. Julia P. Stanley counts 22 terms for promiscuous males (playboy, stud, Don Juan) but more than 200 for promiscuous females (whore, hooker, harlot, concubine, strumpet, and so on); the imbalance suggests social and sexual inequality.[20] Luce Irigaray believes that gender profoundly influences language. Just as consciousness of a phallus shapes male discourse, so does awareness of the clitoris shape female talk; her essays liberally use terms such as "clits" and "pricks."[21] Hélène Cixous urges women to speak honestly about sexuality using their "labial" consciousness to undermine masculine dominance.[22] Once deliberately coopted, derogatory words can empower. Porn actresses and Riot Grrls rehabilitate terms such as "slut" as proud labels, in much the same way that Eve Ensler's play *The Vagina Monologues* attempts to appropriate "cunt" as a term of endearment instead of denigration.

During the 1980s, pressure groups defined pornography as a tool for oppressing women; during the 1990s, women, minorities, gays, and lesbians have recast pornography as a method for discovering and enhancing sexual identities. Lack of polite discourse suitable for articulating sexual acts endows obscene language with power. Telling a sexual story helps to construct a sexual self,[23] create a sense of community among similar individuals, and—by giving weight to constructed identities—foster social acceptance. Since the larger culture for decades automatically classified gay and lesbian speech as pornographic, an obvious strategy is to embrace the language and turn it to different purposes.[24] The key is conscious agency. Moving alternative visions of eroticism into arenas of popular culture allows straight women, lesbians, gays, African Americans, Asian Americans, and so on to compete for attention and acceptance. Given enough effort, say advocates, such groups can assert their own preferences and advance their own mythologies. If pornography were not important, of course, it would not be worth hijacking.

Those intent on constructing identities can draw on veins of sexual humor. Women's sexual humor, for instance, offers social criticism and cohesion in the guise of fun.[25] Conventional studies report stereotypical conclusions: men tell jokes to subordinate women as compensation for emotional inferiority whereas women prefer nonaggressive jokes that deflate pretense or send-up expectations.[26] More thoughtful examinations conclude that women can find men's sexual jokes funny depending on teller, audience, and social setting.[27] The rich, earthy speech and images of African Americans fill collections of black sexual language, tales, verse, jokes, songs, insults, and legends in unexpurgated form. Daryl Cumber Dance believes that for African Americans, obscenity serves to reduce stress, loss, and disappointment and—at another extreme—to verbalize exuberance, affection, or hostility.[28] In any case, highly sexualized language and imagery has flowed for centuries from African American subcultures into American mainstreams.

Sexual humor in fact constitutes a vast folkloristic continent whose exploration has only begun. The major domestic cartographies are the studies by Gershon Legman of dirty jokes and limericks,[29] but historians and ethnographers have looked at coarse satire, religious bawdy, political invective, jestbooks, almanacs, scurrilous poetry and verse, and salty and scatalogical jokes from the American colonial period onward.[30] Most of the scholarship dates from the sub-rosa publication in 1927 of *Anecdota Americana, Being Explicitly an Anthology of the Tales in the Vernacular* by Joseph Fliesler under the pseudonyms "J. Mortimer Hall" and "William Passemon,"[31] a work reprinted many times. The tradition continues today with the long-delayed printing of sexual folklore gathered by folklorists such as Vance Randolph, whose *Roll Me in Your Arms: "Unprintable" Ozark Folksongs and Folklore* and *Blow the Candle Out: "Unprintable" Ozark Folklore* have appeared only in the past few years.[32]

New channels transmit sexual humor more widely than before. For a brief period, the photocopy machine mass-duplicated nasty jokes, racy stories, and ethnic and gender slurs, a more rapid medium than samizdat, the practice of passing handwritten or typed manuscripts hand-to-hand. Scholars marveled at the circulation of photocopied dirty jokes.[33] In a culture of "secondary orality," a McLuhanesque term for the recycling of oral discourse by electronic media, sexual jokes now move with lightning speed. An E-mail box can fill in minutes with off-color jokes generated by events. In 1991, when the actor Paul Reubens (a.k.a. Pee Wee Herman) was arrested for indecent exposure, the *New York Times* was astonished at the speed with which jokes about the incident circulated by E-mail.[34] When Robert Mapplethorpe's portrait of himself with the handle of a bullwhip inserted in his anus triggered the outrage of conservative senator Jesse Helms, E-mail correspondents swiftly suggested that Helms was angry because he thought the photographer had shown disrespect to the state flower of North Carolina. Swapping jokes about the Clinton-Lewinsky scandal created a warm ritual even in office environments normally chary of speech that might be construed as harassment; women shared dirty jokes with men in rational response to a national crisis.[35] Ethnic and female comedians now specialize in ribald, incisive social comment, taking their cues from the greatest of all obscene comedians, Lenny Bruce.

Finally, American musicians have long incorporated sexuality in their compositions. Puritans regarded music as suspect because of its sensuality, but American immigrants have treasured the bawdy music of their ancestors, which has crossed and recrossed borders to form a rich pornographic heritage. The indefatigable John S. Farmer privately published *Merry Songs and Ballads Prior to the Year 1800 and Musa Pedestris* in 1896–1897 to comment on obscene ballads, rhymes, and songs popular in English,[36] but since that time collections of naughty, lewd, and dirty cowboy songs, sea chanteys, college songs, prison songs, workhouse songs, and so on have circulated mostly in expurgated or asterisked editions. When A. Reynolds Morse anonymously and privately published an uncensored *Folk Poems and Ballads, an Anthology: A Collection of Rare Verses and Amusing Folk Songs Compiled from Scarce and Suppressed Books as Well as from Verbal Sources, Which Modern Prudery, False Social Customs and Intolerance Have Separated from the Public and Historical Record* in 1948, it was instantly seized and suppressed for forty years. In 1989, Guy

Logsdon's *"The Whorehouse Bells Were Ringing," and Other Songs Cowboys Sing* escaped prosecution, a circumstance that may eventually lead to recovery of more "unprintable" lyrics. Massive collections, usually in typescript duplicated at several sites to avoid loss, still repose in folklore archives in universities throughout the United States.

During the nineteenth century, says Sandra Perry, Americans were unable to sing of truly adult themes in public. Bawdy songs sung in private thus filled a vacuum, at least for lower classes comfortable with them.[37] Although officials tolerated bawdy songs, raucous marches, and wild fiddling at fairgrounds and private celebrations, in the 1890s ragtime, the music of minstrel shows, spilled over into the streets. "A wave of vulgar, filthy and suggestive music has inundated the land," warned authorities, who excoriated the "obscene posturings" and "lewd gestures"[38] that accompanied ragtime's beat.

In 1911, politicians investigated the licentious pronoun in composer Irving Berlin's song "Everybody's Doing It Now," the first legislative scrutiny of song lyrics. Manners loosened by the chaos of World War I manifested themselves in jazz, a form of music invented in whorehouses, as men and women began to dance in styles that struck their elders as lascivious. "Jazz," a vulgar term for sexual intercourse, became the popular name (Jazz Age) for the 1920s. Its rhythms seemed to inflame rebellious youths with desire; jazz records acquired a reputation as pernicious as prohibited liquor, and no radio station would air them. Nor would broadcasters play the sexy blues lyrics of artists such as Bessie Smith or Ma Rainey ("Need a Little Sugar for My Bowl"), or double-entendre titles such as "Please Warm My Wiener" and "Your Biscuits Are Big Enough for Me."

Ragtime, blues, and jazz merged in the 1950s in rock 'n' roll, a hybrid music that revolted older Americans. Conservatives denounced the gyrations of Elvis Presley and, later, the lyrics of the Beatles, much as their counterparts today lash out at MTV. Police arrested Jim Morrison, Jimmy Hendrix, Wendy O. Williams, and dozens of other performers for public lewdness. When the Senate held hearings on explicit and violent lyrics in 1985, a frightened National Association of Recording Merchandisers "voluntarily" placed warning labels on their products. The rap group 2 Live Crew successfully appealed a 1990 Florida obscenity conviction, but offended fundamentalists and feminists prodded the Senate to hold yet another hearing in 1993.

Erotic Newspapers and Magazines

In 1690 the Massachusetts Bay Colony seized the very first issue of the New World's first newspaper, *Publick Occurrences*, on grounds that its front page, which contained a lurid story about the French monarch, was obscene. Despite the Zenger trial of 1735, which set no clear legal precedents governing libel, newspapers remained vulnerable to attack. In 1798 Congress passed the Alien and Sedition Acts (ostensibly aimed at French partisans) to strike at editors who lambasted political enemies with anatomical slurs, jokes about gender and hygiene, stories of debauchery and lewdness, and accusations of seduction, rape, incest, and paternity. Thomas Jefferson, himself a victim of scurrilous reports regarding his suspected affair with his slave Sally Hemings, nonetheless as president pardoned publishers convicted under the Alien and Sedition Acts, and Congress allowed the acts to lapse in 1800. The rowdy press continued to sling scandal.

The other kind of pornography—intended to titillate rather than excoriate—was slower to develop. Colonial Americans read imported European magazines such as the *Onania*, which deplored the evils of "self-abuse" in language that promoted masturbation. American publishers widely pirated the *Onania* in the 1700s.[39] Most American editors declined to transgress so boldly, although Benjamin Franklin, who printed several scatalogical texts, also perpetrated an amusing newspaper hoax about a woman ("Polly Baker") accused of fornication in 1747.[40] Sailors smuggled ribald British and French broadsheets and pamphlets to eager customers in the nation's transatlantic harbors.

Domestic pornography appeared in the late 1820s and early 1830s as part of the boisterous politics swirling around Andrew Jackson's presidency (1829–1837). Homegrown pornography grew out of the brothels of lower Manhattan. Printers on Ann and Nassau Streets ran off stories and engravings, most of them salacious and most of them tinged with radical but crude republicanism that sought to expose the upper-classes as corrupt. This was pornography in the best—or worst—political tradition of peeping or spying on those with clout. Both Whigs and Democrats spewed venom at each other; privilege and pretense depended on where one stood, and sex, the great leveler, could serve as a weapon for either party.

Benjamin Day's *New York Sun* (1833) and James Gordon Bennett's *New York Herald* (1835) shoveled sensationalism for a penny, but even sleazier newspapers followed. The sporting scene of New York City—and other metropolises—was a masculine realm of prize fighting, billiards, cock fights, horse and dog racing, music halls, saloons, and bordellos.[41] The *Whip*, the *Flash*, the *Weekly Rake*, and the *Libertine*,[42] called "sporting papers," attacked leading citizens for patronizing brothels and provided juicy details. (New Orleans's *Mascot* was similar in its devotion to erotic nightlife.[43]) When the *Sun* lashed at its competition (pots calling kettles black), authorities seized several sporting papers. Decades later, the *Police Gazette* (1878–1897) refined the genre by mixing cartoons, illustrations, and stories of prostitutes, chorus girls, and athletes,[44] though the *Gazette* also revived sex-crime reporting from the previous century.[45] Philadelphia prosecuted newsdealers for selling the *Gazette* in 1889.

Rancorous slavery issues generated sexual invective also. Most abolitionists declined to overemphasize miscegenation by slave owners, though they did express concern about casual nudity and sex among slaves whose family structures had been destroyed. In perhaps the strongest attack, the abolitionist paper *Liberator* charged that "the sixteen slave States constitute one vast brothel," but let matters go at that.[46] Less-restrained proslavery sheets ran stories and drawings depicting licentious abolitionists fondling the female slaves they had "freed."

Predictably, given the penchant for soldiers to read about sex before dying, the Civil War boosted pornographic periodicals. Cheap magazines carried racy stories and engravings, mixing dirty jokes with antimilitary obscenity and "spicy" songs.[47] After the war, new rotogravure techniques and high-speed steam presses enabled backstreet publishers to turn out cheap, lurid rags such as *Day's Doings, Last Sensation, Stetson's Dime Illustrated* (all 1868), *Fox's Illustrated Week's Doings* (1883), and *Illustrated Day's Doings and Sporting World* (1885). In their pages were gravures of burlesque queens clad in tights and corsets, although editors avoided actual nudity in favor of drawings of topless but nippleless women. Given the period's buttoned-up fashions, glimpses of flesh satisfied voyeurs.

Censors drew no distinction between materials that might arouse and materials designed to regulate population. Because birth-control techniques could remove the stigma of pregnancy outside marriage, they were thought by some to encourage sexual immorality. Society could maintain order, so the argument went, only by ostracizing promiscuous women and their bastards; logic thus forbade the circulation of books and pamphlets

on family planning. In 1900 Congress formally defined the sending of contraceptive information through the mails as a criminal
act of obscenity. Not until 1983, in *Bolger v. Young Drug Products,*
463 U.S. 60, did the Supreme Court at last end the ban on advertising contraceptive devices through the mail—almost half a century after the American Medical Association endorsed birth
control in 1937.

Post–Civil War obscenity prosecutions targeted magazines
espousing feminism, "free love," and birth control.[48] The U.S.
Post Office again and again seized the *Word,* an anarchist magazine published in Massachusetts by Ezra Heywood and his wife,
on the grounds that contraceptive advice promoted promiscuity.[49] The U.S. Attorney General joined the U.S. Postmaster General in arresting feminists such as Victoria Woodhull and
free-thought crusaders like Moses Harmon, who published *Lu-
cifer, the Light Bearer* (1883–1907), a voice of "radical" sexuality.
Anthony Comstock's raids swept up birth-control pamphlets,
racing forms, playing cards, and treatises on hygiene along with
"lewd" books and pictures; all were contraband.

Most of the tabloids Comstock seized *were* prurient, having
been run off after-hours by job printers and sold from stalls and
push-carts in seedy districts. During the 1890s, however, the upscale *Munsey's* magazine (1889–1929) ran "nude art," chiefly reproductions of paintings but occasionally photos of decorously
posed models, as did the magazines *Nickell* (1894–1905), *Metropolitan* (1895–1911), and *Peterson's* (1842–1898). The original *Life*
magazine (1883–1936) ran pinups drawn by Charles Dana Gibson; so did *Collier's* in 1903. In 1896, the Supreme Court upheld
the obscenity conviction of Lew Rosen, publisher of *Broadway*
magazine (1898–1911). Using a popular dodge, Rosen obscured
with lampblack the nipples in a drawing of a woman he called a
"tenderloineuse." Readers knew how to wipe off the lampblack.[50]

Global war liberalized expression in America. Soldiers
brought home French magazines featuring women in states of un-
dress. American publishers imitated them: *Breezy Stories* and *Flap-
per* sandwiched drawings or photographs of women in bathing
suits between cartoons and sexy stories. The amazingly popular
Captain Billy's Whiz Bang grew out of a list of jokes that William
Fawcett distributed to American troops during the war; the magazine built the Fawcett publishing house. Jazz Age pornography
for women blended emotional upheaval and social transgression
into popular formulas carried by the magazines *True Story*
(started 1919), *True Confessions* (1922), *True Experiences* (1922), *Love*

and Romance (1923) and *Modern Romance* (1930). Hardly explicit, these heated "confessions" nonetheless titillated. The first major American sociological survey (1929) estimated that 20 to 40 percent of American homes subscribed to *Captain Billy's Whiz Bang, True Story,* or *True Romance,* and lots of other households purchased *Hot Dog, Art Lovers, Breezy Stories,* and *La Vie Parisienne.*[51]

Samuel Roth, beginning a notorious career, came under scrutiny for publishing *Beau: The Man's Magazine* (1924), *Two Worlds Monthly: Devoted to the Increase of the Gaiety of Nations* (1926–1927), and *Casanova Jr.'s Tales* (1929). These sophisticated magazines reproduced classic erotica by authors such as Boccaccio and Ovid (*Two Worlds Monthly* also sanitized and condensed James Joyce's *Ulysses*) and illustrated them with suggestive drawings by artists such as Alexander King. Much lower in tone were the sex-suffused newspapers *New York Daily News, New York Mirror,* and *New York Evening Graphic.* New Yorkers referred to the latter tabloid—the brainchild of Bernarr Macfadden—as the *New York Evening Pornographic* because of its fondness for pictures of criminals and undressed women.[52] Macfadden also published *Physical Culture,* whose pictures of nude men and articles on enemas distressed some readers.[53] Anthony Comstock arrested but failed to convict Macfadden in 1908.

Erotica distracted audiences during the Depression. "Pulps" mutated into the sexy—and sexist—*Spicy Detective, Spicy Western,* and *Spicy Adventure.*[54] Magazine prurience triggered outcries similar to later responses to television; spicy stories were said to be "training manuals" and "equipment catalogs" for criminals.[55] The President's Commission on Obscenity and Pornography in 1970 would decide that police, detective, and thriller types were harmless "barber shop magazines." To compete with their appeal, however, *Wild Cherries, Love's Revels, Broadway Brevities, Smokehouse Monthly, Wow, Jazza-Ka-Jazza, Zest,* and *Army Fun* ran lightly obscured photos of breasts but still avoided nipples, let alone pubic hair, in favor of sniggering humor. From time to time there circulated what were called "Tijuana bibles," a term applied to stapled pages of dirty stories, sometimes illustrated with gamy photos, as well as to eight-page comic books.[56] The printing was atrocious, the paper the lowest grade of pulp; they were inked by printers who ordinarily ran off whisky labels.[57] Mayor La Guardia of New York City gleefully invited residents to watch him set fire to piles of these and other seized magazines (*Garter Girls, Scarlet Confessions, Keyhole Detective Cases*) until advisers reminded him that the Nazis had given book-burning a bad name.[58]

Few magazines of high sexual content appeared during World War II, partly because of paper shortages, partly because there were few men at home to read them, and partly because the war crowded everything else off the public agenda. The war's aftermath forced editors to decide how to report on genuine obscenity, as stories and photographs of the liberated concentration camps came flooding over wire services.[59]

The 1950s, a decade torn by the Korean War and Cold War paranoia, gave rise to exploitation magazines that institutionalized the exposé. *Confidential, True Life Secrets,* and *Police Dragnet* pried into private lives of celebrities. The headlines of the *National Mirror* retailed articles on gory crimes and suburban sin for housewives. Over the next decades, tabloids such as the *National Enquirer,* the *Weekly World News,* the *Globe,* the *Sun,* the *National Examiner,* and the *Star* competed for supermarket readers. The most notorious scandal magazine publisher, Robert Harrison, started out with Macfadden's *Graphic,* launched girlie magazines such as *Beauty Parade* and *Eyeful,* and in 1952 began *Confidential,* whose circulation soared to almost four million.[60] The range of gossip was so enormous that modern collectors have created an index to those "exposed."[61] In the meantime, Harrison's *Flirt, Titter,* and *Wink,* along with other men's magazines such as *Bare, Dare, Sir, Pose, Argosy,* and *Male,* reverted to the light fiction, mild sadism, and cheesecake of prewar decades. They peddled an older generation's version of what psychologist Albert Ellis called "the folklore of sex," the title of his ethnographic survey of magazines of the 1950s and 1960s.[62]

Playboy, started in 1953 by Hugh Hefner, pushed fresher folklore. Few magazines have so changed sexual climates. Critics compared *Playboy* to *Esquire,* also an upscale periodical; indeed, Hefner worked there before editing his own magazine. Moreover, *Esquire* had paved the way when in 1943 it won a case against Postmaster General Frank Walker, who tried to deny second-class mailing privileges to *Esquire* because it was obscene, a charge received with incredulity by the Supreme Court. Hefner's achievement was to make *Playboy* into the liberal voice of a masculinized middle class and to marshal advertisers behind his "Playboy Philosophy," a long-winded (it ran in endless installments) justification of a postwar good life that, he said, included sex as recreation.

High-quality fiction, artwork, and reporting and its later promotion of women writers and women's causes gave *Playboy* a high profile. These very qualities offended feminists and conservatives, who seemed far more upset with *Playboy*'s acceptance by large audiences than they were with the hard-core images in other magazines that followed a decade later. Catharine MacKinnon would charge the magazine with objectifying women and extolling intercourse, the origin of inequality between men and women.[63] Some groups and individuals accused Hefner of conspiracy to destroy American morality.[64] Other detractors claimed that *Playboy* constructed standards of attractiveness damaging to women who unwillingly compare their own bodies to centerfolds. Imitators of *Playboy* rejected its urbanity. *Hustler*, representing itself as the voice of the working class, reveled in a sexism that many middle-class males found difficult to stomach. (For pictorial aspects of magazines, see the Erotic Photography section further in this chapter.)

Success in marketing skin led *Vogue* and *Harper's Bazaar* to show more in fashion layouts and ads and to accentuate sex in articles. *Redbook* and *Ladies' Home Journal*, not known for frankness, began running advice departments on sexual matters.[65] Betty Friedan observed that such advice simply turned women into better consumers of cosmetics and clothes.[66] Familiar riffs on sex and marriage, sex and family, and sex and religion increased circulation of confession magazines during the 1950s and 1960s. These tropes, salacious in intent but innocuous in execution, bewildered investigators for the President's Commission on Obscenity and Pornography (1970), who decided that the confession magazine's appeal was as much emotional as sexual.[67] By 1965, *Cosmopolitan* hired Helen Gurley Brown, author of *Sex and the Single Girl*, as editor, intent on bringing a "candy-sex" orientation to the woman's magazine. Brown ran a centerfold of nude Burt Reynolds in the April 1973 issue. When the brasher *Playgirl* followed suit, its pictorials, ostensibly aimed at women, attracted a gay audience as well.

More important for women in terms of consciousness-raising were the tabloids of the "underground press." During the 1960s and 1970s the *Los Angeles Free Press*, the *East Village Other*, the *Berkeley Barb*, the *Chicago Seed*, and hundreds of counterculture rags condemned the Vietnam war at the same time that they exalted drugs, music, and carnality. Some of these, like Ed Sanders's *Fuck You! A Magazine of the Arts* (1959), were modestly literary; others reprinted pornographic works by writers as famous as W. H. Auden.[68] The sexism of radical papers appalled many women. Even the most intellectually exuberant, like Paul Krassner's *Realist* (1958), suffered from a masculinity that, though hardly macho, excluded women as anything but handmaidens of the revolution. It was one thing for women to be second-class citizens of the larger society; it was another to be an underclass in the counterculture. From this point on, it would be difficult to associate pornography with meaningful liberation.[69]

Many hard-core tabloids hardly bothered to assume counterculture postures, although their "dildo journalism," to use a term coined by cartoonist Jules Feiffer, found plenty of things to complain about. (Even the *Los Angeles Free Press*, most political of all, wound up being bought by Marvin Miller, the pornographer who gave his name to a famous court decision.) Of all these spin-offs from the underground political press, the most outrageous was *Screw*, founded in New York in 1968 by Jim Buckley and Al Goldstein; the latter still publishes it. A reincarnation of sporting papers of the 1840s, *Screw* inspired imitators in New York and California—*Bang, Kiss, New York Review of Sex, Luv, Pleasure, Fun, Cocksure, Ecstasy, Desire*. Most guided readers to local pleasures while complaining about hypocrisy or official malfeasance. Modern counterparts can be found everywhere: *Atlanta Xcitement, Texas Connection* (Dallas), *Rocky Mountain Oyster* (Denver), *Oregon T & A Times* (Portland), *Spectator* (San Francisco), *Stranger* (Seattle). All are legal, thanks to precedent set by *Screw*. Prosecuted in Wichita, Kansas in 1976, Goldstein won his case on appeal on political grounds.

Emboldened upscale entrepreneurs ventured into candor. Andy Warhol began *interView*, a sex-and-celebrity monthly, and Grove Press started the *Evergreen Review*, a literary journal that included erotic art and photographs. In 1962 Ralph Ginzburg brought out the first issue of *Eros*, a slick bimonthly that, among other milestones, printed nude photos of Marilyn Monroe. Although *Eros*'s contents were not obscene, Ginzburg's practice of mailing prurient advertisements from Blue Balls, Montana, and Middlesex, Pennsylvania, subjected him to charges of pandering; the Supreme Court upheld his 1963 conviction in 1966.

Legal climates changed so quickly, however, that by the late 1960s Gourmet Editions, Parliament, American Erotica, Swedish Erotica, and Le Baron were issuing streams of hard-core picture magazines from San Francisco and New York, though they did not circulate widely in the hinterlands. At the end of the decade, investigators of the President's Commission on Obscenity and Pornography estimated that the annual revenues of all hard-core magazines did not add up to the revenues of one month's issue of *Reader's Digest*.[70] In one of those ironies that always seem to grow out of official commissions, when Greenleaf Classics brought out *The Illustrated Presidential Report of the Commission on Obscenity and Pornography* (San Diego, 1970) laced with explicit photographs of the sort the commission had examined, the publisher was promptly sentenced to two years in prison.[71]

Photo magazines multiplied. Often compilations of still photos taken on the sets of hard-core movies, they split into straight and gay categories; ersatz "lesbian" magazines were actually aimed at heterosexual males. Not surprisingly, by the time a market for hard-core images developed among actual lesbians, those audiences preferred videos; authentic hard-core lesbian magazines are still few. Parliament News of Los Angeles, founded by Milton Luros; Peachtree Enterprises of Atlanta, founded by Michael Thevis; and Sovereign News of Cleveland, founded by Reuben Sturman, controlled distribution and in most cases production; all were connected to organized crime. Most Americans have forgotten that the 1973 *Miller v. California* decision (setting community standards as a test for obscenity) is named after Marvin Miller, another "connected" publisher (Collectors' Publications) arrested for advertising explicit photo-books and magazines through the mails. Hard-core magazines followed the trend toward niche-marketing that overtook mainstream periodical publishing. Whereas Irving Klaw had only to use bondage and discipline and whatever costume fetishes came to hand for *Model Parade* in the 1940s and 1950s, hard-core publishers of the 1970s and 1980s tailored their photos to narrow tastes. The fetishes occupied specific coordinates in erotic landscapes, but not all of them involved actual sex.

From the 1970s date such sadomasochism (S/M) periodicals as *Amazon* (Philadelphia), and *Latent Image, Aggressive Gals*, and *Bitch Goddesses* (Los Angeles). Their pictures of dominatrices paddling hapless males recalled the hand-drawn panels of mistresses tormenting slaves in *Bizarre* and *Exotique* (see the Erotic Art section in this chapter) during the 1940s and 1950s whereas their stories recalled the narratives in *Spanking Digest* from the 1960s. From the 1950s date "leg art" magazines, edited by photographer Elmer Batters, whose images filled the pages of *Black Silk Stockings, Thigh High, Leg-O-Rama, Tip Top*, and *Sheer Delight*.[72] The doyenne of fetish magazines today is Dian Hanson, editor of *Juggs, Bust Out, Leg Show*, and *Big Butt*. Formerly an editor for the hard-core *Puritan*, Hanson changed jobs because she was intrigued by sexual specialization. Hanson thinks it is important for people to indulge their sexualities and believes pornography encourages men to masturbate instead of bothering women who have no interest in their fetishes. In fact, she thinks pornography flourishes only in advanced cultures.[73] Valerie Kelly, a sex magazine writer, advises novices to imitate the formulas in *Ass Parade, Bottom, Leggs, Big Boobs, Silky, Pet Pussy, Baby Doll, Naked Nymphs, Roommates, Milk Maids, Bondage Life, TV Tricks, Outlaw Biker, Stallion, Stroke, Leg Parade, Chunky Asses, Lesbian Lovers,* and *Big Mama* in order to pinpoint fetishes.[74] Companies often cover several niches. The publisher of *Celebrity Skin*, for example, also produces *Playgirl, High Society, Cheri, Live Young Girls, Candy Girls, Hawk,* and *Purely 18.*[75]

In 1986, the *Final Report* of the Attorney General's Commission on Pornography listed more than 2,000 hard-core titles, with particular emphasis on the bizarre (*A Cock between Friends, Anal Squeeze, Dildo Fever, Milk Shooters, Ripe Nipples,* and *Young Slit Slurpers*), all carefully alphabetized, much to the amusement of critics, who saw in the report the prurience it lamented. The large number of titles notwithstanding, the commissioners surveyed the field just as the hard-core pictorial magazine market was collapsing, a victim of the surging videocassette industry. The Internet delivered the coup de grâce. Backdate inventories of hard-core periodicals are still available by mail, but most still images—often recycled from magazines—are now distributed electronically.

Homosexual tabloids such as *Gaytimes* appeared during the 1960s, their editors less concerned with correcting mainstream journalism's distortions of gay and lesbian life than with simply establishing lines of communication within subcultures. The fiction, essays, and cartoons of papers such as *Gay Sunshine* (1970–1982) replaced the cautious content of the much slicker *One: The Homosexual Viewpoint*, a New York gay magazine that managed to survive from 1956 to 1965, and the *Ladder* (1956–1972), the principal lesbian periodical. (*Vice Versa*, the first real lesbian magazine, lasted only two issues in 1947.) Today *Out/Look: The National Lesbian and Gay Quarterly* and *OutWeek: The Lesbian and Gay News Magazine* aim at substantial national audiences. Others that focus only on lesbians, such as *On Our Backs* and *Girlfriends*, are still struggling. Lesbians produce small-circulation print and electronic "zines" (as in maga*zines*) in profusion, with titles such as *Poppin' Zits, Holy Titclamps,* and *Slippery When Wet.*

Zines remain the most demotic forms of erotica today. In them Americans share information on alternative social, political, and sexual lifestyles[76] limited only by the imaginations of those who run them off. Frederic Wertham, better known for his critiques of comic books, traced one of these categories, the "fanzine," stapled-together pages of fantasy fiction based on imagined encounters with celebrities, back to the 1930s.[77] For the pages of modern versions, amateurs write gender-bending scenarios around reimagined characters from popular media. Female fans of the *Star Trek* TV series and movies have created a genre called slash/zines or K/S for Kirk/Spock. Writers and artists of K/S zines cast Spock and Captain Kirk as gay or hermaphroditic lovers in congress with galaxies of aliens; other popular TV shows are also used as erotic springboards.[78]

Categories stake out fetishes, issue sexual manifestos, or allow their editors to ride erotic hobbyhorses. The staggering range shifts so quickly that no one can inventory it, although *Factsheet Five*, itself a zine that can be accessed electronically, attempts to keep track of examples such as *Diseased Pariah News* (HIV updates), *Libido* (upscale arty), *On Our Rag* (lesbian menstruation), *Scream Box* (lesbian kinkiness), *Frighten the Horses: A Journal of the Sexual Revolution* (fetishes), *Whorezine* (sex workers), and *Taste of Latex* (pansexuality). *Bust*, a recent zine aimed at young women, celebrates "the f-words (feminism, fucking, fashion)."[79]

Americans unfamiliar with zines can still encounter "pornography" as scandal journalism, advertising, personal ads, and sexual advice columns. According to a recent study of *Newsweek, Time, Cosmopolitan, Redbook, Esquire,* and *Playboy*, of all ads picturing at least one man and one woman in 1993, 17 percent either depicted or implied intercourse between them, whereas only 1 percent of ads did so in 1983 editions of the same magazines. In ads from 1983, only 28 percent of the female models and 11 percent of the males were dressed "provocatively" (a subjective judgment); in 1993, the numbers were 40 percent and 18 percent, respectively.[80] Personal ads coded for gender preferences routinely appear in city magazines and mall weeklies, not to mention slicker journals. Many college newspapers carry "Savage Love," written by Dan Savage to inform correspondents on gay and fetish sex,[81] and alternative newspapers from the *Village Voice* to municipal weeklies such as the Columbus, Ohio, *Other* carry "Pucker Up" by Tristan Taormimo, who advises her readers on the latest techniques of anal sex.

Erotic Literature

American colonists imported erotic books. From England came sex guides by "Aristotle" (*Masterpiece, Compleat Midwife, Problems*) to rivet the randy; in 1744 Jonathan Edwards fulminated against them in Northampton, Massachusetts.[82] Easily the most popular import was *Fanny Hill, or Memoirs of a Woman of Pleasure*, by John Cleland. Benjamin Franklin of Pennsylvania, William Byrd of Virginia, and Samuel Tilden of New York owned copies.[83] Isaiah Thomas, founder of the American Antiquarian Society, author of *History of Printing in America* (1810), and a contender for title of the first American book publisher, probably pirated Cleland's book sometime between 1786 and 1814; certainly later American publishers did.[84] In the first (1821) recorded prosecution for literary obscenity—there may well have been others—the state of Massachusetts sentenced two book peddlers to six months in jail for selling copies of *Memoirs of a Woman of Pleasure*.

Importation was brisk enough for Congress to pass the Tariff Act of 1842, the first federal prohibition of traffic in erotica. Because the late 1830s and early 1840s marked the stirrings of a domestic trade in candid newspapers, books, and engravings, the Tariff Act afforded American pornographers a degree of protectionism and thus assisted the establishment of an industry that would one day dominate the global market. Just who wrote the first American pornographic novel is a matter of dispute. One scholar nominates George Lippard, author of *The Quaker City, or The Monks of Monk Hall, a Romance of Philadelphia Life, Mystery and Crime* (1844), which attacked the licentiousness of upper-class hypocrites. Lippard's characters fondled enough heaving, milky-white bosoms to suggest that a fascination with large breasts is an American fetish of long standing; the breasts in question caused Lippard's book to sell 300,000 copies.[85] A second candidate for first "native erotic novel" is *The Libertine Enchantress, or The Adventures of Lucinda Hartley* (1863), the tale of a seductress whose social status deepened her lubricity.[86] The most likely "first" is George Thompson, who, though a radical himself, did not let his politics obscure a fascination with sex. Thompson's *Venus in Boston* (1849) achieves a degree of explicitness unprecedented in American literature, with as many erect male members as Fanny Hill herself could wish. Its success fostered a series of similarly large-selling works by the author, with titles such as *The G'hals of Boston* (1850) and *The Delights of Love* (1850).[87]

The publisher of *Venus in Boston* was James Ramerio, who according to the New York Society for the Suppression of Vice published half a dozen others with titles such as *Anna Mowbray, or Tales of the Harem* (1854?, also by Thompson) and *Flora Montgomery, the Factory Girl, a Tale of the Lowell Factories* (1856, author unclear). The latter, which dealt with the evils to which working girls were exposed at the nation's chief industrial laboratory, and *Fanny Greely, or The Confessions of a Free-Love Sister Written by Herself* (ca. 1852, Thompson again), which detailed scandals surrounding a communitarian movement, were calls for reform, hack works not bereft of sincerity. Their readers, however, bought them for the sex.

The great erotic bibliographer Henry Spencer Ashbee, writing under his pseudonym Pisanus Fraxi, thought that Americans started producing their own pornography only in 1846; he credited William Haynes (a.k.a. Haines), a former surgeon, with being the first publisher.[88] Haynes built his inventory, however, by pirating *Memoirs of a Woman of Pleasure*. Although Haynes and other publishers reprinted other classics such as *The Lustful Turk*, Cleland's book took pride of place because his heroine seemed so confidently American, so animated by discovery, so intrepid in her sexual adventures that she was admired by male and female readers alike. No bibliographer has been able to track all the British and American editions that circulated in the United States, but the saga of *Fanny Hill* did not climax until 1966, when courts at last cleared the novel for open publication.

In any case, Haynes began commissioning works by American authors, and he wrote a number himself. By 1871 Haynes had supposedly published more than 300 volumes, at which point Anthony Comstock picked up his trail. According to one story, Haynes killed himself just as Comstock closed in.[89] Another bibliographer took note of a New Orleans publisher who began operations about the same time as Haynes,[90] and soon there were many. That fact is significant, because histories of pornographic books in the United States have dealt in the main with the publishers who commissioned subliterary genres, not the authors who actually wrote them. The writing of porn books is industrial piecework, not an artistic calling. Despite the occasional sensational book by a recognized name, deliberately pornographic books are generally pseudonymously written.

Although Comstock sometimes identified authors, he was preoccupied with tracing the histories of suspect publishers.[91] The Civil War created a huge market for pornographic reading matter by soldiers on both sides of the conflict and, more important, lowered prices. Volumes from cheap series such as *Cupid's Own Library* (1862–1865) flooded the trenches. *Fanny Hill* was still just as popular as *The Libertine Enchantress*,[92] but native authors scribbled *Confessions of a Washington Belle; Beautiful Creole of Havana; Adventures of Anna P., or The Belle of New York;* and *Child of Passion, or The Amorous Foundling.* Until the International Copyright Law of 1891 was created, most legitimate U.S. publishers preferred to publish the works of foreign writers because they did not have to pay for them, as they did when the authors were American. In a sense, American pornographers thus helped to establish a legitimate domestic industry by creating a class of writers who expected to be paid.

The market remained strong after the war. In 1885, according to one report, New Yorkers alone bought more than 100,000 pornographic books.[93] From this period date semidocumentary erotic genres such as the "urban sewer" story, like F. M. Lehman's *The White Slave Hell, or With Christ at Midnight in the Slums of Chicago* (1910), an exposé of vice dens and city lowlife; and the "madam's memoir," like *Memoirs of Dolly Morton* (1904), a reminiscence of sometimes distinguished visitors to brothels; modern versions of these two types might include Ivo Dominguez's *Beneath the Skins: The New Spirit and Politics of the Kink Community* (1994) and Sydney Barrows's *Mayflower Madam: The Secret Life of Sydney Biddle Barrows* (1986). In the category established by "Aristotle" were sex and marriage manuals, such as James Teller's *Doctor's Pocket Companion and Marriage Guide* (1864). One of the confirmed suicides Anthony Comstock boasted of having caused was that of Ida Craddock, author of marriage manuals suggesting that sexual pleasure for women was normal and desirable. In 1902, convicted of sending *The Wedding Night* through the mails, she took her own life.[94]

The explicit physical descriptions of *The Horn Book: A Girl's Guide to the Knowledge of Good and Evil* (1899) led to its proscription. By contrast, *Light on Dark Corners* (1894), a manual by B. G. Jefferies and J. L. Nichols, retailed polite folklore; it sold more than a million copies in several editions.[95] Similar texts by physicians, ministers, utopians, educators, public health officials, and quacks advised abstinence, cold compresses or showers, and the thinking of pure thoughts. The strangest doctor was John Harvey Kellogg, a disciple of Sylvester Graham, after whom Kellogg named the Graham cracker, a snack allegedly designed to curb masturbation. Kellogg (1852–1943) also invented granola and corn flakes to prevent erections, which he thought shortened male lives, and insisted that his patients take five enemas a day.[96] Some physicians gave better advice, of course, and some of it gradually reached the public. Much later, in the twentieth century, thanks to the success of David Reuben's *Everything You Al-*

ways Wanted to Know about Sex But Were Afraid to Ask (1970), sex manuals would fill a lucrative niche market.

Canonical American writers occasionally made headlines. Boston authorities merely attacked Nathaniel Hawthorne's *Scarlet Letter* (1852) but banned Walt Whitman's *Leaves of Grass* (1882) outright. In 1890, in a warning shot to writers, Attorney General Miller and Postmaster General Wanamaker banned Leo Tolstoy's *Kreutzer Sonata* from the mails. The publisher of Theodore Dreiser's *Sister Carrie* withdrew the novel in 1900 after it was charged with immorality. Critics who insist that sexual scenes are central to American literature can marshal masses of evidence: Herman Melville's symbolizing of homosexuality through sailors kneading spermaceti (whale oil wax) in *Moby Dick*, Edgar Allen Poe's reworking of a sensational prostitute murder in *The Mystery of Marie Roget*, William Faulkner's foregrounding of Caddy's traumatically remembered underpants in *The Sound and the Fury*, Thomas Pynchon's equating Slothrop's erection with the phallic V-2 rocket in *Gravity's Rainbow*.

Mainstream writers were cautious when they expected trouble. In 1876, Mark Twain surreptitiously wrote the scatalogical *1601*; in 1879 he followed with *Some Thoughts on the Science of Onanism* (in which he recalled Ben Franklin's remark that "masturbation is the mother of invention").[97] An abbreviated list of notorious works might include Eugene Field's *Only a Boy* (1886), James Gibbons Huneker's *Painted Veils* (1920), Ben Hecht and Max Bodenheim's *Cutie: A Warm Mama* (1924), Djuna Barnes's *Nightwood* (1936), and Anaïs Nin's *Delta of Venus* (1940–1941). Edith Wharton hid the pages of her "Beatrice Palmato Fragment" (ca. 1917?), in which a father and daughter kiss each other's genitals. Charles Scribner at first refused to publish the "dirty book" that became Hemingway's *The Sun Also Rises* (1926).[98] Different cities ruled that James Branch Cabell's *Jurgen* (1919) and Theodore Dreiser's *An American Tragedy* (1925) were obscene. In 1901, Claude Hartland wrote *The Story of a Life*, the first published autobiography of an admitted American homosexual; the following year a lesbian published her autobiography as *The Story of Mary MacLane*. Comstock seized both. Two decades later, Radclyffe Hall's lesbian novel, *The Well of Loneliness* (1928), would spur widespread outrage.

The number of "good" books targeted by concerned citizens and organizations is in fact beyond counting, and censors remained adamant no matter how often they were rebuffed. In 1894, Comstock tried to seize the entire stock of the Worthington

Publishing Company on the grounds that its elegantly bound translations of classics such as *The Arabian Nights, The Decameron, Aladdin,* and *The Heptameron* were obscene, only to lose in court.[99] But in 1920 another judge fined Jane Heap and Margaret Anderson $100 each for publishing excerpts from Joyce's *Ulysses* in their avant-garde *Little Review*. The decision delayed publication of the novel in the United States for another eleven years.

Given the sometimes conservative reputations of censors, modern Americans assume that Comstock exaggerated the number of dirty books. In fact, there were a lot, and their authors were usually not in the same league as Joyce or Dreiser. Moral panics notwithstanding, censorship on so magnified a scale does not arise unless there is perceived threat. Jay Gertzman, the principal authority on pre–World War II pornography, has studied marginal publishers from 1920 to 1940 such as Esar Levine (Panurge Press), Benjamin Rebhuhn (Falstaff Press), Louis Shomer (American Ethnological Press), Jake Brussel (Brussel and Brussel), and Samuel Roth (many presses). Vice investigators, postal inspectors, and prosecutors dogged all of them, and several spent time in prison. Gertzman categorizes their materials as "curiosa," which included mild erotic fiction, expurgated classics, jestbooks, and treatises on women, love, and relationships; "sex pulps," which included raunchy romances and mysteries; "erotology and sexology," which included scientific texts on health, contraception, prostitution, nudism, and bizarre sexual customs and practices; "sleaze," which included explicit stories of sex; and classic but proscribed works, which included *Lady Chatterley's Lover, Tropic of Cancer,* and *Fanny Hill.*[100]

During the Great Depression, many booksellers stayed in business only because of demand for erotic fiction.[101] Argus Books in Chicago, Gotham Book Mart in New York, and Casanova Book Store in Milwaukee, Wisconsin, to name just a few, sold serious books considered obscene because their owners thought them important. Those dealers occasionally handled blatantly pornographic works by lesser authors, such as Whidden Graham's parody of detective genres, *Crimson Hairs* (1938), or Val Luten's *Grushenka* (1933), a parody of nineteenth-century Russian novels. Some works circulated only in samizdat, that is, as mimeographed typescripts hand-sewn together. In this category were "Jane of the Bouncing Bottom" and "Liza the Lesbian," stories written by Robert Sewall and bound to form *An Oxford Thesis on Love* (1938). Sewall and Gershon Legman together wrote a sequel, *The Oxford Professor* (ca. 1948), and also *The Devil's Advo-*

cate (1942); both have endured. For sophisticated readers, however, the source of erotica was Paris, France. There Sylvia Beach published the unexpurgated *Ulysses* (1922) and Jack Kahane published Henry Miller's *Tropic of Cancer* (1934). Kahane's Obelisk Press printed high-quality books forbidden in the United States during the 1930s. After the war Kahane's son Maurice Girodias began the Olympia Press, whose cheap "Traveller's Companion" paperbacks boasted titles by Vladimir Nabokov, Jean Genet, William Burroughs, Samuel Beckett, Harriet Daimler, Alexander Trocchi, Terry Southern, and James Sherwood.

During the postwar golden age of pulp fiction, Beacon, Boudoir, Venus, Quarter, Midwood Books, and other paperback publishers returned to the sure-fire American formula of sex and violence. *Commie Sex Trap, Marijuana Girl, Sin Cruise, Dance Hall Girl, Love-Hungry Doctor, White Slave Racket, Hitch-Hike Hussy,* and *Commuter Wives* widened the boundaries of the permissible. Although lesbian pulp can be traced to the 1920s,[102] Gold Medal virtually reinvented it with Tereska Torres's *Women's Barracks* (1950), whose rapid sales led Fawcett, Beacon, Avon, Bantam, and Pyramid to issue dozens more by Ann Aldrich, Valerie Taylor, and Ann Bannon. Bannon recalls that lesbian readers had to study the covers carefully to determine whether they were in fact aimed at lesbians. So many covers pandered to male fantasies of two women making love that one never knew whether the pages inside spoke authoritatively.[103] Even so, lesbian and gay pulps circumspectly depicted homosexual characters as tormented misfits. Among other erotic forms, the period produced hard-boiled detective novels such as John D. MacDonald's *The Brass Cupcake* and Mickey Spillane's *Kiss Me Deadly*, but also candid classics such as Jack Kerouac's *On the Road*.

By the end of the 1950s, it was apparent to mainstream publishers that censors had to be neutralized if their industry were to survive. In 1932, James Joyce had sold *Ulysses* to Random House on condition that publisher Bennett Cerf would fund its legal battles; Cerf won when Justice John M. Woolsey declared one of the greatest novels of the century not obscene. Three decades later Barney Rosset's Grove Press saw *Lady Chatterley's Lover* (1960) through the courts and followed that success with *Tropic of Cancer* (1961; cleared in 1964). Emboldened, Putnam championed the "deathless lady"[104] herself; in 1966 the Supreme Court declared *Fanny Hill* not obscene. Trying desperately to find a legal compass, the Court that same year also upheld the conviction of Samuel Mishkin for publishing *Swish Bottom, Mistress of Leather,* and *So Firm and Fully Packed* because the books were sado-masochistic. The following year the Court in effect threw up its hands; it exonerated Robert Redrup for selling *Shame Agent* and *Lust Pool* on the grounds that consenting adults had the right to read what they pleased. For all practical purposes, literary censorship was now dead in the United States.

Encouraged by those decisions, Maurice Girodias moved Olympia Press from Paris to New York in 1967. He was none too soon, for Collectors' Publications, Essex House, and Brandon House, all California publishers, were bringing out works by Angelo d'Arcangelo (*The Homosexual Handbook*, 1969), Harriet Daimler (*Darling*, 1973), Alexander Trocchi (*White Thighs*, 1967), Marco Vassi (*Pro Ball Groupie*, 1974), and Charles Bukowski (*Notes of a Dirty Old Man*, 1969). Richard Amory's *Song of the Loon* (Greenleaf Classics, 1968) became the first gay porn novel to soar, selling more than 2 million copies by 1982.[105] During the "sexual revolution," virtually everyone in New York seemed to have written a porn book to cover student loans or pay for a trip to Spain. Pornographic tropes surfaced in many genres. Weird sexual encounters between humans and extraterrestrials appeared in science fiction.[106] Anne Rice, author of psychological vampire novels, adopted the pseudonyms A. N. Roquelaure ("Beauty" trilogy, 1983–1985) and Anne Rampling (*Exit to Eden*, 1985) to write "the kind of delicious S&M fantasies I'd looked for but couldn't find anywhere."[107] In the "pornogothic" category also is the fiction of antiporn crusader Andrea Dworkin's other persona; many feminists masturbate to Dworkin's *Ice and Fire* and *Mercy*.[108] Mainline writers as diverse as Norman Mailer, Erica Jong, Gael Greene, Robert Coover, John Colleton, Philip Roth, Mary Gaitskill, and Kathy Acker experimented with the themes and fetishes of pornographic fiction.

Pornography also freshened the woman's romance, or "bodice-ripper," which previously had limited itself to heavy petting above the waists of its characters. Virtually all subgenres (e. g., Regency, gothic, confessional) of the woman's romance became more explicit, sometimes to the distress of older readers unprepared for moist genitals.[109] Most significant perhaps was Odyssey Books's introduction of the African American romance.[110] Novels and short stories are important media for women and minorities to advance sexual agendas through pornographic fantasies. Strong sales have greeted anthologies such as *Erotique Noire: Black Erotica, On a Bed of Rice: An Asian-American Erotic Feast*, and *Under the Pomegranate Tree: The Best*

New Latino Erotica.[111] Similar collections of extravagant gay and lesbian porn number in the dozens. Anthologist Tee Corinne says that her intent is to share fantasies of "warm, comforting, garden-variety sex that nourishes year after year."[112]

Erotic Art

Aside from the erotic pottery, weapons, costumes, and petro-glyphs crafted by Native Americans,[113] the first artisans to craft sexual representations in what became America were untutored colonists. Call them folk or "outsider" artists or just amateurs; they carved, painted, or constructed an astonishing variety of sexual artifacts in media from scrimshaw and wood to canvas, glass, and metal. In another reminder of the anonymity of pornography, few signed their names to what they made.[114] Explicit outsider art still flourishes on regional margins, somewhat obscured by the mass-produced kitsch (toothbrushes in the shape of women's bodies, statuettes of little boys urinating, key chains in the shape of breasts and penises, and so on) increasingly generated by industrialization.

Defending a sexual representation, however, requires attributing it to an artist of training and talent and avowing that the work has intellectual and esthetic merit, that it is "high" art rather than low. The one-of-a-kind uniqueness of a work of art protects it from those who condemn mass-produced expression. Constructing a work *as* art elevates its status, as does displaying it in a place that ensures veneration. When educated Americans look at a painting of copulation by Rembrandt or Picasso in a museum, they regard it differently than they would a canvas that has no provenance or prestige. A sculpture of a penis mounted on marble in the Whitney Museum is art; a richly detailed, handmade dildo on a counter in Al's Adult Arcade is simply an appliance.

Museums—media that can attract crowds—have never been invulnerable, of course. No one knows how many works have been removed from exhibit halls because some moral arbiter paid a "courtesy" visit to a gallery or museum, perhaps in company with police, to offer a curator an "opportunity" to repair a misjudgment of taste. Often institutions forestalled intervention by announcing firm policies. In 1806, the Pennsylvania Academy of Fine Arts, having borrowed classical statutes from the Louvre in Paris, closed its galleries to women visitors except on Mondays, when curators draped the sculptures with cloth so that the ladies would not be harmed by the sight of marble breasts and penises. In 1815, conservatives denounced American John Vanderlyn's nude *Ariadne* as "European depravity" when it was exhibited in New York, but did not try to jail the painter.

Censors often use an economic ruler; if a particular painting costs a lot, that means that someone values it, and its expensiveness also means that the unwashed are not likely to see it. That same year, Philadelphia imprisoned a man named Sharples and five confederates for selling cheap drawings of two lovers that no critics wanted to defend; these were clumsy smudges, with no pretense to status or scarcity. And, expensive or not, everyday objects were fair game: in 1843, customs inspectors confiscated nine imported snuff boxes because their covers were decorated with painted nudes. This was the first of thousands of seizures carried out by customs inspectors under the Tariff Act of 1842.

Prudery also stalked art schools. During the eighteenth century artists Benjamin West, Gilbert Stuart, and John Singleton Copley had to learn to paint nudes in England; studying anatomy in the United States was not possible. The National Academy of Design in New York allowed male students to paint from discreetly draped live female models in 1845, but five years later, a Boston art school still refused to allow female artists to do so. A determined Harriet Hosner left for Europe, then returned in triumph to chisel her classical sculptures.[115] In 1884, Anthony Comstock had a dealer named August Muller arrested for selling photographs of French paintings of nude women that had just been hung in the Salon de Paris, one of which had been exhibited at the Philadelphia Centennial.[116] The University of Pennsylvania fired Thomas Eakins in 1886 when he removed the loin cloth from a male model in order to exhibit musculature for a painting class.[117] Eakins would prevail, and other artists defied conservatives as well, but even Nathaniel Hawthorne and Mark Twain, who should have known better, condemned such paintings.[118] Cincinnati, Ohio, just embarking on a long history of regulating the morality of its citizens, hired a craftsman to construct fig leaves for any nude statues that came its way.[119] Sanity prevailed in time for painters George Luks, George Bellows, William Glackens, and Robert Henri to invent new ways of looking at bodies by the turn of the century.

Truly pornographic pictures in colonial America were nestled in private libraries, where well-to-do collectors could page through editions of *Memoirs of a Woman of Pleasure* featuring Antoine Borel's engravings of Fanny Hill's adventures. Many volumes of classical erotica available to Americans carried explicit drawings commissioned by eighteenth-century European publishers.[120] Few American artists specialized in erotic illustration of texts until the twentieth century. Although Keene Wallis, David Plotkin, and Alexander King are among the best known, two others, Mahlon Blaine and Clara Tice, are the most notable. Blaine illustrated a collection of Ben Franklin's naughty works as well as American editions of the works of French poet Paul Verlaine, philosopher Voltaire, and novelist Gustav Flaubert.[121] During the 1920s and 1930s Tice (1888–1973) drew voluptuous scenes for special American editions of erotica, especially the work of Pierre Louÿs. Easily the greatest of all female erotic book illustrators, Tice was arrested in 1915 by John Sumner of the New York Society for the Suppression of Vice.[122] The *covers* of books and magazines were another matter. Scholars are just now deciphering the codes with which erotic artists alerted readers to the sexual content within mystery novels, science fiction stories, lesbian potboilers, and so on.[123]

Citizens of Boston, Philadelphia, and New York could easily find anonymous engravings of sexual scenes run off by presses in newspaper districts and sold from seedy newsstands, bars, barber shops, music halls, and pushcarts during the 1830s and 1840s. Henry R. Robinson, a Manhattan printer and political caricaturist of the Whig persuasion, sold pornographic etchings and lithographs, some imported, some drawn in the United States. By modern standards these were more satiric than explicit.[124] A typical engraving caricatured a recognizable Wall Street financier clutching a whisky bottle in one hand, a disheveled prostitute in the other. A few years later, entrepreneurs on both sides of the Civil War sold troops vast numbers of vulgar drawings along with sexy playing cards, stories, novelties, and condoms.[125]

From 1916 to 1918, Charles Demuth wove homosexual images into his "Turkish Bath" paintings and his "decadent" illustrations for books by Émile Zola, Honoré de Balzac, and Henry James. During the 1920s Demuth experimented with pornographic drawings of gays and watercolors of urinating sailors, none of them exhibited. Demuth's contemporary Marsden Hartley also ventured into gay erotica but was even more circumspect in his public art. Artist and photographer Carl Van Vechten drew inspiration from twenty private "scrapbooks" of pornography.[126] Radical socialists focused on sexuality during the Progressive Era. John Sloan painted the prostitutes of New York's Tenderloin District; as editor of *The Masses* he encouraged George Bellows,

Boardman Robinson, Stuart Davis, Glenn Coleman, Art Young, and Robert Minor to illustrate similar scenes.[127] A decade later, the women in erotic urban landscapes caught the eye of Reginald Marsh, who painted voluptuous shoppers, burlesque queens, and prostitutes of New York's Union Square.[128] The intellectual voyeurism of painter Edward Hopper's *Girlie Show* (1941) and Thomas Hart Benton's *Persephone* (1939) raised nudity to new planes of meaning.

Well below levels of social realism, however, pornographers critiqued an industrialized middle class in their own way, using the eight-page comic book, or Tijuana bible. "Blue" comics were graffiti pitched at lower-class audiences; they circulated quietly, below official radar. According to Gershon Legman, the eight-page Tijuana bibles are America's single "original contribution to the development of the comics."[129] Some scholars argue that they appeared first (despite the Mexican nickname) in Cuba; others insist they were indigenous to the United States. By any account they were "pure" pornography, that is, vulgarity hurled at icons of respectability. Virtually all the bibles satirized celebrities— "Doug Fairybanks" and "Mae Breast" are examples—or parodied characters in mainstream comic strips—Moon Mullins, Dagwood Bumstead, Dick Tracy, and Little Orphan Annie.

Although racism abounded, with African Americans relegated to humorous stereotypes,[130] there is virtually no aggression in their pages; their intent was to level, not to maim.[131] Familiar cartoon characters humped, sucked, and buggered each other with a single-mindedness that destroyed pretense to status or authority. That audiences adored their exuberant obscenity is certain; almost 900 of the fragile artifacts survive.[132] Even today they inspire affection not so much for what they are as for what they tried to do—to eroticize and thus to democratize.[133] Sold for a quarter at truck stops, bus stations, and seedy newsstands, they passed hand to hand. The artists who created them remain largely anonymous, although collectors note that some were signed by "Rhangild" (Susan Aguerra?).[134]

By midcentury, mainstream comics were in trouble. Swept along by moral panic over juvenile delinquency, the Gathings and Kefauver Commissions accused comic books of corrupting youth. Journalists exaggerated charges by psychologist Frederic Wertham that *Batman* and horror comics carried aggressive, deviant, and antisocial messages,[135] but comics of the period *were* seamy, having aped other sectors of popular culture by substituting violence for sex. Senate investigators eventually got around to

cartoons and drawings of corset-clad mistresses and their submissive male victims, many of them commissioned by Irving
Klaw, the "Pinup King," from artists such as Ruiz, Mario, Stanton,
Eneg, "Jim," and John Willie. Willie (J. A. S. Coutts) was the publisher of *Bizarre* (1946–1961), perhaps the most famous of all fetish
magazines, full of serial comics (*The Adventures of Sweet Gwendolyn*) involving bondage and domination. Eric Stanton continued
these serials (*Sweeter Gwen* and *Sweeter Gwen and the Return of
Sweeter Gwendoline*). The magazine *Exotique* (1957 to 1963), by
Leonard Burtman, also specialized in drawings of the outlandish
appliances and claustrophobic sexuality of sadomasochism.

Although they often drew voluptuous women that resembled figures in fetish serials, artists such as C. D. Gibson, George
Petty, and Alberto Vargas furnished pinups for the respectable
Life and *Esquire* magazines. This trio inspired bolder artists during the 1940s and 1950s, the golden age of the painted or drawn
pinup featured in men's magazines and on calendars. Major
artists included Vargas, Rolf Armstrong, Billy DeVorss, Gil Elvgren, Harry Aikman, Earl MacPherson, Peter Driben, Fritz Willis,
Bill Randall, and Zöe Mozert. The latter reproduced her own
body for paintings and advertisements, notably for the posters
for Howard Hughes's movie *The Outlaw* (released 1946). Mozert's emphasis on actress Jane Russell's cleavage aggravated
Hughes's battle with censors over the film, just as two decades
earlier Florence Kosell's provocative painting of Mae West in *Sex*
had set off conservatives.[136] The exaggerated sexuality of cheesecake paintings parodied rather than set standards of sexiness.
The Spencer Museum of Art at the University of Kansas houses a
collection of classic pinups by Petty, Vargas, and other artists that
is now worth millions.[137]

The energies of Harvey Kurtzman and Wally Wood, who created *Mad* magazine, spilled over into erotica. Kurtzman created
Little Annie Fanny for *Playboy*, and Wood exuberantly parodied
mainstream funnies as "Prince Violate," "Perry and the Privates,"
"Flasher Gordon," and "So White and the Six Dorks."[138] Kurtzman and Wood godfathered what came to be known as underground "comix," the cartoon flowering of the counterculture of
the 1960s. The major artist here was R. Crumb, who stunned audiences with *Zap* in 1967. Crumb was quickly joined by S. Clay
Wilson, Gilbert Shelton, Dave Sheridan, "Spain" Rodriquez, Rick
Griffin, and Victor Moscoso. Their comix sexualized memorably
rendered characters, of which the most emblematic was probably
Larry Welz's Cherry Poptart, a voluptuous, scantily clad bimbo

posed as the Statue of Liberty holding aloft a vibrator. Comix satirized lust and anxiety as much as political authority and social absurdity. Gallery shows and widespread acceptance have by now confirmed the talent of many of the artists: R. Crumb drew the cover for the 21 February 1994 anniversary issue of the *New Yorker*.

Underground comix matured in the 1980s as "alternative" comics, a gender-bending form receptive to women and homosexuals. Diane Noonin and Aline Kominsky (Crumb's wife) began drawing *Twisted Sisters*, a comic zine, in 1976, and about the same time Trina Robbins, Lee Mars, Patricia Moodian, and others formed the Women's Cartoonist Collective. In 1982, Chin Lyvely and Joyce Farmer began *Tits and Clits*, in whose installments Robbins, Mary Fleener, and Dori Seda lampooned the sexism of their male counterparts. Shary Flenniken, Badanna Zack, and Phoebe Gloeckner laced their panels with autobiographical reflections on menstruation, courting, childbirth, feminine roles, and emotional relationships.[139] Some set out to educate; Tee Corinne published *Cunt Coloring Book*, a collection of drawings of vaginas designed to be crayoned so that women could appreciate their own genital beauty,[140] and more than a hundred cartoonists drew explicit panels on HIV for *Strip AIDS, USA*.[141] Some opted for raucous satire, like the illustrators of *Weenie-Toons: Women Cartoonists Mock Cocks*.[142]

Gay Comix, begun by Howard Cruse in 1980, printed the work of Roberta Gregory, editor of the first lesbian underground serial, *Dynamite Damsels*, and Mary Wings, editor of *Dyke Shorts*. Diane DiMassa (*Hothead Paisan: Homicidal Lesbian Terrorist*), Rupert Kinnard (*B. B. and the Diva*), and Craig Maynard (*Up from Bondage*) feature themes and characters aimed at gays and lesbians. The popularity of comic zines led to hybrid erotic forms centered on porn stars such as Annie Sprinkle (Rip Off Press) and Sarah Jane Hamilton (Renegade Press). Prosecution, however, remains a threat. When corporate representatives try to suppress pornographic parodies of Disney characters, gremlins take revenge, most recently by adding nipples and vagina to Jessica Rabbit in the laserdisk version of the animated movie.[143] More controversial is Florida's conviction of Michael Diana for obscenity for drawing the explicit *Boiled Angel* in 1994.

The sexual revolution encouraged artists to draw inspiration and materials from pornography during the 1960s and 1970s. Mel Ramos borrowed pinups as "metaphors, parodies, [and] travesties" of classic styles.[144] Pinups also furnished Richard Lindner with models for robotic, sexy nudes.[145] Erotic urges clearly drove Pop Art; Claes Oldenburg drew his explicit fantasies,[146] Andy Warhol silk-screened his,[147] and Roy Lichtenstein made prints and posters of his.[148] London police seized Jim Dine's penis and vulva drawings in 1966,[149] but Americans seemed more amused than offended by the erect penis of the artist's "Oo La La" (1970) and his riff on "Four Kinds of Pubic Hair" (1971).[150] Probably the two most notorious works of the period were Larry Rivers's "Lampman Loves It" (1966), a sculpture in which a male figure is sodomized by a mechanical assemblage with a light bulb for a penis, and Tom Wesselman's "Great American Nude #87," (1967) in which a pastel female figure fellates a male. Because Wesselman painted genitals the way Warhol painted soup cans, his *Great American Nude* series "made erotic art history."[151] Forays into candor increased; in 1970, a special issue of *Art and Artists* tried to capture the excitement of erotic experimentation among artists as diverse as Henriette Francis, Morton Kaish, Robert Andrew Parker, William de Kooning, Robert Broderson, Martha Edelheit, George Segal, Jasper Johns, William Rauschenberg, and Louise Bourgeois.[152]

American artists may have gravitated toward pornography precisely because postmodern schools were leaching traditional images of meaning. Loaded as it is with biological, esthetic, social, and moral baggage, sexual intercourse carries its own meaning, though it may ultimately be indecipherable in any but the most existential of terms. In any case, by the 1980s it was clear that pornography was powerfully shaping mainstream art. Thematic and stylistic traces of the muscular gay intercourse drawn by Tom of Finland (Touko Laaksonen, 1920–1991) for *Physique Pictorial* are visible in the paintings of Paul Cadmus and David Hockney. Strains of pornography tinge the nudes of dean of American realists Philip Pearlstein. In its objectivity, says one critic, Pearlstein's work "has its greatest affinity with pornography in its use of persons for its own ends, though those ends seem so utterly different from simple sexual arousal."[153] Once a layout artist for *Stag* magazine, David Salle has used pages of pinups in his collages and other compositions. In exploring a sexualized banality associated with pornography, Salle uses vulgarity not so much to shock as to probe reality.[154] Startling images recur in the work of Eric Fischel, an apostle of postmodern esthetic exhaustion. Fischel has painted many scenes of intercourse, most notably the "Dog Days" sequences of 1985, which feature open legs and erections. The most pornographically inspired artist of recent years is Jeff Koons. The chief merit of

Koons's candy-colored paintings and sculptures of himself and his former wife Cicciolina (the Italian porn star and member of Italy's Parliament) engaged in explicit oral, vaginal, and anal intercourse may have been to demonstrate that images can still shock.[155]

"Why Have There Been No Great Women Pornographers?" asks critic Naomi Salman, who answers that personal and social insecurities have prevented women from endowing bodies with the requisite degrees of lust.[156] The charming penis constructions of Louise Bourgeois and the voluptuous sculptures of Mary Frank prefigured the erotic women's "event" of 1979, Judy Chicago's *Dinner Party* gallery/museum installation. For this work, Chicago assembled thirty-nine hand-painted ceramic plates and needle-pointed place mats, all constructed of explicit vaginal images. Each table setting represented a famous woman from history and symbolized the degree to which feminine achievements have been overshadowed. Although members of Congress denounced Chicago's work as pornographic as late as 1990, few works have had such impact on artistic achievement. The *Dinner Party* set erotic precedents for the most distinguished of recent American women artists.[157] These include Eleanor Antin, Lynda Benglis, Judith Bernstein, Hannah Wilke, Nancy Grossman, Joan Semmel, Kathe Kowalski, Jacqueline Livingstone, Carolee Schneemann, Clarisse Sligh, and Anita Steckel, most of whom have encountered censorship.[158]

If there is such a thing as a mainstream feminist erotic school, says Maryse Holder, it embraces all those women and Nikki de Saint Phalle, Silvianna Goldsmith, Kiki Kogelnik, Sara d'Allesandro, Shelly Lowell, Marge Helenchild, Anne Sharp, Arlene Love, Juanita McNeely, and Martha Edelheit as well.[159] Such artists invent, appropriate, invert, or reconfigure erotic themes and images. According to supporters, feminist artists can reclaim disputed erotic terrain in order to demystify sex and gender. Detractors insist that they are merely exploiting stereotypes, recapitulating sexism, and producing bad art. As usual, doctrinaire convictions lead to extreme esthetic judgments. Feminist ideologues insist that since all art is masculine—even that so far produced by women—it should all be destroyed until gender justice can prevail.[160] In contrast, art terrorists advocate using pornography as a weapon to traduce convention and complacency.[161] In the meantime, as Vanessa Beecroft, Sue Williams, Nicole Eisenman, and Sarah Lucas have recently discovered, explicit art sells very well.[162]

Controversy bubbles on. In September 1999, Mayor Rudolph Giuliani of New York City, running for the Senate against Hillary Rodham Clinton and trying hard to woo upstate conservatives, threatened to cut off the city's subsidy of the Brooklyn Museum of Art if it went ahead with the opening of a show that the mayor thought violated standards of public decency.[163] The court ruled against the mayor, but critics observed that the issue was complicated by economics (various deals concerning the exhibit came to light). As Vicki Goldberg has observed, speaking of a current lack of originality in sexual expression, "it is not art but commerce that breaks most of the rules" in modern America.[164]

Erotic Performance

Strippers, cross-dressers, Mardi Gras "tit-flashers," barely clad supermodels, naked mud wrestlers, nude performance artists, and erotic actors are all sexual *impersonators*, a concept that puts performance in the category of representation. They play roles that define, exaggerate, or explode concepts of gender and desire, using their bodies as texts. When a critic spoke of Mae West as "the world's greatest female impersonator," he was referring not simply to the exaggeration she brought to her persona of sex queen but also to her parodies of eroticism. West's counterparts today are the doyennes of hard-core videos, the balloon-breasted women who leer at their fans. The body itself can function as a medium—as a canvas that can be written upon, as with tattoos, piercings, or other modifications—or as a kinetic ensemble that communicates through motion.

Public sexual performance is as old as the species. Women in ancient cultures prostituted themselves in temples of fertility goddesses in order to worship the spirit of generation (one reason that prostitution is called the oldest profession). The priests of Baal practiced ritual homosexuality as a form of veneration (one reason that victorious Christian rivals of Baal still oppose homosexuality). Sexual exhibition and orgiastic dance have flourished from Saturnalias in ancient Rome to festivals of Misrule in medieval England and Mardi Gras revels in the United States, Brazil, and elsewhere. Because drama turned on fantasy, the stage encouraged lasciviousness, or so critics believed. Actresses were often prostitutes, and popes forbade women to appear on stage until well past the age of Shakespeare, a restriction that necessitated castrating boys so that they could play roles that required women's voices. The equation of actress and whore persisted into the Victorian period, when the stereotype became a staple of pornography.[165] The tradition helps explain why the sexual lives of celebrities and movie stars continue to mesmerize audiences.

Mooning, bawdy theatricals, cavorting in the nude, and quasipublic intercourse took place in early America at carnivals and fairs but also in private clubs, bordellos, waterfront dives, and rough taverns. Lewd exhibitions were part of the male "sporting world" comprised of prize fights, circuses, and dance halls,[166] but such unsavory amusements rarely spilled over into venues open to respectable women.[167] In more visible domains, however, entrepreneurs exhibited freaks with physical abnormalities and offered ersatz medical lectures on sexual anomalies to attract audiences.[168] White males attended slave auctions to inspect male and female slaves displayed nude on the block. Such practices shaped both racism and eroticism in the United States,[169] helped establish American preferences for sexual expression as objectification and spectacle,[170] associated nudity with vulnerability, and fostered sexual exploitation of weaker members of society. Americans are still more prone to tolerate nudity when it is linked to primitivism, an association referred to as the *National Geographic* syndrome.

Obscene performances were common enough before the Civil War for Mark Twain to satirize them in the story of the duke and the dauphin in *Huckleberry Finn* (1884). Transvestite reviews, cooch dancers, raunchy joke marathons, pissing and farting contests, and group masturbation are all part of this tradition. They survive in annual Halloween hijinks of Greenwich Village, New York, and Key West, Florida; "doo-dah parades" in Pasadena, California; masturbation derbies called "jerk-offs" and "jill-offs"; and stag parties during which the groom has intercourse with a prostitute the night before the wedding. Well into the 1960s, strippers traveled with carnivals on routes into rural heartlands.[171] Sometimes, after the dancers finished grinding away in midway tents, rubes could pay extra for private shows of intercourse.

Women scandalously attired in tights appeared on stage in 1842 as tableaus—that is, "frozen pictures." Crowds flocked to see "Little Egypt" belly dance at the Chicago Exposition of 1893. A craze for hula dancing led to topless performers in wilder urban cabarets in 1906.[172] In 1907, impresario Florenz Ziegfeld began spectacular revues that filled a stage with singers, comedians, and scantily clad dancers. By 1916, his showgirls would stand nude but unmoving for the finale of his annual *Follies*. Soon the Shuberts, George White, Earl Carroll, and the Minskys competed to eroticize the stage. During the 1920s Minsky performers gyrated into the audience along runways, removing their clothing as they danced. Parisian entrepreneurs actually invented striptease, but Americans raised it to an artform structured into distinct dance phases. American ingenuity created the flash panels, breakaway brassieres, and sequined g-strings; the latter replaced the uncomfortable *cache-sex* (springloaded with a bicycle clip) pioneered by the French. By way of recompense, the American Josephine Baker became the toast of Paris for prancing at the *Follies Bergère* dressed only in bananas.

Vaudeville metamorphosed into burlesque for economic reasons, so that theatrical producers could recapture audiences lured away by movies. Unemployment during the Depression drew women onto the runways; cheap tickets drew audiences of all classes. Economics also ended the golden age. When Mayor La Guardia banned burlesque in New York City in 1937, he did so to placate property owners whose buildings had lost value because of their proximity to theaters (zoning adult businesses to remote areas is the modern-day equivalent). Toned-down versions returned sporadically, with strippers who were also extraordinary entertainers. Tempest Storm, Ann Corio, and Gypsy Rose Lee thrilled audiences as late as the 1960s; Lee's career inspired a Broadway musical and a Hollywood movie, both called *Gypsy*.

Urbanization created sheltered spaces for homosexuals and permitted public performances in the guise of transvestite revues, some of which traveled nationally from the 1930s onward. (These would become extremely popular in the 1990s.) So long as homosexuals were presented as freaks, or could be rationalized as comic travesties of femininity, they seemed unthreatening. Otherwise, to the official culture gays and lesbians were simply invisible *except* as pornographic presences. Homosexual characters on Broadway stages triggered prosecutions.[173] When the publisher Horace Liveright produced Edouard Boudet's *The Captive* in 1927, a drama with a lesbian theme, he had to fight off censors. Bowing to police pressure, Mae West decided not to move *The Drag*, which dealt with an unhappy homosexual, from its try-out in New Jersey to Broadway. America's first porn diva, West seemed poised to loose moral chaos upon terrified conservatives. A judge acting on a complaint by the New York Society for the Suppression of Vice sentenced her to eight days in jail for writing, producing, and starring in *Sex* (1927). Her incarceration, a triumphant performance raucously reported by the press, merely added to her legend as "The Empress of Sex." The carnality she symbolized overwhelmed her critics, who seemed diminished by her aura; always in character, West emerged from prison like the Queen of May surrounded by sour dwarves.

Once the Jazz Age ended, however, American theater eschewed sexual candor in favor of misdirection for the next three decades. The blandness of the nation's theatrical fare thus magnified the effects of the sexual revolution of the 1960s and 1970s as it exploded in Bruce Jay Friedman's *Scuba Duba*, Jerome Ragni and James Rado's *Hair*, Kenneth Tynan's *Oh! Calcutta!*, and Earl Wilson Jr.'s *Let My People Come*. Nude actors cavorted, simulated intercourse, even interacted with members of the audience, using shock to deconstruct modesty. Spectacles of flesh, said Tynan, forced audiences to develop a vocabulary to discuss the impact of private acts performed in public.[174] Depicting the outrageous, said critic Martin Esslin, had the effect of reassuring the orthodox, soothing their fears of deviancy; candid theater contributed to social health.[175]

Less commercial, more avant-garde performances flourished as well. Rochelle Owens's *Futz*, Michael McClure's *The Beard*, and Paul Foster's *Tom Paine* pelted middle-class audiences with raw language and bare flesh. Nude performers stalked the stage in Robert Wilson's *The Life and Times of Sigmund Freud* (1969) and Richard Foreman's *Birth of the Poet* (1985). Richard Schechner, a professor at Yale, designed *Dionysus in '69*, a modern version of Euripedes's *The Bacchae*, to allow nude actors to crawl over members of the audience. Schechner's "Pornography and the New Expression," celebrating an esthetics of shock, became a document of license in the service of drama. Manifestoes by Jerzy Grotowski, Peter Brook, and Jan Kott urged performers toward romantic, revolutionary, frenzied physicality. John Vaccaro and Charles Ludlam founded the Theater of the Ridiculous to mount bizarre comedies of gender inversion and obsessive desire. Similarly influential was the Living Theater, a commune-like troupe led by Julian Beck and Judith Malina. Malina was actually raped on stage by an audience member during a performance of *Paradise Now*, the group's most famous performance piece. Revolutionaries must be brave, she said later, marking the assault down to the price of being misunderstood.[176]

From 1962 to 1966 members of the Judson Dance Troupe at the Judson Church in Greenwich Village, the nation's avant-garde laboratory, experimented with nudity, as when Yvonne

Rainer appeared nude with Robert Morris. A year later, Ann Halprin presented "Parades and Changes" at Hunter College. In this milestone, all the dancers disrobed. The lead in *Oh! Calcutta!*, Margo Sappington, went on to choreograph for the Joffrey Ballet. The new physicality led to dance troupes such as Pilobolus, whose athletic nudity still rivets audiences, and that of Martha Clarke, whose compositions of flesh stun intellectually and sensually. Professional dancers learned that taking off their clothes affirmed the body's beauty, vulnerability, and logic; nudity in motion creates semiotics of gender and sexuality.[177]

Dancers without classical training followed different paths to a similar place. After its exile from New York, striptease divorced itself from burlesque and took refuge in middle-class bars in the hinterlands. The Theater Lounge in Dallas, run by Jack Ruby (before his assassination of Lee Harvey Oswald, presumed assassin of President John Kennedy) was typical. During the 1950s, patrons dined and danced between acts in which women serenely disrobed down to g-strings and pasties. A few blocks away, Candy Barr twirled her matched six-guns in a Western act. Barr became one of the major symbols of Dallas; the Colony Club plastered pictures of her in her trademark white cowgirl costume on huge billboards. Her sweet face and perfect breasts, coupled with notoriety over the stag film *Smart Alec*, enraged Texas conservatives. According to some sources, authorities set her up on a marijuana charge, for which she was sentenced to prison.[178] In a twist ironic even for Texas, however, the judge delayed her imprisonment long enough to allow Barr to tutor Joan Collins in the art of stripping so that the actress could star in Twentieth-Century Fox's *Seven Thieves* (1959).[179] Lacking the stature of Mae West, Barr disappeared from the public eye.

One by-product of the hippie movements of the 1960s was public nudity in parks, on beaches, at rock concerts. To compete, strippers stopped using pasties to cover their nipples. Bare breasts became statements, and bigger seemed better. Reporters covered the unveiling of the siliconed breasts of Carol Doda, lead dancer at the Condor Club in San Francisco. When topless joints became bottomless, naked dancing began to look like "hard-core pornography set to music."[180] By the mid-1970s in New York, totally nude male and female dancers cavorted on bar-counters in clubs clustered near Chinatown, Times Square, and the Garment District. San Francisco offered similar attractions. For a dollar, dancers would permit patrons to fondle or suck nipples or genitals, just as did their counterparts in adult arcades. In the latter, patrons stood at little windows constructed around a central stage. Depositing a quarter lifted an opaque screen so they could view the nude dancers; a dollar purchased a grope.

If executives in San Francisco took clients to restaurants with topless waitresses, construction workers in Manhattan could order lunch while dancers gyrated over blue-plate specials. In one nude cafe in the Meatpacking District, dancers "seasoned" a hot dog (sold at inflated prices) using a technique later perfected by Monica Lewinsky to accent President Clinton's cigars. Critics found such scenes revolting.[181] The country, or at least the urban parts of it, seemed bent on eroticizing (or, depending on one's perspective, vulgarizing) the most pedestrian sectors of life. Topless or nude women (and, less often, men) shined shoes, washed cars, worked as office cleaners, and sold pizzas.

Urban entrepreneurs recruited performers for sex shows in rented New York storefronts owned by organized crime. Needle tracks stippled the arms and buttocks of every second or third body listlessly opening its legs. Makeshift theaters were filthy, poorly heated, or damp. In 1980, when a journalist visited the upscale Show World theater complex (42nd Street at Eighth Avenue), he found women performing sex in front of audiences for $130 a week. The exploitation was the result of supply outstripping demand[182] but was also a reminder, not lost on entrepreneurs of the present, that below levels of subsistence, eroticism dwindles quickly into ugliness and despair. At this end of the scale, New York's Times Square resembled the wretched Patpong District of Bangkok, Thailand.

Most performers have long since disappeared into the anonymous history that is the hallmark of low porn, though a few achieved modest fame. Veronica Hart, considered by some to be one of the most talented actresses to appear in hard-core pornographic films, began her career coupling with partners on a 42nd Street mattress, and so did Wendy O. Williams, later the lead singer of the punk music group the Plasmatics. Among celebrated performers were Monica Kennedy, who stripped while her butler passed around champagne, then invited members of the audience to have intercourse with her on stage; and Honeysuckle Divine, who shot ping-pong balls from her vagina at targets held by patrons. Divine's act attracted an upscale crowd because she claimed to have enjoyed affairs with Republican Illinois Senator Everett Dirksen and presidential speechwriter Pierre Salinger.[183] Fascinated by her muscular control, critics compared Divine's ability to spray clouds of talcum powder to the farting virtuosity of Le Pétomane, the famous Parisian music hall entertainer.[184] As the popularity of hard-core pornographic films created stars in the 1980s, urban arcades signed them for a week or two of live sex. The O'Farrell Theater in San Francisco, run by the Mitchell brothers (*Behind the Green Door*, 1972), showcased performers such as Marilyn Chambers in S/M acts.

Ritualized sadomasochism usually attracted participants rather than voyeurs. Few types of sexual expression evoke such controversy. Some opponents of pornography believe that the power currents that drive S/M are typical of all sexual representations. Other observers point out that S/M relationships are too precise, too narrow, and too self-conscious to refer to anything other than themselves. The astute Ann McClintock distinguishes between casual brutality or domestic abuse and the theatrical aggression that is the stuff of pornographic expression. She also draws lines between *"reciprocal* S/M for mutual pleasure, and *consensual* S/M organized as a commercial exchange"; the former she thinks is more acceptable than the latter. Reciprocal S/M resembles Christianity, with whom it shares a great deal of symbology and imagery, McClintock says, because it involves mortification of the flesh and expiation of sin to secure the approval of a master. S/M can thus be a profoundly liturgical experience.[185]

Lynda Hart suggests that the S/M ritual is a way of "bearing witness" to the power of sexuality. S/M permits individuals to "recover" a self by transgressing normal relationships.[186] Sadomasochism most often casts males rather than females as the submissives; the logic of S/M demands that the powerful be punished, not the other way around. Though statistics refute claims that S/M pornography incites males to violence, "mistresses" merely note that when they have finished whipping a client's buttocks raw, he has little aggression left.[187] The issue is complicated, however, by S/M's popularity in both gay and lesbian circles. Indeed, one of the most heated skirmishes in the porn wars of the 1980s was that involving antiporn feminists against lesbian S/M enthusiasts.[188] Far from merely imitating masculine behavior, say spokeswomen, sadomasochism allows lesbians to construct a sexual universe of their own[189] and to cast themselves as "sexual outlaws" in order to establish their own identities.[190]

During the 1970s the Chateau (133 West 19th Street) and the Eulenspiegel Society, which floated from location to location in Manhattan, held nightly or weekly events. Audience members joined in fantasies enacted on a stage furnished with ropes, racks, rods, and whips. Another famous S/M venue was the Toilet, a gay bar in the Meatpacking District frequented by Andy Warhol and Robert Mapplethorpe, who there recruited models for his notorious photographs. Today's S/M establishments have escaped the zoning regulations with which New York City has pushed most sex businesses to the fringes of the metropolis. Because very little actual sex takes place in the clubs, and because they are expensive enough to keep out riff-raff, police do not regard them as a nuisance. Typical clients are CEOs of corporations who pay dominatrices $200 a session to be imprisoned in a dungeon or led about on a dog leash.[191] The Vault and Paddles, two of the more expensive, thus remain open, as does a popular restaurant called La Nouvelle Justice (24 First Avenue, New York), in which waitresses tie guests to their chairs or force them to eat from the floor; the latter shares premises with a Chinese restaurant catering to drag queens.

Sadomasochism is a minority interest, albeit curiously domesticated. A spate of how-to books addresses both curiosity and fashion.[192] HBO's *Real Sex* series has interviewed enthusiasts who customize their whips, tie up their naked friends, and spend their weekends whacking each other instead of watching football on television. The *New Yorker* published an article by Daphne Merkin, one of the magazine's columnists, who confessed that her only truly satisfying orgasms derive from her being ritually spanked by lovers, and another by novelist Paul Theroux on a Manhattan dominatrix who petulantly insisted that a proper whipping for a powerful executive involved more than just a fancy corset and good wrist action.[193]

The sexual revolution kicked off quasipublic performances of the sort detailed by Gay Talese in the best-selling *Thy Neighbor's Wife* (1981). Americans in several states joined sexual freedom leagues or swingers' groups to experiment with controlled promiscuity, visited New York clubs such as Plato's Retreat and Night Moves to participate in orgies involving multiple genders, or signed up at the Sandstone Sex Commune for tutoring in sexual anarchy. The Ansonia 73 Baths, located in New York's Ansonia Hotel, catered to homosexuals; it became chic when rising star Bette Midler began singing there between sex sessions. After a decade, however, the specter of AIDS began to slow casual exchanges of fluids in the baths.

Fear of AIDS has increased demand for sexual representation. If one has to give up participation, then he or she can enjoy voyeuristic spectacles. Top-grossing headliners are female porn stars, who make porn films to publicize their stripping; their fans welcome the opportunity to see them in the flesh. "Lap-danc-ing," that is, a stripper's writhing on a fully clothed lap in an at-tempt to bring the lap's owner to orgasm, has become so popular that it has crossed over to lesbian clubs. Lesbian establishments are still limited to cities with large subcultures (e.g., Baybrick's in San Francisco), and gay bars are still circumspect outside New York and San Francisco. According to one report, 2,000 clubs now offer male striptease for women (sometimes only on special nights).[194] Chippendales, a chain of male strip clubs for women, is a blatant exercise in erotic engineering, where managers ensure an atmosphere that is comfortable and fun but also—the hard part—transgressive. In these settings, women bond in the same ways that men do, whooping and joking as dancers take it off, enjoying the illusion of control.[195]

Stripping fosters its own folklore. Legends proliferated in the wake of Blaze Starr's affair with Earl Long, governor of Louisiana, and Fannie Foxe's Washington Tidal Basin hijinks with Wilbur Mills, chairman of the House Ways and Means Com-mittee. These and other stories crop up in stripping memoirs, a well-rehearsed biographical genre. Examples range from Georgia Southern's *Georgia: My Life in Burlesque* (1972), the story of a poor girl's rise to fame during the Depression, to Heidi Mattson's *Ivy League Stripper* (1995), the story of a Brown University under-graduate who enjoyed the stripping that paid her tuition. Strip-ping has also furnished numerous graduate students with dissertations, the most tiresome of which analyze the clubs in terms of Foucauldian surveillance and sexism, or argue over whether audience member or dancer has the most power over the other. Sociologists patronize strippers by assuming that the profession is deviant, that all strippers were abused as children, and that all are animated by the need for male approval, but some probe more deeply. Astute critics point out that stripping pays well, that the women dress and dance as much for each other as for male audiences, and that *nobody* dancing on stage or sitting in the audience has *any* power—otherwise neither would be there.

Circumstances and working conditions, of course, vary sub-stantially. Some clubs are abysmal, and all suffer from their tawdry status, however glittering and expensive the location. Some are run by the Mob, some by moms and pops; some treat employees with respect, some do not. Some performers are edu-cated, focused, ambitious, smart; some are addicts, alcoholics, victims. Aware of the range of clubs in the United States, critics at last are beginning to compare and contrast strippers and audiences of all genders in terms of the psychological, esthetic, sexual, and cultural impulses that drive participants toward erotic dramaturgy.[196] But no comment can top Marshall McLuhan's insight, delivered on a visit to a nude show: "They're *not* naked. They're wearing *us*."[197]

Frequent newspaper stories—themselves an indicator of widespread tolerance—highlight drives to unionize the profession and report on "tits for tots" campaigns, in which dancers launch charity drives, or cover stripper pressure groups in local elections. Popular business monthlies run articles on dancers as "independent contractors" and take note that female executives do not feel comfortable taking clients to strip clubs, as their male counterparts routinely do.[198] Under Tina Brown's editorship, the *New Yorker* reviewed trendy strip clubs for both male and female patrons. Going out for an evening of variously gendered striptease may eventually seem as casual as stopping by Hooters restaurants for a burger or renting *Sorority Sex Kittens* for home viewing.

In the meantime, low and high forms of sexual performance have vectored together in postmodern dynamic. Stripping has revitalized performance art, a fact first recognized by Senator Jesse Helms. The history of avant-garde performance art, a category of creative expression in which a performer consciously manipulates his or her body or persona to convey esthetic, moral, or political messages, reaches back to the theatrical components of the Fluxus movement in the 1920s and Futurism, Dadaism, and Surrealism in the 1930s and 1940s. During the 1960s, Allan Kaprow and Merce Cunningham staged kinetic "happenings," semispontaneous evocations of social and political issues, for counterculture audiences. Yoko Ono and Nam June Paik mounted multimedia amalgams of music, body sculpture, action painting, installation art, and nudity to disorient. Probably the most riveting event was Carolee Schneemann's lurid "flesh celebration," *Meat Joy* (1964), which featured naked human bodies covered with blood from animal carcasses.

Today performers use their bodies to deconstruct and subvert conventions of gender and sex and standards of age and beauty. Performance artists such as Colette, Karen Finley, Robbie McCauley, and the late Hannah Wilke have confronted the nature of eroticism itself through shock. In the early 1990s Senator Helms inveighed against the National Endowment for the Arts (NEA) for supporting performers such as Finley and Holly Hughes. When Congress passed a law restricting NEA funds to

artists who pledged not to be indecent, artists challenged the provision but eventually lost in court. Performers such as Annie
Sprinkle and Veronica Vera have supported their serious endeavors by working in porn films or stripping. Another performer,
Lilly Burana, says that sex work burns out performers, and,
worse, mirrors only the most clichéd reflections on the body.[199]
    That pornographic performance has been mainstreamed is
obvious. It is inconceivable that current New York stagings of *The
Vagina Monologues*, with its riffs on slang terms for female genitals, or *Naked Boys Singing*, with chorus lines of young men
bouncing their penises to show tunes, could take place had not
once-anathematized sexual expression made such profound in-
roads in the American theater.[200]

Erotic Photography

To make nude images acceptable, professional photographers
have usually pretended that they are not arousing. As the critic
John Berger has observed, a formal sitting converts nudity to "a
form of dress": "A naked body has to be seen as an object in
order to become a nude. (The sight of it as an object stimulates
the use of it as an object.) Nakedness reveals itself. Nudity is
placed on display."[201] The artistic nude justifies itself if viewers
agree that it does. Pornographic nudes are unapologetically
naked; because they do not justify themselves, they relieve the
viewer of the burden of approval. Pornographic photos are free
to arouse—or to repel.
    Louis Daguerre exhibited the first daguerreotype in 1839.
Within six years, daguerreotypists produced images of naked
humans.[202] "Warts and all" realism offended viewers schooled by
familiarity with the brush but appealed to those tired of idealized
nudes by polite painters.[203] What made the photographed nude
so significant, says Abigail Solomon-Godeau, was that it "disrupted . . . the propriety of the [painted] nude." Solomon-Godeau
dismisses arguments that the photograph objectified women: the
photograph of the nude exposes and undermines objectification,
and "potentially subverts the very authority it apes."[204] Of all
criticisms directed at pornography, the charge that it objectifies
women, she says, is the most meaningless. Any representation of
any subject objectifies.
    By the 1850s, Americans made three million daguerreotypes
each year,[205] some of naked people. Although daguerreotypes

could be reproduced only with difficulty, a panicked U.S. Congress in 1857 amended the Customs Act of 1842 to add explicit daguerreotypes to the list of prohibitions.[206] The next year, one of the very first photography magazines denounced the widespread appearance of erotic stereographs.[207] During the Civil War, erotic stereographs sold for $9 a dozen, pricey for the time.[208] Rapid technological developments led to erotic calotypes, ambrotypes, tintypes, and eventually celluloid prints. Post–Civil War proliferation of single prints and picture sets inspired censors to mount sting operations. By 1877, arrests of bookstore clerks, hotel concierges, and cigar store owners were commonplace.[209]

Prosecutors did not distinguish between soft-core shots of nude men or women and hard-core scenes of intercourse or penetration. The erotic photo archive of the Kinsey Institute, the most comprehensive in the world, contains many early nudes now regarded as high art, by recognized masters such as Edward Weston and Arnold Genthe; like the scruffy hard-core prints shot by amateurs, they bear docket numbers and dates of seizure. Given such threats, hundreds of photographers shot salon nudes from which they carefully leached traces of sexuality. Ironically, it is those very images that American culture has discarded. Museums and galleries today celebrate portraits of flesh whose eroticism made them endure. First among sensual explorers was Edward Weston, who shot nudes glowing in deserts or erect against architectural angles; probably more than any other photographer he educated Americans to the ravishing contours of the human body. E. J. Bellocq took starkly empathetic portraits of naked prostitutes in the New Orleans whorehouse district in 1912, but no one saw the lost prints until decades later.[210] In 1918, the wisps of pubic hair in Alfred Stieglitz's photographs of his lover (and later wife), the artist Georgia O'Keeffe, affronted Americans who saw them; in 1995, a single Stieglitz shot of O'Keeffe in a coy lingerie pose sold for $400,000.[211]

Paul Outerbridge experimented with gender masquerade, manipulating the labia of his female nudes and dressing them in male accoutrements, and F. Holland Day, another artist, shot explicit male nudes in religiously homoerotic settings. Carl Van Vechten photographed "fetish and fantasy" images of interracial homosexuality in the 1930s and 1940s.[212] The late Paul Cadmus, working with fellow artist Jared French and his wife Margaret French, produced homoerotic photos as well.[213] Comparing the formal male nudes of Minor White,[214] who began shooting in the

1940s, with the misshapen bodies captured by the talented George Dureau, working in the same period, reveals in the first a cold estheticism, in the second a helpless desire—on the part of models, viewers, and photographer.[215] Other classic professionals to push against limits include Tony Sansone, who photographs his own body; Bill Brandt, whose frames constantly reconceive landscapes of flesh; Robert Farber, whose studies of women reeroticize them decade by decade; Lee Friedlander, who portrays genitals in stark, edgy frames; Lucas Samaras, who makes eerie Polaroids of erotic tableaux; and Duane Michaels, who shoots differently gendered models to create a complex sensuality.

Less-skilled nude photographs very gradually made their way toward the center of culture in the early decades of this century. Prior to 1900, newspapers and magazines resisted such photographs partly because of the technical difficulty of reproducing them, and partly because it was safer to print drawings or paintings of burlesque queens. Postcard formats, by contrast, were ideal. Just before the turn of the century the collecting of postcards became an international craze, principally among women; one historian suggests that eroticizing the postcard was a marketing strategy designed to encourage men to collect.[216] Unlike postcards of lynchings of African American men and women, which were just fine with postmasters until 1908,[217] postcards of nude people could not be sent through the mails. Most posed stiff models against classical columns or mythological backdrops; a few revealed pubic hair, and the boldest captured women astride partners, but these were rare.[218]

Erotic postcards were not an American form, and they were often called "French" (though many were from Budapest, Berlin, or Vienna) after the alleged lasciviousness of that nation.[219] Even delegates to the League of Nations, which held an international conference on the traffic in obscene materials in 1910, believed that most dirty photos were French.[220] Many nude photographs came from Germany, especially during the 1920s and 1930s, the so-called *schonheit* (beauty) period of the Weimar Republic, which in turn was followed by a period that celebrated *naturkeit* (nudism). Marginal American publishers collected German images, air-brushed the pubic hair, bound them into covers, and sold them under titles such as *A Private Anthropological Cabinet of 500 Authentic Racial-Esoteric Photographs and Illustrations*.[221] Mail-order businesses sold full-frontal nudes of both sexes, though again with genitals retouched, through advertisements in men's magazines. Of newsstand fare, only "art" magazines such as

Artists and Models and *Art Inspirations* revealed nipples, and sellers usually kept these away from minors. Equally circumspect nudist magazines appeared as early as 1931, but their circulation was small until the 1950s.[222]

One could, of course, sexualize bodies through fetishes. The largest producer of fetish photographs was Irving Klaw, owner of Movie Star News in New York. The rationale behind fetish publications of the time was a simple variation on Gershon Legman's thesis that Americans prefer violence as a surrogate for sex. Klaw's photos contained no real nudity and absolutely no sex; his female models simply boxed, wrestled, caged, tied-up, and spanked each other. During the 1940s and 1950s, Klaw sold *Movie Star News* and *Model Parade* and also individual prints featuring bondage and discipline garb—lingerie, high heels, and leather costumes—worn by models such as Bettie Page, Donna Brown, and Joann Rydell. Klaw photos boosted the careers of strippers Blaze Starr, Tempest Storm, and Lili St. Cyr. Before being forced out of business by the Kefauver Commission, Klaw may have begun to lose sales when courts upheld the right of nudist magazines such as *Sunshine and Health* to reveal genitals. Within a few years, the nipples on display in *Dazzle, Frolic, Caper, Escapade, Dude, Scamp,* and *Monsieur* made the bondage and discipline stratagems seem silly. Even so, Bettie Page, Klaw's favorite model, ignited the libidos of a generation of American males. Articles and books on Page, many of them rhapsodic, now number in the hundreds.

Seminude photos began to appear in garages and barber shops as the pinup, which at first featured drawn or painted figures. (A St. Paul, Minnesota, company issued the first American pinup calendar in 1904.) The chief purveyors were the Hollywood studios, who used pinups to advertise movies and balloon the careers of major stars; the practice circumvented the restrictions of the Motion Picture Production Code by making both films and performers seem sexier than they really were.[223] Some 50,000 American soldiers per month asked for the over-the-shoulder shot of the bathing-suit-clad Betty Grable, whose sweetly sexy image was more ubiquitous than any other in the 1940s.[224] Pinups continued to piqué a postwar middle class. In 1949, Tom Kelley shot the most famous nude of the twentieth century. First published as the "Golden Dreams" Calendar by the John Baumgarth Company of Melrose Park, California, in 1953, it was instantly reproduced as *Playboy*'s first centerfold. Marilyn Monroe's sexiness overshadowed even Bettie Page's, and her im-

ages generated an even larger industry. (One enterprising volume now lists all the known Monroe magazine appearances; a
price guide assists investors.)[225]

Perhaps more than any other magazine, *Playboy* convention-
alized poses and constructed ideals of sexiness in the United
States. Dozens of articles have examined the layouts, the lighting,
and the air-brushing of Playmates. Bunny Yeager and Russ
Meyer photographed bare-breasted starlets such as Jayne Mans-
field and Mamie Van Doren for its pages, and thus set in motion
the now-familiar public relations cycle in which celebrities pose
for lavish pictorials timed to promote a movie, a television series,
or a book. Patty Reagan, for example, the daughter of former
president Ronald Reagan, appeared nude in 1994, just before her
new book came off the presses. Posing for *Playboy* and similar
magazines has generated a subgenre of memoirs.[226]

Though it is obvious that *Playboy* rose to success by depicting
women's bodies as objects of male desire, the magazine's relentless "objectification" of women accelerated the destruction of
sexual mystery that kept women "property" for so long. Stripped
of clothing imposed by males, her nudity made public and social,
and thus liberated from private claims by individual males, a
woman's body becomes hers once again, a substrate for a repertoire of nonsexual identities that are simply not possible when
the body is hidden from view. In their letters to *Esquire*, *Playboy*,
Life, and *Ebony* in the 1950s and 1960s, some housewives
protested against pictures they thought degrading, whereas others approved because the images seemed at last to recognize
women's sexuality. The debate has not diminished.[227]

Increasingly Americans see the centerfolds as just pictures of
pretty women in their birthday suits. More than one study indicates that men find *Playboy*'s pictorials "monotonous and te-
dious."[228] Rationales for nudity always inform displays. Nudist
magazines became legal because of their rationale: a healthy
mind in a healthy body had nothing to do with sex, and the pictures of naked women washing dishes or naked men playing golf
were perversely innocent. Hefner's philosophical justification for
depicting nude women in effect denied them *real* sexuality; the
Playmates were trophies of the good life, and they were posing
to show the effects of good grooming and high spirits on their
stunning chests. *Playboy* airbrushed crotches for years, until *Penthouse*, casually photographing pubic hair in 1970, at one stroke
shifted the focus of desire from breasts to a point several degrees
further south. Now *Penthouse* photographs women urinating,

performing oral sex, and engaging in intercourse. By contrast, *Playboy's* photos are more modest now than five years ago.

Given pervasive homophobia, male pinup photos developed cautiously. Heterosexual viewers can more readily accept a hardcore image of intercourse, in which a penis is depicted entering a vagina, than a shot of a male posed with his penis in the foreground. Theories of phallus-display abound. Lacanian psychologists insist that Western culture shrouds the penis in order to preserve its mystery and power, that male dominance rests on keeping the member hidden, hiding it behind the concept of the phallus, a sceptered symbol of heterosexual male oppression of familiar rosters of victims. But such nudes are problematic for gay viewers as well. Because one penis pretty much looks like any other, gays must search for cues that the photo is aimed at them. Signifiers of gender and desire must be learned, and that is one of the great contributions of pornographic images.[229]

"Academic" photographers shot male nudes during the nineteenth century, but salon studies were reticent.[230] American gays collected erotic prints by the German Wilhelm von Gloeden, whose youthful models posed outdoors, sometimes provocatively. Collectors also favored the prints of German-American George Platt Lynes, whose nudes appeared in highly theatrical erotic frames during the 1930s and 1940s. What to do with the penis, whose depiction could bring down authorities, remained a problem. Most photographers continued the practice, begun in the 1890s, of using "posing straps" to cover the genitals of body builders. The popularity of physique shots turned in part on their "deniability": the subjects were pumped, ripped, and chiseled, so healthy and uneffeminate that looking at them did not betray the viewer's orientation. Bernarr Macfadden promoted "beefcake" in *Physical Culture* after the turn of the century. By the 1930s, photographers such as Earle Forbes, Robert Gebhart, and Edwin Townsend shot dozens of nude muscle poses for body-builder magazines. Not until after World War II, however, did this genre come into its own.

According to Thomas Waugh, creating a subversive pornographic sensibility in the midst of a society that despised homosexuals was one of the great achievements of gay culture. Because masked desire bonded a homosexual community under adversity, the pioneering muscle photographers now enjoy gallery shows and belated recognition for their art.[231] More than a dozen California studios, with names such as the Western Photography Guild and "Bruce of Los Angeles," marketed physique photos. From the 1940s until the 1960s, Robert Mizer, head of the Los Angeles Athletic Model Guild, shot more than one million nudes; he sold them as single prints, as sets, and as pages for *Physique Pictorial* (1951–1990). Harassed by the U.S. Post Office, Mizer won a landmark case in 1962 when the Supreme Court decided that a penis by itself did not make a photo obscene and in any event was not sufficient reason to ban it from the mails. In recent years, Mizer has emerged as a pornographer who helped to define gay consciousness; Strand Films has just released *Beefcake*, a documentary on his life,[232] and a German publisher has reprinted every issue of his magazine.[233] By the 1960s, thanks to Mizer's efforts, the editors of more explicit pictorial magazines such as *Male Man* and *Yearling* could allow models to dispense with subterfuge and sport erections.

Eroticism crept into photography through yet another genre, however, as fashion photographers acknowledged the potential of clothing to excite. To say that eroticism often owes more to clothing than to nudity is to pay homage to the obvious. As painters and photographers have always known, nudes per se rarely stimulate; they are figures bereft of the erotic cues normally furnished by apparel. A pinup in *Penthouse* magazine, for example, will foreground the model's labia but almost always frame them with some kind of garment, however skimpy, however draped. Glamour photography, the kind that produces pinups, is really an offshoot of the fashion industry. The photographs of mannequins that filled fashion magazines month after month did as much to eroticize the culture as those in men's magazines.

Separating glamour and fashion was easier in the past, when photographers had to be more circumspect. In fact, George Platt Lynes shot fashion as a way of subsiding his homoerotic pictures.[234] During the late 1940s, the Conde Nast fashion photographer John Rawlings asked model Evelyn Frey to stay after clothing shoots. His *100 Studies of the Figure* (1951) explored her body in studio shots that emphasized Frey's sensuality. In the 1970s, the fashion photographer George M. Hester included amateur models among professional mannequins in *The Classic Nude*. In the 1980s, Pat Booth, a fashion model turned self-photographer, teased riveting emotional states from poses of her own body. Today virtually all major high-fashion photographers—Rebecca Blake, Bruce Weber, Guy Bourdin, Deborah Turbeville, Ellen von Unwerth, and Herb Ritts—also work in erotic genres. Helmut Newton frequently shoots layouts for *Playboy*, and supermodels such as Naomi Campbell and Cindy Crawford pose nude for men's magazines, though *Harper's Bazaar* and *Vogue* reveal almost as much. *Penthouse* annually runs at least one pictorial on the transparent fashions parading down the runways of Milanese or Parisian couturiers. In 1993, when the Eileen Ford Model Agency published its picture book (from which designers and photographers select their clothes horses), it included full-frontal nudes of many contract models.[235]

These indicators bolster the claim of Valerie Steele, historian of American fashion, that pornography has profoundly influenced the fashion industry by promoting fetishes. Although Steele has in mind S/M garb, leather and fur, stiletto heels, and tastes in hips and bosoms, the influence of fetishes is probably most clear in the distinct category of lingerie, easily the best-documented genre of erotic photography. By the end of the nineteenth century, photographs of women in intimate garments had multiplied to the point that aficionados could specialize. Their collections (e. g., the Bourgeron[236]) in turn attracted scholars.

Folklore also sprang up immediately, with photographers advising each other to hire models just beginning to menstruate, so that their breasts would be larger, or to ask them to cross their ankles so as to part and round the buttocks.[237] Until 1976, when Guy Bourdin shot the Bloomingdale's catalog *Sighs and Whispers*, glamour protocols specified demure poses, medium focal-lengths, and healthy skin-tone lighting. Bourdin shot sallow models starkly posed against blanched tile and metal faucets, with nipples and pubic hair visible through fabrics. More recently, taking note of the millions of Victoria's Secret catalogs stuffed into America's mailboxes, *American Photo* asked Sante D'Orazco, who shoots them, to contribute an essay to a special issue on the history of lingerie photography. That special issue graphs a curve of eroticism toward respectability.[238]

The investigators for the Kefauver Committee (1954–1955) who persecuted Irving Klaw found that bogus art studies and shots of topless models circulated in some profusion, but hard-core examples were uncommon. The Kinsey Institute's photo archive contains few hard-core examples from this period, and reports from the 1950s suggest that the boldest prints limited exposure to displays of pubic hair.[239] Even so, the President's Commission on Obscenity and Pornography (1970) decided that hard-core prints had a longer life, so that pictures of human intercourse shot in the 1930s still circulated in the 1960s.[240] The Feminist Anti-Censorship Task Force (FACT) gathered hard-core period examples from the Joseph Vasta, Richard Merkin, and

Bélier Press archives to illustrate the essays in *Caught Looking: Feminism, Pornography, and Censorship*; they seem familiar because they have been reproduced so often.[241]

Early hard-core prints were deliberately crude. For the most part their shock was unmitigated by skill, unsoftened by nuance, uncushioned by context. Well before 1900, low, vulgar, highly explicit, and often ugly close-ups—a weathered prostitute furtively sucking a penis, say—went deep underground to avoid prosecution. Judging from annual reports of vice societies and the U.S. Post Office, the channels of circulation were primitive and erratic. Some dealers sold them through the mails, changing addresses frequently to thwart postal inspectors, or sold them directly to customers they met face to face. Amateurs shooting stag films in the 1930s and 1940s shot still photographs at the same time. Unlike films, photos could be reproduced easily. About a dozen shots depict Candy Barr, a.k.a. Juanita Slusher, star of the most famous of all stag films, *Smart Alec*, made in 1951 when she was sixteen. Sold one at a time, or in sets, the prints of her in intercourse with the film's co-star eventually ended up in attics in virtually every state, left there by fans of the striptease legend that Barr became, but the total number of reproductions could not have exceeded 10,000. Before the 1970s, the largest seizure of individual different photos ever made in the United States took place in Jamaica, New York, in 1957, when two women were arrested with 3,000 photographic plates and 50,000 copies,[242] a paltry figure by mass media standards. With the widespread adoption of the Polaroid in the 1970s, Americans began taking pornographic pictures in numbers impossible to estimate.

Two other media, however, have most elevated what might be called the photography of erotic realism: the museum/gallery exhibition and the coffee-table book, both of which can function subversively. World-class photographers bring new perspectives to sexual domains, and they no longer pretend that their interest is sociological. Nan Goldin's *The Ballad of Sexual Dependency* (1986) chronicles the intimacies of Goldin's friends and relatives; their sexuality seems "real," vulnerable, and touching. Later volumes such as Goldin's *The Other Side* (1993) and *I'll Be Your Mirror* (1996) explore the pain of transvestites and transsexuals, and question the very idea of gender. For her show/volume *Dirty Windows* (1995), Merry Alpert secretly shot through the window of a Manhattan sex club; her images connect sex and money and surveillance in postmodern cultural comment. Before he turned filmmaker (*Kids*, 1995), Larry Clark shot graphic scenes of intercourse and drugs

(*Larry Clark*, 1992, and *Teenage Lust*, 1983); their power has influenced other photographers of his generation.[243] Joyce Baronio doc-
umented the lives and careers of male and female sex performers
in the compassionate frames of *42nd Street Studio* (1980). Della
Grace published the lesbian images of *Love Bites* (1991) first in England, only to have the volume seized by customs agents when the
publisher shipped a copy to the United States for reproduction
here. Says Grace, "I don't set out to take erotica and I don't set out
to do pornography. I'm happy if someone gets an erotic buzz."[244]
Other examples of lesbian erotic creativity by various photographers appear in *Her Tongue on My Theory: Images, Essays and Fantasies*, a collection of essays and images that explode popular and
academic stereotypes of lesbians.[245] Aware of the need to engineer
fantasies for neglected groups, artists such as Rundu L. Staggers
now produce photographic erotica for African Americans.[246]

The most notorious of major photographers in recent years
was Robert Mapplethorpe, although it is still unclear as to
whether conservatives were more offended by the homosexuality or the race of his subjects. Critical opinion is divided among
those who think that Mapplethorpe's images are revolutionary
and those who find them contrived; no one denies their force. His
several photo volumes, a CD-ROM collection of hundreds of
prints, and three biographies of the artist are now available from
book clubs. Whatever any given viewer might think of his work,
Mapplethorpe demonstrated that explicit images could refresh
debate on sexuality, gender, race—and pornography. Cincinnati,
Ohio, unsuccessfully prosecuted Dennis Barrie, director of the
Contemporary Arts Center there, for bringing a traveling exhibit
of Mapplethorpe photographs to the city in 1990. More recently,
the *New York Times*, commenting on Mayor Rudolph Giuliani's
attempt to eradicate sex industries, observed that Manhattan's
galleries had taken up the slack by displaying explicit photographs by Andres Serrano and other major artists.[247]

Erotic Motion Pictures and Videotapes

If performance art lends itself to the impersonation of women,
pornographic movies are the realm of the male impersonator.
This medium caricatures males by reducing them to penises,
which, obviously, must be as large as those once drawn by
Aubrey Beardsley for much the same purpose. Male performers
in hard-core films and videos exist almost entirely as penises

whose purpose is to ejaculate. Male performers are the second-class citizens of the video industry, valued almost exclusively for their ability to maintain erections amidst chaos on a set. In terms of status, salaries, and followings, they lag behind female counterparts; veterans make a fifth of what women are paid for the same scene. Male performers make visible what the culture at large has always taken pains to disguise: that men, at base, are pricks. Given the insignificance of average genitalia, only the magic of the cinema can raise penises to full fetishistic glory.

Moralists denounced motion pictures as soon as they were invented, charging the new medium with promoting sloth, sacrilege, and indecency in those who peered through peepshow cabinets. A few years later, ministers inveighed against projections in theaters whose darkness could hide imagined sexual fumbling between the boys and girls mingling there. The first (1896) public exhibition of Thomas Edison's projector took place in a former bawdy house (Koster and Bial's Theater on New York's 34th Street), a venue that conservatives found appropriate. A year later, in *People v. Doris*, New York convicted a filmstrip of indecency, which led other cities and states to establish censorship boards. Rumors of immorality led the mayor of New York City in 1908 to shut down *all* movie theaters in the city.

The miraculous new technology was frightening because it was sensual and accessible. Entrepreneurs were seedy, corrupt, and violent. Edison hired Pinkerton detectives to beat up his rivals and destroy their equipment, but pirates stole prints, cheated distributors (and vice versa), and swindled investors.[248] Though they claimed to move to California because of the Pacific light, producers also fled to escape their unsavory reputation back East, but not before the Supreme Court ruled in 1915 that movies were spectacles similar to carnival shows and thus not entitled to the protection of the First Amendment. Although politics influenced the decision (the movie was *Birth of a Nation*), some of the scandal-ridden movies on "white slavery" and miscegenation emerging from cheap studios *were* pretty seamy.[249] To prevent the establishment of a federal censorship agency, studio heads created the Motion Picture Producers and Distributors of America (MPPDA), a self-policing organization begun in 1922, with Will Hays as its head. For the next thirty years, Hollywood coped with capricious rulings of local censorship boards chiefly through the MPPDA. Under pressure from Catholic groups, the MPPDA adopted its Production Code in 1930 to eliminate allusions to sex and reproduction from mainstream movies.

To compensate for these absent elements, Hollywood adopted violence on a massive scale. Mayhem became America's surrogate for sex, a strategy pioneered by filmmakers such as Cecil B. DeMille, whose Biblical epics featured scenes of torture sanctioned by religious fervor. Directors without DeMille's sado-masochistic genius learned to cut away from a heated embrace to phallic images of locomotives penetrating tunnels, or to replace love scenes altogether with shootings or stabbings. This trend became so pronounced by 1949 that Gershon Legman denounced the syndrome as a distinctive American pathology.[250]

As usual, economics ruled. The threat of censorship meant that Hollywood could not depict sex openly, so producers emphasized aggression. In the 1920s and 1930s, burlesque impresarios headlined seminude dancers to lure back to Broadway the crowds siphoned off by the kinetic violence of the cinema. In the 1950s, however, Hollywood faced competition from two fronts. The first was domestic, as television laid siege to movies. The second was global, as foreign films marshaled frank themes, sexual repartee, and flashes of nudity to challenge Hollywood's domination of world markets. Sex, motion picture veterans realized, was the only thing that could save the mainstream film. Fortunately, the Supreme Court reversed itself in 1952,[251] deciding that motion pictures were a category of speech, and thus allowed Hollywood to wield the First Amendment against censors immediately up in arms over director Otto Preminger's sexy *The Moon Is Blue* (1953). A series of court decisions allowed Hollywood to offer a candor forbidden to American television but familiar to audiences in Europe.

The stalking horse was the "exploitation" film. This type can be traced to "exposés" of white slave traffic as early as 1913, and to "educational" films on the subjects of venereal disease, birth, premarital sex, interracial marriage, and contraception during the 1930s and 1940s. These "teased" by promising but rarely delivering lurid content. When the Supreme Court in 1955 cleared the modest nudist film *Garden of Eden*, filmmakers shot dozens of movies featuring women who bared their breasts in improbable places. *The Immoral Mr. Teas* (1959) launched the directing career of Russ Meyer, who promptly wedded nudity to violence in a series of "roughie" movies with titles such as *Mudhoney* (1965), *Faster Pussycat, Kill! Kill!* (1966) and *Vixen* (1968). The bra sizes of his stars grew with each film. David Friedman, another director to see the commercial possibilities of mammoth breasts and graphic gore, shot *Blood Feast* (1963) and other features to symbolize sex through phallic brutality. Herschell Gordon Lewis, Ted V. Mikels, Joe Sarno, and Doris Wishman—an incomplete roster—began inventing genres of exploitation: Nudie Films, Biker Films, Juvenile Delinquency Films, Beach Party Films, Women in Prison Films, and half-a-dozen others, some of which still delight audiences.[252] More important, they schooled American audiences to accept sex at neighborhood movie houses. In 1945, the major studios reorganized the industry censor into the Motion Picture Producers' Association (MPPA). In 1966, the MPPA issued a new PG, R, and X rating system. The X-rated *Last Tango in Paris* (1972), starring Marlon Brando in nude embraces with Maria Schneider, drew large audiences.

Exploitation movies have engendered legends that still resonate. The most enduring is the "snuff film," a hoax inadvertently created by the most notorious of exploitation directors, Roberta Finley. Her unfinished 1971 film *Slaughterhouse* was recut by its distributor and released under the title *Snuff*. The film's publicist falsely hinted that the female protagonist had actually been murdered during a sex scene. The rumor brought out feminist pickets, who thus ensured financial success for a film too incoherent to watch. Both the Federal Bureau of Investigation (FBI) and the Adult Film Association investigated reports of snuff films for years; despite persistent urban myth, none has ever turned up. Historians now characterize the furor as the second stage of the moral panic triggered by the radical feminist indictment of looking as an act of male oppression; *Snuff* seemed to confirm the thesis that the male gaze itself is lethal.[253] Another bit of folklore, potentially more serious, grew out of research conducted by sociologists investigating the alleged antisocial effects of pornography. Several studies indicated that male audiences exposed to exploitation horror films (carelessly called "pornographic") were more likely to tolerate violence directed at women than groups who had not seen the films.[254] Journalists and antiporn critics concluded that the studies proved that pornography leads to rape, a mistaken surmise that researchers themselves tried in vain to correct.[255]

Scholars have generally ignored hard-core films, whose single-minded obsession with sex makes them unsuitable for theories of social aggression. Researchers prefer to analyze the soft-core exploitation film, with its obvious blending of sex and aggression, in the hope of demonstrating that at least some forms of pornography lead to violence. Hard-core films can claim an ironic purity because they reject symbolism in favor of the literal

mechanics of intercourse; hard-core has no need for violent images. Instead of raping or hurting his partner, as might be the
case in an exploitation film, the protagonist in typical hard-core
films makes genital contact with a willing lover. A viewer might
recoil in disgust from such images, of course, but rarely because
the sequence is violent.

In fact, historical controversies over morality and decency in
mainstream films had little to do with actual pornographic reels,
which went underground after the turn of the century. The mainstream legitimate cinema developed its own genres; the pornographic imagination instantly parodied them. From the beginning
the pornographic film functioned as a deliberate alternative to the
public cinema and evolved parallel to it, albeit secretly and anonymously. Stag films circulated first in Europe and in South America.
Around 1911, during his sailing career, future playwright Eugene
O'Neill sold tickets to a pornographic theater in a whorehouse
during a stay on the beach in Buenos Aires, Argentina.[256] The first
recorded raid on a showing of stag films in America took place in
Manhattan in 1912.[257] The first surviving American stag film, *A
Free Ride* (a.k.a. *A Grass Sandwich*) dates from 1915. By the end of
the decade, producers on the fringe of Hollywood brought forth
The Casting Couch (1920) and *Strictly Union* (1919), both with ac-
complished comic scenarios. During the 1920s, however, the
shooting of stag films in America became an amateur pursuit.

Because they rarely made much money, their circulation
being limited to secret gatherings, early stag films were labors of
love. Shot at first on 35-millimeter film as single reels of twelve
minutes, stags featured plain-vanilla sex between prostitutes and
males recruited from waterfronts or bars. Sometimes the men
wore masks or fake mustaches, and both men and women often
kept on their shoes, the better—according to legend—to run if
police appeared on the set. These quaint elements aside, stags
coupled self-parodic formulas with the technical incompetence
(poor lighting, stupid editing, ungrammatical titles, wretched
camera angles) that became their hallmark. The more inept the
film, the more the performers tripped over themselves, the more
"authentic" the eroticism seemed.

Watching a stag film was a social event of male bonding, not
the occasion for solitary masturbation that videocassettes would
later make possible. Projectors were expensive, so distributors—
who were sometimes the filmmakers—usually rented their stock
of films along with projectors, with themselves as operators. By
observing the reaction of the men in the American Legion Hall,

they could determine what audiences liked. They did not care for films featuring minors; the men in the audiences tended to be middle-aged fathers. Somewhat surprisingly, audiences preferred comic plots in which males were the butt of the joke.[258] The plots frequently turned on tales or jokes from folklore, while intertitles sniggered at the silent action. A typical example of 1923 depicted a man driving a date ten miles out of town, then threatening to force her to walk back unless she agreed to intercourse. She refuses and walks back. On the second night he drives her twenty miles out. She refuses again and walks back. On the third night, he stretches the distance to fifty miles. This time she complies. Satisfied after the explicit intercourse, the driver asks her why she gave in. Her reply, in bold intertitle: "I don't mind walking ten miles or even twenty miles, but I'll be dammed if I'll walk fifty miles just to avoid giving a man the clap!"[259]

If the gathering were an Elks Club or similar organization, the police chief of the town might show the films himself, having confiscated the reels from an itinerant exhibitor, and thus removed them from the sight of the "wrong people." Because middle-class audiences recoiled from homosexual acts, the hard-core film bifurcated. Gay filmmakers shot fewer films because they were uncertain of their audience and more fearful of prosecution. It was safer to produce body-building reels, in which oiled bodies posed in jockstraps. Over the years, studios such as the Athletic Model Guild of Los Angeles would turn out dozens of these. For a time, authorities were bewildered by these and fetish films for straights, because they did not show nipples, labia, or penises.

Middle-class fantasies generated stags in which Fuller Brush Men or plumbers seduced housewives (and vice versa), or—as women moved into the workplace—office managers seduced secretaries or doctors their patients (and vice versa). By the 1930s, when amateurs switched to 16-millimeter formats, the number of stags rose. In Manhattan, police arrested famous madam Polly Adler not for running a whorehouse but because she screened stag films there.[260] Stags were still crude: Before 1965, only five were shot in sound, and only four in color.[261] American amateurs turned out more stags than any other nationality and continued to do so until the 1950s, when they were outpaced by the English. During the 1960s, the Scandinavians legalized pornography and pulled ahead, only to drop behind in the 1970s as Danes and Swedes tired of the stuff.

Despite their reputation, stag films were pretty tame. They were almost uniformly nonviolent. Garden-variety sex, its depiction on screen a violation of taboo, was quite enough to shock and to satisfy. The first genuine sadomasochistic film, *Song of the Lash*, an import from Germany, did not appear in the United States until 1956. After the war, the "cum shot," the penis's ejaculation outside the vagina, became nearly universal, a phenomenon still debated. Since producers called it the "money shot," some critics seized on visible ejaculation as an expression of capitalism; others thought that producers included fancy ejaculation to "prove" that orgasm had taken place; still others thought that gushing orgasms structured the genre like the songs in a musical comedy.[262] The most plausible analysis, that males spray semen to demonstrate control, seems closer to the mark.[263] Since characters in a typical hard-core film succumb to the chaos of passion, cum shots symbolize restoration of sexual order through virtuoso performance.

When cheap 8-millimeter film projectors allowed individuals to take the films home, production of ten-minute reels soared. Now producers could cater to preferences of specific audiences by covering fetishes of all sorts. The sexual revolution of the 1960s and 1970s opened the door to theatrical distribution of feature-length hard-core. The first hard-core feature to be shown publicly in the United States was an untitled, hour-long, 16-millimeter reel exhibited for three days at the Avon Theater in New York City in 1968; neither it nor a homosexual feature shown at the Park Theater in Los Angeles a few months later was prosecuted. The first feature to be nationally distributed was Bill Osco's *Mona* (1970). "Documentaries" like *Sexual Freedom in Denmark* (1970), under the guise of "socially redeeming importance," made theaters safe for pornography, as did Alex de Renzy's *A History of the Blue Movie* (1970). The feature market bifurcated into heterosexual and homosexual types, the latter pioneered by Wakefield Poole's *Boys in the Sand* (1972). Imaginative plots suddenly mattered, as did production values for the large screen.

Pornographic features benefited from avant-garde mystique. Carolee Schneemann shot *Fuses* (1964–1967), featuring the performance artist herself in explicit intercourse with James Tenney. Kenneth Anger's *Scorpio Rising* (1964) and Andy Warhol's *Blow Job* (1963) and *Taylor Mead's Ass* (1964), all shown in storefront theaters in major cities, claimed new sexual territory for serious artists. Jack Smith made *Flaming Creatures* (1963), whose homosexual images so upset a Congress chagrined by liberal decisions on pornography that its members refused to confirm Abe Fortas as Chief Justice.[264]

In 1972, in a mass phenomenon called "porn chic," urban audiences flocked to see *Deep Throat* and *Behind the Green Door*. For the first, a Queens hairdresser named Gerard Damiano borrowed $25,000 from mobster Louis Peraino, hired an actress named Linda Lovelace, and shot the film in two weeks in Miami. *Deep Throat* centered on Lovelace's ability orally to engulf large penises, a technique that seemed a counterpart to the male "cum shot" as an example of control. *Behind the Green Door*, shot by Jim and Artie Mitchell of San Francisco, featured model Marilyn Chambers, whose face was familiar to Americans from having been reproduced millions of times on Ivory Snow soap boxes. Chambers's character indulged fantasies of being ravished by multiple partners simultaneously. Both films thus traded on sex as athletic performance, a concept that lifted eroticism to spectacle. Lovelace briefly traded on her fame by publishing *Inside Linda Lovelace*, a book on techniques of oral and anal sex, but soon claimed that she had been forced to perform, and denounced pornography.[265] By contrast, Chambers made other porn movies (*Never a Tender Moment*, 1979; *Insatiable*, 1980), polished a Las Vegas stage act, starred in a couple of grade-B mainstream movies, and eventually found her way back into hard-core.

From 1973 to 1975, Americans shot one hundred hard-core features a year, at a time when Hollywood averaged fewer than 400 films annually, and shot almost 500 8-millimeter shorts per year during the same period. Before hard-core films declined, they built a global American market and created the video cassette recorder (VCR) industry. Because the first VCRs were expensive and copyright issues remained unsettled, most film producers were reluctant to transfer movies to the new format. Not so pornographers, who seized on prospects for home viewing; the majority of early cassettes were pornographic. The Sony Corporation' s refusal to license its Beta technology to pornographers guaranteed the triumph of the VHS format marketed by JVC.[266] Today, on the cusp of another format shift, CD-ROM professionals believe that erotic movies and images are crucial to growth in that sector of the video-computer industry.[267] In any case, theatrical exhibition of pornography is already obsolete.

The market for videos is enormous, with American production estimated at 10,000 videos in 1999 (see "The Economics of Pornography," Chapter 5). America's porn companies shoot about 150 hard-core videos per week; all other countries combined shoot a hundred per month.[268] Producers address audiences through standard gender categories but also through crossover and transsexual fare. As one might expect, quality varies sharply, as do types. Consumers can find costume dramas and well-developed plots, softly lit "couples" tapes, comedies and melodramas, gonzo cassettes of raw sex, fetish videos from foot-worship to nude wrestling, and scabrous examples that defy description. African Americans, Hispanics, and Asian Americans are forming porn video companies with the announced intention of pushing the sexualities of people of color into popular consciousness.[269] None of this means that pornographers have become positive role models, conscious agents of social responsibility, or even enlightened capitalists. Video companies are only now introducing safety measures, for instance. Afraid that audiences did not want to see penises clad in condoms, studios failed to insist on basic protection. High-profile HIV-positive cases, most notably John Stagliano, head of Evil Angel, have led to more performers insisting on condoms. And, lest they be forgotten, other erotic videos are doing well also. Soft-core films and videos draw their own audiences, along with occasional respectful notices from the *New York Times*.[270]

Porn stars make regular appearances on television talk shows, operate huge fan clubs and Web sites, endorse erotic products, dress extravagantly for premieres, and generally carry on like their counterparts in the legitimate cinema. For a certain class of Americans, porn actresses such as Jenna Jameson and Juli Ashton are as much the nation's sweethearts as are Julia Roberts and Drew Barrymore. Like their Hollywood counterparts—and like football players—performers enjoy short careers bounded by youth, beauty, and litheness. Because their peak earning years are short, they tend to pursue their celebrity hard and burn out quickly. Jameson has made millions as a performer,[271] but most women and men in the industry make far, far less, though they flock to the business as an alternative to working in fast-food chains.

Most veterans leave when they can no longer draw fans, or move to the other side of the camera. John Leslie, Candida Royalle, and many others now direct. In 1999, a fifty-year-old Marilyn Chambers starred in *Still Insatiable*, a film directed by veteran actress Veronica Hart. The durability of these first-generation performers (others include Ginger Lynn, Jamie Gillis, Joey Silvera, and Sharon Mitchell) suggests that they feel a sense of pride in the fantasies with which they have cindered the imaginations of their fellow citizens.

Erotic Electronic Media

Dial-a-Porn Services

Although therapists in larger cities during the 1960s established telephone "hot lines" to offer sexual advice, especially to young people confused by the sexual revolution, the encounters were not pornographic. The marketing possibilities became obvious only in the next decade, when companies began selling prerecorded fantasies to callers.

Prodded by Senator Helms and other conservatives, Congress in 1983 amended Section 223 [b] of the 1934 Telecommunications Act to prevent the transmission of obscene or indecent messages to minors. When pornographers began delivering messages by leased lines, Congress added an amendment to the 1988 Education Bill outlawing 800-number Watts line dial-a-porn services. Pornographers promptly switched to 900-number party lines instead. When courts struck down a law that prohibited "indecent" messages—which are protected—along with "obscene" ones, Congress passed a law requiring that telephone companies block access unless the subscriber asked for it in writing. Gays and lesbians protested that the provision restricted their rights, especially when people afraid of AIDS needed nonphysical forms of sexuality.[272] A series of court decisions resulted in the de facto legalization of dial-a-porn, except for a requirement that phone companies block access by minors at the request of parents.

Explosive growth generated a need for sexual scripts, especially for prerecorded messages, and thus provided work for writers.[273] As these audiotexts gave way to interactive encounters in the 1990s, demand rose for skilled operators who could ask for credit-card numbers, then smoothly respond to cues provided by the callers. Veterans learned to recognize patterns and to incorporate precise motifs demanded by callers into the fantasy.[274] Dial-a-porn fills a niche for callers seeking fantasies built around specific fetishes that other pornographic media ignore. Whereas males may think they have reached nubile young women when they call, some of the most successful operators are retirees working part-time or female impersonators adept at building gendered fantasies.[275] Gays and lesbians report satisfactions and frustrations common to heterosexual consumers.[276] Every night in 1996, 250,000 Americans of all genders made dial-a-porn calls lasting from six to eight minutes.[277]

Broadcasting

Section 1464 of the U. S. Criminal Code prohibits profane, indecent, or obscene language on a broadcast medium. Section 326 of
the 1934 Communications Act, written to comply with the First
Amendment, however, prohibits the Federal Communication
Commission (FCC) from censoring program content. Judges
have preferred to finesse this contradiction by treating infractions
as civil rather than criminal cases. Since courts have upheld the
FCC's authority to fine stations guilty of transmitting "indecency" (a much vaguer term than obscenity), the broadcast industry has found it prudent to regulate itself. Starting in 1923, the
National Association of Broadcasters (NAB) enforced stringent
rules governing expression. Courts eventually declared the
NAB's policies unconstitutional, but network censors still clear
scripts before airtime.

Where radio is concerned, incidents have been few. In 1937,
when ventriloquist Edgar Bergen invited Mae West to visit with
his dummy Charlie McCarthy on the *Chase and Sanborn Hour*
(NBC), "Diamond Lil" delivered her lines so "suggestively" that
congressmen threatened an investigation of radio. Panicked, the
networks banned appearances by West. (In 1959, when Charles
Collingwood taped an interview with West—at sixty-six still too
sexy—for *Person to Person*, CBS-TV canceled the show.) During
the 1960s, deejays experimented with suggestive remarks, and a
few college radio stations lost their licenses for pushing limits,
but the major radio incident was the "Seven Dirty Words" case.
In 1973, Pacifica station WBAI broadcast a radio monologue in
which comedian George Carlin speculated on why certain taboo
words carried shameful connotations, and enunciated the seven
words he had in mind. When a single listener complained, the
FCC sanctioned WBAI. On appeal, the Supreme Court ruled that
since radio was a "guest in the home" where there might be children, the FCC could punish the station for violating propriety.
Actually, in 1971, Dr. Hip Pocrates lost his job on Metromedia's
KSAN for saying the word "cock,"[278] and in 1972, a year before
the WBAI scandal, announcer Harry Shearson lost his for saying
the word "penis" (neither of these words was among Carlin's
seven) on an FM station.[279] In 1991, "shock jock" Howard Stern
played word games with "penis" himself, then moved onto masturbation, sodomy, and the mating habits of celebrities. By 1995,
Infinity Broadcasting, Stern's employer, owed the FCC $2 million
in fines for Stern's off-color remarks. A few years later, President

Clinton's affair with former White House intern Monica Lewinsky made sexual terminology inevitable.

Broadcast television has been even more circumspect, although one critic notes that since 1973, sitcom writers have tried to insert the word "ass" as often as possible into scripts for sure-fire laughs.[280] For most of its history, television followed Hollywood by substituting violence for sex in its programming, replacing orgasms with gunfire or car chases. The principal exceptions were the afternoon soap operas, often called "pornography for women," which serve a steady diet of steamy embraces and talk of infidelity, incest, and rape. About a dozen television soap operas attract an audience of about 25 million viewers. Since soap operas appear to endorse male dominance, heterosexuality, racism, and rigid social class, academic feminists are bewildered by their appeal to women. One critic finds that constant themes of infidelity and mistaken paternity remind women of their power to control reproduction and thus function as subversive fantasies.[281] Other theories hold that women are attracted by the constantly eroticized relationships among the characters rather than by explicitness. The formulas are aging nonetheless, and Proctor and Gamble (the reason the genre is called "soap"), which owns and produces *As the World Turns, Another World,* and *Guiding Light,* is searching for novel forms of titillation.[282]

In the 1960s, writers inserted double-entendre dialogue into risqué plots for *The Beverly Hillbillies* (1962–1971) and *Laugh-In* (1968–1973). Hugh Hefner's *Playboy After Dark* (1968–1969) and Johnny Carson's *Tonight Show* (1962–1992) in their different ways smirked at sex without being explicit. Broadcasters had to cope with unprecedented images of protest, war, and assassination during the decade; they were just as unprepared for sexual candor. Network censors refused to allow Barbara Eden to reveal her navel in *I Dream of Jeannie* (1965–1970), and an advertiser called for censorship when white singer Petula Clark touched black singer Harry Belafonte's arm on *Petula* (1968).[283] By the end of the decade, however, the plots of *Love, American Style* (1969–1974) cautiously mentioned massage parlors, wife-swapping, and sexual appliances.

During the 1970s, Norman Lear challenged censors with forbidden topics in *All in the Family,* a landmark program that elevated the intelligence of network fare. More important, Lear joined the Writer's Guild, the Screen Actor's Guild, and the Director's Guild in a 1975 First Amendment suit to force the FCC to abandon the "family viewing" policy designed to keep all television programming at a level acceptable for children. Competition from cable made their plea urgent. That same year, Home Box Office (HBO) began distributing uncut R-rated mainstream movies by satellite to cable systems around the country. Three years later, in 1978, Viacom began satellite delivery of Showtime, another candid premium service.

The most visible change in broadcasting merely set sweater-clad breasts bouncing. The bellwether show here was *Charlie's Angels* (1976–1981), probably a rip-off of an exploitation film called *The Doll Squad* (Ted V. Mikels, 1973).[284] Networks scheduled lots of "jigglies." Brash young comedians on *Saturday Night Live* made a point of saying "penis" as many times as they could. Characters and themes became gradually more adult, and sexual relationships became candid and frequent enough for conservatives to complain.[285] Liberals complained too: the Planned Parenthood Federation accused producers of joking about sex instead of providing educational information on sex, birth control, or sexually transmitted diseases.[286]

Public broadcasters built an audience around British imports such as *The Benny Hill Show* and every now and then showed a female nipple, which commercial broadcasters still will not do. During the 1980s fundamentalists boycotted advertisers on shows such as *Married with Children*, which traded in vulgar comedy, and in the 1990s protested *NYPD Blue*, which showed bare buttocks. According to the Parents Television Council, the incidence of "foul language" on prime-time network TV shows increased 30 percent from November 1996 to November 1998; sexual content increased 42 percent during the same two-year period.[287] In recent years, the public has become convinced that sex saturates prime-time.[288]

Networks still shy from homosexuality, although *La Cage aux Folles* has aired. Some PBS affiliates declined to broadcast *Tongues Untied*, a 1989 documentary on black gays, and *Tales of the City* (1994), a dramatization of Armistead Maupin's San Francisco stories, both of which showed penises. When commercial television does present programs involving gays or lesbians, the characters are persistently stereotyped.[289] Some gays have found their way onto tabloid and scandal programs such as the *Jerry Springer Show*, where they join other "freaks" showcased by the program's host. *Geraldo, Oprah, Hard Copy, Inside Edition, Confessions of Crime,* and *Current Affair*—not an exhaustive list—are hardly spontaneous; the National Talk Show Registry, a database of freaks, will furnish bizarre program guests when the show's own staff runs out of applicants.[290] Even so, says Joshua Gamson, freak shows offer a service that pornographic genres have always provided: in addition to providing therapeutic discussion for the sexually challenged, they alter attitudes toward deviant, marginal, or alternative sexual lifestyles.[291] Trash television, in other words, subverts class, gender, and other social categories.

Rapid technological change, strong public feeling, and political grandstanding have deepened the constitutional confusion surrounding issues of indecency on broadcast media. In 1991, a federal court ruled that indecency could be forbidden between 6 A.M. and 10 P.M., but that a 24-hour prohibition was unconstitutional because that would reduce the content to levels suitable for five-year-olds, but networks have been tentative about exploiting "safe harbor" late evening hours. CBS broadcasts a late-night television version of the *Howard Stern Show* but optically censors the nudity of his porn star guests, arguably making the images more prurient.

Cablecasting and Satellites

Cable television flourished because it could show materials networks could not, one factor in broadcasting's loss of one-third of its audience to cable. In 1972, when municipalities tried to ensure democratic reach by mandating community access channels, amateur hosts of cable shows in New York and California invited their guests to remove their clothes and even to engage in intercourse. By 1975, the FCC pressured local systems to curtail sex programs even though state laws forbade censorship of public access channel content. Squeezed by contradictions, cable operators shifted sexy public access programs to leased channels. At first Congress tried to help by passing the 1984 Cable Communications Policy Act, which promised operators immunity to prosecution for obscene materials because they could not legally exercise control over content. Senator Helms amended the 1992 Cable Television Consumer Protection and Competition Act to give operators the right to ban indecent programming, and hold them accountable if they did not.

Some programs, slightly toned down, survived. The most venerable is *Screw* magazine's *Midnight Blue*. Callers discuss fantasies with the semiclothed hostess of *Voyeurvision*, a program on Channel J (leased-access) of Manhattan Cable in New York; the program now appears on European cable systems as well. In California, Dr. Susan Block, a Yale Ph.D., also takes calls dressed in a

Merry Widow. For over ten years Channel J (Manhattan) has carried weekly gay soap operas, erotic movie reviews, and other subjects of interest to gays on the Gay Cable Network.

Because cable customers must subscribe, censors cannot claim that such shows are unwelcome intruders in the home. Family-oriented channels routinely edit sex out of mainstream movies whereas premium services such as HBO and Showtime do not. Services such as Spice and Playboy provide soft-core adult material. Recently the E! Channel began offering adult programming but obscured nipples, buttocks, and genitals.[292] Fundamentalists aside, however, critics have been less concerned about R-rated or soft-X movies than with Music Television (MTV), launched in 1981 by Warner Cable, because of alleged influence on youth. Conservative action groups such as the Parents' Music Resource Center attack MTV for promoting antisocial values, and feminists attack it for images degrading women. Typical studies find that women characters in MTV segments are scantily clad, mindlessly affectionate, and clearly dependent on aggressive male musicians.[293]

By building studios, premium services turn out their own candid movies and programs to pull audiences away from broadcast channels. Late-night HBO delivers *Real Sex* and *Shock Video*; the first documents sexual representations (video performers, dancers, S/M enthusiasts, performance artists, erotica collectors, and fetishists of all sorts), and the second compiles raunchy television shows from other countries. The two largest-drawing HBO shows were *Breasts* (1996) and *Private Dicks* (1998), both of them filled with naked body parts. Sheila Nevins, vice-president and head of HBO's documentary division, is the force behind such shows, about which she says, "We're all divided somewhere between our brains and our groins."[294]

Hotel chains routinely provide pay-per-view, satellite-delivered soft-core adult movies. When cheaper satellite technology emboldened entrepreneurs to deliver hard-core features, the Justice Department, following Attorney General Edwin Meese's directives to prosecute pornographers at all costs, targeted American Exxxstacy in the late 1980s. After shopping for a conservative community in Alabama, prosecutors impaneled a jury certain to find the programming obscene, and bankrupted the national company. New regulations have complicated economics. In 1998, the Playboy Channel purchased its chief soft-core programming competitor, the Spice Channel. Soon after, New Frontier Media (Boulder, Colorado) purchased Exctasy Networks, formed

[handwritten margin note: to pick sex names listing mlune — usenet/ etc.]

The Erotic Network (TEN), a   an-
nel, Pleasure, in 1999. The ri\   in
1998 the FCC began enforcir   on
505) of cable law that requi   ver
Playboy channel programmi   te,
Playboy, which does not sh\.. .....   ica
that appeals to women and multiple ethnic groups. Playboy executives consider their real competition to be shows like HBO's
Real Sex and *Sex in the City*, network programs like *Buffy the Vampire Slayer* and *Ally McBeal*, and the roster of sexy afternoon soap
operas. For its part, New Frontier Media has begun delivering
hard-core on three Direct Broadcast Satellite (DBS) channels (not
available on cable)—Exctasy, TrueBlue, and Gonzo X—to about
165,000 subscribers who pay between $6 and $ 14.95 per month.
New Frontier has also been acquiring adult Web sites to program
with video-streamed material. New Frontier's current annual
revenues exceed $80 million.[295]

Assuming that all program providers eventually agree on a
rating system (NBC and the Black Entertainment Network are
holdouts), the V-chip mandated under section 551 of the Communications Act of 1996 should permit parents to block offensive
material for children. The filtering technology will have one of
two consequences: it will either render moot disputes over unwanted programming, or encourage broadcasters to include
more rather than less sexual expression by shifting responsibility
to the consumers. Because it is so pervasive, television has already undermined childhood, say media scholars, by exposing
them to nonsexual and nonexplicit information that in the past
would have been available only to adults.[296]

Computers and the Internet

Soon after the Internet was established, amateurs began creating
communities of fantasy on the Usenet (electronic bulletin boards
for posting messages) by establishing hierarchies of fetishes in
alt.sex directories and creating chat rooms. Americans adopted
fanciful cyber names (Superstud, Thunder Tits, Creamy Thighs)
for erotic E-mail exchanges and thus refurbished one of the oldest of pornographic traditions—pseudonymity. The practice inspired a thousand pop psychologists to speculate on the
consequences of constructing *sub rosa* sexual identities in cyberspace. Choosing a persona allows one to change gender; a gay
clerk can become a woman in an exchange with a male executive

who is really a woman. Cybersex is representation as representation; it makes possible erotic shape-shifting enshrined by folklore and dreams. Cyberspace has no boundaries; everywhere and nowhere, the environment it creates is comfortable and safe. The 47-year-old housewife pretending to be a 35-year-old male doctor can explore erotic possibilities with an interesting persona willing to share fantasy. Cyberspace, says Brenda Laurel of Interval Research, is a "new representational world that allows people to construct representations of their own sexuality for each other."[297]

Entrepreneurs quickly invented digitalized pornographic games. Most of these, like *Strip Poker II* (Art Work, Inc.), and *Strip Blackjack II* (I. O. Research), were primitive; they were eclipsed in 1986 when Mike Saenz created *Virtual Valerie*, an interactive program. Though still just electronic kitsch, the software allowed its user to plunge a dildo in and out of "Valerie's" vagina. There followed *Leisure Suit Larry, Passionate Patti, Sorcerers Get All the Girls, Sexxcapades,* and *MacPlaymate,* all of which have been made obsolete by CD-ROMS, streamed video on the Net, and DVD. Although thus far the interactivity of DVD is limited to games like *Digital Debutantes* (1998), in which players quest for a white dildo and the right to use it, DVD's capacity for multiple plot lines and specific behaviors will transform hard-core videos into new kinds of narrative.

The World Wide Web, invented by Tim Berners-Lee at the start of the 1990s, lifted pornography to another level. In constructing their Web sites, pornographers swiftly added commercial novelties to net technology: flash, the click-through banner ad, pop-up windows.[298] Three innovations pioneered by pornographic entrepreneurs stand out. The first is the development of "transaction technologies" on the Internet, or electronic protocols for making credit card purchases secure. The best of these methods was established by the Internet Entertainment Group (IEG), producer of pornographic videos and Web sites, and immediately copied by legitimate industries from banks to retail merchandisers. A second is the "streaming" of audio and video content on the Net, another technology advanced by IEG and companies such as Vivid Video.[299] A third involves the creation of "virtual reality" scenarios that will make artificial sex seem "real" to electronic participants. Here again, Vivid seems to be outpacing universities and commercial leaders.[300]

Marketing by Internet shifts viewing and purchasing decisions to the consumer, thus exempting the vendor from the traditional accusation that pornographers prey on the unaware. A

Web site is the merchandising equivalent of the automatic teller machine (ATM), an electronic device that enlists the consumer as the worker for a specific transaction under the guise of greater convenience. The real significance of the Internet, however, lies not so much in its irresistible power to distribute sexual representations without hindrance on a global scale, impressive though that is. The Internet promises true interactivity in the design and execution of fantasies. Already a user can draw representations from a vast storehouse, seeking and downloading still images and full-motion video, adding to them sequences of his or her own making. These operations are prelude to virtual reality—simulations without precedent, in which an individual will actively participate through sensors that mimic human sexual experience.

In 1995, just as Congress geared up to pass the Communications Decency Act, Martin Rimm, a student at Carnegie-Mellon University, published a bogus (prank?) survey claiming that more than 80 percent of all images posted on the Internet were pornographic.[301] When antiporn activist Catharine MacKinnon immediately endorsed the study, the media, in a remarkable illustration of folklore in the making, trumpeted the news. *Time* magazine ran a cover story on the Rimm report[302] and did not retract it when it was exposed as fraudulent, thus leaving the spurious figures hanging in culturespace. According to experts, pornography accounted for about 3 percent of all messages on the Usenet, and less than 0.5 percent of images on the Net itself.[303] The percentage has probably remained flat. There are now more than 10,000 commercial sex sites in a roster of legitimate sites that has itself increased exponentially. As was the case with satellite transmission of hard-core, the Justice Department battled against the tide. It used "forum-shopping" strategies to convict Robert and Carleen Thomas for operating Amateur Action, an on-line pictorial site, when they were entrapped into sending images from their site, located in California, to a government agent in Memphis, Tennessee. The local jury dutifully found obscene images that many Californians would hardly notice.[304] Two developments have slowed prosecutions. First, the Supreme Court decisively rejected the restrictions of the Communications Decency Act (1996) on the grounds that they would cripple the Internet. Second, access to Web sites increasingly requires credit cards not readily available to minors. Moreover, many adult sites now use net filters themselves. These, with names such as Surf-Watch and SurfNanny, can block access. Net filters have led to controversy when installed on public computers in libraries.

Early court decisions have ruled filters unconstitutional in those circumstances, but many libraries continue to use them.

All major men's magazines now operate Web sites, but average citizens publish erotic E-zines as well. *Nerve*, an upscale erotic magazine (advertised as "Literate Smut") run out of a Soho loft in Manhattan, has been recapitalized at $10 million in order to build a Web site and portal that will attract visitors of all genders.[305] According to one research firm, 20 percent of women eighteen and older visit sex sites, as contrasted with 41 percent for males similarly aged.[306] On their site, two lesbian entrepreneurs offer what are essentially porn photos of lesbian sex but sandwich them between "propaganda" for lesbian causes.[307] One voyeur's site allows subscribers to monitor the intimate lives of women (who are paid) in a dormitory through forty miniature cameras.[308] Operating interactive erotic sites, however, requires training. At Virtual Dreams, a Las Vegas–based on-line site, strippers disrobe via Internet videoconferencing software. Leaning how to take off one's bra, move slowly—so as not to outpace the slow-transmission rate of six to ten frames a second—and type messages at the same time makes striptease a pretty mechanical process.[309]

"Ever since the Victorian era the rich and the privileged have always had their erotic bound editions of pornography," says Larry Flynt. "But today the poor man's art museum has become the video store and the newsstand. So with this flow of information, I don't see the government being able to take it away or curtail it. Information is power and the people now have it." Given the Internet, Flynt thinks, the trend will accelerate: "The majority of people will be getting their information off the Net or Direct TV."[310] Whether such tolerance continues depends on a host of factors, of course, not the least of which may be current confusion over just how the Internet operates. According to a study commissioned by the Kaiser Family Foundation, the Kennedy School of Political Science, and National Public Radio, a great many Americans favor restrictions on internet content ranging from classified data and fraudulent information to violent imagery and pornography, without any clear sense of how such restrictions would impact their own unfettered access to any and all kinds of material—which the same surveyees also insist that they want.[311] Within a few decades, the threats of offensive messages, of irresponsible freedom, and even of virtual sexual representation may be dwarfed by a greater menace. The marvels of the Internet prefigure future developments in what Bill Joy, Chief Scientist of Sun Microsystems, calls "GNR"—for genetics, nanotechnology, and robotics. Joy thinks that the artificial systems made possible by GNR engineering may make our species obsolete in the long run.[312]

Notes

1. Legman quoted in Helen Dudar, "Love and Death (and Schmutz): G. Legman's Second Thoughts," *Village Voice*, 1 May 1984, p. 42.

2. Gershon Legman, "Erotic Folksongs and Ballads: An International Bibliography," *Journal of American Folklore* 103 (October/December 1990): 417.

3. See Gershon Legman, "Erotic Folksongs and Ballads: An International Bibliography" and his *The Horn Book: Studies in Erotic Folklore and Bibliography* (New York: University Books, 1964).

4. Bruno Bettelheim, *Symbolic Wounds: Puberty Rites and the Envious Male* (New York: Collier Books, 1962).

5. Richard Dooling, *Blue Streak: Swearing, Free Speech, and Sexual Harassment* (New York: Random House, 1996).

6. *Bilderlexicon der Erotik. Ein bibliographisches und biographisches Nachschlagewerk, eine Kunst– und Literaturgeschichte für die Gebiete der erotischen Belletristik ... von der Antike zur Gegenwart*, 6 vols. (Vienna and Hamburg: Verlag für Kulturforschung, 1928–1931, 1963).

7. See James Axtell, ed., *The Indian Peoples of Eastern America: A Documentary History of the Sexes* (New York: Oxford, 1981); Walter L. Williams, *The Spirit and the Flesh: Sexual Diversity in American Indian Culture* (Boston: Beacon Press, 1986); Fred W. Voget, "Sex Life of the American Indians," *Encyclopedia of Sexual Behavior*, Albert Ellis and Albert Abarbanel, eds. (New York: Hawthorne, 1961), pp. 90–109.

8. Bruce C. Daniels, *Puritans at Play: Leisure and Recreation in Colonial New England* (New York: St. Martin's, 1996).

9. Kate McCafferty, "Palimpsest of Desire: The Re-Emergence of the American Captivity Narrative as Pulp Romance," *Journal of Popular Culture* 27, 4 (Spring 1994): 43–56.

10. See, for example, Frank Hoffmann and Tristram Coffin, eds., "Symposium on Obscenity in Folklore," *Journal of American Folklore* 75 (1962): 187–265.

11. John S. Farmer and William Earnest Henley. *Slang and Its Analogues*, 7 vols. (London: privately printed, 1890–1904), reprinted as *Dictionary of Slang and Its Analogues, Past and Present: A Dictionary Historical and Comparative of the Heterodox Speech of All Classes of Society for More Than Three*

Hundred Years with Synonyms in English, French, German, Italian, etc., Vol. 1, revised and enlarged (New Hyde Park, N.Y.: University Books, 1966), reprinted as *Slang and Its Analogues, Past and Present*, 3 vols. (Millwood, N.Y.: Kraus Reprint, 1989).

12. Adolph F. Niemoller, *American Encyclopedia of Sex* (New York: Panurge Press, 1935).

13. Allen Walker Read, *Lexical Evidence from Folk Epigraphy in Western North America: A Glossarial Study of the Low Element in the English Vocabulary* (Paris: privately printed, 1935), reprinted as *Classic American Graffiti* (Waukesha, Wisc.: Maledicta Press, 1977).

14. Mamie Meredith, "Inexpressibles, Unmentionables, Unwhisperables, and other Verbal Delicacies of Mid-Nineteenth Century Americans," *American Speech* 5 (April 1930): 285–287.

15. See, for example, Thomas E. Murray and Thomas R. Murrell, *The Language of Sadomasochism: A Glossary and Linguistic Analysis* (Westport, Conn.: Greenwood Press, 1989).

16. James W. Chesebro, ed., *Gayspeak: Gay Male and Lesbian Communication* (New York: Pilgrim Press, 1981).

17. R. Jeffrey Ringer, ed., *Queer Words, Queer Images: Communication and the Construction of Homosexuality* (New York: New York University Press, 1994).

18. Catharine MacKinnon, *Only Words* (Cambridge, Mass.: Harvard University Press, 1993).

19. Judith Butler, *Excitable Speech: A Politics of the Performative* (New York: Routledge, 1997).

20. Julia P. Stanley, "Paradigmatic Women: The Prostitute," in *Papers in Language Variation*, David L. Shores and Carole P. Hinds, eds. (Tuscaloosa: University of Alabama Press, 1977), pp. 303–321.

21. Luce Irigaray, *This Sex Which Is Not One*, Catherine Porter, trans., with Carolyn Burke (Ithaca: Cornell University Press, 1985).

22. Hélène Cixous, "The Laugh of the Medusa," Keith Cohen and Paula Cohen, trans., *Signs* 1, 4 (1976): 875–893; and "Veiled Lips," *Mississippi Review* 11 (1983): 93–131.

23. Ken Plummer, *Telling Sexual Stories: Power, Change and Social Worlds* (New York: Routledge, 1995).

24. John Preston, ed., *Flesh and the Word: An Anthology of Erotic Writing*, 2 vols. (New York: Plume, 1992, 1993), II, p. 2.

25. Rayna Green, "Magnolias Grow in Dirt: The Bawdy Lore of Southern Women," *Southern Exposure* 4, 4 (1977): 32–35.

26. See, for example, William F. Fry, "Psychodynamics of Sexual Humor: Men's View of Sex," and "Women's View of Sex," *Medical Aspects of Human Sexuality* 6 (May 1972): 128–131, 133–135.

27. Carol Mitchell, "The Sexual Perspective in the Appreciation and Interpretation of Jokes," *Western Folklore* 36 (1977): 303–329.

28. Alan Dundes, ed., *Mother Wit from the Laughing Barrel: Readings in the Interpretation of Afro-American Folklore* (Englewood Cliffs, N.J.: Prentice-Hall, 1973); Roger D. Abrahams, *Deep Down in the Jungle: Negro Narrative Folklore from the Streets of Philadelphia* (Hatboro, Penn.: Folklore Associates, 1964); Bruce Jackson, *"Get Your Ass in the Water and Swim Like Me": Narrative Poetry from the Black Oral Tradition* (Cambridge, Mass.: Harvard University Press, 1974; Daryl Cumber Dance, *Shuckin' and Jivin': Folklore from Contemporary Black Americans* (Bloomington: Indiana University Press, 1978).

29. Gershon Legman, "Toward a Motif-Index of Erotic Humor," *Journal of American Folklore* 75 (1962): 227–248; *Rationale of the Dirty Joke* (New York: Grove Press, 1968); *No Laughing Matter: Rationale of the Dirty Joke, Second Series* (New York: Breaking Point, 1975); *The Limerick: 1700 Examples, with Notes, Variants, and Index* (Paris: Les Hautes Etudes, 1953); *The New Limerick: 2750 Unpublished Examples, American and British* (New York: Crown Publishers, 1977).

30. See, for example, D. J. Hibler, "Sexual Rhetoric in Seventeenth-Century American Literature," Ph.D. dissertation, Notre Dame University, 1970; Karl Keller, "Reverend Mr. Edward Taylor's Bawdry," *New England Quarterly* 44 (1970): 382–406; William Howland Kenny, *Laughter in the Wilderness: Early American Humor to 1783* (Kent, Ohio: Kent State University Press, 1976); B. L. Granger, *Political Satire in the American Revolution, 1763–1783* (Ithaca: Cornell University Press, 1963); Paul M. Zall, "The Old Age of American Jestbooks," *Early American Literature* 15 (1980): 3–15; J. P. Siegel, "Puritan Light Reading," *New England Quarterly* 37 (1964): 185–199.

31. *Anecdota Americana. Being Explicitly an Anthology of the Tales of the Vernacular. Elucidatory Preface by J. Mortimer Hall* [Joseph Fleisler] (Boston [New York]: Humphrey Adams, 1927; reset and expanded, same publisher, 1932.)

32. Vance Randolph, *Roll Me in Your Arms: "Unprintable" Ozark Folksongs and Folklore*, Vol. 1, edited and with an introduction by Gershon Legman (Fayetteville, Ark.: University of Arkansas Press, 1992), and Vance Randolph, *Blow the Candle Out: "Unprintable" Ozark Folklore*, Vol. 2, edited and with an introduction by Gershon Legman (Fayetteville, Ark: University of Arkansas Press, 1997).

33. Alan Dundes and Carl R. Pagter, *Work Hard and You Shall Be Rewarded: Urban Folklore from the Paperwork Empire* (Bloomington: Indiana

University Press, 1978), and Alan Dundes and Carl R. Pagter, *When You're Up to Your Ass in Alligators* (Bloomington: Indiana University Press, 1987).

34. "Sick Jokes," *New York Times*, nat. ed., 6 August 1991, p. A10.

35. Alex Kuczynski, "In Offices, an Excuse to Talk About S*x," *New York Times*, 2 February 1998, pp. B1, B7.

36. John S. Farmer, *Merry Songs and Ballads Prior to the Year 1800 and Musa Pedestris*, 6 vols. (London: privately printed, 1896–1897; reprinted New York: Cooper Square, 1964, with introduction by Gershon Legman).

37. Sandra Perry, "Sex and Sentiment in America, or What Was Really Going On between the Staves of Nineteeenth Century Songs of Fashion," *Journal of Popular Culture* 6 (Summer 1972): 32–48.

38. Quoted by Richard Harrington in "Exercising the Right to Censor the Censors," in *Messages 3: The Washington Post Media Companion*, Thomas Beel, ed. (Boston: Allyn and Bacon, 1996), p. 99.

39. Peter Wagner, "The Veil of Medicine and Morality: Some Pornographic Aspects of the *Onania*," *British Journal for Eighteenth-Century Studies* 6 (1983): 179–184.

40. Max Hall, *Benjamin Franklin and Polly Baker: The History of a Literary Deception* (Pittsburgh: University of Pittsburgh Press, 1990).

41. See Timothy J. Gilfoyle, *City of Eros: New York City, Prostitution, and the Commercialization of Sex, 1790–1920* (New York: Norton, 1992); Paul S. Boyer, *Urban Masses and Moral Order in America, 1820–1920* (Cambridge, Mass.: Harvard University Press, 1978); Luc Sante, *Low Life: Lures and Snares of Old New York* (New York: Farrar, Straus and Giroux, 1991).

42. Patricia Cline Cohen, Timothy J. Gilfoyle, and Helen Lefkowitz Horowitz, "The 'Sporting' Press in 1840s New York: Three Interpretations," paper presented at the Annual Meeting of the American Studies Association, Montreal, Canada, 29 October 1999.

43. Al Rose, *Storyville, New Orleans: Being an Authentic, Illustrated Account of the Notorious Red-Light District* (University Station, Ala.: University of Alabama Press, 1974).

44. See Edward Van Every, *Sins of America as Exposed by the Police Gazette* (New York: Stokes, 1931), and Gene and Jayne Barry Smith, eds., *The Police Gazette* (New York: Simon and Schuster, 1972).

45. Peter Wagner, "Pornography in the Courtroom: Trial Reports about Cases of Sexual Crimes and Delinquencies as a Genre of Eighteenth-Century Erotica," in *Sexuality in Eighteenth-Century Britain*, Paul-Gabriel Bouce, ed. (Manchester, U.K.: Manchester University Press, 1982), pp. 120–140.

46. Ronald G. Walters, "The Erotic South: Civilization and Sexuality in American Abolitionism," *American Quarterly* 25 (May 1973): 177–201; he quotes the *Liberator* of 29 January 1858, p. 183.

47. Thomas P. Lowry, *The Story the Soldiers Wouldn't Tell: Sex in the Civil War* (Mechanicsburg, Penn.: Stackpole Books, 1994).

48. Hal D. Sears, *The Sex Radicals: Free Love in Victorian America* (Lawrence, Kan.: Regents Press, 1977), p. 28.

49. Martin Henry Blatt, *Free Love and Anarchism: The Biography of Ezra Heywood* (Urbana: University of Illinois Press, 1989).

50. James Jackson Kilpatrick, *The Smut Peddlers* (Garden City, N.Y.: Doubleday, 1960), pp. 44–45.

51. Robert S. Lynn and Helen M. Lynd, *Middletown: A Study in Contemporary American Culture* (New York: Harcourt Brace, 1929), pp. 239–242.

52. John Tebbel, *The Media in America* (New York: New American Library, 1974), p. 362; see also Simon Michael Bessie, *Jazz Journalism: The Story of the Tabloid Newspapers* (New York: Dutton, 1938).

53. Greg Mullins, "Nudes, Prudes, and Pigmies: The Desirability of Disavowal in *Physical Culture*," *Discourse* 15, 1 (Fall 1992): 27–48; see also Robert Ernst, *Weakness Is a Crime: The Life of Bernarr Macfadden* (Syracuse, N.Y.: Syracuse University Press, 1990).

54. See chapter 7 of Tony Goodstone, *The Pulps: Fifty Years of American Popular Culture* (New York: Chelsea House, 1970).

55. Elliott P. Dietz, Bruce Harry, and Robert Hazelwood, "Detective Magazines: Pornography for the Sexual Sadist?" *Journal of Forensic Sciences* 31, 1 (January 1986): 197–211; reprinted in the *Final Report* of the Attorney General's Commission on Pornography (Washington, D.C.: Government Printing Office, 1986), I, pp. 55–69.

56. Douglas H. Gamelin, ed., *The Tijuana Bible Reader* (San Diego: Greenleaf, 1969).

57. Jay A. Gertzman, *Bookleggers and Smuthounds: The Trade in Erotica, 1920–1940* (Philadelphia: University of Pennsylvania Press, 1999), p. 79.

58. "Lewd Magazines Burn Amid Cheers," *New York Times*, 28 January 1941, p. 1.

59. See Barbie Zelitzer, *Remembering to Forget: Holocaust Memory through the Camera's Eye* (Chicago: University of Chicago Press, 1998).

60. James R. Petersen, "Playboy's History of the Sexual Revolution, Part VI: Something Cool (1950–1959)," *Playboy* 45, 2 (February 1998): 78, 104.

61. Alan Betrock and Hillard Schneider, *The Personality Index to Hollywood Scandal Magazines, 1952–1966* (Brooklyn, N.Y.: Shake Books, 1990).

62. Albert Ellis, *The Folklore of Sex*, a.k.a. *Sex Beliefs and Customs* (New York: Charles Boni, 1951), and *The Folklore of Sex* (New York: Grove Press, 1961).

63. Catharine A. MacKinnon, "More Than Simply a Magazine: *Playboy*'s Money," *Feminism Unmodified: Discourses on Life and Law* (Cambridge, Mass.: Harvard University Press, 1987), pp. 134–145.

64. Judith A. Reisman, *"Soft Porn" Plays Hardball: Its Tragic Effects on Women, Children and the Family* (Lafayette, La.: Huntington House, 1991).

65. William Iverson, *The Pious Pornographers* (New York: William Morrow, 1963).

66. Betty Friedan, "The Sexual Sell," chapter 9 in her book *The Feminine Mystique* (New York: Norton, 1963).

67. David Sonenschein et al., "A Study of Mass Media Erotica: The 'Romance' or 'Confession' Magazine," *Technical Report of the Commission on Obscenity and Pornography*, 9 vols. (Washington, D.C.: Government Printing Office, 1971–1972), IX, pp. 99–164.

68. Tuppy Owens, *Politico Frou-Frou: Pornographic Art as Political Protest* (New York: Cassell, 1996).

69. Steven Clay and Rodney Phillips, *A Secret Location on the Lower East Side: Adventures in Writing, 1960–1980* (New York: Granary Books/New York Public Library, 1998); Abe Peck, *Uncovering the Sixties: The Life and Times of the Underground Press* (New York: Pantheon, 1985); Robin Morgan, "Goodbye to All That," in *The American Sisterhood*, Wendy Martin, ed. (New York: Harper and Row, 1972).

70. President's Commission on Obscenity and Pornography, *Report of the Commission on Obscenity and Pornography* (Washington, D. C.: Government Printing Office, 1970), part 3, section D.

71. *New York Times*, 15 October 1974, p. 23.

72. Neil Wexler, "The Master of Leg Art," *Gallery* 22, 9 (September 1994): 36; see also *Elmer Batters: Legs That Dance to Elmer's Tune*, Dian Hanson, ed. (Cologne: Benedikt Taschen, 1997).

73. Quoted in Mark Kramer, "The Mastur Race," *Gauntlet* 5 (1993): 139.

74. Valerie Kelly, *How to Write Erotica for Fun and Profit* (New York: Harmony Books, 1986).

75. Rosalinda Stone, "Porn Yesterday: True Confessions of a *Celebrity Skin* Editor," *Village Voice*, 3 August 1999, p. 66.

76. Stephen Duncombe, *Notes from Underground: Zines and the Politics of Alternative Culture* (New York: Verso, 1997).

77. Frederic Wertham, *The World of Fanzines: A Special Form of Communication* (Carbondale: Southern Illinois University Press, 1973).

78. Joanna Russ, "Pornography by Women for Women, with Love," in *Magic Mommas: Trembling Sisters, Puritans and Perverts: Feminist Essays* (Trumansburg, N.Y.: Crossing Press, 1985), pp. 79–99.

79. Karen Houppert, "My Breast Friend," *Village Voice*, 17 August 1999, p. 125.

80. Tom Reichert, Jacqueline Lambiase, Susan Morgan, Meta Carstarphen, and Susan Zavoina, "Cheesecake and Beefcake: No Matter How You Slice It, Sexual Explicitness in Advertising Continues to Increase," *Journalism and Mass Communication Quarterly* 76, 1 (Spring 1999): 7–20.

81. See Introduction to a collection of columns in Dan Savage, *Savage Love* (New York: Plume, 1998).

82. Peter Wagner, "Eros Goes West: European and 'Homespun' Erotica in Eighteenth-Century America," in *The Transit of Civilization from Europe to America*, Winfried Herget and Karl Ortseifen, eds. (Tübingen: G. Narr, 1986), p. 148.

83. Ralph Thompson, "Deathless Lady," *The Colophon: A Quarterly for Bookmen* 1, 2 (Autumn 1935): 207–220.

84. "A Note on the American History of *Memoirs of a Woman of Pleasure*," in John Cleland, *Memoirs of a Woman of Pleasure* (New York: Putnam, 1963), pp. 19–20.

85. Milton Rugoff, *Prudery and Passion: Sexuality in Victorian America* (New York: Putnam, 1971), pp. 305–306.

86. John W. Tebbel, *The Media in America* (New York: Crowell, 1974), p. 39.

87. David Reynolds, *Beneath the American Renaissance: The Subversive Imagination in the Age of Emerson and Melville* (New York: Knopf, 1988), p. 224.

88. Henry Spencer Ashbee [Pisanus Fraxi], *Index Librorum Prohibitorum* (London: privately printed, 1877), pp. xlix–1.

89. Walter Kenrick, *The Secret Museum* (New York: Viking, 1987), pp. 129–130.

90. [William Laird Clowes], *Bibliotheca Arcana Seu Catalogs Librorum Penetralium: Being Brief Notices of Books That Have Been Secretly Printed, Prohibited by Law, Seized, Anathematised, Burnt or Bowdlerised, by Speculator Morum* (London: privately printed [George Redway], 1885; London: Piscean Press, 1971).

91. See New York Society for the Suppression of Vice, *Annual Reports* (New York: New York Society for the Suppression of Vice, 1874–1940); Anthony Comstock, *Frauds Exposed; Or, How the People Are Deceived and Robbed, and Youth Corrupted* (1880; reprinted Montclair, N.J.: Patterson Smith, 1969); and Gershon Legman, *The Horn Book: Studies in Erotic Folklore and Bibliography* (New York: University Books, 1966).

92. Lowry, *The Story the Soldiers Wouldn't Tell*, p. 55.

93. Ashbee [Pisanus Fraxi], *Index Librorum Prohibitorum*, pp. xlix–1.

94. Edward de Grazia, *Girls Lean Back Everywhere: The Law of Obscenity and the Assault on Genius* (New York: Random House, 1992), pp. 10–12.

95. See the introduction by J. W. Collins and Edward Spear to the reprint of B. G. Jefferies and J. L. Nichols, *Light on Dark Corners* ([1894]; New York: Grove Press, 1967).

96. John Money, *The Destroying Angel: Sex, Fitness, and Food in the Legacy of Degeneracy, Graham Crackers, Kellogg's Corn Flakes, and American Health History* (Buffalo, N.Y.: Prometheus Books, 1985).

97. Mark Twain [Samuel Clemens], "Some Remarks on the Science of Onanism," *The Mammoth Cod, An Address to the Stomach Club* (Waukegan, Wisc.: Maledicta Press, 1976), p. 23.

98. Jonathan Karp, "Decline? What Decline?" *Media Studies Journal* 6, 3 (Summer 1992): 45–53.

99. Kilpatrick, *The Smut Peddlers*, pp. 46–47.

100. Gertzman, *Bookleggers and Smuthounds*, pp. 61–85.

101. Robert McG. Thomas Jr., "Jack Biblo, Used Bookseller for Half a Century, Dies at 91," *New York Times*, 18 June 1998, p. C20.

102. Lillian Faderman, *Odd Girls and Twilight Lovers: A History of Lesbian Life in Twentieth-Century America* (New York: Columbia University Press, 1991).

103. Ann Bannon, "Introduction" to Jaye Zimet, *Strange Sisters: The Art of Lesbian Pulp Fiction, 1949–1969* (New York: Viking Studio, 1999), pp. 11–12.

104. Ralph Thompson, "Deathless Lady," 207–220.

105. Daniel Eisenberg, "Toward a Bibliography of Erotic Pulps," *Journal of Popular Culture* 15, 4 (Spring 1982): 184.

106. Thomas Scortia, *Strange Bedfellows: Sex and Science Fiction* (New York: Random House, 1972).

107. Quoted in Stewart Kellerman, "Other Incarnations of the Vampire Author," *New York Times*, 7 November 1988, pp. C15–16.

108. Naomi Morgenstern, "'There Is Nothing Else Like This': Sex and

Citation in Pornogothic Feminism," in *Sex Positives? The Cultural Politics of Dissident Sexualities*, Thomas Foster, Carol Siegel, and Ellen E. Berry, eds. (New York: New York University Press, 1997), pp. 39–67; see also Susie Bright, quoted in Steven Chapple and David Talbot, *Burning Desires: Sex in America—A Report from the Field* (New York: Signet, 1990), p. 316.

109. Shirley Moretto and Kathleen Weidenburner, "We'll Take Romance," *Library Journal*, 15 September 1984, pp. 1727–1728.

110. Edith Updike, "Publishers of Romance Novels Add Color to Their Lines," *New York Newsday*, 25 July 1994, pp. 23–24.

111. Miriam Decosta-Willis, Reginald Martin, and RoseAnn P. Bell, eds., *Erotique Noire: Black Erotica* (New York: Doubleday, 1992); Geraldine Kudaka, ed., *On a Bed of Rice: An Asian-American Erotic Feast* (New York: Anchor/Doubleday, 1995); Ray Gonzalez, ed., *Under the Pomegranate Tree: The Best New Latino Erotica* (New York: Washington Square Press, 1996).

112. Tee Corinne, ed., *Riding Desire: An Anthology of Erotic Writing* (Austin, Tex.: Banned Books, 1991), p. 156.

113. See the chapters on North America in Philip Rawson, *Primitive Erotic Art* (New York: Putnam, 1973).

114. See Milton Simpson, *Folk Erotica: Celebrating Centuries of Erotic Americana* (New York: HarperCollins, 1994).

115. William H. Gerdts, *The Great American Nude: A History in Art* (New York: Praeger, 1974), pp. 66, 86–89.

116. Kilpatrick, *The Smut Peddlers*, p. 48.

117. Michael Gill, *Image of the Body* (New York: Doubleday, 1989), p. 309.

118. Milton Rugoff, *Prudery and Passion: Sexuality in Victorian America* (New York: Putnam, 1971), pp. 116–117.

119. Bernard Perlman, "A Century of Cincinnati Esthetics: From Fig Leaves to Fines," *New York Times*, 13 April 1990, A31.

120. See Berhard Stern, *Illustrierte Geschichte der Erotischen Literatur aller Zeiten und Völker* (Vienna/Leipzig: C. W. Stern, 1908), and Gordon Grimley, comp., *Erotic Illustrations* (New York: Bell, 1974).

121. See Gershon Legman's introduction in Mahlon Blaine, *The Art of Mahlon Blaine* (East Lansing, Mich.: Peregrine, 1982).

122. Gertzman, *Bookleggers and Smuthounds*, p. 155.

123. See *Spicy: Naughty '30s Pulp Covers* (Princeton, Wisc.: Kitchen Sink Press, 1992); Robert Lesser, *Pulp Art: Original Cover Paintings for the Great American Pulp Magazines* (New York: Grammercy, 1997); Harry Harrison, *Great Balls of Fire: An Illustrated History of Sex in Science Fiction* (New

York: Grosset and Dunlap, 1977); Jaye Zimet, *Strange Sisters: The Art of Lesbian Pulp Fiction 1949–1969* (New York: Viking Studio, 1999).

124, Gilfoyle, *City of Eros*, pp. 145–147.

125. Lowry, *The Story the Soldiers Wouldn't Tell*, p. 55.

126. Jonathan Weinberg, "'Boy Crazy': Carl Van Vechten's Queer Collection," *Yale Journal of Criticism* 7, 2 (1994): 25–49.

127. Suzanne L. Kinser, "Prostitutes in the Art of John Sloan," *Prospects* 9 (1984): 231–254.

128. Ellen W. Todd, "Sex for Sale: Reginald Marsh's Voluptuous Shopper," *The "New Woman" Revisited: Painting and Gender Politics on Fourteenth Street* (Berkeley: University of California Press, 1993), pp. 178–223.

129. Gershon Legman, *Love and Death: A Study in Censorship* (New York: Breaking Point, 1949), p. 46.

130. Phyllis R. Klotman, "Racial Stereotypes in Hard-Core Pornography," *Journal of Popular Culture* 5, 1 (Summer 1971): 221–235.

131. Otis Raymond, *Sex Comic Classics*, 2 vols. (New York: Comic Classics, 1972), I, pp. 6.

132. D. M. Klinger, *Die Frühzeit der Erotischen Comics, 1900–1935.* Auction catalog #8 (Nuremburg, Germany: D. M. Klinger, 1985); this catalog lists 878 American titles.

133. See Bob Adelman, ed., *Tijuana Bibles: Art and Wit in America's Forbidden Funnies, 1930s–1950s* (New York: Simon and Schuster, 1997).

134. C. J. Scheiner, *Compendium*, p. 31.

135. Frederic Wertham, *Seduction of the Innocent* (New York: Rinehart, 1954).

136. Anjelica Huston and Peter Lester, "Mae West 1976," *Interview*, July 1994, pp. 92–93.

137. Shirley Christian, "University's Trove of Pinups Is Admired by All Sorts, Even Some Feminists," *New York Times*, 25 November 1998, p. B3.

138. Wallace Wood, *Gang Bang!* and *Gang Bang! 2* (N. P.: Nuance Publishers, 1980).

139. Jaye Berman Montresor, "Comic Strip-Tease: A Revealing Look at Women Cartoon Artists," *Look Who's Laughing: Women and Comedy*, Gail Finney, ed. (Langhorne, PA: Gordon and Breach, 1994).

140. Tee Corinne, *Cunt Coloring Book* (San Francisco: Last Gasp, 1975; reprinted as *Labiaflowers*, 1981).

141. Trina Robbins et al., *Strip AIDS, USA* (San Juan, Calif.: Shanti Project, 1988).

142. Roz Warren, ed., *Weenie–Toons: Women Cartoonists Mock Cocks* (Bala Cynwyd, Penn: Laugh Lines Press, 1992).

143. Ed Cafasso, "The Chilling Effect of Corporate Extortion on the Arts," *Gauntlet* 1, 5 (1993): 146–162; Michael Fleming, "Freeze Frames: Who Undressed Jessica Rabbit?" *Variety*, 14–20 March 1994, p. 2.

144. Honey Truewoman, "Realism in Drag," *Arts* 48, 5 (February 1974): 44–45.

145. Hilton Kramer, "Lindner's Ladies," *Playboy* 20, 3 (March 1973): 96–101.

146. Claes Oldenburg, *Claes Oldenburg: An Exhibition of Recent Erotic Fantasy Drawings* (London: Mayer Gallery, 1975).

147. Elizabeth Claridge, "Aspects of the Erotic—1: Warhol, Oldenburg," *London Magazine* 19 (February–March 1976): 94–101.

148. Roy Lichtenstein, *The Prints of Roy Lichtenstein: A Catalogue Raisonne, 1948–1993*, Mary Lee Corlett, comp., with introduction by Ruth E. Fine (New York: Hudson Hills Press/National Gallery of Art, 1994).

149. Robert Fraser Gallery, *Dine* (London: Fraser, 1966).

150. Jim Dine, *Prints 1970–1977* (New York: Williams College/Harper and Row, 1977).

151. Tom Gardner, "Tom Wesselman: 'I Like to Think that My Work Is about All Kinds of Pleasure,'" *Art News* 81 (January 1982): 67–72.

152. "Erotic Art," special issue of *Art and Artists* 5, 5 (August 1970).

153. Janet Hobhouse, *The Bride Stripped Bare: The Artist and the Female Nude in the Twentieth Century* (New York: Weidenfeld and Nicolson, 1988), p. 275.

154. Lisa Phillips, essay on David Salle, in *David Salle*, Janet Kardon, ed. (Philadelphia: Institute of Contemporary Art, University of Pennsylvania, 1986).

155. Adam Gopnik, "Lust for Life," *New Yorker* (18 May 1992): 76–78.

156. Naomi Salman, "Why Have There Been No Great Women Pornographers?" in *New Feminist Art Criticism*, Katy Deepwell, ed. (Manchester, U.K.: Manchester University Press/St. Martin's, 1995), pp. 119–125.

157. See the essays in Amelia Jones, ed., *Sexual Politics: Judy Chicago's Dinner Party in Feminist Art History* (Berkeley: University of California Press/Hammer, 1996).

158. Carol Jacobsen, "Redefining Censorship: A Feminist View," *Art Journal* 50 (Winter 1991): 42–55.

159. Maryse Holder, "Another Cuntree: At Last, a Mainstream Female

Art Movement," *Off Our Backs* 3, 10 (September 1973): 11–17, reprinted in *Feminist Art Criticism: An Anthology*, Arlene Raven, Cassandra Langer, and Joanna Frueh, eds. (New York: Harper/Collins, 1991), pp. 1–20.

160. Susanne Kappeler, *The Pornography of Representation* (Minneapolis: University of Minnesota Press, 1986).

161. See Mark Dery, *Culture Jamming, Hacking, Slashing and Sniping in the Empire of Signs* (Westfield, N.J.: Open Magazine Pamphlet Series, 1993), and Linda S. Kauffman, *Bad Girls and Sick Boys: Fantasies in Contemporary Art and Culture* (Berkeley: University of California Press, 1998).

162. Michelle Falkenstern, "What's So Good about Being Bad? Women to Watch," *ArtNews* 98, 10 (November 1999): 159–163.

163. Dan Barry and Carol Vogel, "Guiliani Vows to Cut Subsidy over 'Sick' Art," *New York Times*, 23 September 1999, pp. A1, A25.

164. Vicki Goldberg, "Testing the Limits in a Culture of Excess," *New York Times*, 29 October 1995, pp. 2:1, 40.

165. Tracy C. Davis, "The Actress in Victorian Pornography," *Theatre Journal* 41 (October 1989): 294–315.

166. See Gilfoyle, *City of Eros*, pp. 15–19.

167. Abe Laufe, *The Wicked Stage: A History of Theater Censorship and Harassment in the United States* (New York: Frederick Ungar, 1978).

168. Robert Bogdan, *Freak Show: Presenting Human Oddities for Amusement and Profit* (Chicago: University of Chicago Press, 1988).

169. Sander L. Gilman, "Black Bodies, White Bodies: Toward an Iconography of Female Sexuality in Late Nineteenth-Century Art, Medicine, and Literature," *Critical Inquiry* 12, 1 (1985): 205–243.

170. Patricia Hill Collins, *Black Feminist Thought* (New York: Routledge, 1990), pp. 21–25.

171. Charles Fish, *Blue Ribbons and Burlesque: A Book of County Fairs* (Woodstock, Vt.: Countryman Press, 1998).

172. See Lewis Erenberg, *Steppin' Out: New York Nightlife and the Transformation of American Culture, 1890–1930* (Westport, Conn.: Greenwood, 1981) for information on the period.

173. See Kaier Curtin, *"We Can Always Call Them Bulgarians": The Emergence of Lesbians and Gay Men on the American Stage* (Boston: Alyson Publications, 1987).

174. Kenneth Tynan, *The Sound of Two Hands Clapping* (New York: Holt, Rinehart and Winston, 1975), pp. 143–144.

175. Martin Esslin, "Nudity: Barely the Beginning?" *Reflections: Essays on Modern Theatre* (Garden City, N.J.: Doubleday, 1969), pp. 181–182.

176. Quoted in Sarah Boxer, "Enter, the Audience," *New York Times*, 29 August 1998, p. A15.

177. Deborah Jowitt, "Getting It Off: Why Dancers Bare All for Art," *Village Voice*, 5 May 1998, p. 143.

178. Gary Cartwright, "Candy: Taking the Wrapper Off a Texas Legend," *Texas Monthly* 4 (December 1976): 99–103, 188–192.

179. Joan Collins, *Past Imperfect: An Autobiography* (New York: Simon and Schuster, 1984), pp. 160–161.

180. Marilyn Salutin, "Stripper Morality," in *The Sexual Scene*, John H. Gagnon and William Simon, eds., 2nd ed. (New Brunswick, N.J.: Transaction/Dutton, 1973), p. 172.

181. Blair Sabol, "This Box Lunch Will Kill Your Appetite," *Village Voice*, 20 September 1976, pp. 16, 23.

182. Henry Schipper, "Filthy Lucre," *Mother Jones* 5 (April 1980), pp. 30–33, 60–62.

183. "As Slime Goes By," *Screw* 819 (12 November 1984), p. 6.

184. Ricky Jay, *Learned Pigs and Fireproof Women* (New York: Villard Books, 1987), p. 307.

185. Ann McClintock, "Maid to Order: Commercial S/M and Gender Power," in *Dirty Looks: Women, Pornography, Power*, Pamela Church Gibson and Roma Gibson, eds. (London: British Film Institute, 1993), pp. 227.

186. Lynda Hart, *Between the Body and the Flesh: Performing Sadomasochism* (New York: Columbia University Press, 1998), p. 202.

187. Mistress Lilith Lash, "Pain, Pleasure and Poetry," in *Sex Work: Writings by Women in the Sex Industry*, Frédérique Delacoste and Priscilla Alexander, eds. (Pittsburgh: Cleis Press, 1987), pp. 50–52.

188. See Robin Ruth Linden, Darlene R. Pagano, Diana E. H. Russell, and Susan Leigh Star, eds., *Against Sadomasochism: A Radical Feminist Analysis* (East Palo Alto, Calif.: Frog in the Well, 1982).

189. Pat Califia, *Public Sex: The Culture of Radical Sex* (Pittsburgh: Cleis Press, 1994).

190. Julia Creet, "Daughter of the Movement: The Psychodynamics of the Lesbian S/M Fantasy," *differences* 3, 2 (Summer 1991); 135–146.

191. Denise Kiernan, "Spank You Very Much," *Village Voice*, 21 November 1995, p. 8.

192. See Dottie Easton and Catherine A. Liszt, *The Bottoming Book, or How to Get Terrible Things Done to You by Wonderful People* and *The Topping Book, or Getting Good at Being Bad* (San Francisco: Greenery Press, 1995).

193. Daphne Merkin, "Unlikely Obsession: Confronting a Taboo," *New Yorker* (26 February and 4 March, 1996 [double issue]): 98–100, 102, 104, 111–115; Paul Theroux, "Nurse Wolf," *New Yorker* (15 June 1998): 50–60, 62–63.

194. Marianne Macy, *Working Sex: An Odyssey into Our Cultural Underworld* (New York: Carroll and Graf, 1996), p. 39.

195. Judith Brackley, "Male Strip Shows," *MS* 9, 5 (November 1980): 68–70, 84.

196. See, for example, Katherine H. Liepe-Levinson, "Striptease: Desire, Mimetic Jeopardy, and Performing Spectators," *TDR* 42, 2 (Summer 1998): 9–37.

197. Quoted in Tom Wolfe (writer/narrator), *The Video McLuhan: Cassette 2, 1965–1970* (Toronto: McLuhan Productions, 1996), at 56 minutes.

198. Mary MacKinnon, "How Topless Bars Shut Me Out," *Sales and Marketing Management* 147, 7 (July 1995): 52–53.

199. Lily Burana, "The Old Bump and Grind: Can Stripping Support the Arts?" *Village Voice*, 5 May 1998, pp. 138–140.

200. See Dinitia Smith, "Today the Anatomy, Tomorrow the World," *New York Times*, 26 September 1999, sec. 2, pp. 7, 20.

201. John Berger, *Ways of Seeing* (London: BBC/Penguin, 1986).

202. The photo archives of the Kinsey Institute for Research in Sex, Gender, and Reproduction at Indiana University hold early examples.

203. Bill Jay, "The Erotic Dawn of Photography," *The Image* (London: Baroque Press, 1972), pp. 40–46.

204. Abigail Solomon-Godeau, "The Legs of the Countess," in *Fetishism as Cultural Discourse*, Emily Apter and William Pietz, eds. (Ithaca: Cornell University Press, 1993), pp. 299, 306.

205. Robert Taft, *Photography and the American Scene* (New York: Macmillan, 1938), p. 76.

206. John Tebbel in *The Media in America* (New York: NAL, 1974), p. 142, suggests that the original 1842 Customs Act was aimed at photographs, but that hardly seems likely.

207. "Questionable Subjects for Photography," *Photographic News* 1 (26 November 1858), pp. 135–136.

208. Lowry, *The Story the Soldiers Wouldn't Tell*, p. 55.

209. "Dealers in Obscene Pictures," *New York Tribune*, 10 July 1877, p. 2.

210. E. J. Bellocq, *Storyville Portraits: Photographs from the New Orleans*

Red Light District, Circa 1912 (New York: Museum of Modern Art, 1970); the prints were pulled from the original glass plates by Lee Friedlander.

211. Peter H. Halpert, "Fantasy Buys," *American Photo* 6, 5 (September 1995): 27–28.

212. James Smalls, "Public Face, Private Thoughts: Fetish, Interracialism, and the Homoerotic in Some Photographs by Carl Van Vechten," in *Sex Positives? The Cultural Politics of Dissident Sexualities*, Thomas Foster, Carol Siegel, and Ellen E. Berry, eds. (New York: New York University Press, 1997), pp. 144–193.

213. Jack Woody, ed., *Collaboration: The Photographs of Paul Cadmus, Margaret French, and Jared French* (Santa Fe, N.M.: Twelvetrees Press, 1992).

214. Minor White, *Minor White: Rites and Passages* (New York: Aperture, 1978).

215. George Dureau, *George Dureau: New Orleans*, Edward Lucie-Smith, ed. (London: GMP, 1985); reprinted as *New Orleans* (East Haven, Conn.: InBook/GMP Publishers UK, 1991).

216. Richard Carline, *Pictures in the Post*, rev. ed. (London: Gordon Fraser, 1971), pp. 5–6.

217. Roberta Smith, "An Ugly Legacy Lives On, Its Glare Unsoftened by Age," *New York Times*, 13 January 2000, pp. B1, B8.

218. Patrick Waldberg, *Eros Modern Style* (New York: Grove Press, 1969), pp. 23–26.

219. See Leo Schidrowitz, ed., *Sittengeschichte des Hafens und der Reise*, vol. 8 of *Sittengeschichte der Kulturwelt und ihrer Entwicklung in Einzeldarstellungen* (Vienna/Leipzig: Verlag für Kulturforschung, 1927) for accounts of traffic in obscene photos around the world.

220. Reissued as United Nations, *Agreement for the Suppression of the Circulation of Obscene Publications, Signed at Paris on 4 May 1910/Amended by the Protocol Signed at Lake Success, New York, 4 May 1949* (Lake Success, N.Y.: United Nations, 1950); see also League of Nations, *Records of the International Conference for the Suppression of the Circulation of and Traffic in Obscene Publications Held at Geneva from August 31st to September 12th, 1923* (Geneva: League of Nations, 1923), for follow-up conferences.

221. Robert Meadows, *A Private Anthropological Cabinet of 500 Authentic Racial-Esoteric Photographs and Illustrations* (New York: Falstaff Press, 1934).

222. Philip G. Stewart, *The New-Genre Nude: A New Fine Art Motif Derived from Nudist Magazine Photography* (Ph.D. dissertation, Ohio State University, 1986), p. 6.

223. Mary Beth Haralovich, "Film Advertising, the Film Industry and

the Pin-Up: the Industry's Accommodations to Social Forces in the 1940s," in *Current Research in Film: Audiences, Economics, and Law*, Bruce A. Austin, ed., 4 vols. (Norwood, N.J.: Ablex, 1985), I, pp. 127–164.

224. *American Photography: A Century of Images*, PBS special, 13 October 1999, section 2.

225. Clark Kidder and Madison Daniels, eds., *Marilyn Monroe unCovers* (Edmonton, Alberta: Quon Editions, 1994); Denis C. Jackson, *The Price and Identification Guide to Marilyn Monroe*, 2nd ed. (Sequim, Wash.: privately printed, 1995).

226. Gloria Gale, *Calendar Model* (New York: Frederick Fell, 1957); Surrey Marshe, *The Girl in the Centerfold: The Uninhibited Memoirs of Miss January* (New York: Delacorte, 1969); Liz Renay, *My First 2,000 Men* (Fort Lee, N.J.: Barricade Books, 1992); see also *Posing: Inspired by Three Stories* (Los Angeles: An Alta Loma/Republic Pictures Television/Gillian Production, 1989).

227. Joanne Meyerowitz, "Women, Cheesecake, and Borderline Material: Responses to Girlie Pictures in the Mid-Twentieth Century United States," *Journal of Women's History* 8, 3 (Fall 1996): 9–35.

228. N. M. Malamuth and R. D. McIlwraith, "Fantasies and Exposure to Sexually Explicit Magazines," *Communication Research* 15, 6 (December 1988): 753–771; Marvin Zuckerman, "Physiological Measures of Sexual Arousal in the Human," *Psychological Bulletin* 75 (1971): 297–310.

229. See, for example, Hal Fischer, *Gay Semiotics: A Photographic Study of Visual Coding among Homosexual Men* (Berkeley: NFS Press, 1978).

230. Stephen Boyd, ed., *Life Class: The Academic Male Nude, 1820–1920* (London: Éditions Aubrey Walter/GMP Publications, 1989).

231. See Tom Waugh, *Hard to Imagine: Gay Male Eroticism in Photography and Film from Their Beginnings to Stonewall* (New York: Columbia University Press, 1997); see also Vince Aletti, "Physique Pictorial: The Rise, Fall, and Revival of Lon of New York," *Village Voice*, 2 March 1999, pp. 55–56.

232. Thom Fitzgerald, director, *Beefcake* (Los Angeles: Strand Films, 1999).

233. *The Complete Reprint of Physique Pictorial, 1951–1990*, 3 vols. (Berlin: Benedikt Taschen, 1997).

234. James Crump, with an introduction by Bruce Weber, *George Platt Lynes: Photographs from the Kinsey Institute* (Boston: Bulfinch, 1993).

235. Woody Hochswender, "Pins and Needles," *Harper's Bazaar* (September 1992): 411.

236. *Petit Catalogue des Fetichismes* (Paris: Le Club Livre Secret, 1980); see

also Gilles Néret, *1000 Dessous: A History of Lingerie* (Berlin: Benedikt Taschen, 1998).

237. Peter Barry, *Erotic Lingerie* (Guildford, Surrey, U.K.: Arlington House/Crown, 1984).

238. "Lingerie," *American Photo* 6, 5 (September 1995).

239. Kilpatrick, *The Smut Peddlers*, pp. 51–77.

240. *Technical Reports of the Commission on Obscenity and Pornography* (Washington, D. C.: Government Printing Office, 1971–1972), III, p. 197.

241. Feminist Anti-Censorship Task Force, *Caught Looking: Feminism, Pornography, and Censorship* (New York: Caught Looking, Inc., 1986).

242. "Pornography Seized," *New York Times*, 19 December 1957, p. 26.

243. Vince Aletti, "Arrested Development: Larry Clark Pins Adolescence to the Wall," *Village Voice*, 13 October 1997, pp. 99–100.

244. Quoted in Gillian Rodgerson, "Lesbian Erotic Explorations," in *Sex Exposed: Sexuality and the Pornography Debate*, Lynne Segal and Mary McIntosh, eds. (New Brunswick, N.J.: Rutgers University Press, 1993), p. 277.

245. Kiss and Tell Lesbian Collective [Persimmon Blackbridge, Lizard Jones, and Susan Stewart], *Her Tongue on My Theory: Images, Essays and Fantasies* (Vancouver: Press Gang Publishers, 1994; East Haven, Conn.: InBook Publishing, 1994).

246. See Rundu L. Staggers, *Body and Soul: Black Erotica by Rundu* (New York: Crown, 1998).

247. "Peep Galleries," *New York Times Magazine*, 6 September 1998, p. 19.

248. Lewis Jacobs, *The Rise of the American Film: A Critical History* (New York: Teachers College Press, 1968), pp. 52–66, 81–94; Richard Meyers, *For One Week Only: The World of Exploitation Films* (Piscataway, NJ: New Century, 1982), pp. 5–17; Gerald Mast, *A Short History of the Movies* (Indianapolis: Bobbs-Merrill, 1976), pp. 46–49.

249. Richard Meyers, *For One Week Only: The World of Exploitation Films* (Piscataway, N.J.: New Century, 1982).

250. Gershon Legman, *Love and Death: A Study in Censorship* (New York: Breaking Point, 1949).

251. *Joseph Burnstyn, Inc., v. Wilson, Commissioner of Education of NY* (343 U.S. 495 [1952]).

252. Andrea Juno and V. Vale, eds., *Incredibly Strange Films* (San Francisco: RE/Search, 1986).

253. Eithne Johnson and Eric Schaefer, "Soft Core/Hard Core: *Snuff* as a

Crisis in Meaning," *Journal of Film and Video* 45, 2-3 (Summer-Fall 1993): 40–59; see also Avedon Carol, "Snuff: Believing the Worst," in *Bad Girls and Dirty Pictures: The Challenge to Reclaim Feminism*, Alison Assiter and Avedon Carol, eds. (Boulder, Colo.: Pluto Press, 1993), pp. 126–130.

254. See, for example, Dolf Zillman and Jennings Bryant, "Pornography, Sexual Callousness, and the Trivialization of Rape," *Journal of Communication* 32(4) (Fall 1982): 10–21; no other researchers were able to confirm the conclusions.

255. Daniel Linz and Edward Donnerstein, "Research Can Help Us Explain Violence and Pornography," *The Chronicle of Higher Education* (30 September 1992): B3–B4.

256. Louis Sheaffer, *O'Neill: Son and Playwright* (Boston: Little, Brown, 1968), pp. 175–177, 267.

257. "Police to Run Down All Illegal Films," *New York Times*, 17 January 1912, p. 13.

258. The information on preferences was gleaned by Eugene Slabaugh and George Huntington, who conducted interviews in the 1960s with the aging producers of vintage stags and deposited the tape recordings in the Kinsey Institute.

259. *The Pick Up* (1923), in the Kinsey Institute's Film Archives, Bloomington, Indiana.

260. James R. Petersen, "Playboy's History of the Sexual Revolution: Hard Times: Part IV, 1930–1939," *Playboy* 44, 7 (July 1997): 154.

261. Joseph Slade's forthcoming book *Shades of Blue* recounts the history of stag films.

262. Linda Williams, *Hard Core: Power, Pleasure, and the Frenzy of the Visible* (Berkeley: University of California Press, 1989).

263. Cindy Patton, "The Cum Shot: Three Takes on Lesbian and Gay Sexuality," *Out/Look* 1, 3 (Fall 1988): 72–76.

264. J. Hoberman, "The Big Heat," *Village Voice*, 1 November 1991, pp. 61, 72.

265. Linda Lovelace, *Inside Linda Lovelace* (Los Angeles: Pinnacle, 1973); Linda Lovelace, *Out of Bondage* (Secaucus, N.J.: Lyle Stuart, 1986); Linda Lovelace and Mike Brady, *Ordeal* (New York: Citadel, 1980).

266. Kayte Van Scoy, "Sex Sells, So Learn a Thing or Two from It," *PC Computing* 13, 1 (January 2000): 64.

267. Martin Jay Tucker, "How Pivotal Is Porn in Developing the Market for CD-ROM?" *CD-ROM Professional* 8, 11 (November 1995): 64–72.

268. Joseph W. Slade, "Pornography in the Late Nineties," *Wide Angle* 19, 3 (July 1997): 9.

269. Donald Suggs, "Hard Corps: A New Generation of People of Color Penetrates Porn's Mainstream," *Village Voice*, 21 October 1997, pp. 39–40.

270. Peter M. Nichols, "Working the Angles in Low-Budget Paradise," *New York Times*, 3 August 1997, sec. 2, pp. 11, 20.

271. "Jenna," *Penthouse* 31, 1 (September 1999): 75.

272. Carlos Briceno, "'Dial-a-Porn' Industry Battles U.S. Restrictions," *New York Times*, 13 April 1990, p. B5.

273. Valerie Kelly, "Writing Telephone Sex Calls," *How to Write Erotica* (New York: Harmony Books, 1986), pp. 209–215.

274. Chapple and Talbot, *Burning Desires: Sex in America*, chapter 8; see also Kathleen K., *Sweet Talkers* (New York: Waite Group, 1995).

275. Gary Anthony with Rockey Bennett, *Dirty Talk: Diary of a Phone Sex "Mistress"* (Buffalo, N.Y.: Prometheus Books, 1997).

276. Steve Abbott, "Dialing for Sex," in *Men Confront Pornography*, Michael S. Kimmel, ed. (New York: Crown, 1990), pp. 285–287; Carrington McDuffie, "A Gay Girl's Guide to Phone Sex," *On Our Backs* 7, 3 (January-February 1991): 20–22, 44–45.

277. "Time Capsule," *Playboy* 46, 11 (November 1999): 150.

278. Jack Boulware, *Sex American Style: An Illustrated Romp through the Golden Age of Heterosexuality* (Venice, Calif.: Feral House, 1997), pp. 180–181.

279. Paul Krassner, "Dicks in the Media," *Penthouse* 23, 8 (April 1992): 54.

280. Paula Yoo, "Tales from the Backside," *People Weekly* 45, 13 (1 April 1996): 5.

281. Laura Stempel Mumford, *Love and Ideology in the Afternoon: Soap Opera, Women and Television Genre* (Bloomington: Indiana University Press, 1995).

282. Dana Canedy, "P. & G. Is Seeking to Revive Soaps: Shaking Up TV Serials as Audiences Dwindle," *New York Times*, 11 March 1997, pp. C1, C4.

283. Gail Blasser Riley, *Censorship* (New York: Facts on File, 1998), p. 77.

284. Boulware, *Sex American Style*, pp. 101–102.

285. Richard Viguerie, *The New Right: We're Ready to Lead* (Falls Church, Va.: Viguerie Company, 1980).

286. Louis Harris and Associates, *Sexual Material on American Television during the 1987–88 Season* (New York: Planned Parenthood Federation of America, 26 January 1988).

287. Quoted in "Ticker," *Brill's Content* 2, 7 (September 1999): 128; the survey for each year was conducted in the first two weeks of each November "sweeps" period.

288. Gary Levin, "TV Turns On," *USA Today*, 24 September 1999, pp. E1–2.

289. *Off the Straight and Narrow: Lesbians, Gays, Bisexuals, and Television* (Northampton, Mass.: Media Education Foundation, 1998).

290. J. Max Robins, "Talkshow Producers Find Dial-a-Dilemma," *Variety*, 11–17 April 1994, pp. 45–46.

291. Joshua Gamson, *Freaks Talk Back: Tabloid Talk Shows and Sexual Nonconformity* (Chicago: University of Chicago Press, 1998).

292. Warren Berger, "That's E! for Entertainment (and Erotica?)," *New York Times*, 26 June 1998, p. 27.

293. Steven A. Seidman, "An Investigation of Sex-Role Stereotyping in Music Videos," *Journal of Broadcasting and Electronic Media* 36, 2 (Spring 1992): 209–216.

294. James Sterngold, "HBO Programmer Likes to Kindle Both Heat and Light," *New York Times*, 15 April 1998, p. B2.

295. "Playboy Weathers 505 Storm," *Cable World* (Pay Per View Special Report), 6 December 1999, pp. 38A–39A.

296. See Joshua Meyrowitz, *No Sense of Place: The Impact of Electronic Mediation on Social Behavior* (New York: Oxford University Press, 1985), and Neil Postman, *Amusing Ourselves to Death* (New York: Viking, 1985).

297. Quoted in Suzanne Stefanac, "Sex and the New Media," *New Media* 3, 4 (April 1993): 38–45.

298. Van Scoy, "Sex Sells, So Learn a Thing or Two from It," 64.

299. Frank Rose, "Sex Sells—Young Ambitious Seth Warshavsky Is the Bob Guccione of the 1990s," *Wired* (12 December 1997): 5.

300. Julian Dibbell, "The Body Electric," *Time Digital* (12 April 1999): 24–27.

301. Martin Rimm, "Marketing Pornography on the Information Superhighway: A Survey of 917,410 Images, Descriptions, Short Stories, and Animations Downloaded 8.5 Million Times by Consumers in Over 2000 Cities in Forty Countries, Provinces, and Territories," *Georgetown Law Review* 83 (June 1995): 1849–1958.

302. Philip Elmer-Dewitt, "Cyberporn," *Time* (3 July 1995): 38–45.

303. Jeffrey Rosen, "Cheap Speech," *New Yorker* (7 August 1995): 75–80.

304. Wendy Cole, "The Marquis de Cyberspace," *Time* (3 July 1995): 43.

305. Mark Boal, "A Lot of Nerve," *Village Voice*, 31 August 1999, pp. 31–32.

306. Pamela Licalzi O'Connell, "Web Erotica Aims for New Female Customers," *New York Times*, 13 August 1998, p. D6.

307. Donna Ladd, "Porn Pays," *Village Voice*, 12 October 1999, p. 35.

308. Mark Boal, "Surveillance Sorority," *Village Voice*, 10 August 1999, pp. 55–56.

309. Daniel Eisenberg, "Sex, Bytes, and Video Dates," *Time Digital* (12 May 1997): 23–24.

310. Larry Flynt, "Larry Flynt: Hell on Wheels [an interview with Russell T. Orenstein]," *Gallery* 28 (June 2000): 74–79.

311. Reported on "All Things Considered," National Public Radio, March 2–4, 2000.

312. Bill Joy, "Why the Future Doesn't Need Us," *Wired* 8(4) (April 2000): 238–263.

Chronology 3

Given the threat of prosecution, producers and distributors of sexual representations have cherished anonymity and generally secured it by circulating their materials secretly. Historians still know little about many pornographers and their genres. Pornographic photographers and early "stag" cinematographers, for all their eagerness to document sexuality, have left few traces of themselves. Some producers and dealers attracted the attention of authorities early on, of course, whereas others became visible only when they collided with the laws and mores of mainstream culture. The dates below refer chiefly to institutional response to materials as they surfaced from still-uncharted undergrounds in the United States.

500   Scenes of intercourse are put on ceramics by Mimbres peoples in what will later become the state of New Mexico.

950   Fremont petroglyphs of copulating couples are drawn by Native Americans residing in what will later become the southwestern United States.

1690   The Massachusetts Bay Colony seizes the first issue of the first colonial newspaper, *Publick Occurrences*, published by Benjamin Harris in Boston, because of a story about the alleged philandering of the French king.

1712 Massachusetts passes the first colonial law against obscene writing and pictures.

1750s Colonists begin to produce anonymous erotic folk art (figurines, walking sticks, pipes), some of which will be passed down to descendants and eventually purchased by collectors.

1780s Advertisements for imported erotic novels appear in New York and Massachusetts newspapers.

1791 The Bill of Rights is adopted; these ten amendments to the Constitution begin with the right of free speech.

1798– Alien and Sedition Acts, ostensibly aimed at French sym-
1800 pathizers (war with France seems imminent), are used to jail editors in Boston and New York for accusing politicians of sexual improprieties.

1806 The Pennsylvania Academy of Fine Arts drapes statues of human figures on Mondays, the only day women are permitted to visit the academy.

1815 Philadelphia prosecutes six men for selling drawings of naked women.

1821 Boston prosecutes two book peddlers for selling John Cleland's novel *Fanny Hill*, which contains explicit passages that seem obscene to many Americans.

1839 Charles Goodyear vulcanizes rubber and makes possible not only improved condoms but a wide variety of fetish items.

1840s Women in loose drapes and thick tights begin to appear on New York stages as *tableaux vivants*.

1841 "Sporting" papers such as the *Whip, Rake,* and *Libertine* appear as quasipornographic guides to the New York sexual scene.

1842   The Tariff Act, the first federal obscenity law, gives the U.S. Customs Department authority to ban importation of obscene contraband.

1843   Prosecutors secure the first federal conviction under the Tariff Act in a case involving snuff boxes lacquered with pictures of nude women.

1846   Publishers in New York and New Orleans sell thousands of reprints of pornographic European works.

1849   George Thompson writes *Venus in Boston,* the first domestic pornographic novel, published that year in New York by James Ramerio.

1852   Boston prosecutors attack Nathaniel Hawthorne's novel *The Scarlet Letter* as obscene.

1857   The rapid spread of a new technology leads Congress to amend the Tariff Act of 1842 to prohibit salacious daguerreotypes.

        The noun *pornography* appears for the first time in English in a medical dictionary.

1865   Congress amends the Tariff Act to prohibit traffic in pornographic novels among Union troops.

1866   When Broadway stages *The Black Crook,* featuring a dance by performers in opaque full-body tights, audiences "gasp" at "nudity."

1868   English courts establish the Hicklin decision prohibiting "obscene libel," which will for years form the basis for U.S. prosecutions.

1873   Congress passes the Comstock Act, named after Anthony Comstock, who as head of the New York Society for the Suppression of Vice becomes a national symbol of censorship. The Comstock Act expands the 1865 postal law to include penalties against publishers as well as distributors of offensive material by revising Title 18 of the U.S. Code. Section 1461 prohibits materials dealing with lewd expression or immoral purposes, especially birth control advice or articles designed to prevent conception or produce abortion; Section 1462 prohibits the importation of obscene matter and its interstate transportation; and Section 1463 forbids advertising immoral products or using obscene language to promote immoral artifacts. Comstock himself becomes a special agent of the U.S. Post Office, but also holds wide censorship powers in the state of New York.

1876   The U.S. Post Office becomes the nation's chief internal censor when Congress amends the Comstock Act to give the agency that power.

1879   Mark Twain writes *1601* and *Some Thoughts on the Science of Onanism.*

1882   Boston bans Walt Whitman's *Leaves of Grass* as obscene.

1885   New York City dealers sell 100,000 pornographic books.

1890   Postmaster General Wanamaker bans Leo Tolstoy's *Kreutzer Sonata* from the mails.

1895   Inventor and filmmaker Thomas Edison films "Fatima's serpentine dance" in his studio; authorities later censor it by drawing black bars across her (clothed) undulating bosom and buttocks.

1896   The Supreme Court upholds the obscenity conviction of Lew Rosen, publisher of *Broadway* magazine, the first federal prosecution under the Comstock Act.

1897   In *People v. Doris,* a New York court rules that *Orange Blossoms,* a motion picture "pantomime," is indecent because it depicts a wedding night.

1900   The U.S. Congress defines the sending of contraceptive information through the mails as a criminal act of obscenity.

The publisher of Theodore Dreiser's *Sister Carrie* withdraws the book after attacks on it.

1901   Claude Hartland writes *The Story of a Life,* the first published autobiography of an American homosexual, which is considered obscene by definition at the time.

1902   Publication of *The Story of Mary MacLane*, the first autobiography of an American lesbian.

1904   The first American pinup calendar is published by Brown and Bigelow in St. Paul, Minnesota, to advertise the products of Belding Brothers Silk Manufacturers of Cincinnati, Ohio; the pictures featured breasts barely hidden by long hair or loose silken garments.

1907   Florenz Ziegfeld stages *Follies*, featuring chorus girls with bare breasts.

1908   On Christmas Day the mayor of New York City closes all cinemas on grounds of immorality.

1910   Hundreds of thousands of pornographic photos circulate clandestinely in the United States.

1912   The first recorded police raid on an exhibit of pornographic films as they are being shown takes place in a storefront in Manhattan.

        The first issue of *Snappy Stories*, a mildly pornographic magazine, is circulated.

1913   Judge Learned Hand, though upholding the Hicklin principle in the prosecution of Daniel Goodman's *Hagar Revelly* (a novel of social comment), expresses doubt about the wisdom of suppressing a work of ideas.

        Anthony Comstock seizes copies of *September Morn*, a highly idealized painting by Paul Chabas of a nearly nude woman bathing in a lake; the seizure causes sales to soar.

1914   Anthony Comstock indicts Margaret Sanger for writing "obscene" articles about contraception.

1915   *A Grass Sandwich*, a.k.a. *A Free Ride*, the first surviving American hard-core pornographic film, is shot (according to legend) in New Jersey.

The U.S. Supreme Court rules in *Mutual Film Corporation v. Industrial Commission of Ohio,* 236 U.S. 230 (the case involves the film *Birth of a Nation*), that cinema is unprotected by the First and Fourteenth Amendments.

1916   Cincinnati bans Theodore Dreiser's novel *The Genius.*

1919   In New York, Joseph Patterson begins publishing the *Daily News,* whose sensationalism boosts circulation to one million in six years.

    True Story, the first of the "confession" magazines, is launched.

1920s   Eight-page pornographic comic books called Tijuana bibles, a term applied also to pages of fiction stapled together, multiply in urban areas.

1920   The judge deciding on *Halsey v. New York Society for the Suppression of Vice,* 180 N.Y. S. 836, rules that a book "must be considered broadly, as a whole," not just in terms of isolated passages, by qualified critics.

1922   The Motion Picture Producers and Distributors of America is created, with Will H. Hays as the Hollywood censorship czar.

1923   Senator Jimmy Walker speaks against a proposed "clean books" amendment to the New York State Penal Code: "I have never yet heard of a girl being ruined by a book."

1925   Prodded by the New York Society for the Suppression of Vice, police raid *Minsky's Burlesque* show at the National Winter Garden Theater in New York.

    The nation's animators honor pioneer cartoonist Winsor McCay by creating *Everready,* the most famous of all animated pornographic films.

1926   Boston bans the sale of H. L. Mencken's collection *American Mercury* because of a story called "Hatrack," which concerns the experiences of a prostitute.

1927   Joseph Fliesler clandestinely publishes *Anecdota Ameri-*

cana, the first authoritative collection of the nation's erotic folklore.

Entertainer Mae West goes to jail for ten days for doing an "obscene" dance as part of the play *Sex* that she had written.

1929 Radclyffe Hall's lesbian novel, *The Well of Loneliness,* is declared obscene in New York.

Katherine Bement Davis publishes a survey called *Factors in the Sex Life of Twenty-Two Hundred Women;* some subjects confess that they enjoy recreational sex more than dutiful reproduction and enjoy reading about it too.

1930 Massachusetts declares Theodore Dreiser's *An American Tragedy* and D. H. Lawrence's *Lady Chatterley's Lover* obscene.

Federal Judge Augustus Hand reverses the conviction of an educational pamphlet, *The Sex Side of Life,* by Mary Ware Dennett.

Motion Picture Producers and Distributors of America adopts the Production Code for Hollywood movies as a way of heading off federal censorship.

The National Organization for Decent Literature is founded.

The New Tariff Act transfers authority for determining obscenity from the U.S. Customs Department and U.S. Post Office to the courts.

Drugstores rent pornographic books to citizens desperate for cheap entertainment during the Depression.

1931 Georgia Southern, one of the most talented American strippers, while still in her teens, takes off her clothes for the first time to *Hold That Tiger!*

1933 District Court Judge John M. Woolsey in *United States v. One Book Called "Ulysses"* (5F Supp. 182) reverses a conviction of James Joyce's stream-of-consciousness novel on grounds that the book must be considered as a whole.

Sally Rand, the celebrated fan dancer, grosses $6,000 a week at the Chicago World's Fair.

The Payne Fund, a private philanthropic agency, agrees to fund a series of studies by the Motion Picture Research Council to chart the moral effects of motion pictures on children.

Mae West's sly performance in the film *She Done Him Wrong* triggers the formation of the Catholic Legion of Decency.

1934 Judge Augustus Hand of the Court of Appeals upholds Woolsey's decision on *Ulysses.*

1938 The National Organization for Decent Literature prosecutes *Life* magazine for publishing an illustrated article, "The Birth of a Baby," because the mother's labia are visible.

1941 New York City holds public burnings of pornographic books and magazines but stops when critics note parallels with the Nazis.

1942 Anaïs Nin and Henry Miller write pornography for an American collector.

1943 Howard Hughes invents a cleavage-emphasizing bra for Jane Russell, star of *The Outlaw,* then launches an advertising campaign featuring a suggestive portrait of Russell rendered by the leading female pinup artist, Zöe Mozert, with the result that the Legion of Decency forces withdrawal of the film.

1944 Robert Sewall writes *The Devil's Advocate,* a.k.a. *The Sign of the Scorpion,* perhaps the most important American erotic novel.

1945 Municipal Justice Elijah Adlow of Boston rejects as idiotic the Watch and Ward Society's contention that readers of

Erskine Caldwell's *Tragic Ground* will be harmed by passages in which a young woman sees a bare male chest.

1946 The U.S. Supreme Court rules in *Hannegan v. Esquire* (327 U.S. 146) that the U.S. Postmaster General does not have authority to deny mailing privileges to *Esquire* without a prior judicial hearing.

The Federal Communications Commission issues its "Blue Book," which codifies "responsibilities" of broadcasters, who fear censorship.

1948 Alfred C. Kinsey and colleagues publish *Sexual Behavior in the Human Male.*

Frederick's of Hollywood markets the first crotchless panty.

1949 Photographer John Kelley shoots pinup of a nude Marilyn Monroe and godfathers the practice of starlets posing in order to launch careers.

1951 *Confidential* magazine, which runs seamy exposés of celebrities, begins publication.

Sixteen-year-old Juanita Slusher (stage name Candy Barr) is forced to perform in the stag film *Smart Alec.*

The television soap opera *Search for Tomorrow* begins its multidecade run on CBS.

The U.S. Post Office attempts to ban Gershon Legman's scholarly book *Love and Death.*

1952 The U.S. Supreme Court decides that cinema is protected by the First and Fourteenth Amendments in the case of *The Miracle,* a motion picture prosecuted for sacrilege in *Joseph Burstyn, Inc. v. Wilson,* 343 U.S. 495.

Comedian Lucille Ball incorporates her pregnancy into her TV show *I Love Lucy.*

1953 Kinsey and his colleagues publish *Sexual Behavior in the Human Female.*

In December, Hugh Hefner publishes the first edition of *Playboy*.

The Motion Picture Producer's Association refuses to grant a censor's certificate to *The Moon Is Blue*, a film about a "professional virgin" who attempts to sexually tease a man into marrying her; when director Otto Preminger releases the movie without this seal of approval, other directors also ignore the Production Code.

Make Room for Daddy is the first TV show to depict a married couple in bed together.

1954   Comics Magazine Association publishes the Comics Code, to which publishers must subscribe in order to receive its seal of approval.

1955   Senator Estes Kefauver's subcommittee holds hearings on the relationship of pornography and juvenile delinquency, and calls Irving Klaw, America's leading producer of fetish materials, as a witness.

1956   Beat poet Allen Ginsberg publishes *Howl*, which is denounced as obscene.

Cameramen on the *Ed Sullivan Show* focus on rock singer Elvis Presley's torso to avoid showing his gyrating hips.

1957   In *Roth v. United States*, 354 U.S. 476, the Warren Supreme Court upholds Samuel Roth's conviction 5–4 on grounds that the material appeals to prurient interest; in *Butler v. Michigan*, however, the Court rejects the argument that distribution of adult material must be restricted because it might harm minors.

Garden of Eden (1955), the first of the nudist colony films, is cleared for exhibition by the New York State Court of Appeals (*Excelsior Pictures Corporation v. Regents of the University of the State of New York*) on grounds that nudity is not obscenity.

Two women in Jamaica, New York, are arrested with 3,000 photographic plates and 50,000 copies, touted as the largest single seizure of pornographic materials ever made.

1959 The U.S. Supreme Court rules that *Lady Chatterley's Lover* by D. H. Lawrence is not obscene, that the adultery theme of a French movie is "ideological obscenity" and therefore protected speech, and that to be found guilty of selling an obscene book, the seller must know ahead of time that the book *is* obscene, a burden that would cause the public to suffer from a limited stock of information.

William Burroughs publishes *Naked Lunch.*

Russ Meyer directs *The Immoral Mr. Teas*, the first exploitation film to emphasize voyeurism for its own sake.

Ed Sanders of the musical group the Fugs publishes *Fuck You! A Magazine of the Arts* (later known as *Intercourse*).

1961 The National Council of Churches endorses birth control.

1962 The U.S. Supreme Court rules in *Manual Enterprises v. Day*, 370 U.S. 478, that the U.S. Post Office cannot ban homosexual magazines from the mails.

1963 Jack Smith screens *Flaming Creatures*, featuring a homosexual orgy, and Andy Warhol shows his film *Blow Job*.

1964 The U.S. Supreme Court rules in *Jacobellis v. Ohio*, 378 U.S. 184, that the test of obscenity requires national standards, which leads the Illinois Supreme Court to overturn comedian Lenny Bruce's 1963 conviction for obscenity.

Leading topless dancer Carol Doda surgically enlarges her breasts.

The Federal Bureau of Investigation (FBI) launches an investigation of "obscenity" in the lyrics of *Louie Louie*, the popular song by the Kingsmen.

Conservatives attack the brochures of the newly founded Sex Information and Education Council of the United States (SIECUS) as pornographic.

In *Grove Press v. Gerstein*, 378 U.S. 577, the U.S. Supreme Court finally brings to an end the prosecution of Henry Miller's *Tropic of Cancer*, "the most litigated book in the history of literature."

Police arrest avante-garde artist Jonas Mekas for screening Jack Smith's *Flaming Creatures* in New York.

1965   Thelma Oliver bares her breasts in Sidney Lumet's *The Pawnbroker*.

More than three hundred antipornography organizations agitate against sexual expression.

1966   Sex researchers William H. Masters and Virginia E. Johnson publish the clinical study *Human Sexual Response*.

The U.S. Supreme Court upholds the conviction of Ralph Ginzburg in *Ginzburg v. U. S.*, 383 U.S. 463, on grounds that though the works in question were not obscene, Ginzburg did pander through the mails. The Court also reverses the Massachusetts finding that the novel *Fanny Hill* is obscene in *Memoirs v. Massachusetts*, 383 U.S. 413, but affirms the conviction of Edward Mishkin of New York for publishing "sadistic and masochistic" books.

The Hollywood Production Code is amended to permit more explicit speech and behavior.

The National Organization for Women, which lobbies for birth control, better sex education, and reproductive rights, among other issues, is founded. These stances are so controversial in the first few years of its operation that many women leave the organization to form other women's organizations.

1967   Performance artist Charlotte Moorman is arrested at Cinemathéque, New York City, for playing a cello topless as she accompanies Nam June Paik's *Opera Sextronique*.

Congress creates the Commission on Pornography and Obscenity in an unsuccessful attempt to forestall President Lyndon Johnson's appointment of the President's Commission on Obscenity and Pornography.

Chronology **153**

R. Crumb draws the first issue of *Zap*, first of the genre of explicit comix.

Maurice Girodias moves Olympia Press to New York from Paris to take advantage of relaxed American book censorship.

Anne Halprin's dance troupe performs nude "Parades and Changes" at Hunter College in New York City.

Tom Wesselman's *Great American Nude* shocks audiences with its display of genitalia.

1968 Al Goldstein and Jim Buckley publish the first issue of *Screw*, the sex and politics tabloid.

New York's Hudson Theater in February shows the first heterosexual hard-core film (untitled) in theatrical release in the United States.

In June, Los Angeles's Park Theater shows the first homosexual hard-core feature in theatrical release.

Richard Amory publishes the first of his *Song of the Loon* series of explicit homosexual novels, which have sold more than two million copies in the United States.

Dionysius in 69, Richard Schechner's version of Euripedes's *The Bacchae*, is presented by the sometimes nude members of the Performance Group in New York City.

The Motion Picture Producers Association adopts PG, R, and X rating system for movies.

Singer-composers John Lennon and Yoko Ono appear nude on the album cover of *Two Virgins*.

Feminists picket the Miss America Pageant for displaying women as sex objects but contrary to legend do not burn bras.

Hair is staged on Broadway.

1969　*Oh! Calcutta!*, featuring totally nude performers, opens in New York for a run of many years.

A group of writers publish *Naked Came the Stranger* to spoof porn genres.

Homosexuals revolt against a police raid on the Stonewall Bar in Manhattan.

The First American edition of *Penthouse* magazine is published.

The U.S. Supreme Court in *Stanley v. Georgia*, 394 U.S. 557, overturns the conviction of a man accused of possessing pornographic films for his private use.

Rock singer Jim Morrison is arrested at a Doors concert for exposing himself.

The playwright and performers of *Che!* are arrested for obscenity in New York City.

1970　The President's Commission on Pornography and Obscenity publishes a report recommending abolishing restrictions on distributing sexual expression to consenting adults, a conclusion rejected by President Richard Nixon.

Bill Osco releases *Mona, the Virgin Queen*, the first hardcore feature film to be distributed nationally.

Penthouse's April issue reveals pubic hair, which causes a sensation.

The U.S. Post Office receives its highest number of complaints (284,000) about obscenity in the mails.

The TV show *All in the Family* deals with sexual subjects such as impotence and abortion.

1972　Gerard Damiano makes the film *Deep Throat* for $25,000 in organized crime money, and the Mitchell Brothers shoot *Behind the Green Door* for $18,000; both render hard-core pornography "chic."

Bernardo Bertolucci releases *Last Tango in Paris,* with Marlon Brando and Maria Schneider, both of whom appear nude in simulated intercourse.

Burt Reynolds poses nude for *Cosmopolitan* magazine.

Chin Lyvely and Joyce Farmer found the all-women underground comic book *Tits and Clits.*

The Federal Communications Commission (FCC) mandates community access channels, which in some cities air shows by amateurs making porn.

Performance artist Vito Acconci performs *Seedbed* at a gallery in New York, during which he masturbates.

1973   Phyllis and Eberhard Kronhausen open the Museum of Erotic Art in San Francisco.

Charlene Webb shoots *Goldenrod,* the first hard-core feature film made by a female director.

Boston establishes its Adult Entertainment District, or "Combat Zone," to contain sex-oriented businesses.

WBAI (Pacifica) broadcasts a monologue by George Carlin in which the comedian reflects on the meaning of "filthy words," for which the FCC imposes sanctions.

In *Miller v. California,* the U.S. Supreme Court tries to formulate criteria by which works can be suppressed, ruling that community standards can be determined by states.

The American Psychiatric Association drops homosexuality from its list of mental disorders.

The U.S. Supreme Court rules in *Roe v. Wade* that women have a constitutional right to abortion, the most extreme form of family planning, long anathematized as obscene under the Comstock Act.

PBS airs *Steambath,* in which Valerie Perrine bares her breasts, a first for American broadcast television.

1974 Barbara Hammer makes *Dyketactics*, the first explicit film shot by a lesbian.

Screw magazine launches its sex show, *Midnight Blue*, on Manhattan Cable Television.

Emmanuelle, a French soft-core film, draws huge American audiences.

The publisher of Greenleaf Classics, William Hamling, is sentenced to prison for publishing *The Illustrated Presidential Report of the Commission on Obscenity and Pornography* (1970).

In *Jenkins v. Georgia*, 413 U.S. 496 (1973), the U.S. Supreme Court reverses Georgia's conviction of the mainstream film *Carnal Knowledge*, a seizure inspired by the *Miller* (1973) decision.

Larry Flynt launches *Hustler* magazine first as a newsletter.

The first issue of *Playgirl* is published.

1975 Sony introduces the Betamax, but refuses to license the format to video pornographers.

Time Inc. begins Home Box Office, which distributes R-rated movies by satellite.

Organized crime families move to control various distributorships of pornographic materials.

Performance artist Carolee Schneemann presents *Interior Scroll*, in which she stands naked while pulling a feminist manifesto from her vagina.

Hustler runs nude photos of Jackie Kennedy Onassis (August).

1976 The U.S. Supreme Court rules that Detroit may limit the establishment of sex-related businesses by zoning in *Young v. American Mini-Theatres* (427 U.S. 50).

Al Goldstein, publisher of *Screw*, is convicted of obscenity in Wichita, Kansas, in a verdict that will be overturned. Radley Metzger shoots *The Opening of Misty Beethoven,* touted by some as the best porn feature ever made.

Women Against Violence Against Women, a group in California, successfully protests a Warner Brothers billboard image of a woman in chains, captioned "I'm black and blue from the Rolling Stones and I love it," a move that leads to the formation of Women Against Violence in Pornography and Media.

Publication of *The Hite Report,* which debunks the vaginal orgasm in favor of clitoral stimulation.

The Slaughter (1970), a low-budget film shot in Argentina by Michael and Roberta Findlay, is recut and retitled as *Snuff,* then marketed in a sensational hoax that causes feminist groups to picket theaters and receipts to soar.

Carolee Schneemann stages the orgiastic *Meat Joy.*

In the encyclical *Declaration on Certain Questions Concerning Sexual Ethics,* the Vatican reaffirms its condemnation of masturbation as a source of physical ills.

JVC introduces the VHS video recorder/player, and licenses the format to pornographers, dooming the Beta format.

1977   The U.S. House of Representatives holds hearings on sex and violence on TV.

Billy Crystal stars in *Soap* (ABC) as the first openly gay character on TV, which triggers protests by right-wing antiporn groups.

1979   Tara Alexandar has public, filmed intercourse with 83 men at the highly promoted "Spermathon" held at Plato's Retreat in New York City.

Women Against Pornography is founded in New York City.

Andrea Dworkin publishes *Pornography: Men Possessing Women.*

Steve Banerjee opens Hollywood Chippendales, the first of a chain of clubs for women that feature male dancers.

1980   The first issue of *Gay Comix* is released.

The Great American Lesbian Art Show is held in Los Angeles.

Women Against Violence in Pornography and the Media holds a Berkeley conference attacking sadism and masochism (S/M) and is picketed by lesbian S/M enthusiasts.

1981   The U.S. Supreme Court places limits on zoning of sex-related businesses in *Schad v. Mt. Ephraim*, 452 U.S. 61, by forbidding a municipality to eliminate such businesses entirely.

A special issue on sexuality by the journal *Heresies*, published by a feminist group, begins to undercut the ideological solidarity of antiporn feminist groups by insisting on a human dimension, rather than an exclusively male dimension to sexual expression.

Warner Cable launches Music Television (MTV), combining rock and roll and sex in a music video format.

1982   "Women and Sexuality," a controversial Barnard College conference, attracts a variety of feminists with myriad views about pornography.

The number of obscenity complaints to the U.S. Post Office falls to 5,000.

1983   In *Bolger v. Young Drug Products*, 463 U.S. 60, the U.S. Supreme Court at last ends the ban on advertising contraceptive devices through the mail.

The dial-a-porn industry begins, with recorded messages.

1984   Performance artist Annie Sprinkle performs the first version of her "Boob Ballet" at Franklin Furnace Studios in New York.

The Minneapolis City Council passes the MacKinnon/ Dworkin ordinance defining pornography as discrimination against women, which is immediately vetoed by the city's mayor; when radical feminists write an Indianapolis version, other feminists found the Feminist Anti-Censorship Taskforce to counter the ordinance.

The first issues of *Bad Attitude* and *On Our Backs*, lesbian journals endorsing sexual freedom, are published.

Lesbian performance artist Holly Hughes stages her play *Well of Horniness*.

Candida Royalle, a former porn performer, begins directing hard-core porn films for women and couples.

1985   Federal Judge Sarah Evans Barker of the Seventh District Court rules that the Indianapolis ordinance, which attempts to ban speech characterized as pornographic (i.e. as discrimination against women), violates the First Amendment.

Virginia passes a law prohibiting the display of magazines such as *Playboy* and *Penthouse* on newsstands, to be struck down the following year by the U.S. Supreme Court as unconstitutional.

San Francisco police arrest Marilyn Chambers for lewd acts in the O'Farrell Theater.

Tigress Productions and Blush Productions, two lesbian porn film companies, begin production.

The first New York Women's Erotic Film Festival is held.

After congressional hearings on disturbing lyrics in rock music, the Recording Industry Association of America agrees to a rating system.

1986   Attorney General Edwin Meese empanels a commission to overturn the findings of the 1970 Presidential Commission on Pornography and Obscenity; the new commission recommends Project Post Porn to harass sex businesses and encourages the Justice Department to entrap consumers of pornography in what the American Civil Liberties Union (ACLU) calls "a constitutionally renegade operation."

Meese creates the National Obscenity Enforcement Unit, but Playboy Enterprises, the American Booksellers Association, and other groups sue Meese and the members of the commission to stop harassment.

The U.S. Supreme Court upholds the right of a municipality to zone sex-related businesses to remote areas in *Renton v. Playtime Theatres* (475 U.S. 41).

Playboy Enterprises, the American Council of the Blind, the Blinded Veterans Association, and the American Library Association sue to force the Library of Congress to offer Braille versions of *Playboy*.

Mike Saenz creates *Virtual Valerie*, an interactive porn computer disk.

Intimidated by the Justice Department and badgered by fundamentalist groups, the Southland Corporation removes *Playboy* and *Penthouse* from newsstands in 7-Eleven Stores, which leads U.S. District Judge John Penn to order the Justice Department to end its assaults on the First Amendment.

Characterizing rock music as "degenerate filth" and a threat to family values, evangelist Jimmy Swaggart persuades the Wal-Mart chain of stores to purge its shelves of offensive records and music magazines.

John Holmes, star of more than 2,000 porn loops and films, tests positive for HIV.

The U.S. Supreme Court upholds the right of the state of Georgia to prohibit homosexual acts even in the privacy of the home and upholds a Texas state law whereby homosexual and lesbian acts are criminalized.

In *Valerie* (NBC), a character displays a condom on TV.

Performance artist Karen Finley does *I'm An Ass Man.*

1988   Congress passes the Telephone Indecency Act.

Jimmy Swaggart confesses to an addiction to pornography and loses his pulpit.

1989   Conservatives launch attacks on the National Endowment for the Arts (NEA) for funding museums displaying the photos of Robert Mapplethorpe.

Annie Sprinkle performs *Public Cervix Announcement* by inviting audiences to inspect her cervix through a speculum.

1990   Cincinnati arrests Dennis Barrie, the director of the city's Contemporary Arts Center, for exhibiting a show of the photographs of Robert Mapplethorpe.

Charles H. Keating Jr., a major crusader against pornography, is convicted of swindling hundreds in a savings and loan scam; Father Bruce Ritter, another vocal opponent of pornography, resigns from Covenant House because of accusations of sexually abusing minors in his care.

The U.S. House of Representatives cuts the budget of the District of Columbia by the exact amount required to install in a museum Judy Chicago's *The Dinner Party,* described by one congressman as "ceramic 3-D pornography."

1991   The U.S. Supreme Court overturns the FCC's 24-hour ban on indecent broadcasting.

Anita Hill accuses Clarence Thomas, Supreme Court nominee, of sexually harassing her by boasting that his penis is as impressive as that of Long Dong Silver, a minor porn star of the late 1970s, which leads to revival of the latter's films.

In *Barnes v. Glen Theater, Inc.* (115 L Ed 2nd 504), the U.S. Supreme Court rules that it is permissible for Indiana to prohibit "expressive performance" on the grounds that "traditional moral belief" in the demoralizing effects of nudity on public order provides a "rational basis" for requiring dancers to wear pasties on their nipples.

The National Obscenity Enforcement Unit conducts massive sting operations and extensive "forum shopping" so as to convict pornographers by prosecuting them in conservative communities.

Jeff Koons creates paintings and sculptures of himself and his wife (the porn-star Cicciolina) in explicit intercourse.

1992   Canada adopts a stringent new antiporn law at the urging of Catharine MacKinnon, and Canadian Customs promptly seizes *Bad Attitude,* published by a Boston lesbian collective, then confiscates as obscene books by Andrea Dworkin but returns them as a professional courtesy.

The U.S. Supreme Court sentences Reuben Sturman, the largest porn entrepreneur, to prison for tax evasion.

Paul Reubens (stage name Pee Wee Herman) is arrested for masturbating in a porn theater by Miami police permanently assigned to watch for throbbing penises in the audience.

Singer-actor-entertainer Madonna publishes the explicit photo book *Sex.* Communities around the country attempt to have it banned from their libraries.

A federal judge overturns a Florida court's ruling that "As Nasty as They Wanna Be," an album by 2 Live Crew, is obscene.

A federal court overturns restrictions on AIDS information prohibited as obscene.

Congress overrides George Bush's presidential veto of the Cable Television Consumer Protection and Competition Act, which contains provisions banning indecency.

The U.S. Supreme Court rules in *Jacobson v. United States,* 503 U.S. 540, that the government had illegally entrapped a purchaser of child pornography by badgering him for years to buy it.

Seinfeld (NBC) airs "The Contest," about masturbation.

1993   In *Alexander v. U. S.*, 113 S. Ct. 2766, the U.S. Supreme Court holds that federal agents may seize assets of adult businesses under the RICO Act after some items are declared obscene, but in *Austin v. U. S.*, 113 S. Ct. 2801, the Court appears to place limits on how many assets may be seized.

Lorena Bobbitt slices off her husband John's penis, and the television networks cover every aspect of his trial for wife abuse and hers for assault, both of which end in acquittal.

The Conference on Women, Censorship, and "Pornography" is held by Libertarian feminists opposed to MacKinnon/Dworkin formulations at the Graduate Center of the City University in New York City.

The German company Cyber SM clothes a man and a woman in data suits so that they can engage in virtual-reality intercourse.

The University of Chicago Law School Conference on Pornography in March divides feminists.

1994   Patti Reagan Davis, daughter of former President Ronald Reagan, poses nude for *Playboy*.

Memphis, Tennessee, convicts on obscenity charges the California operators of the Amateur Action Bulletin Board accessed by the Internet.

Prostitutes in Washington state and Arizona begin advertising on the World Wide Web.

Playboy launches its Web site.

1995   An amendment to U.S. Code Title 18 (Sexual Exploitation and Other Abuse of Children, Section 2257, "Record Keeping Provisions") requires that producers of porn films keep precise records of the ages of performers, even if they are clearly elderly, in films made after July 3.

Rentals of *Playboy*'s Pamela Anderson videotape outnumber those of mainstream blockbuster *Forrest Gump*.

Live videoconferencing in the form of person-to-person audio and video appears on the Internet, which leads instantly to striptease and mutual masturbation.

Some 200 businesses sell erotica on the World Wide Web.

FCC fines against controversial radio personality Howard Stern total $2 million.

1996   President Bill Clinton signs a new telecommunications act with a provision requiring all future TV sets to incorporate a V-chip for blocking objectionable programming, and with other provisions forbidding indecency on the Internet.

The Military Honor and Decency Act forbids the sale on military bases of magazines and videos that depict nudity in a "salacious way."

1997   The U.S. Supreme Court upholds a Court of Appeals decision that anti-indecency provisions of the Telecommunications Act dealing with the Internet are unconstitutional.

Some 10,000 Internet sex sites are in operation.

Television networks agree to more detailed ratings designating nudity, sex, and violence, with NBC the only holdout.

The Women's Studies Program at the State University of New York–New Paltz sponsors a "Revolting Behavior" Conference featuring porn in a positive light.

Oklahoma City police seize as child pornography the film *The Tin Drum*, winner of the 1979 Academy Award for Best Foreign Picture, and take names of citizens who rented the videotape.

1998   The World Pornography Conference brings academics and sex industry workers together at Universal City, California.

Kenneth Starr releases a "pornographic" report on Bill Clinton's trysts with Monica Lewinsky that leads to a Republican impeachment of the president. Porn publisher Larry Flynt retaliates by exposing sexual secrets of some prominent Republicans.

Revenues of women's romance novels reach $1 billion per year in the United States, as do revenues from Internet sex sites; some 2,500 clubs employ 250,000 strippers per year; the magazine *The Economist* predicts that pornography will become a legitimate component of the global entertainment industry within a few years.

The U.S. Supreme Court, rejecting a challenge brought by "the NEA Four," rules that the provision imposing decency tests by the National Endowment for the Arts is constitutional.

1999   Karen Finley poses nude for *Playboy* (July).

The number of on-line Internet users reaches 179 million.

The mayor of New York City threatens to withhold funding from the Brooklyn Museum if it mounts "Sensation," an exhibit of outrageous art.

Former porn star Veronica Hart directs two other veterans, Marilyn Chambers and Ginger Lynn, in *Still Insatiable* and *Torn*.

The adult video industry produces 10,000 new cassettes during this year.

The New York State Court of Appeals rules that New York City has been too zealous in zoning adult businesses, and reins in police.

FREE-SEX
PORNOSHOP
OKS MAGAZNES ATHER FILMS
X-TOYS VIDEOCASSETTES CLOTHES
FILMSHOWS
N COLOR WITH SOUND

Biographical Sketches 4

The number of Americans who have commented on pornography is beyond counting. Those sketched below are among the most celebrated, in some cases because they have been active as producers of sexual materials, in other cases because they have opposed the circulation of such materials, and in still others because they have actually studied the subject rather than merely pontificated about it.

Lenny Bruce (1925–1966)

Lenny Bruce was the Tom Paine of American comedy. When he laughed at the establishment, the establishment responded with an outrage usually reserved for capital crimes. The city of Chicago alone arrested him seven times for obscenity; England deported him for the same reason in 1963. Continuous arrests led to four major obscenity trials (in Philadelphia, Beverly Hills, Chicago, and New York), in addition to at least one other for narcotics. Unfortunately, Bruce chose to regard these trials as a form of theater, declining counsel to defend himself in routines as spontaneous and sometimes as brilliant as his comedy acts. Conservative judges were unsympathetic audiences, however, and courtroom defeats became part of

167

Bruce's legend. Convicted in absentia in Chicago in 1963, Bruce appealed to the Illinois Supreme Court, which reluctantly decided in 1964 that his comedy might possess some socially redeeming importance. That did not prevent New York from convicting him again the following year. Obsessed with his right to free speech, Bruce was preparing an appeal to the U.S. Supreme Court when he died of a heroin overdose in 1966. (The decision was overturned eighteen months later.) Since his death, the theater world has made him into a cultural icon, virtually canonizing him in a Broadway play and a film. His humor, called "black" and "sick," has profoundly influenced both stand-up comedians and writers.

Lenny Bruce was born Leonard Alfred Schneider on 13 October 1925, into a Mineola, New York, home disrupted by his father's constant change of professions and his mother's desire to become a dancer (eventually under the stage name Sally Marr). The divorce of his parents, a succession of homes, and youthful rebellion filled his Depression-era childhood with scrapes with teachers and authorities. At age sixteen he dropped out of school. He volunteered for the Navy in 1942, experienced three years of combat in World War II, then, bored, asked for a discharge on the grounds that he was a transvestite (thus indirectly creating a famous role for the TV sitcom *M*A*S*H**). After the war he drifted from coast to coast, told jokes when he could find jobs at clubs, wrote screenplays, studied acting, scrounged (he was arrested for panhandling for a fictitious leper colony while dressed as a priest in 1951), and married the stripper Honey Harlowe, for whom his love was complex. Engagements in marginal clubs honed an outlaw brand of satire—improvisational, manic, scatological, caustic, destructive—directed at everybody and everything; he offended white Southerners, blacks, Northern liberals, Jews, and conservatives by ridiculing religion, the body, education, politics, and complacency. Bruce mocked hypocrisy, sneered at stupidity, and probed the corruption of everyday life, diagnosing the nation's diseases in a raw voice that articulated the moral concerns common to both the Beat Generation and counterculture. By 1963, thanks to his notoriety, he had redefined humor in America; his autobiography, *How to Talk Dirty and Influence People* (1965), defends satirical obscenity as an expression of moral rectitude. After his death, he was called the conscience of America and one of its most optimistic voices.

Pat Califia (1954–)

Where sexual representation is concerned, perhaps no topic spurs so much controversy as sadomasochism, especially lesbian sadomasochism. Several years ago, antiporn feminists attacked lesbian sadomasochism as perverse and masculine and thus triggered a discussion that has focused on issues of sexuality and gender. Pat Califia emerged as a prominent spokesperson for lesbian sadomasochism and gay rights. Many critics regard her as the finest lesbian erotic fiction writer in America, citing her *Macho Sluts* (1989), *Doc and Fluff* (1990), and *Sensuous Magic* (1993) as stimulating to audiences of all genders. Califia takes her profession seriously, insisting that she has an obligation to arouse her readers. She does not believe that sex will "transform" the world, or that pleasure is necessarily an anarchic force for good, or that frequent intercourse will lead to genuine freedom. She maintains nonetheless that pornography can help people confront their psyches and help them break the bonds of a repressive culture, even if the rebellion is more symbolic than real. Given the power of that culture, Califia feels an obligation to challenge it.

Califia describes her political stance as "radical pervert" and her religion as "pagan." Born in Texas on 8 March 1954, she attended San Francisco State University, graduating in 1977. She has been a columnist for the *Advocate,* a gay newspaper, since 1981, and editor of *Advocatemen* since 1990; a collection of her columns, praised for their verve and common sense, has been published as *The Advocate Adviser* (1990). She is a member of the board of directors of the National Leather Association, a fetish group. In *Sapphistry: The Book of Lesbian Sexuality* (1978) and *The Lesbian S/M Safety Manual* (1988), Califia has attacked various women-against-pornography groups for making "illogical" and "misleading" arguments, for employing questionable tactics, and for trying to censor the expression of lesbians—especially lesbians who practice consensual sadomasochism. Pornography is chock-full of misinformation about sexuality and gender, she says, and so is its mirror opposite, the antipornography diatribe. As large categories, she believes, both porn and antiporn are reductionist and sometimes mean-spirited: both promote stereotypes (the one of females, the other of males) as adolescent sources of pleasure to their consumers. Erotic expression is crucial nonetheless, she writes in *Public Sex: The Culture of Radical Sex* (1994). Americans must strive for tolerance and civility because they can only learn of experimentation through public or semi-public channels. Califia points out that erotica may replicate some of the power structures in society, but that its messages simultaneously can undermine the control of authoritarian institutions; truly subversive (i.e., extreme) pornography is always instantly suppressed.

Califia believes that pornography produced by minorities serves as a channel of information about erotic nonconformity. When historians consider that the larger American culture has routinely condemned the everyday speech of gays and lesbians as obscene, the value of pornography becomes apparent: it has over time created authentic communities out of gender subcultures. For Califia, however, politics takes a backseat to pleasure, although she is currently writing a history of American obscenity laws. In general, her works demystify the rituals and pleasures, spiritual and physical, of sadomasochism as practiced by women. (Califia is now the transgendered Patrick Califia-Rice.)

Anthony Comstock (1844–1915)

Though slightly revised now, sections 1461, 1462, and 1463 (prohibiting the circulation of lewd materials and birth control information and devices) of Title 18 of the U.S. Code are still known as the Comstock Codes after the man who first parlayed the search for obscenity into celebrity and power. Born in New Canaan, Connecticut, on 7 March 1844, Anthony Comstock went to school there and in nearby New Britain. At nineteen he joined the Union Army; after mustering out in 1865, he worked at odd jobs in New England and the South. He ended up as a grocery clerk in New York City, which to his moralistic eye seemed a sewer of degeneracy. Backed by wealthy patrons, Comstock built his Young Men's Christian Association (YMCA) connections into an organization he called the New York Society for the Suppression of Vice. In 1868 Comstock persuaded the New York State Legislature to pass a law to punish local retailers of material Comstock thought pernicious and to give his society the authority to investigate complaints concerning blasphemy, gambling, theatrical performance, lewd writings and pictures, scientific treatises on hygiene and anthropological customs, tracts on birth control and family planning, feminist tracts, sex education treatises, and other offenses against public decency. In return, the Society for the Suppression of Vice received half of all fines levied against convicted offenders, a provision that led Comstock to redouble his zeal.

More important, Comstock lobbied Congress to expand the 1865 postal law to include federal penalties against publishers as well as distributors of offensive material. Following this new federal legislation (commonly called the Comstock Act of 1873), some thirty states adopted more stringent obscenity laws, and local Watch and Ward societies sprang up to ferret out smut. As a special agent of the U.S. Post Office, Comstock himself conducted seizures and prosecutions against thousands over several decades. He attacked marginal enterprises rather than carriage-trade publishers, though he certainly pressured the latter. The *Annual Reports* of the New York Society for the Suppression of Vice listed pornography by weight, as so much trash, always with a reference to the nationality of those arrested for making or selling it. This practice illustrated the society's conviction that the United States was vulnerable to infection by "inferior" (primarily Eastern European) races alleged to be more "sexually active" than "real" Americans.

When the Society of American Artists condemned him as "incompetent" to judge artistic expression, Comstock wrote in *Morals and Art* (1887) that no expertise was required to spot "impure" thought in paintings or literature, and he declared in "Vampire Literature" (1891) that even world classics (e. g., *The Aeneid*) should be accessible only to mature scholars. He tried to prevent the staging of George Bernard Shaw's *Mrs. Warren's Profession* in 1905 and seized the school catalog of the New York Art Students League because it contained illustrations of famous nude paintings. Although he had wide public support at first, such actions stereotyped Comstock as a bigot, the crusader who ensured the success of that which he strove against, and ultimately subjected him to ridicule because he was reacting to a culture being reshaped by industrialization, immigration, and education. He died in Summit, New Jersey, on 21 September 1915, before the United States entered a war in aid of the Europeans that Comstock considered morally diseased. His censorship society lasted for many more years before metamorphosing into the New York Police Athletic League.

Mary Ware Dennett (1872–1947)

In 1926, in *Birth Control Laws,* Mary Ware Dennett attacked the official ignorance, mean-spiritedness, and moral obtuseness that equated family planning with obscenity by lampooning the rationale for laws prohibiting contraceptives and information about birth control: "Some perverts use contraceptives, therefore the law should not allow any one at all to secure them or know anything about them, and besides, as most of those who are not perverts can't be really trusted anyhow, hearing about or seeing contraceptives would be pretty sure to make them go to the devil, especially young people, so the complete prohibition is after all the safest."

Mary Coffin Ware was born on April 4, 1872, in Worcester, Massachusetts, but moved with her family to Boston when her father died in 1882. After public school in Boston, she attended Miss Capen's School for Girls in Northampton and then the school at Boston's Museum of Fine Arts. Her talent led to her becoming chair of the Department of Design and Decoration at Philadelphia's Drexel Institute. In 1900 she married William Hartley Dennett, a Boston architect. Her political activism probably contributed to their divorce in 1913; she was a feisty crusader. She resigned frequently from organizations as a form of protest, most notably in 1915 as secretary of the National American Women's Suffrage Association, when the organization would not support pacifism, and again in 1917 as secretary of the Women's Section of the Democratic National Committee, when the United States entered World War I. Her causes included the single tax movement, peace, free trade, and civil rights, but she became most notorious for her advocacy of reproductive rights.

Unlike crusaders such as Margaret Sanger, Dennett insisted that the individual's control of her own body did not require justification in terms of hygiene; it was her right. As one of the founders of the National Birth Control League in 1915, Dennett rejected Sanger's call for class agitation and civil disobedience in favor of legislative reform to amend the Comstock laws on obscenity. In 1919, Dennett founded the Voluntary Parenthood League, serving as director and editor of its magazine. When Sanger's birth control movement agreed to a strategy that would restrict authority to distribute information and contraception to doctors, Dennett declined to compromise, insisting that Americans should enjoy choice as individuals. When the birth control movement endorsed eugenics and population control, she denounced both as paternalistic and racist. Convicted of distributing obscenity in 1928 for sending her educational pamphlet, *The Sex Side of Life*, through the mails, she and the American Civil Liberties Union took the case to the Circuit Court of Appeals, which overturned the decision. Dennett's *Who's Obscene?* (1930) recounted her legal battles. More than any other reformer of the period, Dennett insisted that choices about sex and reproduction were inalienable rights of individuals. Social and economic reform were keys to morality, not government intervention, she wrote in *The Sex Education of Children* (1931). For the last years of her life she worked with the National Council on Freedom from Censorship and the ACLU. She died in Valatie, New York on 25 July 1947.

Edward Donnerstein (1945–)

Edward Irving Donnerstein was born 4 May 1945 in New York City. He attended the University of Florida as an undergraduate and Florida State University as a graduate student, receiving his Ph.D. in 1972. A communications psychologist, he has taught at Southern Illinois University, Iowa State University, the University of Wisconsin, and the University of California at Santa Barbara, where he is currently dean of social sciences. He has received numerous research grants and has authored eight books, some forty book chapters, and more than 150 articles, many of them on aggression, sexuality, and mediated behavior.

Donnerstein's work on erotica came to public attention when he conducted a series of experiments with colleagues such as Daniel Linz in the early 1980s to determine whether sexually explicit films desensitized audiences toward rape and encouraged the objectification of women. In most of these experiments, the researchers showed films to a group of young males, then artificially angered the subjects and tried to assess the impact of viewing the materials. When the researchers showed R-rated violent movies such as *Halloween* and *Friday the 13th*, subjects with prolonged exposure exhibited some desensitization toward rape and the objectification of women (the researchers did not construe desensitization as an increased likelihood *to* rape). Subsequent experiments with actual pornography (i.e., hard-core sex films) refined Donnerstein's conclusions. In "The Effects of Long-term Exposure to Violent and Sexually Degrading Depictions of Women" (1988), Linz, Donnerstein, and Stephen Penrod did not find a significant relationship between exposure to *nonviolent* pornography and the tendency to view women as sex objects.

Although conservatives and antiporn feminists seized on Donnerstein's early research as evidence of a causal link between pornography and violence directed against women, Donnerstein pointed out that films appear to have negative effects *only* when sexual content is combined with violence, a qualification omitted by media reports. Moreover, Donnerstein and Linz found in separate studies, narrative context counts: when male audiences see a *complete* film, rather than excerpts, they are no more tolerant of violence than any other group. When one treats erotic film as a carrier of messages, say Linz and Donnerstein in "The Effects of Counter-Information on the Acceptance of Rape Myths" (1989), then it becomes apparent that exploding the myth that women actually enjoy being raped depends directly on better education. In his testimony before the Meese Commission, Donnerstein said flatly that no reputable researchers have linked ordinary hardcore films, that is, those primarily concerned with depicting sexual intercourse, with violent behavioral effects. In other public statements, Donnerstein and Linz have cautioned that that there is little evidence that sexual aggression calibrated in laboratory studies is similar to violence in actual assaults, and that there is no scientific evidence connecting pornography to serial murders.

Andrea Dworkin (1946–)

During the 1970s, Andrea Dworkin electrified a radical wing of feminists seeking a cause for gender inequity. Dworkin's thesis, that pornography—defined as the exclusive expression of males—both enshrines and causes misogyny, became the rationale for the antiporn feminist movement. Dworkin swiftly became an activist as well as a theoretician. Working with attorney Catharine A. MacKinnon, Dworkin helped construct the Minneapolis and Indianapolis (and other) ordinances that attempted to punish pornographers for discriminating against women as a class. Although the strategy has not fared well in U.S. courts, which determined that it violates the First Amendment, Dworkin continues to advocate it.

Dworkin was born 26 September 1946 in Camden, New Jersey. Her parents were Harry Dworkin, a guidance counselor, and Sylvia Dworkin, a secretary. Perhaps because she read a great deal, Dworkin early decided that she wanted to become a writer, but not a passive one: she joined antiwar demonstrations in 1964, when she was eighteen, and spent several days in jail. The young radical's arrest caused a furor when she loudly protested a humiliating and unnecessarily painful body-cavity search by police. After graduating from Bennington College in 1968, she left for Europe partly because she was disgusted with the Vietnam War and American racism and partly to learn to write. A traumatic marriage to a wife-battering Dutchman provided the writer with a subject and a cause. Returning from the Netherlands to the United States in the 1970s, Dworkin supported herself with a succession of jobs ranging from waitress to teacher before becoming an assistant to poet Muriel Rukeyser, who encouraged her writing. The success of *Women Hating* (1974) led to demand for speeches by Dworkin at various feminist rallies. Some of these she collected in *Our Blood: Prophecies and Discourses on Sexual Politics* (1976). Her most important book, *Pornography: Men Possessing Women* (1981), asserted that male sexuality can only be understood as "the process of killing," a mindset visible in all male sexual expression according to her. Dworkin argued that men's hatred of women is the only reason for pornography's appeal.

Skeptical readers suggest that Dworkin merely combats hatred with hatred, while sympathetic ones find that her observations do echo the experience of many women. In her best early work, she uses resonance and originality to offset polemics that can otherwise seem single-minded. Critics concede her consistency and her sincerity, and readily acknowledge that she has provoked valuable reexamination of gender issues. They are less inclined to believe that Dworkin's ideas have added much to discussions of sexuality, noting that they often recall puritanical repugnance toward sex as nasty; here her extreme positions usually forestall debate. An unrepentant vision animates *Intercourse* (1987), a diatribe against the brutality of the sex act itself; as she sees it, women are victimized because they are penetrated, and they will escape outrage only by inventing some other form of reproduction.

Although Dworkin and MacKinnon collaborated on *Pornography and Civil Rights: A New Day for Women's Equality* as late as 1988, Dworkin broke ranks with her coauthor in 1992 over the antipornography legislation—based on their critique of pornography—adopted by Canada. MacKinnon decided that any kind of censorship was better than none, while Dworkin predicted, correctly, that the Canadian statute would simply ban degrees of explicitness rather than male sexual expression in general. Not surprisingly, Canadian customs instantly seized two of Dworkin's own books as obscene. Dworkin's fiction contains familiar pornographic tropes; she has been called the "de Sade of our time." She denies that the cruel "pornogothic" sexuality that so many women find erotically stimulating in her own fiction such as *Ice and Fire* (1986) and *Mercy* (1990) is similar to that in stories by males, insisting that she is more skilled than ordinary pornographers.

A long-time resident of Brooklyn, New York, Dworkin continues to attack male lust and the "terrorism" of a pornography that she sees as a blueprint for degrading women. Recent works include *Letters from a War Zone: Writings, 1976–1989* (1993) and *Life and Death: Unapologetic Writings on the Continuing War against Women* (1997).

Morris Ernst (1888–1976)

Among attorney Morris Ernst's more notable books are those that sought to understand the impulses of censors. With William Seagle, Ernst published *To the Pure . . . : A Study of Obscenity and the Censor* (1928), which delineated the abuses of power by the U.S. Post Office and other government agencies; given the impossibility of defining obscenity, said Ernst, censorship was irrational. With Pare Lorentz, an anthropologist, Morris satirized the absurdities of film suppression during the 1920s in *Censored: The Private Life of the Movie* (1930). With Alexander Lindley, Ernst reviewed significant court cases in *The Censor Marches On: On Recent Milestones in the Obscenity Laws in the United States* (1940), and again, a quarter-century later, with Allan Schwartz in *Censorship: The Search for the Obscene* (1964). These books, a dozen others, and well over 100 articles established Ernst as one of the most formidable champions of artistic freedom. By studying the tactics of antiporn crusaders, Ernst learned to counter their attempts to entrap booksellers, try defendants in the press, and bring cases before conservative judges. Ernst engineered a series of postponements, for example, until he got Judge John M. Woolsey to preside over the trial of James Joyce's novel *Ulysses*, probably the most famous case of both men's careers. Such maneuvers lent credibility to his argument that censorship was arbitrary.

Morris Leopold Ernst was born in Uniontown, Alabama, on 23 August 1888, moved at age two with his family to New York City, and attended New York City public schools. He received his B.A. from Williams College in 1909, earned his LL.B in 1912, and three years later cofounded the firm of Greenbaum, Wolff, and Ernst, where he worked for the rest of his life. Because Ernst believed that the Constitution protected even offensive ideas, he took on cases from which other attorneys shied away, such as the defense of Radclyffe Hall's lesbian novel *The Well of Loneliness*. Ernst's thinking would be encapsulated in Woolsey's decision, which held that a book must be judged on its merits in its entirety, not condemned for specific passages. Ernst's victory in the

1933 *Ulysses* trial, perhaps the most far-reaching of all decisions regarding obscenity, brought him many clients, among them Margaret Sanger and Dr. Marie Stopes, crusaders for birth control information, which was categorized in the United States as a species of obscenity. His successful defenses of reproductive freedom made possible the circulation of Sanger's *Birth Control* and Stopes's *Married Love*. Ernst served from 1929 to 1954 as general counsel for the American Civil Liberties Union, and for the Planned Parenthood Federation from 1929 to 1960. He died in New York on 21 May 1976. His papers, now housed at the University of Texas, provide an incomparable record of First Amendment law.

Larry Flynt (1942–)

Unlike Samuel Roth, another publisher of questionable materials, Larry Flynt has been transformed from sleazy pornographer to mainstream champion of free speech, largely because of an attempted assassination that left Flynt in a wheelchair, which earned him some sympathy; Milos Forman's film, *The People Versus Larry Flynt* (1996), which cast him as a First Amendment crusader; Flynt's own autobiography, *An Unseemly Man: My Life as Pornographer, Pundit, and Social Outcast* (1996), which attacks his enemies as self-serving and promotes himself as a working-class hero; and his exposés of hypocritical congressmen during the Clinton impeachment, which struck some Americans as overdue fair play. Now head of a $100 million empire of thirty magazines, including *Maternity Fashion* and *Beauty*, Flynt became notorious for *Hustler*, a magazine whose depiction of America as a land of hypocrisy resonated with a blue-collar audience but galvanized feminists who accused him of demeaning women. Perhaps more than that of any other single individual in recent history, Flynt's career illustrates the cultural dynamics by which society first marginalizes the pornographer/outsider, then rehabilitates and defangs him through capitalistic appropriation and commodification. That fate, in fact, may be society's ultimate revenge.

Larry Flynt was born 1 November 1942 into Appalachian poverty in Magoffin County, Kentucky. He sold moonshine at age ten, moved with his divorced mother to Hamlet, Indiana, dropped out of school after the eighth grade to join the army (and was booted out because of poor education), and held a variety of odd jobs in Ohio before joining the navy. At 23 he bought a Dayton bar from his mother, then parlayed it into a string of

Hustler go-go clubs across Ohio. *Hustler* magazine began in 1971 as a newsletter advertising the clubs. Each issue aimed at "Joe Lunchbox": its vulgar text sneered at upper-class pretense; its nasty cartoons targeted women, children, do-gooders, and Santa Claus; and the open-crotch pictorials focused on naked "women-next-door," not the more elegant models recruited by *Playboy.* Surreptitiously snapped photos of a nude Jackie Kennedy Onassis in the August 1975 issue caused a furor, partly because they seemed to trash a national icon and partly because of the subtext—Flynt's conviction that the working class should share in the hedonism of the sexual revolution. Convicted in 1977 by Cincinnati prosecutors of pandering, obscenity, and organized crime for publishing the magazine, Flynt won a reversal. In 1978, during another trial for publishing *Hustler* in Lawrenceville, Georgia, Flynt was shot and paralyzed by a White Supremacist angered by an interracial photo in the magazine. Outrageous even in a wheelchair, Flynt fought charges of libel, fraud, and contempt and briefly ran for president in 1983. Perhaps the most significant controversy to envelope Flynt resulted from *Hustler's* vile parody of Jerry Falwell, leader of the Moral Majority, which caused Falwell to sue. The Supreme Court's 1988 decision, exonerating Flynt, significantly expanded freedom of the press.

Spurred by the rehabilitation of his reputation, Flynt announced that he would once again put himself on the line by selling explicit materials in Cincinnati, but he quickly cut a deal with prosecutors in 1999. Unrepentant, convinced that *Hustler's* sexual representations are authentic because they have no pretense to art, Flynt continues to push against standards of "decency," to offend feminists, conservatives, and fundamentalists, and to disgust even his defenders.

David F. Friedman (1923–)

David Friedman, affectionately known as "The Sultan of Sleaze," is candid about his trade. The exploitation film, he says, is "a con-game," advertised to persuade movie patrons that they will see something sensational instead of the hokum they actually get. Friedman describes himself as "the senior citizen of the second of four generations of exploitation." Junk films aimed at lonely men made him a millionaire. Although he refuses to take himself or his products seriously, his films helped shaped the sexual sensibilities of a generation of Americans, and some critics have discovered artistic merit in Friedman's soft-core scenarios. Certainly they are better-made than most examples of the genre, full of humor, verve, and crisp homilies on hypocrisy and sin.

Friedman was born 24 December 1923 in Birmingham, Alabama. His father, a newspaper editor, and his mother, a former piano player in silent movie houses, divorced when he was eight. The young Friedman hung around movie theaters owned by his uncle, lived in hotels with his father, and traveled with circuses during the summer. Graduating from Cornell University with a degree in electrical engineering, he joined the army and served during World War II, then after the war worked as a craps dealer, wrote speeches for Alabama Governor Jim Folsom, and drifted into publicity for the Chicago office of Paramount studios. In 1954 he became an independent distributor, learned that the money was in sex, and formed Apex Attractions to distribute semisalacious hygiene films in an era when on-screen nudity and sex were strictly forbidden. Friedman's disarming autobiography, *A Youth in Babylon: Confessions of a Trash-Film King*, recalls his partnership with exploitation pioneer Kroger Babb (one of the original "Forty Thieves," as the early exploitation producers were called) who shot *Mom and Dad* (1944), the "supreme birth-of-a-baby film," for about $40,000 but marketed it so skillfully that it generated about $90 million at admission prices of only 35 to 50 cents.

The New York State Supreme Court's *Garden of Eden* decision legalizing nudist films (1955) led Friedman to team with Herschell Gordon Lewis to shoot movies that featured topless women recruited from burlesque and nudist camps. Because the vogue for these did not last long, Friedman helped to invent what is usually called "the roughie," a movie that uses sadism as a substitute for intercourse, a strategy perfectly suited to an American sensibility that tolerated violence but censored sex. The success of his *Blood Feast* (1963) spawned others with titles such as *Color Me Blood Red* and *Two Thousand Maniacs*. When censors accepted brutality in place of sex, hundreds of roughies (sometimes called "women in danger" films) poured from sleazy studios. Friedman's *Ilsa, She Wolf of the SS* (1974) still stands as a monument of bad taste, despite serious competition from similar films by contemporaries such as Russ Meyer. In 1964, Friedman merged his company with the oldest exploitation company in the country, Sonney Amusement, founded by Louis Sonney, another of the Forty Thieves. The renamed enterprise (Entertainment Ventures) became the largest distributor of sex films in the United States. Between 1958 and 1984, Friedman produced fifty-eight features, only a half dozen of which were hard-core, a genre he does not think erotic. As president of the Adult Film Association (1970–1975), however, he lobbied strenuously for the right to make and view graphic sexual films. He still thinks that Americans prefer sex scenes that are "put-ons" over depictions of hard-core.

Al Goldstein (1936–)

The most notorious of hard-core sex tabloids is *Screw*, published since 1968 by Al Goldstein, who also produces erotic programs (*Midnight Blue*) for Manhattan Cable Television. *Screw*'s immense sales in the 1960s inspired a host of imitators: *Bang, Kiss, New York Review of Sex, Luv, Pleasure, Fun, Cocksure, Ecstasy, Desire*, and so on, mostly published in New York, Los Angeles, or San Francisco. Often attacked, *Screw* has survived in part because Goldstein combines the salacious with political protest, since the latter is clearly protected speech: a typical issue is just as likely to criticize an agency of the State of New York for some backward social policy as to scream about censorship. The genius of *Screw* is its deliberate mythologizing of New York City to suggest that the seamy undergrounds it so meticulously chronicles somehow furnish the energy that drives the metropolis. For years, audiences have read *Screw* as a guide to the sexual consciousness of alternative political subcultures; the magazine helped to construct the "sexual revolution" of the late 1960s and early 1970s by shaping its folklore.

Al Goldstein was born in Brooklyn in 1936, the son of a Hearst newspaper photographer. He attended Pace College in New York without graduating, then worked as a taxi driver, an encyclopedia salesman, and a freelance photographer for newspapers and wire services in the United States and abroad. His most notable experiences as a photojournalist included being arrested in Cuba in 1960 and accompanying Jacqueline Kennedy to Pakistan on an assignment for *Travel Digest* in 1962. After working for several months for the *National Mirror*, a supermarket tabloid, he met Jim Buckley, editor of the *Underground Free Press*. The two each contributed $150 to launch the first issue of *Screw*, a freewheeling tabloid with a commitment to tastelessness and—somewhat surprisingly, considering policies often derided as sexist—a penchant for hiring female editors. (In 1975 Goldstein bought out Buckley to become sole owner of Milky Way Productions, the tabloid's parent company.) *Screw*'s abrasiveness led to at least ten arrests for obscenity, which Goldstein fought aggressively. In 1969, for example, police raided *Screw*'s editorial offices when the tabloid ran a composite photo of Mayor John Lindsay with a huge penis alleged to be more effective than his political skills. Goldstein won. In 1976, forum-shopping prosecutors persuaded a conservative jury in Wichita to convict Goldstein of obscenity after Kansas postal inspectors ordered a copy of *Screw* by mail. Higher courts overturned the conviction on appeal. *Screw* still boldly reports on sexual fiction, magazines, and sex toys and appliances, and, most famously, it reviews hard-core videos using its trademark "Peter Meter," on which the reviewer assesses the videotape's likelihood to induce erections. It also comments on topics ranging from public safety to campaign financing. During the 1970s Goldstein himself ran against Mayor Ed Koch for the U.S. House of Representatives.

In 1974, Goldstein started *Midnight Blue,* a late-night show on a public access channel operated by Manhattan Cable. Programs featured nudity and simulated sex; interviews with porn stars, strippers, and writers; visits with the weird; Goldstein's diatribes against politicians and institutions; and lots of ads for escort services. Two years later, the FCC forced Manhattan Cable to remove *Midnight Blue* from the public access channel, but Goldstein, taking advantage of a New York state law forbidding censorship of cable program content, moved his program to a leased-access channel, where it remains. Goldstein makes no claims for the intellectual basis of pornography. He merely point outs, usually in vulgar language, that freedom to say what one wants is the real test of a democracy and its politics. Now almost an institution himself, he writes articles for *Playboy* and a film review column for *Penthouse* and shows up on various panels on freedom of speech as a formidable opponent of would-be censors.

Mary Elizabeth "Tipper" Gore (1948–)

In 1985, the U.S. Senate held hearings on explicit and violent lyrics on audio recordings; by 1990, a frightened National Association of Recording Merchandisers "voluntarily" stuck warning labels on record, disc, and cassette jackets. At first the labels increased sales, at least in urban areas, but over time they resulted in de facto censorship for rural regions because chains such as Wal-Mart and Blockbuster, often the only stores in town, refuse to carry products with the labels, thus blocking access for many Americans. The chief lobbyist for "sticker" labels was Tipper Gore, wife of Vice President Al Gore.

Tipper Gore was born in Washington, D.C., on 19 August 1948 and grew up in Arlington, Virginia. She married Albert

Gore Jr. in 1970, the same year she graduated from Boston University with a degree in psychology. She earned her master's degree (1975, also in psychology) at Vanderbilt University while her husband attended Vanderbilt Law School, then became a part-time newspaper photographer and chairperson of the Congressional Wives Task Force when Al Gore was elected to Congress. Aware that she herself had been stimulated by rock music in her teens, she became alarmed at explicit lyrics of heavy-metal rock that seemed to her a form of "cultural strip-mining" destroying the innocence of American children. Her husband, now a senator, convened the U.S. Senate hearing in response to charges that "porn rock" causes promiscuity, unwanted pregnancies, devil worship, drug addiction, alcoholism, and many other evils in teenagers. After founding the Parents' Music Resource Center (PMRC) with Susan Baker, wife of the secretary of state, and thirteen other Washington wives, Tipper Gore wrote *Raising PG Kids in an X-Rated Society* (1987), a criticism of sex and violence in popular music. Although law enforcement officials in several states began prosecuting targets identified by the PMRC, and although right-wing and anti-Semitic fundamentalists began campaigns against musicians on the PMRC's list, Gore insisted that she was not in favor of censorship, only self-policing by the industry of perverse material inappropriate for adolescents. Nonetheless, both she and Senator Gore, running for president in 1988, tried to distance themselves from the center's activities.

Since then, Tipper Gore has become a mental health adviser to President Bill Clinton, published *Picture This: A Visual Diary* (1996), and with the National Mental Health Association produced *Homeless in America: A Photographic Project* (1996).

Learned Hand (1872–1961)

Judges routinely cite the decisions of Learned Hand under his name rather than by docket number in deference to perhaps the greatest jurist to sit on a federal bench. Billings Learned Hand was born in Albany, New York, on 27 January 1872, the son, nephew, and grandson of attorneys. After graduating from Albany Academy, Hand went in 1889 directly to Harvard, where he studied philosophy under William James, Josiah Royce, and George Santayana. After receiving an M.A. in 1893, he moved to the Harvard Law School, graduated, and returned to Albany to practice law in 1896; after marrying, he and his wife moved to New York City in 1902. President William Taft appointed him a district judge in

1909 because of Hand's brilliant articles in law journals. Carefully reasoned decisions advanced a career whose energies overflowed into political comment, especially in *The New Republic* magazine, of which Hand was virtually a cofounder in 1914, and into the creation of the American Law Institute, which still advises the legal profession, in 1923. After 1924, when President Calvin Coolidge named him to the Court of Appeals for the Second Circuit, Hand avoided politics altogether except in the early 1950s to speak out against Joseph McCarthy when other officials feared to. Hand became Chief Justice of the second appellate court in 1939 and held that office until his retirement in 1951.

Hand's precedent-setting opinions ranged from negligence, bankruptcy, and intellectual property to antitrust and immigration, but he is popularly remembered for his interpretations of the First Amendment. Only speech that incited others to commit illegal acts could be prosecuted, he said. "The spirit of liberty is the spirit which is not too sure that it is right," he declared, a conviction that reinforced his belief in the necessity for tolerance. Hand guided American courts toward a new interpretation of the forbidden. The Hicklin principle, permitting conviction of a book on the basis of a single passage, remained the touchstone of obscenity until 1913, when Hand, though upholding the conviction of *Hagar Revelly,* a sociological novel by Daniel Goodman, expressed doubts about the wisdom of suppressing what was clearly a work of ideas on the basis of isolated parts. In 1930, Judge Augustus Hand, drawing on his cousin Learned's reservations, reversed the federal conviction of Mary Ware Dennett's sex education pamphlet, *The Sex Side of Life,* and thus set in motion the final assault on the Hicklin principle. When Judge John Woolsey reversed the conviction of James Joyce's *Ulysses* on the grounds that a book must be judged as a whole, not on the basis of offensive passages, the government appealed. Appellate Justices Learned and Augustus Hand upheld Woolsey's interpretation. Two years later, in still another case, Learned Hand once again rejected narrow tests and in effect destroyed the Hicklin principle for good. After spending his retirement lecturing and writing, Hand died in New York on 18 August 1961.

Nina Hartley (1961–)

Journalists and critics often write about sex performers, but few performers write about their own experiences and ideas. Although profiled frequently in a wide variety of media, Nina Hartley is herself an articulate columnist, lecturer, and essayist. She acknowledges that the porn industry is still dominated by males but asserts that women have only recently begun to advance their own sexual agendas. According to Hartley, society does its best to turn out sexually twisted Americans, then acts surprised when the fantasies exhibited in pornography are unpleasant. Nevertheless, says Hartley, violence is rare in pornography. Moreover, to despise sexual expression because it has been commercialized is to argue with the ethos of capitalism, which commodifies all speech and images in order to distribute them. She believes that pornography can help alleviate widespread sexual ignorance.

Raised in Berkeley, California, by "leftist liberal" parents, Hartley attended San Francisco State University, dancing nude at the O'Farrell Theater to help pay her way. She graduated *magna cum laude* in 1985 with a degree in nursing. At some point her girlfriend, Bobby Lilly, an anticensorship activist, became part of a ménage à trois with Hartley and her husband, Dave. Both mates are supportive of her work as a stripper and hard-core film star, and Lilly helps produce Hartley's educational sex films. Hartley's porn career began in 1984 with *Educating Nina,* a film produced, directed, and written by Juliet Anderson, a popular performer of the 1980s. Since then she has made more than 400 pornographic features. Although she was arrested for "felony lesbianism" in Las Vegas in 1993 for giving an illustrated lecture on how to make love to a woman (her trial ended when she agreed to contribute to a Las Vegas charity), she has become a respected unofficial spokesperson for pornography.

Hartley says that she appears in films in order to gratify her exhibitionism, improve as a performer, furnish herself with erotic representations that she can enjoy, and celebrate female sexuality. Pornography does not victimize women, she insists, but she denounces those who refuse to permit women the prerogative of consent. Hartley says that no one in the industry forces women to perform, nor do most women do so out of desperate economic need. According to her, pornography, like any other industry, can function as a route to self-expression and achievement. She is a strong advocate of safe sex and monthly AIDS tests for performers.

Donna Rice Hughes (1958–)

Believing that parental effort can prevent children from being exposed to pornography, Donna Rice Hughes attempts to give parents the tools they need to deal with sexual materials on the

Internet. She has appeared on television shows such as *Oprah Winfrey, Crossfire,* and *Dateline* to advocate her position. Hughes was born Donna Rice in 1958 in Florida. Her father, William Rice, a federal highway engineer, and her mother, Miriam, a secretary, moved the family first to Atlanta and then to Columbia, South Carolina, where Donna attended school from the sixth grade through high school. Rice, making an early start on a modeling career, appeared in her first television commercial, for Pizza Hut, in the ninth grade. After graduating in 1980 from the University of South Carolina as both a cheerleader and a Phi Beta Kappa student, she entered and won the Miss South Carolina beauty pageant. Then her life took a turn toward the wild. Newspapers linked her romantically with movie star Warren Beatty, with Prince Albert of Monaco, with drummer Don Henley of the Eagles, and with arms dealer Adnan Khashoggi. In 1982 she took a job as a pharmaceutical saleswoman in Miami, where she hoped to pursue a career as a model and actress. For two years she lived with the narcotics trafficker James Bradley Parks (imprisoned in 1984) while she modeled for television ads and secured small parts on *One Life to Live, Dallas,* and *Miami Vice.*

In 1987, on a trip to Aspen, Colorado, Rice met Senator Gary Hart, then seeking the Democratic presidential nomination. When newspapers hinted at romantic involvement, Hart issued his famous challenge to journalists to prove the allegations. The results were stories supplemented by photographs of Rice sitting in Hart's lap on board the yacht *Monkey Business.* Although the scandal destroyed Hart's political ambitions, Rice tried to capitalize on her notoriety by hiring a press agent, selling her story to *Life,* appearing on the cover of *People,* and being interviewed by Barbara Walters for ABC's *20/20* TV news magazine. Agents made a deal for ABC to shoot and air *The Donna Rice Story* as a two-hour movie, but household-goods behemoth Proctor and Gamble canceled an ad that she had made for Folger's Coffee. She shot commercials for jeans manufactured by No Excuses Sportswear, but that company too dismissed her, and the ABC movie never appeared. Feeling "exploited" and "hunted," Rice returned to her job selling pharmaceuticals.

At some point, Rice experienced a religious conversion, and in 1994 she married business executive Jack Hughes. That same year she began working for Enough Is Enough, a nonprofit organization devoted to stopping "illegal pornography" and to shielding children from sexual materials on the Internet; in 1996 she became director of marketing and communications. With

Pamela T. Campbell, Rice wrote *Kids Online: Protecting Your Children in Cyberspace* (1998), a handbook for parents. The text offers advice to parents on preventing exposure of children to sexual materials on the Internet, reviews various software packages and filtering agents designed to intercept sexual materials, and recounts the experience of some schools in attempting to block student access to sexual sites. Hughes argues with the ACLU, which takes a First Amendment position on such issues as public libraries' attempting to restrict patrons' access to materials of which the library staffs disapprove, and occasionally repeats misinformation about pornography (contrary to her claims, there is no reliable research demonstrating links between pornography and antisocial behavior), but overall her approach is to place responsibility for what children encounter on the Net with parents.

Irving Klaw (1911–1966)

Although ignored by most historians, Irving Klaw remains an important figure because he defined important elements of sexual expression during the 1940s and 1950s. Klaw focused on desire for specific fetishes at a time when Americans could not speak openly about sex or register their appreciation of nude bodies. No one seems to have noted much about his Brooklyn childhood or upbringing, but Klaw's ability to identify and expand a niche market, coupled with just enough talent to craft a durable product and a flair for merchandising it, was quintessentially American. In fact, Klaw has been eclipsed by Bettie Page, the woman he turned into a cult figure, perhaps the most famous pinup model of all time. Today, more than two dozen books and 200 Web sites reproduce Klaw's photos of her.

In 1939, after an unsuccessful career in the fur business, Klaw and his younger sister Paula opened a second-hand basement bookstore on 14th Street in Manhattan. Not only did they not handle the erotic books that kept bookstores afloat during the Depression, they soon dispensed with books altogether. Noticing that patrons of the movie palaces on 14th Street swiftly bought out the publicity photos of stars he offered as an experiment, Klaw added to his stock and began issuing catalogs. Success led to a new store—Movie Star News—on the street level across 14th, under a sign reading "Irving Klaw, the Pin-Up King." When customers began asking for lingerie, spanking, and bondage shots of their favorite Hollywood actresses, Klaw at first packaged photos on fetish themes and then began commissioning photos of burlesque queens such as Lili St. Cyr and Tempest Storm and pinup models such as Joan Rydell and Julie Cartier. Renting a floor above the store, he and Paula built a studio to shoot photos and 8-millimeter movies themselves. At first Paula merely assisted Irving, but as her confidence behind the camera grew, she herself turned out thousands of pinup shots. The Klaws shot no nude photographs, and never even hinted at intercourse. Paula and the models sewed the costumes, which featured bathing suits, corsets, brassieres, satin panties, silk stockings, and high heels, all exaggerated as fetishes. In about 1951 Bettie Page, a stunning brunette graduate of Peabody College in Tennessee, joined their repertoire of models. A few years earlier, John Willie (J. A. S. Coutts) had arrived from Australia to draw fetish cartoons for Klaw. Because of the enormous appeal of Willie's "bondage and discipline" drawings, the Klaws began shooting "tease and tumble" scenarios, with models wrestling, spanking each other, or being tied up with ropes with enormous knots. Fans all over the world awaited each issue of Klaws' *Cartoon and Model Parade,* an illustrated catalog of the comic books, photo sets, and films with which the Klaws sublimated sexuality.

In 1955, Senator Estes Kefauver impaneled a U.S. Senate subcommittee on pornography and juvenile delinquency. Kefauver subpoenaed Irving Klaw, accused him of running a $1.5 million annual business (an exaggeration) to peddle obscenity, and called witnesses to testify that watching the Klaws' movies would turn "normal" juveniles into homosexuals. The U.S. Post Office, struggling to maintain its authority to censor against a series of court decisions that characterized the agency's policies as illegal, promptly informed the public that all mail addressed to Irving Klaw or Movie Star News would be returned stamped "unlawful." Klaw pleaded the Fifth Amendment, then moved his business to New Jersey. In 1963, a year Ralph Ginzburg called "an obscenity panic" in America, prosecutors arrested Klaw and prepared to try him for obscenity. Too ill to defend himself, Klaw burned his entire stock of photos and films in exchange for having the charges dropped. Because Paula Klaw had kept the masters, she later reopened Movie Star News and ran it until her death in December 1996. (Movie Star News today does a lively trade in these artifacts of nostalgia.) Klaw himself died in 1966.

Klaw's cheesecake was good-naturedly adolescent, even dopey. The photos and films are clumsily shot, badly lit, and tediously paced. What redeems them is an unaffected voyeurism that nonfetishists mistake for deliberate stupidity rather than the cheerful incompetence that is the hallmark of "low" pornography. Although Klaw's pictorials are as silly as they are naughty, they helped shape contours of desire for a nation suddenly aware of "sex appeal." More important, as fashion historians have noted, Klaw's photographs of fetish costumes have profoundly influenced today's fashion industry in much the same way that the movies of the Three Stooges, say, defined a brand of comedy. Klaw's career is a reminder that sexual appeal arises as much from lower-class, amateurish, and yet authentic representations as from the higher-class eroticism of a Picasso or a D. H. Lawrence.

Gershon Legman (1918–1999)

According to the late Gershon Legman, easily America's greatest scholar of erotica, "All folklore is erotic," by which he means that the oral traditions of humans revolve around sexuality. In fact, "folklore" is often the name used to distinguish venerable stories that contain obscenity from equally old narratives that aspire to literary status. "Folklore," said Legman, "is the voice of those who have no other voice, and would not be listened to if they did." To become a pioneer in erotic folklore required courage and enormous learning, and over the course of Legman's career he became an authority on stories, songs, ballads, limericks, and jokes. Legman's bibliographies and essays trace the influence of sexual themes and motifs around the world, identify the genres of sexual expression, and chart the migrations of materials in and out of archives.

Legman was born in 1918 to East European immigrants in Scranton, Pennsylvania. He claimed to have gone to university for a year but dropped out to pursue his fascination with sexuality, working as an advocate for birth control, an activity for which he was arrested several times. In New York City he worked in bookstores and in other odd jobs to support his research in the New York Public Library. As editor of *Neurotica*, a periodical of popular psychology that lasted only from 1947 to 1948, he published essays by Allen Ginsberg, Marshall McLuhan, and himself. Some of that work became the basis for *Love and Death: A Study in Censorship*, a book he published himself when no publisher would accept it. Its thesis was that suppressing sexual expression and representation leads directly to expressions or representations of violence. Since for many years Americans could not watch humans making love, they gravitated toward aggression instead, assisted by a Hollywood that would cut away from a human embrace to depict a locomotive rushing through a tunnel or a man firing a gun. Legman worked briefly as researcher and archivist at the Kinsey Institute of Sex, Reproduction, and Gender but, hounded by the U.S. Post Office for sending *Love and Death* through the mails, moved to France in 1953.

From Opio, France, where his home became the world's unofficial headquarters for academic study of erotica, he conducted a voluminous correspondence, collected vast quantities of pornographic ephemera, and wrote numerous essays and books. *The Horn Book: Studies in Erotic Folklore and Bibliography* (1964) explored the creative impulses of obscenity and chronicled the traditions of "low" expression. Legman's studies of obscene and pornographic humor, published as *The Rationale of the Dirty Joke: An Analysis of Sexual Humor* (1968) and *No Laughing Matter: Rationale of the Dirty Joke, Second Series* (1975), are exhaustive analyses of ribald categories. Here Legman unearths hidden meaning, traces derivations, ferrets out aggressiveness, and does not shrink from judgments such as "venomous," "nasty," and "sexist." Legman thinks that dirty jokes originate with males, who use them as a form of colorful plumage for public display, and often denigrate women. Such humor, in short, is masculine, the product of a "voice as phallus." His *The Limerick: 1700 Examples, with Notes, Variants, and Index* (1953) and *The New Limerick: 2750 Unpublished Examples, American and British* (1977) annotate a verse form that combines intellectual ingenuity with fondness for obscenity. Legman's "Erotic Folksongs and Ballads: An International Bibliography" (1990) lists samizdat versions, spin-offs, reprints, paperback editions, and other mutations of jokes, stories, songs, ballads, and broadsides. His two last major volumes were editions of Southern sexual folklore gathered by fellow folklorist Vance Randolph and published as *Roll Me in Your Arms: "Unprintable" Ozark Folksongs and Folklore* (1992) and *Blow the Candle Out: "Unprintable" Ozark Folklore* (1997). Legman died on the Riviera on 23 February 1999 before he could finish his autobiography, tentatively titled *Peregrine Penis: An Autobiography of Innocence,* an account of his experiences as a writer, dealer, and bibliographer of erotica.

Catharine A. MacKinnon (1946–)

Catharine MacKinnon, who teaches law at the University of Michigan and the University of Chicago, is the theorist most responsible for creating legal remedies for sexual harassment in the workplace. For MacKinnon, sexual harassment is sexual discrimination, and therefore illegal, a strong argument that compels assent and that has profoundly reshaped the way Americans—and American jurists—think about the issue. Her attempts to persuade others that pornography is also sexual discrimination have been less successful, but no one would deny that MacKinnon has sharpened debate on sexual representation.

Catharine MacKinnon was born in 1946. Her father, George E. MacKinnon, was a federal appellate judge, a congress-member from Minnesota, and a one-time Republican candidate for governor of that state. MacKinnon graduated from Smith College in 1969 with a B.A. in government, from Yale University in 1977 with a J.D., and from Yale again in 1987 with a Ph.D. in political science. Her activism as a student flowed into various causes: the Black Panthers, the women's movement, and legal representation for the poor. Beginning to practice law in Connecticut in 1977, she took an immediate interest in cases of sexual harassment and published her rationale for changes to the law as her first book, *Sexual Harassment of Working Women: A Case of Sexual Discrimination* (1979). As cocounsel in *Meritor Savings Bank v. Vinson*, MacKinnon persuaded the U.S. Supreme Court in 1986 that sexual harassment on the job included not just quid pro quo types (i.e., sexual favors demanded in exchange for continued employment or advancement) but also the persistence of a sexually hostile environment, and that both were illegal under Title VII of the 1964 Civil Rights Act. Subsequent litigation has further refined her arguments.

With Andrea Dworkin, an antipornography activist, MacKinnon wrote or provided language for ordinances in various states, most notably in the cities of Minneapolis and Indianapolis. These would have enabled women to sue producers and distributors of pornography if they could prove they had been harmed by specific examples. In *Feminism Unmodified: Discourses on Life and Law* (1987), MacKinnon argues that gender itself is not a "natural" distinction but merely a rationalization of inequalities of power, a form of discrimination. Some critics maintain that MacKinnon makes no distinction between ordinary intercourse and rape as exercises of male power; reading MacKinnon's books is not likely to resolve the confusion. In *Pornography and Civil Rights: A New Day for Women's Equality* (1988), MacKinnon and Dworkin argue that women as a class suffer as a consequence of gender and that the agent of harm is pornography that embodies, encourages, and perpetuates sexual discrimination. Controversy ensued when MacKinnon brusquely attacked feminists who disagreed. When the U.S. Supreme Court let stand a lower court's 1985 rejection of the Indianapolis ordinance (the last surviving piece of MacKinnon-inspired legislation) on the grounds that it attacked free speech, MacKinnon wrote *Only Words* (1993) to insist that words can be equivalent to actions. Some of her views have been upheld in Canada, in the *Regina v. Butler* decision (1992) that added materials that subordinate or degrade women to the list of forbidden forms of expression.

Robert Mapplethorpe (1946–1989)

Always controversial, Robert Mapplethorpe became even more notorious just as he died, when conservatives attacked the National Endowment of the Arts for funding a 1988 retrospective exhibit of the photographer's work that was scheduled to travel. Mapplethorpe's explicit images of gay subcultures, including one that depicted himself in a graphic pose, struck some audiences as offensive. Senator Jesse Helms led a loose coalition that included the American Family Association, the 700 Club, Concerned Women for America, and other groups in an effective protest against using public funds to support objectionable art, especially art that featured "deviant sexuality." In 1989, Washington, D.C.'s, Corcoran Gallery of Art canceled the show; in 1990, Cincinnati brought obscenity charges against the city's Contemporary Arts Center and its director (both were acquitted) because one of the photos was of a young girl. The battle pitted artistic freedom against social responsibility, or so it seemed to the combatants.

Robert Mapplethorpe was born 4 November 1946 in Floral Park, Queens, New York. Robert was the third of six children of his Roman Catholic father (an electrician) and mother; the mysteries of their faith, Mapplethorpe observed many times, influenced his images. At age sixteen he enrolled at Brooklyn's Pratt Institute to study art. There he met Patti Smith, the musician, and lived and collaborated with her for some years; he graduated from Pratt in 1970. Although he toyed with other genres, Mapplethorpe experimented increasingly with photographs, first as collages he assembled from images ripped from gay pornographic magazines, then as Polaroids of models he chose himself, using a camera given him by John McKendry, his mentor, the photography curator at the Metropolitan Museum of Art. In 1975, his lover, Sam Wagstaff, also a former curator, built Mapplethorpe a studio in Manhattan. Mapplethorpe's first show, in 1976, attracted attention for the "sculptural" qualities of his prints of nudes and flowers and his studio portraits of many luminaries of the art scene. He soon moved on to large-format cameras, especially the Hasselblad, with which he began to photograph friends in Manhattan's homosexual S/M culture. Blending studio and journalistic styles, the formal composition of these photographs heightened the shock of their sexuality, especially since they indicated that Mapplethorpe was a part of this scene rather than merely an objective observer. But his frames invested his subjects with curious grace and dignity.

During the 1980s he returned to shooting flowers that seemed as sexually symbolic as the flower paintings of Georgia O'Keeffe. Still fascinated with bodies, however, he photographed Lisa Lyon, a female body-builder, as if she were male, for a famous volume, *Lady: Lisa Lyon* (1983), and collected his photographs of black nudes in *Black Males* (1980) and *Black Book* (1986), depicting them as stylized, abstract sculptures, often startling in their genital exposure. At the same time, Mapplethorpe's skill as a studio portraitist earned him respectability and income (he charged $10,000 for a sitting). His shots of celebrities, often brilliantly characterized by Mapplethorpe's eye for essentials, appeared in upscale magazines and made him a celebrity too. One after another, the world's major museums held one-man exhibits of his work, and critical assessments multiplied. Some held that the risks the photographer took were always self-serving and calculated; others parsed his innovations as revolutionary. When Sam Wagstaff died of AIDS in 1987, he left his former lover a multimillion-dollar estate with which Mapplethorpe, also ill with AIDS himself, established the Robert Mapplethorpe Foundation to support photographic arts and AIDS research. Mapplethorpe died 8 March 1989 in Boston.

Edwin Meese, III (1931–)

As U.S. attorney general under Ronald Reagan, Meese became famous for his description of the American Civil Liberties Union (ACLU) as the pawn of a nationwide "criminals' lobby," his advocacy of preventive detention, and his assertion that suspects would not have been arrested if they weren't guilty. In 1986, Meese impaneled the Attorney General's Commission on Pornography, an event designed, said his critics, to divert attention from his own involvement in the Wedtech scandal. The commission attempted unsuccessfully to link pornography with violence, harassed stores for selling *Playboy,* and published a report so prurient that its critics called it pornographic. Investigated by the Office of Government Ethics, Meese resigned in 1988 after an independent counselor asserted that he had probably violated criminal law on several occasions. Several members of the commission also fell into disgrace.

Meese was born 3 December 1931 in Oakland, California, the oldest of four sons of an Alameda County tax collector. After graduating from Oakland High School, he attended Yale University, graduating in 1953. Two years of army service interrupted his study at Berkeley Law School, from which he received his LL.B in 1958. As deputy district attorney in Alameda County he combated the free speech movement that swept Berkeley and Oakland in 1964; his reputation as a "law and order" prosecutor appealed to Governor Ronald Reagan, who in 1967 chose Meese as his secretary and (in his second term) executive assistant. From 1976 to 1980, Meese worked in private industry, practiced law, and taught criminal justice at San Diego Law School before joining Reagan's presidential campaign. Meese served as counselor to the president, a cabinet-level appointment, until 1985, when he became attorney general. He argued strenuously for expanding the secrecy classification to cover many government documents not previously so designated and for forcing government workers with access to those documents to sign pledges of permanent secrecy.

Finding new ways to restrict expression was also the mandate of the Meese Commission on Pornography, which functioned chiefly as political theater despite a lack of interest by the rest of the country (Maine rejected new antiporn legislation as the Meese hearings were taking place). The government invited antiporn feminists, conservatives, religious groups, and academics to testify. Upon hearing the disappointing testimony of some scholars who denied that research could establish links between ordinary pornography and aggression, the commissioners conceded that pornographic books were no longer dangerous but spent a great deal of time on the sexual content of visual and electronic media that some witnesses thought imperiled morality. Even supporters, however, were disturbed by the commissioners' apparent fondness for hearing about bizarre fetishes at great length. The report's legal recommendations were that dealers in adult materials be harassed until they went out of business, intimidated when they would not, imprisoned when the government could make a case, and rendered bankrupt through the Racketeer Influenced and

Corrupt Organizations statute (RICO, 1970) as often as possible. Meese endorsed its findings and called for reeducating the public to the evils of sexual representation and encouraging censorship groups to act as surrogates for the Justice Department by conducting boycotts and picketing stores. The commission's most lasting consequence was the creation of a special unit of the Justice Department with instructions to circumvent the First Amendment by treating all erotic expression as a form of contraband. Courts have since rebuked these vigilante tactics.

Henry Miller (1891–1980)

Henry Miller's *Tropic of Cancer* (1934) holds the distinction of being "the most litigated book in the history of literature." Perhaps the last major American writer to believe in the wisdom of romantic rebellion, Miller insisted that his fiction was not pornographic but obscene. Obscenity, he claimed, is the cosmic wellspring of creativity; exploring obscenity is redemptive.

Henry Valentine Miller was born in Manhattan on 26 December 1891 to an immigrant tailor and his wife, who moved to Brooklyn while the child was an infant. After a lackluster schooling hampered by the German that was his first language, Miller spent a few months at City College before lapsing back into chores at his father's tailor shop, where he spent his time reading Nietzsche, Hamsun, London, Spencer, and Bergson. He drifted from California to Washington, D.C., between 1913 and 1917, married Beatrice Wickens and fathered a child to avoid the draft, and worked as employment manager for Western Union in Brooklyn, where he learned to study the underclass, from 1920 to 1924. In 1924 he divorced Beatrice and married June Edith Smith, whose sexuality and morality would spur his literary ambitions. The two drifted along the Eastern seaboard, working at odd jobs, some of them borderline criminal, as Miller wrote one bad novel after another. In 1930, Miller traveled alone to Paris (June joined him later), where he descended into a poverty whose despair inspired him to write *Tropic of Cancer* as "a gob of spit in the face of Art, a kick in the pants to God, Man, Destiny, Time, Love, Beauty." Hailed by T. S. Eliot, Ezra Pound, Lawrence Durrell, Edmund Wilson, George Orwell, and George Bernard Shaw as a work of genius, *Tropic of Cancer* was immediately banned almost everywhere because of its raw scenes and language. Anaïs Nin, a young artist and writer who became close to Henry and June, paid for Obelisk Press to issue the novel in Paris.

Miller himself wrote in a steady stream, most notably *Black Spring* (1936), *Tropic of Capricorn* (1939), *The Air-Conditioned Nightmare* (1945), and the trilogy called *The Rosy Crucifixion* (1949, 1953, 1960). Some of these also encountered censorship. In 1961, Grove Press published *Tropic of Cancer* in the United States, an act that precipitated a series of obscenity trials that ended in 1964, when the U.S. Supreme Court cleared it in a decision that erased most of the restrictions on literature in America. Miller himself married three more times but rejected the sexual liberation of the 1960s and 1970s as tepid and self-serving. He died in Big Sur, California, his coastal home, on 7 June 1980. As befits so controversial a figure, Miller is still roundly condemned by his critics as sexist and nasty, and praised by his admirers as Whitmanesque and avant-garde.

Samuel Roth (1894–1974)

The case of Samuel Roth symbolizes the American practice of martyring individuals along the route to free speech. Roth is all the more valuable as an example because he has proved difficult to romanticize or sentimentalize. Pirate, swindler, perpetrator of frauds, outlaw, Roth embodies the classic role of the outsider/scapegoat who serves society by providing services that people want and then being condemned for doing so. Easily the most notorious pornographer in American history, Roth's name is attached to a famous U.S. Supreme Court decision (*Roth v. United States*, 1957) upholding the publisher's conviction for mailing materials that appealed to prurient interest. Every history of censorship in the United States discusses Roth's case in terms of the evolution of obscenity law, but his literary career is no less deserving of attention.

Roth was born in a village in Austria on 17 November 1894 and immigrated to the United States in 1904. His precocious achievements in a New York City high school secured a scholarship to Columbia University. After graduation, he began publishing a series of magazines, *Beau: The Man's Magazine* (1924); *Two Worlds Monthly: Devoted to the Increase of the Gaiety of Nations* (1926–1927), notable for its unauthorized condensation and expurgation of James Joyce's *Ulysses* but also for stories by writers as diverse as Boccaccio and Clement Wood, and for erotic illustrations by Austin Spare, Alexander King, and Cecil French; *Casanova Jr.'s Tales* (1929); *American Aphrodite* (1951–1955), a quarterly containing works of erotica by well-known writers such as

Henry Miller, G. S. Viereck, Frank Harris, and Roth himself, often illustrated; and *Good Times: A Review of the World of Pleasure* (1954–1956), whose content was similar. In 1930, when Roth published unexpurgated passages from *Ulysses*, he was sentenced to sixty days in jail; in 1935, when he published *The Kama Sutra* and *The Perfumed Garden*, he was sentenced to ninety days; in 1936, when he sold *Lady Chatterley's Lover* through the mails, he was sentenced to three years.

Roth himself wrote *The Private Life of Frank Harris*, a study of the English-American author of erotica; *Diary of a Smut Hound* (under the pseudonym Hugh Wakem), an attack on vice officers; *Stone Walls Do Not: The Chronicle of a Captivity*, an account of his imprisonment and a plea for free speech; and a number of erotic works. Though he tried to protect himself by changing the names of his presses and using other dodges to diversify his enterprises, his refusal to stop publishing made him a target for the New York Society for the Suppression of Vice, for the U.S. Post Office, and for other federal agencies. In 1954, after courageously defending himself and the First Amendment before a U.S. Senate committee investigating pornography and juvenile delinquency, Roth was indicted for selling copies of Aubrey Beardsley's *Venus and Tannhauser*. When the U.S. Supreme Court upheld his conviction, the 63-year-old publisher went to jail for five years. Ironically, the Supreme Court's opinion, which included the argument that the "dominant theme of the material taken as a whole appeals to the prurient interest" of "the average person," led rapidly to other decisions that cleared the very works Roth had sold. Roth, however, remained in jail. He died in New York on 3 July 1974.

Annie Sprinkle (1954–)

In recent years, women working in sex industries have drawn on their experiences to become performance artists, appearing on avant-garde stages to dramatize esthetic, moral, and political issues. Probably the best known is Annie Sprinkle, veteran porn film actress and creator of startling performance art. On stage, Sprinkle "deconstructs" and demystifies women's sexuality, usually by appearing nude and inviting members of the audience to inspect her genitals ("A Public Cervix Announcement") while she speaks about masturbation, menstruation, and discrimination against women. In the performance piece "Bosom Ballet," for example, she bounces her large breasts rhythmically until the sheer exaggeration reveals the absurdity of human self-consciousness and desire. (Prints made from the performance are now in venues such as the Columbus, Ohio, Museum of Art.) Her critics attack her for objectifying women's bodies and thus reinforcing sexism. Her admirers believe that her subversions of convention return control of women's bodies to themselves by breaking the "male gaze." If there were no controversy, observes Sprinkle, there would be no point to her performances.

Sprinkle was born Ellen F. Sternberg on 23 July 1954 in Philadelphia. After attending high school in Panama when her father took a job there, she began a series of sexual experiments, first in a commune in Tucson, Arizona, then as a prostitute there. A meeting with Gerard Damiano, director of *Deep Throat*, led to a career in pornographic films. Over several years she worked as a model, dominatrix, and stripper in New York, and began a mail order business for sexual materials, including various fetish publications of her own (especially one called *Piss Art*, the magazine that celebrated her nom-de-plume). In the mid-1980s, Richard Schechner, a drama professor at New York University, invited her to participate in *The Prometheus Project*, a performance series dealing with, among other things, sex. Soon she was collaborating with other performance artists, such as Veronica Vera, Linda Montano, and (tattooist) Spider Webb, with whom she experimented with installations and artistic events. Her odd photographs, especially those that transformed ordinary women into "sex goddesses," earned Sprinkle exhibitions in galleries and coverage on cable channels. Her documentary film *Linda/Les and Annie: The First Female to Male Transsexual Love Story* (1995), though graphic in its depiction of intercourse between Sprinkle and her surgically altered lover, probably says more about transgender issues than any academic text on the subject.

The protean Sprinkle, whose intercourse with the widest possible number of humans and objects invests her with enormous authority, asserts that virtually all important female performance artists have come out of sex industries and that pornographic genres profoundly influence culture today. Numerous critics have observed that her cheerful and sincere stage presence demonstrates her conviction that sex at base is performance; she seems entirely untouched by sexual experiences that many Americans think of as degrading. Sprinkle's autobiography, *Post Porn Modernist*, recaps her experiences as actor in and director of porn films, author of some 300 articles, editor of outrageous 'zines, professional photographer, feminist, and relentless explorer of sex, gender, eroticism, and obscenity. She opposes censorship but declines to indulge in the name-calling so common to current debate.

Nadine Strossen (1950–)

Free speech takes precedence over everything, says Nadine Strossen, president of the American Civil Liberties Union, especially where pornography is concerned. Although males have historically been dominant in the production of pornography, and while male sensibilities have traditionally skewed sexual representation toward gratification for males, says Strossen, pornography can also empower women by giving their sexual fantasies and aspirations a voice. Suppressing sexual expression in the name of gender equity, then, is not simply unconstitutional but also mistaken. Strossen's *Defending Pornography: Free Speech, Sex, and the Fight for Women's Rights* (1995) encountered not simply the ire of conservative Americans but also the rancor of many antiporn feminists, who accused her of defending those who foster discrimination by objectifying women.

Strossen was born 18 August 1950 in Jersey City, New Jersey, to a family noted for taking unpopular positions. A champion debater in high school, she frequently defended minority positions. From Harvard-Radcliffe College, where she graduated in 1972, she moved on to Harvard Law School, where she became editor of the *Law Review*, one of the school's top honors. In 1984, after nine years of practicing law, she began teaching civil rights and constitutional law at the New York University Law School, then became a law professor there. Her career with the ACLU began in 1983, when she joined its board of directors; she became a national general counsel in 1986 and its first female and youngest president in 1991.

Like it or not, says Strossen, many people use pornographic genres to express discontent, to subvert the status quo, and to convey unpopular ideas, all activities specifically protected by the Constitution. She rejects as myth the radical feminist position that pornographers invariably force women to appear in visual porn and says that the Constitution and common sense deny that the Fourteenth Amendment (which antiporn feminists invoke to counter speech that discriminates against women as a class) can take precedence over the First. According to Strossen, speech is not equivalent to action, as antiporn feminists maintain, nor is there any scientific evidence supporting the antiporn feminist claim that garden-variety pornography leads to violence against women. Also, she points out, censorship—however rational-ized—always targets the weakest voices, and women's voices will be the first (she points to Canadian antipornography legisla-tion that does just that). Women must be free to produce and con-sume pornography themselves, to enjoy the pleasure and the communication it offers, and to alter the tropes and conventions of sexual expression to suit themselves. Given human ignorance about sexuality and gender, Americans must be free to explore these subjects however they wish, limited only by demonstrable harm to others, she believes.

Reuben Sturman (1924–)

Until recently, the three largest dealers in pornography in the United States were Parliament News of Los Angeles, founded by Milton Luros; Peachtree Enterprises of Atlanta, founded by Michael Thevis; and Sovereign News of Cleveland, founded by Reuben Sturman. To one degree or another, all had connections with organized crime. Sturman, generally acknowledged to be in first place, once owned (in addition to Sovereign News) Auto-matic Vending, a company that manufactured peep machines; Western Amusements, a chain of peep arcades; *Eros*, a magazine (not to be confused with Ralph Ginzburg's famous journal); and a chain of 800 adult bookstore outlets. In 1989, Sturman was con-victed of tax evasion; in 1991 he went to prison.

A classic example of American entrepreneurship, Sturman's career also illustrates the process by which marginalized indus-tries move from criminal fringe to mainstream enterprises. Born in 1924 in Cleveland, Ohio, Sturman attended Western Reserve University on the GI Bill after service in the Army Air Corps dur-ing World War II. Operating at first out of his Cleveland home, he delivered comic books and magazines to retail stores; by 1959 he had built Sovereign News into a giant distributorship covering eight states. Realizing that the sex magazines that began to ap-pear in the 1960s were far more lucrative than other kinds, he gradually established a near-monopoly that, according to prose-cutors, attracted the attention of the Gambino crime family, which demanded a share.

Sturman vertically integrated his companies by publishing magazines, controlling their distribution, and opening his own sex stores to sell them. Sovereign News of Cleveland secretly controlled Bon-Jay Sales of Baltimore, for example, and Sturman operated other companies through more than twenty aliases.

Similar strategies captured the market for pornographic films. Sturman devised the peep booth, a coin-operated projector in a cubicle so that patrons of his stores could view 8-millimeter "loop" films in private. His subsidiary Automatic Vending built the booths, maintained them, and placed them in his own and other arcades across the nation, taking in return a percentage of the revenues from exhibition of films that Sturman's companies had shot. Always technologically ahead of his competition, Sturman moved aggressively into sexual aids and appliances (he founded the Doc Johnson Company, largest supplier of novelties in the world) and into videotape formats that began to displace movies. By 1980, he had become the quintessential American capitalist; Sturman controlled the lion's share of his product market in every state and in more than forty countries.

Beginning in 1964, however, the Justice Department raided his warehouses and indicted him again and again on obscenity charges. These Sturman easily brushed aside. Fearing that it would not be able to prove antitrust abuses or racketeering charges, the government chose instead to demonstrate that Sturman had evaded taxes on the millions in profits that his enterprises generated. (One prosecutor ingeniously weighed containers of quarters from the peep-booths to estimate actual income.) In 1992 Sturman escaped from prison but was recaptured after eight weeks. Now in his seventies, he is serving a nineteen-year sentence. The effect of legal action against Sturman and other crime-connected figures has been to diminish the role of organized crime and to open pornographic industries to standard business and accounting practices. Where pornographic videos are concerned, for instance, the big six companies (VCA, Evil Angel, Western Visuals, and so on) now dominate the industry after the model set by their major Hollywood studio counterparts in the legitimate film industry.

Donald Wildmon (1938–)

Donald Wildmon founded the American Family Association (AFA) as a watchdog group devoted to reducing depictions of sex and violence on television. One of the most well-organized and well-financed political action lobbies, the American Family Association employs efficient direct-mail operations to combat expressions endorsing promiscuity, abortion, homosexuality, and blasphemy. Over the years the group has called for restrictions on the content of broadcast and cable television programming, movies, books in libraries, videotapes, and audio recordings. The AFA's tactics have been aggressive. In 1989 it circulated the names and phone numbers of all members of Congress who voted against restricting the funds from the National Endowment for the Arts to artists who signed a "decency" pledge. In 1990, David Wojnarowizc successfully applied for an injunction preventing Wildmon from isolating images from the artist's exhibitions, then displaying them in a pornographic configuration that the organization sent out as direct-mail, although some legal scholars believe that the injunction improperly constituted prior restraint. In 1991, *Damned in the USA*, a documentary by British journalists Paul Yule and Jonathan Stack, depicted Wildmon as one of the most rancorous of partisans. Wildmon tried unsuccessfully to ban showings of the documentary in the United States.

Wildmon was born in 1938 in Ripley, Mississippi, a rural town in northeastern Mississippi. His mother was a schoolteacher, and his father was the venereal disease investigator for the Mississippi Health Department. After graduating from Millsaps College in 1960 and serving in the army, he took a graduate divinity degree at Emory University in 1965. While minister of a Methodist Church in Southhaven, Mississippi, in 1976, he became outraged at the anti-Christian content of national television programming, gave up the formal ministry, and moved to Tupelo, Mississippi, to start the National Federation for Decency (which changed its name in 1987). In 1978 he launched his first boycott of advertisers who sponsored programs such as *Charlie's Angels, Three's Company,* and *All in the Family.* Wildmon and Jerry Falwell of the Moral Majority created the Coalition for Better Television and urged members and affiliates to monitor programming for incidents of sex, violence, and profanity. Although Falwell pulled out after a year, Wildmon has continued to pressure companies ranging from Holiday Inn to Pepsi, Waldenbooks, Clorox, and Mennen. Perhaps the most famous boycotts coordinated by the AFA were those directed at *The Last Temptation of Christ*, the film version of Nikos Kazantzakis's novel, and *Mighty Mouse*, the television cartoon series. Wildmon has written more than twenty books, chiefly on religious themes, including *The Case against Pornography* (1986), which argues that explicit sexual representation is anti-Christian because of its emphasis on the body.

Documents and Statistics 5

Court Decisions

The evolution of judicial tolerance is an important strand in the history of pornography in the United States. At present, pornography is quite legal in this country. Obscenity is not. Along with ordinary citizens, American jurists have tended to confuse the two terms, and many decisions have turned on whether the works in question inspired disgust or sexual arousal. Study of historical periods and cultural contexts does not always clarify matters.

Regina v. Hicklin (L.R. [3 Q.B.C.] 360 1868)

Until well into the twentieth century, American judges followed English common law concerning obscenity, consistently citing the Hicklin decision, the first judicial response to Lord Campbell's Act of 1857 forbidding the sale and distribution of what was called "obscene libel."

> The test for obscenity is this, whether the tendency of the matter charged as obscenity is to deprave and corrupt those whose minds are open to such immoral influences,

and into whose hands a publication of this sort may fall.—Lord Cockburn

People v. Doris (14 A.D. 117 appeal dismissed, 153 N.Y. 678 [1897])

Just how the Hicklin principle was applied is visible in a New York State Supreme Court opinion upholding the conviction of a filmstrip seized soon after the motion picture camera was invented. Fear of the new technology sharpened condemnation.

> The pantomime "Orange Blossoms" is considered a "representation" which "suggests indecency." That test is whether the picture presented to the eye "is naturally calculated to excite in a spectator impure imagination, and whether the other incidents and qualities, however attractive, were merely accessory to this as the primary or main purposes of the representation. . . . We need only say that the test to which reference has been made embraces any picture which tends to deprave and corrupt the morals of those whose minds are open to such influences. . . . Such a performance as that under consideration is really more dangerous to public morals than any mere vulgar exhibition of nudity. The latter may arouse impure thoughts, but is more apt to excite disgust. The greater danger lies in an appeal to the imagination, and when the suggestion is immoral the more that is left to the imagination the more subtle and seductive the influence.—Judge Barnett

Mutual Film Corp. v. Industrial Commission of Ohio (236 U.S. 230 [1915]

Faced with the State of Ohio's desire to ban D. W. Griffith's film *Birth of a Nation* as immoral, the U.S. Supreme Court perhaps thought to end such litigation entirely by relegating motion pictures to the status of carnival shows, tainted by profit motives, and thus not entitled to the protection of the First Amendment.

> It cannot be put out of view that the exhibition of moving pictures is a business, pure and simple, originated and conducted for profit, like other spectacles, not to be

regarded by the Ohio constitution, we think, as part of the press of the country or as organs of public opinion. They are representations of events, of ideas and sentiments published and known, vivid, useful and entertaining, no doubt, but as we have said, capable of evil, having power for it, the greater because of their attractiveness and manner of exhibition.—Justice McKenna

Halsey v. New York Society for the Suppression of Vice (180 N.Y.S. 836 [1920])

By 1920, smut-hunting had become a profession attractive to the sincere and the hypocritical alike. Censors searched through a book for the passages that made the work obscene in order to testify to the pernicious effects that exposure to such words would occasion. In 1920, however, a judge in New York cast doubt on this practice.

In the first place, I think it was improper to allow the attorney to select such quotations as he desired to read, which may never have been in the mind of the complaining witness, Sumner [head of the New York Society for the Suppression of Vice], when he made the charge against the plaintiff. The most he could have testified to under any conditions was what he honestly believed were indecent or lascivious passages, or the general character of the book, when he made the complaint. What counsel might think were indecent passages, selected months or years afterwards, was quite immaterial. In the second place, counsel for defendant had already agreed that the court should pass upon the character of the book as a question of law. He did not ask the court to decide the question then, nor ask that the jury be allowed to decide the character of the book. The book (as a whole) was already regarded by the community as a standard literary work.

No work may be judged from a selection of such paragraphs alone. Printed by themselves, they might, as a matter of law, come with the prohibition of the statute. So might a similar selection from Aristophanes or Chaucer or Boccaccio, or even from the Bible. The book, however, must be considered broadly, as a whole.—Judge Andrews

United States v. One Book Called "Ulysses" (5 F. Supp. 182 [1933])

One threat to expression was the condemnation of a book, magazine, or film before it had actually been published or distributed, on suspicion that the expression in it was obscene. The Customs Department and the U.S. Post Office sometimes prohibited works on that basis, but other agencies tried also. Here the courts sensed the need to assert their function as arbiters, and in *Near v. Minnesota* (283 U.S. 697 [1931]) one of them ruled that *prior restraint* infringed on freedom of the press.

Judge John M. Woolsey of the District Court of New York hammered the growing fissures in previously monolithic obscenity laws by ruling that a book must be considered as a whole, not just as the sum of isolated parts. Perhaps because it involved one of the world's great literary works, Woolsey's is the most famous of all American decisions regarding obscenity.

> In any case where a book is claimed to be obscene it must first be determined, whether the intent with which it was written was what is called, according to the usual phrase, pornographic, that is, written for the purpose of exploiting obscenity.
>
> Reading *Ulysses* in its entirety, as a book must be read on such a test as this, did not tend to excite sexual impulses or lustful thoughts, but that its net effect on them was only that of a somewhat tragic and very powerful commentary on the inner lives of men and women.
>
> But my considered opinion, after long reflection, is that, whilst in many places the effect of *Ulysses* on the reader undoubtedly is somewhat emetic, nowhere does it tend to be an aphrodisiac.—Judge Woolsey

United States v. One Book Entitled Ulysses by James Joyce (Random House Inc.) (72 F.2d 705 [1934])

When the *Ulysses* decision was appealed by the government, the case went to the appellate court of Augustus Hand, who upheld Woolsey's argument.

> That numerous long passages in *Ulysses* contain matter that is obscene under any fair definition of the word can-

not be gainsaid; yet they are relevant to the purpose of depicting the thoughts of the characters and are introduced to give meaning to the whole, rather than promote lust or portray filth for its own sake. The net effect even of portions most open to attack, such as the closing monologue of the wife of Leopold Bloom, is pitiful and tragic, rather than lustful.

The book as a whole is not pornographic and, while in a few spots it is coarse, blasphemous, and obscene, it does not in our opinion, tend to promote lust.

We think that *Ulysses* is a book of originality and sincerity of treatment and that it has not the effect of promoting lust. Accordingly, it does not fall within the statute, even though it justly may offend many.—Justice Hand

Hannegan, Postmaster General v. Esquire, Inc. (327 U.S. 146 [1946])

Other forces were at work, among them interagency rivalry over which agencies of government held the privilege of censoring expression. The prohibitions against contraband in the 1930 Tariff Act transferred authority for determining whether an article is obscene from the Customs Department and the U.S. Post Office to the courts. The Post Office resisted the erosion of its power. Members of the House Subcommittee on the Post Office and Post Roads held hearings in 1935 to assert the necessity of having postal inspectors censor obscenity in the mails, especially forbidden birth-control materials. When the Post Office continued to interdict materials, the courts began to take notice. In 1943 Postmaster General Frank Walker denied second-class mailing privileges to *Esquire*, a magazine he said was immoral. The case reached the Supreme Court in 1946, by which time a new postmaster general was in office. The Court rebuked the agency by deciding that the Post Office could not exercise prior restraint, that is, prohibit material unless it had been ruled obscene by a court. The ruling diminished the power of the Post Office.

It is plain, as we have said, that the favorable second class rates were granted periodicals meeting the requirements of the Fourth condition, so that the public good might be served through dissemination of the periodicals described. But that is a far cry from assuming that a

Congress had any idea that each applicant for the second-class rate must convince the Postmaster General
that his publication positively contributes to the public
good or public welfare. Under our system of government
there is an accommodation for the widest varieties of
tastes and ideas. . . . But a requirement that literature or
art conform to some norm prescribed by an official
smacks of an ideology foreign to our system.This is not
to say that there is nothing left to the Postmaster General
under the Fourth condition. . . . But the power to determine whether a periodical (which is mailable) contains
information of a public character, literature or art does
not include the further power to determine whether the
contents meet some standard of the public good or welfare.—Justice Douglas

Joseph Burnstyn, Inc., v. Wilson, Commissioner of Education of New York (343 U.S. 495 [1952])

In 1952, the Supreme Court reversed its 1915 decision on the status of motion pictures. When the State of New York charged the
motion picture *The Miracle* with sacrilege, the Court ruled that
cinema is protected by the First and Fourteenth Amendments because it is a channel of information and ideas.

It cannot be doubted that motion pictures are a significant
medium for the communication of ideas. They may affect
public attitudes and behavior in a variety of ways, ranging from direct espousal of a political or social doctrine to
the subtle shaping of thought which characterizes all
artistic expression. The importance of motion pictures as
an organ of public opinion is not lessened by the fact that
they are designed to entertain as well as to inform.
    That books, newspapers and magazines are pub-
lished and sold for profit does not prevent them from
being a form of expression whose liberty is safeguarded
by the First Amendment. We fail to see why operation
for profit should have any different effect in the case of
motion pictures.
    It is further urged that motion pictures possess a
greater capacity for evil, particularly among the youth of
a community, than any other mode of expression. Even if

one were to accept this hypothesis, it does not follow that motion pictures should be disqualified from First Amendment protection. If there be capacity for evil it may be relevant in determining the permissible scope of community control, but it does not authorize substantially unbridled censorship such as we have here.

For the foregoing reasons, we conclude that expression by means of motion pictures is included within the free speech and free press guarantee of the First and Fourteenth Amendments.—Justice Clark

Butler v. Michigan (352 U.S. 380 [1957])

In 1957, the Supreme Court repudiated the Hicklin principle by observing in *Butler v. Michigan* that it discriminated against adults.

The State insists that, by thus quarantining the general reading public against books not too rugged for grown men and women in order to shield juvenile innocence, it is surely exercising its power to promote the general welfare. Surely, this is to burn the house to roast the pig.

We have before us legislation not reasonably restricted to the evil with which it is said to deal. The incidence of this enactment is to reduce the adult population of Michigan to reading only what is fit for children.—Justice Frankfurter

Roth v. United States (354 U.S. 476 [1957])

That same year the Court began building a new constitutional test for obscenity, starting with the famous *Roth* case, named after a veteran and unrepentant pornography publisher. To suggest that the Court achieved unanimity, however, would be misleading. Between 1957 until 1967, when the Court decided thirteen major obscenity cases, the nine justices filed fifty-five *different* concurring or dissenting opinions.[1] The premise of *Roth* was that obscenity, being "utterly without redeeming social value," was not entitled to First Amendment protection. By the same token, material with any such value could not be obscene. Roth's conviction was upheld nonetheless, on the grounds that the materials (copies of Aubrey Beardsley's *Venus and Tannhauser*) appealed to prurient interest. Some justices observed that the majority opinion did not define "the average person," the specific "community" or the process for determining its standards, or "prurient interest."

The fundamental freedoms of speech and press have contributed greatly to the development and well-being of our free society and are indispensable to its continued growth. Ceaseless vigilance is the watchword to prevent their erosion by Congress or by the State. The door barring federal and state intrusion into this area cannot be left ajar; it must be kept tightly closed and open only the slightest crack to prevent encroachment upon more important interests. It is therefore vital that the standards for judging obscenity safeguard the protection of freedom of speech and press for material which does not treat sex in a manner appealing to a prurient interest.

All ideas having even the slightest redeeming social importance—unorthodox ideas, controversial ideas, even ideas hateful to the prevailing climate of opinion—have the full protection of the guarantees, unless excludable because they encroach upon the limited area of more important interests.

[The test for obscenity is] whether to the average person, applying contemporary community standards, the dominant theme of the material taken as a whole appeals to prurient interest.

Roth's argument that the federal obscenity statute unconstitutionally encroaches upon the powers reserved by the Ninth and Tenth Amendments to the State and to the people to punish speech and press where offensive to decency and morality is hinged upon his contention that obscenity is expression not excepted from the provision of the First Amendment that "Congress shall make no law . . . abridging freedom of speech or of the press. . . ." That argument fails in light of our holding that obscenity is not expression protected by the First Amendment. We therefore hold that the federal obscenity statute punishing the use of the mails for obscene materials is a proper exercise of the postal power delegated to Congress.—Justice Brennan

Excelsior Pictures Corp. v. Regents of the University of the State of New York (3 N.Y. 2d 237 [1957])

The Supreme Court's more liberal interpretation made itself felt in lower courts that same year, as in one involving the *Garden of Eden*, a nudist film. The decision had the effect of warning censors not to seize on mere nudity as a reason for suppression.

> Since the Constitution forbids any prior restraint of a motion picture which is not obscene and since this film has not been found to be obscene or rejected because of obscenity and since it is not obscene by any standard we ever heard of, we could end this opinion right here. Nudity in itself and without lewdness or dirtiness is not obscenity in law or in common sense. . . . For more than a century the New York courts have held that exposure of the body to the view of others is not criminal if there be no lewd intent. . . . Nothing sexually impure or filthy is shown or suggested in *Garden of Eden* and so there is no legal basis for censorship.—Judge Desmond

Kingsley Int'l Pictures Corp. v. Regents of the University of the State of New York (360 U.S. 684 [1959])

In 1959, the Supreme Court reversed the conviction of a distributor of a French movie based on *Lady Chatterley's Lover* on grounds that "ideological obscenity," in this case adultery, is an "idea" and therefore protected speech. In other words, authorities could not ban a work simply because it dealt with sexual themes.

> What New York has done, therefore, is to prevent the exhibition of a motion picture because that picture advocates an idea—that adultery under certain circumstances may be proper behavior. Yet the First Amendment's basic guarantee is of freedom to advocate ideas. The State, quite simply, has thus struck at the very heart of constitutionally protected liberty.—Justice Stewart

Smith v. California (361 U.S. 147 [1959])

In another refinement, the Supreme Court ruled that to be found guilty of selling an obscene book, the seller must know ahead of time that the book is obscene. Since it would be impossible for the dealer to read every book in the store before offering it for sale, the requirement would constitute a burden that would cause the public to suffer from a limited stock of information.

> If the contents of bookshops and periodical stands were restricted to material of which their proprietors had made a inspection, they might be depleted indeed. The bookseller's limitation in the amount of reading material with which he could familiarize himself, and his timidity in the face of his criminal liability, thus would tend to restrict the public's access to forms of the printed word which the State could not constitutionally suppress directly. The bookseller's self-censorship, compelled by the State, would be a censorship affecting the whole public, hardly less virulent for being privately administered. Through it, the distribution of all books, both obscene and not obscene, would be impeded.
>
> It is plain to us that the ordinance in question, though aimed at obscene matter, has such a tendency to inhibit constitutionally protected expression that it cannot stand under the Constitution.—Justice Brennan

Manual Enterprises, Inc., v. Day, Postmaster General (370 U.S. 478 [1962])

To some Americans, homosexual materials remained obscene by definition. The Supreme Court decided, however, that the U.S. Post Office could not ban homosexual magazines from the mails, using Section 1461 of the U.S. Code, simply because they were about homosexuals or addressed to a homosexual audience. More to the point, the *Manual* decision strengthened the "prurient interest" test of *Roth*: a work had to appeal to "prurient interest" in "a patently offensive way."

> For we find lacking in these magazines an element which, no less than "prurient interest," is essential to a valid determination of obscenity under 1461, and to which neither the Post Office Department nor the Court

of Appeals addressed itself at all: these magazines cannot be deemed so offensive on their faces to affront current community standards of decency—a quality that we shall hereafter refer to as "patent offensiveness" or "indecency." Lacking that quality, the magazines cannot be deemed legally "obscene," and we need not consider the question of the proper "audience" by which their "prurient interest" appeal should be judged.

The words of 1461, "obscene, lewd, lascivious, indecent, filthy or vile," connote something that is portrayed in manner so offensive as to make it unacceptable under current community mores. While in common usage the words have different shades of meaning, the statute since its inception has always been taken as aimed at obnoxiously debasing portrayals of sex. . . . These particular magazines are not subject to repression under 1461.—Justices Harlan and Stewart

Jacobellis v. Ohio (378 U.S. 184 [1964])

A 1964 ruling set the stage for greater controversy when Justice William Brennan, writing for the majority, added that a work to be judged obscene must be shown to lack "redeeming social importance" according to "national contemporary standards," not merely local ones.

It is true that local communities throughout the land are in fact diverse, and that in cases such as this one the Court is confronted with the task of reconciling the rights of such communities with the rights of individuals. Communities vary, however, in many respects other than their toleration of alleged obscenity, and such variances have never been considered to require or justify a varying standard for application of the Federal Constitution.

The Court has explicitly refused to tolerate a result whereby the constitutional limits of free expression in the Nation would vary with state lines; we see even less justification for allowing such limits to vary with town or county lines. We thus reaffirm the position taken in *Roth* to the effect that the constitutional status of an allegedly obscene work must be determined on the basis of a national standard. It is, after all, a national Constitution we are expounding.—Justices Brennan and Goldberg

Ginzburg v. United States (383 U.S. 463 [1965])

Although it was still following the standards set in *Roth*, the Court decided in the case of publisher Ralph Ginzburg that the motive of the seller mattered. It upheld Ginzburg's conviction on the grounds that though the works in question were not obscene, he did pander through the mails by advertising them salaciously and postmarking them from places such as Blue Balls, Montana, and Intercourse, Pennsylvania.

> Where the purveyor's sole emphasis is on the sexually provocative aspects of his publications, that fact may be decisive in the determination of obscenity. Certainly in a prosecution which, as here, does not necessarily imply suppression of the materials involved, the fact that they originate or are used as a subject of pandering is relevant to the application of the Roth test.
> We perceive no threat to First Amendment guarantees in thus holding that in close cases evidence of pandering may be probative with respect to the nature of the material in question and thus satisfy the Roth test. . . . The fact that each of these publications was created or exploited entirely on the basis of its appeal to prurient interests strengthens the conclusion that transactions here were sales of illicit merchandise, not sales of constitutionally protected matter.—Justice Brennan

Memoirs v. Massachusetts (383 U.S. 413 [1966])

That same year, the Court reversed the finding of a Massachusetts court that the novel *Fanny Hill* was obscene, and thus brought to an end the seemingly endless litigation over the "big three": *Lady Chatterley's Lover* (cleared 1959), *Tropic of Cancer* (cleared 1964), and *Fanny Hill, or Memoirs of a Woman of Pleasure*. Moreover, the decision in *Memoirs* established that a work had to fail *all* three *Roth* principles: it must (1) have a prurient interest that (2) appeals in a patently offensive way, and (3) lack socially redeeming value.

> The Supreme Judicial Court erred in holding that a book need not be "unqualifiedly worthless before it can be

deemed obscene." A book cannot be proscribed unless it is found to be utterly without redeeming social value. This is so even though the book is found to possess the requisite prurient appeal and to be patently offensive. Each of the three federal constitutional criteria is to be applied independently; the social value of the book can neither be weighed against nor canceled by its prurient interest appeal or patent offensiveness. Hence, even on the view of the court below that *Memoirs* possessed only a modicum of social value, its judgment must be reversed as being founded on an erroneous interpretation of a federal constitutional standard.—Justices Brennan and Fortas

Redrup v. New York (386 U.S. 767 [1966])

Henceforth it would be difficult to prosecute works of fiction for obscenity in the United States. It might be possible, said the Court in 1967, to prosecute the *distribution* of questionable works if (1) they were clearly aimed at children, (2) they were marketed so aggressively that unwilling audiences could not escape exposure, or (3) the distributor was clearly pandering. In *Redrup v. New York*, the Court reversed three state obscenity convictions but offered those categories as possible grounds for prosecution in future.

> In none of the cases was there a claim that the statute in question reflected a specific and limited state concern for juveniles. . . . In none was there any suggestion of an assault upon individual privacy by publication in a manner so obtrusive as to make it impossible for an unwilling individual to avoid exposure to it. . . . And in none was there evidence of a sort of "pandering" which the Court found significant in *Ginzburg v. United States.*— Justice Fortas

Stanley v. Georgia (394 U.S. 557 [1969])

In an effort to recapture some of its power to regulate expression, the State of Georgia convicted a man of possessing pornographic films for his private use. Police discovered the films when they raided the man's home on an entirely unrelated bookkeeping charge. The Supreme Court overturned his conviction, ruling that it was not illegal to own obscene materials for one's own personal use, especially in light of the right to privacy in one's own home.

> But we think that mere categorization of these films as obscene is insufficient justification for such a drastic invasion of personal liberties guaranteed by the First and Fourteenth Amendments. Whatever may be the justification for other statutes regulating obscenity, we do not think they reach into the privacy of one's own home. If the First Amendment means anything it means that a State has no business telling a man, sitting alone in his own house, what books he may read or what films he may watch. Our whole constitutional heritage rebels at the thought of giving government the power to control men's minds.
>
> We hold that the First and Fourteenth Amendments prohibit making mere private possession of obscene material a crime. . . . As we have said, the State retains broad power to regulate obscenity; that power does not extend to mere possession by the individual in the privacy of his own home.—Justice Marshall

Miller v. California (413 U.S. 15 [1973])

By now, the composition of what had been called the Warren Court (after Chief Justice Earl Warren, 1953–1969) had shifted under Chief Justice Warren Burger. In a series of decisions, the Warren Court had refined *Roth* to establish the "utterly without redeeming social value" test: a work could be proscribed only if to "the average person," "applying national contemporary standards," "the dominant theme of the material taken as a whole appeals to the prurient interests in a patently offensive way" and "has no redeeming social importance." Burger and his conservative colleagues thought that such decisions had gone too far. They chose to ignore President Lyndon Johnson's Commission on Obscenity and Pornography, which recommended in 1970 that pornography be decriminalized for adults in the United States. The Burger Court in *Miller v. California* and its companion case, *Paris Adult Theatre I v. Slaton*, redefined the prurient interest test as "whether the work depicts or describes, in a patently offensive way, sexual conduct specifically defined by state law." That stipulation in effect invited states to prohibit certain conduct. Writing for the majority, Burger also rejected the "utterly without redeeming social value" test as too broad. He redefined the standard to read "whether the work, taken as a whole, lacks serious literary, artistic, political or scientific value," a much weaker statement of the standard of *any* redeeming value established by *Roth*. Just as significant was his redefinition of "contemporary standards" to mean those of a local, not a national, community.

> We do not adopt as a constitutional standard the "utterly without redeeming social value" test of *Memoirs v. Massachusetts*; that concept has never commanded the adherence of more than three Justices at one time.
> It is neither realistic nor constitutionally sound to read the First Amendment as requiring that the people of Maine or Mississippi accept public depiction of conduct found tolerable in Las Vegas or New York City.
> In sum, we a) reaffirm the *Roth* holding that obscene material is not protected by the First Amendment; b) hold that such material can be regulated by the States, subject to the specific safeguards enunciated above, without a showing that the material is "utterly without redeeming social value"; and c) hold that obscenity is to be determined by applying "contemporary community standards" . . . not national standards.—Justice Burger

Paris Adult Theatre v. Slaton (413 U.S. 49 [1973])

As if to reintroduce the provisions of *Hicklin*, Burger in the *Paris* decision asserted that government may act "to protect the weak, the uninformed, the unsuspecting, and the gullible" from their own weaknesses by prohibiting certain expression. He also attempted to erode the right of privacy; in *Paris*, the Court held that states (in this case Georgia) can close adult theaters.

> Commercial exploitation of depictions, descriptions or exhibitions of obscene conduct on commercial premises open to the adult public fall within a State's broad power to regulate commerce and protect the public environment. The issue in this context goes beyond whether someone, or even the majority, considers the conduct depicted as "wrong" or "sinful." The States have the power

to make a morally neutral judgment that public exhibition of obscene material, or commerce in such material, has a tendency to injure the community as a whole, to endanger the public safety, or to jeopardize . . . the States' right . . . to maintain a decent society.

We have directed our holdings, not at thoughts or speech, but a depiction and description of specifically defined sexual conduct that States may regulate within limits designed to prevent infringement of First Amendment rights. We have also reaffirmed . . . that commerce in obscene material is unprotected by any constitutional doctrine of privacy.—Justice Burger

Jenkins v. Georgia (418 U.S. 153 [1974])

The temptation for conservative states was too great to ignore. On the basis of *Miller*, a Georgia court promptly convicted *Carnal Knowledge* (1971), a mainstream Hollywood film directed by Mike Nichols and starring Ann-Margaret, of obscenity. The Supreme Court reversed the conviction and tried to indicate that it had not intended to declare a field day for every censor offended by any sexual theme.

Our own viewing of the film satisfies us that *Carnal Knowledge* could not be found under the *Miller* standards to depict sexual conduct in a patently offensive way. Nothing in the movie falls within either of the two examples given in *Miller* of material which may constitutionally be found to meet the "patently offensive" element of those standards, nor is there anything sufficiently similar to such material to justify similar treatment. While the subject matter of the picture is, in a broader sense, sex, and there are scenes in which sexual conduct including ultimate sexual acts is to be understood to be taking place, the camera does not focus on the bodies of the actors at such times. There is no exhibition whatever of the actors' genitals, lewd, or otherwise, during these scenes. There are occasional scenes of nudity, but nudity alone is not enough to make material legally obscene under the *Miller* standards.

We hold that the film could not, as a matter of constitutional law, be found to depict sexual conduct in a patently offensive way, and it is therefore not outside the protection of the First and Fourteenth Amendments because it is obscene.—Justice Rehnquist

Young, Mayor of Detroit, v. American Mini-Theatres, Inc. (427 U.S. 50 [1976]

By 1976, municipalities shifted their attack to zoning adult businesses rather than try to suppress the content of expression that even conservatives found difficult to deny was covered by the First Amendment. In a major case, the Court ruled that Detroit could regulate sex-related businesses by requiring them not to cluster together.

> Putting to one side for the moment the fact that adult motion picture theaters must satisfy a locational restriction not applicable to other theaters, we are also persuaded that the 100-foot restriction does not, in itself, create an impermissible restraint on protected communication. . . . In short, apart from the fact that the ordinance treats adult theaters differently from other theaters and the fact that the classification is predicated on the content of material shown in the respective theaters, the regulation of the place where such films may be exhibited does not offend the First Amendment.
>
> Since what is ultimately at stake is nothing more than a limitation on the place where adult films may be exhibited, even though the determination of whether a particular film fits that characterization turns on the nature of its content, we conclude that the city's interest in the present and future character of its neighborhoods adequately supports its classification of motion pictures. We hold that the zoning ordinances requiring that adult motion picture theaters not be located within 100 feet of two other regulated uses does not violate the Equal Protection Clause of the Fourteenth Amendment.—Justice Stevens

FCC v. Pacifica Foundation (438 U.S. 726 [1978])

In a 1978 appeal of the *Pacifica* case (comedian George Carlin's "seven dirty words"), the Supreme Court affirmed the Federal

Communication Commission's power to regulate indecency in broadcasting. Leaving aside the vagueness of the term *indecency* and its shakiness in law, there were other legal problems. Section 1464 of the U.S. Criminal Code provides sanctions against profane, indecent, or obscene language over a broadcast medium. At the same time, Section 326 of the 1934 Communications Act, written to comply with the First Amendment, forbids the FCC from censoring program content; the contradiction is evident.

In 1973, George Carlin had broadcast a comic routine on what makes words taboo over New York's WBAI-FM (Pacifica Broadcasting). A father filed a complaint because his son was listening, and the FCC imposed sanctions on the station. A lower court decided in favor of Pacifica. In reversing the decision, the Justices ruled that the FCC did have the authority to impose sanctions against material that was indecent because (1) the FCC had not edited the broadcast in advance, which would have constituted prior restraint, (2) broadcasting confronts the individual in the home (or car), and prior warnings about content cannot protect a station-hopping listener, and (3) broadcasting is "uniquely accessible to children."

The relevant statutory questions are whether the Commission's action is forbidden "censorship" within the meaning of 47 U.S.C. 326 and whether speech that concededly is not obscene may be restricted as "indecent" under the authority of U.S.C. 1464 (176 ed).

The prohibition against censorship unequivocally denies the Commission any power to edit proposed broadcasts in advance and to excise material considered inappropriate for the air-waves. The prohibition, however, has never been construed to deny the Commission the power to review the content of completed broadcasts in the performance of its regulatory duties.

We have not decided that an occasional expletive in either setting would justify any sanction or, indeed, that this broadcast would justify a criminal prosecution. The Commission's decision rested entirely on a nuisance rationale under which context is all-important. The concept requires consideration of a host of variables. The time of day was emphasized by the Commission. The content of the program in which the language is used will also affect the composition of the audience and differences between radio, television and perhaps closed-

circuit transmissions, may also be relevant. As Mr. Justice
Sutherland wrote, "a nuisance may be merely a wrong
thing in a wrong place—like a pig in a parlor instead of
the barnyard." We simply hold that when the Commission finds that a pig has entered the parlor, the exercise
of its regulatory power does not depend on proof that
the pig is obscene.—Justice Stevens

Schad v. Borough of Mt. Ephraim (452 U.S. 61 [1981])

Returning to the new strategy for regulating sex businesses, the
Court placed limits on the zealousness of municipalities that
wished to use zoning of such enterprises by forbidding authorities from employing the tactic to eliminate such businesses entirely. Zoning for purposes of preventing nuisances, congestion,
or urban blight was one thing; extinction was quite another, because that would infringe on the First Amendment.

> In this case, however, Mt. Ephraim has not adequately
> justified its substantial restriction of protected activ-
> ity. . . . First the Borough contends that permitting live
> entertainment would conflict with its plan to create a
> commercial area that caters only to the immediate needs
> of its residents and that would enable them to purchase
> at local stores the few items they occasionally forgot to
> buy outside the Borough. No evidence was introduced
> below to support this assertion. . . .
>
> Second, Mount Ephraim contends that it may selec-
> tively exclude commercial live entertainment from the
> broad range of commercial uses permitted in the Bor-
> ough for reasons normally associated with live enter-
> tainment, such as parking, trash, police protection and
> medical facilities. The Borough has presented no evi-
> dence . . . that live entertainment poses problems of
> this nature more significant than those with various per-
> mitted uses.
>
> The Borough nevertheless contends that live enter-
> tainment in general and nude dancing in particular are
> amply available in close-by areas outside the limits of the
> Borough. . . . There is no evidence in this record to sup-
> port the proposition that the kind of entertainment ap-
> pellants wish to provide is available in reasonably

nearby areas. . . . "One is not to have the exercise of his liberty of expression in appropriate places abridged in the plea that it may be exercised in some other place." *Schneider v. State*, 308 U.S. 163.—Justice White

American Booksellers Association, Inc., v. William H. Hudnut III, Mayor, City of Indianapolis (771 F.2d 323 [1985])

In the mid-1980s, a flurry of actions by feminists and conservatives led to important court cases. The still-conservative Court offered some hope to censors when it reduced the requirements for searches and seizures in *Maryland v. Macon*, 472 U.S. 463 (1985); reduced the level of knowledge required about a film before a magistrate could issue a warrant in *New York v. P.J. Video, Inc.*, 475 U.S. 868 (1986); and upheld the use of nuisance-abatement ordinances to close bookstores after less drastic measures had failed in *Arcara v. Cloud Books, Inc.*, 478 U.S. 697 (1986).

Antiporn feminists first in Minneapolis and then in Indianapolis attempted to redefine pornography (see further in this chapter) so as to make it possible for women to sue producers and distributors of pornography provided that they could prove the materials harmful. American Booksellers, the trade organization of book publishers and dealers, contested the ordinance and won when a lower court declared the ordinance a form of thought control. The Supreme Court refused to hear Indianapolis's appeal and thus doomed the law as unconstitutional.

> The ordinance discriminates on the ground of the content of the speech. Speech treating women in the approved way—in sexual encounters "premised on equality"—is lawful no matter how sexually explicit. Speech treating women in the disapproved way—as submissive in matters sexual or as enjoying humiliation—is unlawful no matter how significant the literary, artistic or political qualities of the work taken as a whole. The state may not ordain preferred viewpoints in this way. The Constitution forbids the state to declare one perspective right and silence opponents.
>
> Speech that subordinates women . . . is forbidden, no matter how great the literary or political value of the work taken as a whole. Speech that portrays women in

positions of equality is lawful, no matter how graphic the sexual content. This is thought control. It establishes an "approved" view of women, of how they may react to sexual encounters, of how the sexes may relate to each other. Those who espouse the approved view may use sexual images; those who do not, may not.—Judge Easterbrook

American Booksellers, Inc., v. Commonwealth of Virginia (802 F.2d 691 [1986])

The 1986 Attorney General's Commission on Pornography urged prosecutors to harass dealers in pornography, and Virginia complied by passing a law prohibiting display of magazines such as *Playboy* and *Penthouse* on newsstands. Again the American Booksellers Association challenged the law, and won. The Court agreed that such a statute infringed on basic rights. (Even after this ruling, that same year U.S. District Judge John Penn had to order renegade elements of the Justice Department acting at the direction of Attorney General Edwin Meese to end their assaults on the First Amendment.)

If the booksellers attempt to comply with the amendment, they face economic injury; if the booksellers continue to conduct their business in their normal fashion, they face the prospect of prosecution. . . . The Commonwealth suggests a number of ways by which the book retailer may solve these problems, but none appear to us to significantly ease the First Amendment burden. . . . Placing "adults only" tags on books and magazines or displaying the restricted material behind blinder racks or on adults-only shelves freely accessible in the main part of the store would not stop any determined juvenile from examining and perusing the materials. . . . Forcing a bookseller to create a separate, monitored adults-only section . . . interferes with the bookseller's right to sell the restricted materials and the adult's ability to buy them. . . . Contrary to the Commonwealth's argument that the scienter [awareness of prohibited conduct] requirement in the statute allows a book retailer to avoid the hazards of self-censorship, each of these suggested practices would require the seller to read and make a content-based judgment. . . . A retailer cannot rely on the amendment to guide him in deciding what are the least restrictive modifications in display methods which would be sufficient to satisfy the statute. . . . In sum, we feel that the amendment discourages the exercise of first amendment rights in a real and substantial fashion.— Judge Sprouse

Renton v. Playtime Theatres **(475 U.S. 41 [1986])**

By now it was clear that prosecutors seeking to demonstrate that a particular work was obscene would have a hard time of it, particularly since juries in all but the most conservative areas were unlikely to convict. That made zoning, the strategy upheld by the courts, more attractive as a way of controlling sexual expression. In another decision, the Court upheld the right of a municipality to limit sex-related businesses to remote areas and in effect affirmed the use of zoning in most circumstances. Except for topless dance clubs, the issue of where a sex-oriented business was located would soon be somewhat moot, given the rise of the Internet and its ability to deliver sexual materials anywhere instantaneously. (Technology continuously rewrites both practice and law.)

> We hold that Renton was entitled to rely on the experiences of Seattle and other cities . . . in enacting its adult theater zoning ordinance. The First Amendment does not require a city, before enacting such an ordinance, to conduct new studies or produce evidence independent of that already generated by other cities, so long as whatever evidence the city relies on is reasonably believed to be relevant to the problem that the city addresses.
>
> In sum, we find that the Renton ordinance represents a valid governmental response to the "admittedly serious problems" created by adult theaters. Renton has not used "the power to zone as a pretext for suppressing expression," . . . but rather has sought to make some areas available for adult theaters and their patrons, while at the same time preserving the quality of life in the community at large by preventing those theaters from locating in other areas. This, after all, is the essence of zoning.

Hence, as in American Mini-theatres, the city has enacted a zoning ordinance that meets these goals while also satisfying the dictates of the First Amendment.—Justice Rehnquist

Barnes v. Glen Theater, Inc. (501 U.S. 560 [1991])

At the same time, the Court under Chief Justice William Rehnquist clung to its belief that states could and perhaps should regulate public morality, and in a much-lampooned decision ruled that Indiana could require that topless dancers cover their nipples with pasties. The Court said it is permissible to prohibit "expressive performance" on the grounds that "traditional moral belief" in the demoralizing effects of nudity on public order provides a "rational basis" for doing so. Newspapers laughed as the Justices tried—in tortured prose—to prescribe how dancers could be "expressive" and "sexy" without baring their breasts completely.

Respondents contend that even though prohibiting nudity in public generally may not be related to suppressing expression, prohibiting the performance of nude dancing is related to expression because the State seeks to prevent its erotic message. Therefore they reason that the application of the Indiana statute to the nude dancing in this case violates the First Amendment, because it fails the third part of the O'Brien test, viz: the governmental interest must be unrelated to the suppression of free expression.

But we do not think that when Indiana applies its statute to the nude dancing in these nightclubs it is proscribing nudity because of the erotic message conveyed by the dancers. Presumably numerous other erotic performances are presented at these establishments and similar clubs without any interference from the State, so long as the performers wear a scant amount of clothing . . . the perceived evil that Indiana seeks to address is not erotic dancing, but public nudity. The appearance of people of all shapes, sizes and ages in the nude at a beach, for example, would convey little if any erotic message, yet the State still seeks to prevent it. Public nudity is the evil the State seeks to prevent, whether or not it is combined with expressive activity.—Judge Rehnquist

Jacobson v. United States (503 U.S. 540 [1991])

Occasionally the government abused its power to prosecute. In 1992, the Court ruled that the government had illegally entrapped a purchaser of child pornography through a deception that lasted for years. Here prosecutors had virtually begged a man to purchase materials so that they could then arrest him for breaking the law.

> In their zeal to enforce the law, however, Government agents may not originate a criminal design, implant in an innocent person's mind the disposition to commit a criminal act, and then induce commission of the crime so that the Government may prosecute. . . . The prosecution must prove beyond reasonable doubt that the defendant was disposed to commit the criminal act prior to first being approached by Government agents.—Justice White

Alexander v. United States (113 S. Ct. 2766 [1993])

The following year, the Supreme Court reaffirmed the use of an extremely powerful government tool when it held that federal agents may seize assets of adult businesses under the RICO Act after some items are declared obscene. Government agents posing as consumers in a conservative community might order a videotape from a company in New York, obtain a ruling of obscenity from a jury in that community (the practice called "forum-shopping"), and then under RICO seize all the dealer's assets—worth millions, perhaps—even though the tape sold for only $30.

> However, the order here imposes no legal impediment to petitioner's ability to engage in any expressive activity; it just prevents him from financing those activities with assets derived from his prior racketeering offenses. RICO is oblivious to the expressive or nonexpressive nature of the assets forfeited. Petitioner's assets were forfeited be-

cause they were directly related to past racketeering violations, and thus they differ from material seized or restrained on suspicion of being obscene without a prior judicial obscenity determination. . . . His claim is also inconsistent with *Arcara v. Cloud Books, Inc.* . . . in which the Court rejected a claim that the closure of an adult bookstore under a general nuisance stature was not an improper prior restraint.—Justice Rehnquist

Austin v. United States (113 S. Ct. 2801 [1993])

Aware of criticism of what seemed disproportionate punishment, the Court then in *Austin v. U.S.* appeared to place limits on how many assets could be seized on the grounds that the punishment was excessive.

In sum, even though this Court has rejected the "innocence" of the owner as a common-law defense to forfeiture, it consistently has recognized that forfeiture serves, at least in part, to punish the owner. . . . We conclude, therefore, that forfeiture generally and statutory in rem forfeiture in particular historically have been understood, at least in part, as punishment.—Justice Blackmun

American Civil Liberties Union v. Janet Reno, Attorney General of the United States (929 F. Supp. 824 [1996])

The most notable case of the 1990s, however, and the one with the most implications for the new century, involved the Communications Decency Act (CDA) of 1996. A conservative Congress passed the law to forbid indecency on the Internet because children might be able to access such materials. The American Civil Liberties Union headed a coalition of organizations to challenge those provisions of the act. The court of appeals for the 3rd Circuit ruled those provisions unconstitutional.

Cutting through the acronyms and argot that littered the hearing testimony, the Internet may fairly be regarded as a never-ending worldwide conversation. The Government may not, through the CDA, interrupt that conversation. As the most participatory form of mass speech yet developed, the Internet deserves the highest protection from governmental intrusion.

True is it that many find some of the speech on the Internet to be offensive, and amid the din of cyberspace many hear discordant voices they regard as indecent. The absence of governmental regulation of Internet content has unquestionably produced a kind of chaos, but as one of the plaintiffs' experts put it with such resonance at the hearing: "What achieved success was the very chaos that the Internet is. The strength of the Internet is that chaos." Just as the strength of the Internet is chaos, so the strength of our liberty depends upon the chaos and the cacophony of the unfettered speech the First Amendment protects. For these reasons, I without hesitation hold that the CDA is unconstitutional on its face.—Judge Sloviter

Janet Reno v. ACLU (117 S. Ct. 2329 [1997])

The government appealed to the Supreme Court, which upheld the lower court's decision.

The dramatic expansion of this new marketplace of ideas contradicts the factual basis of this contention. The record demonstrates that the growth of the Internet has been and continues to be phenomenal. As a matter of constitutional tradition, in the absence of evidence to the contrary, we presume that governmental regulation of the content of speech is more likely to interfere with the free exchange of ideas than to encourage it. The interest in encouraging freedom of expression in a democratic society outweighs any theoretical but unproven benefit of censorship.—Justice Stevens

Laws and Legislation

The First Amendment (1791)

The First Amendment guarantees all citizens the right to free speech.

Congress shall make no law respecting an establishment of religion, or prohibiting the free exercise thereof; or abridging the freedom of speech, or of the press, or the right peaceably to assemble, and to petition the Government for a redress of grievances.

The Fourteenth Amendment (1868)

The Fourteenth Amendment protects citizens against abuses by the individual states. Section I reads:

All persons born or naturalized in the United States, and subject to the jurisdiction thereof, are citizens of the United States and of the State wherein they reside. No State shall make or enforce any law which shall abridge the privileges or immunities of citizens of the United States; nor shall any State deprive any person of life, liberty, or property, without due process of law; nor deny to any person within its jurisdiction the equal protection of the laws.

This would appear to mean that federal guarantees of free speech take precedence over state attempts to curtail speech. The *Miller* decision (1973), however, allows states to set standards for obscenity.

The Indianapolis Ordinance (1984)

The Indianapolis Ordinance closely resembled the legislation drafted by Catharine MacKinnon and Andrea Dworkin for Minneapolis (vetoed by the Minneapolis mayor) in its concentration on sexual postures and penetration. It was struck down in 1985 by Federal Judge Sarah Evans Barker of the Seventh District Court. The ordinance defined pornography using six criteria.

Pornography shall mean the graphic sexually explicit subordination of women, whether in pictures or in words, that also includes one or more of the following:
(1) Women are presented as sexual objects who enjoy pain or humiliation; or
(2) Women are presented as sexual objects who experience sexual pleasure in being raped; or
(3) Women are presented as sexual objects tied up or cut up or mutilated or bruised or physically hurt or

dismembered or truncated or fragmented or severed into body parts; or
(4) Women are presented as being penetrated by objects or animals; or
(5) Women are presented in scenarios of degradation, injury, abasement, torture, shown as filthy or inferior, bleeding, bruised or hurt in a context that makes these scenarios sexual; or
(6) Women are presented as sexual objects for domination, conquest, violation, exploitation, possession or use, or through postures or positions of servility or submission or display.
The use of men, children or transsexuals in the place of women in paragraphs 1–6 above shall also constitute pornography under this section.

Section 2257, 18 U.S. Code (1995)

The Pornography Victims' Compensation Act, an attempt by Congress to harass pornographers, created an addition to the U.S. Code called Section 2257. The law (Sexual Exploitation and Other Abuse of Children, Section 2257, "Record Keeping Provisions") requires that producers of pornographic films, videotapes, and photos keep precise records of the ages of performers, even if they are clearly elderly, in films made after 3 July 1995. They must also identify the person who keeps those records, and the place where they are kept. As is so often the case, this legislation had the unintended effect of introducing standard accounting practices to an industry much in need of them. Below is a Section 2257 notice of compliance for the videotape entitled *Talent Scout*, produced, directed, and shot in Czechoslovakia by Paul Thomas for Vivid Video, an American company:

In accordance with 18 U.S.C. Sec. 2257
The Production Date of
This Feature is 9.20.98
It was first duplicated on 3.1.99
Documentation Pursuant to 18 U.S.C. Sec. 2257 is maintained by
S. Hirsch and D. James
at 15127 Califa St., Van Nuys CA
91411

The Communications Decency Act (1996)

The Communications Decency Act, 110 Stat. 133–43, amended paragraph 223 of Section 47 of the United States Code to add a new subsection (d) to prohibit an individual or organization from knowingly sending or displaying "indecent" materials to minors (those under the age of 18) by means of computers, and defined "indecency" in terms similar to those that govern broadcasts, as "any comment, request, suggestion, proposal, image, or other communication that, in context, depicts or describes, in terms patently offensive as measured by contemporary community standards, sexual or excretory activities or organs." Though it affirmed the application of obscenity provisions and laws governing child pornography, the Supreme Court struck down this provision as unconstitutional, especially since there are no viable community standards that could apply to the universe of cyberspace.

Reports

The Report of the President's Commission on Obscenity and Pornography (1970)

The President's Commission on Obscenity and Pornography issued a report supplemented with a nine-volume *Technical Report* (Washington, D.C.: Government Printing Office, 1970) that dealt with virtually every facet of the subject, brought massive research to bear on the alleged effects, and reviewed all pertinent state and federal laws (from nuisance and display ordinances to criminal statutes). The three principal recommendations of the commission were succinct:

> The Commission recommends that federal, state and local legislation should not seek to interfere with the right of adults who wish to do so to read, obtain or view explicit sexual materials. On the other hand, we recommend legislative regulation upon the sale of sexual materials to young persons who do not have the consent of their parents, and we also recommend legislation to protect persons from having sexual materials thrust upon them without their consent through the mails or through open public display. (64–65)

The Report of the Attorney General's Commission on Pornography (1986)

The members of the Attorney General's Commission on Pornography could not substantiate a connection between sexual materials and sexual deviance or violence, though they did reiterate links between pornography and organized crime. Even though the Constitution protects pornography, the conservative commission recommended that citizens work with law enforcement officials to suppress it.

Half (49 percent) of the 92 recommendations in the report of the Attorney General's Commission (Washington DC: Government Printing Office, 1986) dealt with child pornography. Among the recommendations for combating pornography for adults were formation of citizens' pressure groups, use of RICO legislation to seize assets of accused pornographers, creation of a National Obscenity Enforcement Unit, and filing of multiple simultaneous prosecutions in different states ("forum-shopping") so that at least one will stick.

Following are selected recommendations (omitting entirely those directed at child pornography) under various categories:

A. Recommendations for Changes in Federal Law

1. Congress should enact a forfeiture statute to reach the proceeds and instruments of any offense committed in violation of the federal obscenity laws.

2. Congress should amend the federal obscenity laws to eliminate the necessity of proving transportation in interstate commerce. A statute should be enacted to only require proof that the distribution of the obscene material "affects" interstate commerce.

3. Congress should enact legislation making it an unfair business practice and an unfair labor practice for any employer to hire individuals to participate in commercial sexual performances.

4. Congress should amend the Mann Act to make its provisions gender neutral.

5. Congress should amend Title 18 of the United States Code to specifically proscribe obscene television programming.

6. Congress should enact legislation to prohibit the transmission of obscene material through the telephone or similar common carrier.

B. Recommendations for Changes in State Law

7. State legislatures should amend, if necessary, obscenity statutes containing the definitional requirement that material be "utterly without redeeming social value" in order to be obscene to conform with the current standard enunciated by the United States Supreme Court in *Miller v. California.*

8. State legislatures should amend, if necessary, obscenity statutes to eliminate misdemeanor statutes for second offenses and make any second offense punishable as a felony.

9. State legislatures should enact, if necessary, forfeiture provisions as part of the state obscenity laws.

10. State legislatures should enact a racketeer-influenced corrupt organizations (RICO) statute which has obscenity as a predicate act.

C. Recommendations for the United States Department of Justice

11. The Attorney General should direct the United States Attorneys to examine the obscenity problem in the respective districts, identify offenders, initiate investigations, and commence prosecution without further delay.

12. The Attorney General should appoint a high-ranking official from the Department of Justice to oversee the creation and operation of an Obscenity Task Force. The Task Force should consist of Special Assistant United States Attorneys and federal agents who will assist United States Attorneys in the prosecution and investigation of obscenity cases.

13. The Department of Justice should initiate the creation of an Obscenity Law Enforcement Data Base which would serve as a resource network for federal, state, and local law enforcement agencies. . . .

17. The United States Attorneys should use all available federal statutes to prosecute obscenity law violations involving cable and satellite television. . . .

H. Recommendations for the Federal Communications Commission

34. The Federal Communications Commission should use its full regulatory powers and impose appropriate sanctions against providers of obscene dial-a-porn telephone services.

35. The Federal Communications Commission should use its full regulatory powers and impose appropriate sanctions against cable and television programmers who transmit obscene programs. . . .
Section III: Victimization
86. State, county and municipal governments should facilitate the development of public and private resources for persons who are currently involved in the production or consumption of pornography and wish to discontinue this involvement and for those who suffer mental, physical, educational, or employment disabilities as a result of exposure or participation in the production of pornography.
Section IV: Civil Rights
87. Legislatures should conduct hearings and consider legislation recognizing a civil remedy for harms attributable to pornography.

The Economics of Pornography

In "The Sex Industry" (1998), the *Economist* pegs the revenues of the worldwide sex industry, which includes activities from prostitution to pornography, at $20 billion a year. The article notes that cheap products have overwhelmed the lowest strata of the market, forcing producers to scramble to find niches. The *Economist*'s writers also predict that global competition will lead governments to criminalize child pornography as a way of ensuring a legal market for sexual representations aimed at adults.[2]

Pornographic Magazines and Books

Increased respectability and infusions of capital will gradually lead to better accounting procedures for some sexual materials. At the moment, however, precise figures for most forms of sexual expression are not always available. Alleged revenues for "the pornography industry" that do not break out specific media are almost never accurate. The reasons are obvious: (1) few people agree on what constitutes pornography, so that one source may lump magazines such as *Cosmopolitan* with hard-core picture periodicals, or merge prime-time television shows such as *NYPD Blue* with triple-X adult videotapes to arrive at wildly inflated totals; and (2) figures may be unobtainable because some enterprises are not open to scrutiny.

It is easy to find accurate revenues for Playboy Enterprises, publisher of *Playboy* magazine and the Playboy Channel; like every other company listed on the New York Stock Exchange, it issues an annual report. Playboy Enterprises in 1995, for example, netted $629,000, a figure that reflected an upswing in the company's fortunes. The magazine itself accounted for only part of the company's revenues, and profits have improved since 1995 thanks to good management by Christie Hefner. It is more difficult to assess Larry Flynt's income from "pornography," however, because in addition to *Hustler* magazine he owns thirty others, the majority nonerotic, and because he is the sole owner of the parent company, which means that unlike publicly held companies, his corporation does not have to inform stockholders. One authoritative source said that in 1993 Flynt's empire generated $100 million a year.[3] The revenues of General Media International, the privately held parent company of Bob Guccione, publisher of *Penthouse*, were $200 million in that same year.[4] *Hustler* and *Penthouse* file circulation figures with the Audit Bureau of Circulation, which makes it possible to estimate revenues for the magazines alone.

The last time anyone tried to estimate the traffic in hard-core magazines, in 1986, the Attorney General's Commission listed more than 2,500 fetish magazines. Despite its reproduction of Justice Department figures, the commission could not come up with aggregate revenues, but it did indicate that various criminal elements involved in their distribution had failed to report as income several millions of dollars.[5] The market for magazines has been seriously eroded since that time by competition from videotapes and Internet sites. Publishers of hard-core pornographic magazines rarely register their periodicals for copyright and do not report profits and losses to stockholders. Pornographic 'zines, in the form of innumerable stapled-together photocopies, escape reporting altogether.

Respectable mainline publishers routinely publish books that at least some Americans consider pornographic, but it would be difficult to break out revenues. The number of American publishers specializing in cheap, clearly salacious paperbacks, however, has fallen substantially.[6] Romances, often called pornography for women, remain a huge and recognized publishing category. According to the *New York Times Magazine*, romances generate revenues of $1 billion a year and account for virtually half of all the paperbacks annually purchased in the United States.[7]

Pornographic Films and Videos

Although the industry itself documents annual sales and rentals, it does not break out soft- and hard-core varieties. According to *Adult Video News*, the trade journal, aggregate sales and rentals for 1998 were $4.1 billion, of which approximately a third was accounted for by foreign trade. (In 1992, the figure was $1.6 billion, but in 1997 it was $4.2 billion, slightly higher than for 1998.) Using the industry's own figures, *Time* magazine estimates porn video industry grosses for 1999 at $5 billion, a figure that includes foreign sales, and compares it to Hollywood's film grosses during the same period at $7.5 billion, a figure that does not include foreign revenues.[8] The adult industry projected 10,000 new titles for 1999, an increase over the 8,950 released in 1998.[9] Most of those will never be seen by most Americans, just as many legitimate movies never make it to neighborhood theaters, because of control of distribution channels by major producers.

Such figures attest to a robust industry. The *Los Angeles Times* recently reported that while mainstream feature film production in Los Angeles County had decreased 13 percent, adult film production had increased by 25 percent. In July 1999, one in five "shoots" in Los Angeles was an adult film. The San Fernando Valley industry includes fifty of the top eighty-five porn film companies, most of them vertically integrated to produce, package, and ship videos. Vivid Video (founded in 1984) has annual sales and rentals of $50 million and is considered a leader in developing interactive DVD (more than a million disks released in 1999) and virtual sex technology for digital interfaces.[10]

Time, however, pegs Vivid's revenues at only $25 million;[11] the discrepancy is a reminder that porn industries may be tempted to inflate their own revenues to acquire respectability in a society that respects wealth more than anything else. According to *Time*, pornographic videos account for 14 percent of all sales and almost 50 percent of the rental industry. Four companies (Metro, Vivid, VCA, and Wicked) dominate distribution. The largest, Vivid, sells its products through increasingly upscale stores and has invested in *Playboy*'s AdulTVision cable channel. Metro Video has traded on the NASDAQ stock exchange since 1994.

The *Los Angeles Times* revealed the pay scales of video sex performers as well. Males average $500 per sex scene, and women three to ten times that. Stars such as Jenna Jameson, Anna Malle, Jenteal, and Lexus charge $5,000.[12] The majority of women who perform in hard-core videos make a good deal more than they would selling burgers at McDonald's, but only the stars pull in more than $500,000 a year, and much of that comes from stripping. Careers generally are brief.

Broadcast and Cable Media

As "guests in the home," broadcasters must observe standards of appropriateness lower than those governing obscenity for other media. In *FCC v. Pacifica Foundation*, 438 U.S. 726 (1978), the courts upheld the FCC's definition of broadcast indecency as materials or language that "in context, depicts or describes in terms patently offensive as measured by contemporary community standards for the broadcast medium, sexual or excretory activities or organs."

Conservatives often charge that broadcast and cablecast television are suffused with sex. One could, of course, separate out the revenues of shows such as ABC's often-attacked *NYPD Blue* or HBO's *Sex in the City*, but since not everyone agrees that those shows are pornographic, doing so seems pointless. Similarly, one could perhaps trace the income of those specific raunchy public access and leased access channel shows that advertise, but the aggregates would not be impressive. Dealing with cable- or satellite-delivered premium "adult" fare, however, makes more sense. According to the trade journal *Cable World*, the revenues of adult services in 1996 were $95 million.[13] For all practical purposes, two companies, Playboy and New Frontier Media, now monopolize adult cable and DBS programming in the United States.[14] New Frontier Media alone took in $80 million in 1999.[15] Playboy's largest channel, Playboy TV, reaches 24 million homes, and its AdulTVision, Adam & Eve, and Spice channels reach several more million. Now that the Supreme Court has overturned restrictions that would have limited its programming to late evening hours, Playboy (and its competitor) will surely grow.[16]

Dial-a-Porn Services

According to *Sable Communications of California, Inc., v. FCC*, 492 U.S. 115, 126, 128–30 (1989), *Information Providers' Coalition v. FCC*, 928 F.2nd 866, 872 (9th Cir. 1991), and *Dial Information Services Corporation of New York v. Thornburgh*, 938 F.2nd 1535 (2nd Cir. 1991), telephone pornography is defined as "the description or depiction of sexual or excretory activities or organs in a patently offensive manner as measured by contemporary community standards for the telephone medium." The courts have upheld provisions that access to such material can be regulated by forcing the service provider to require of the adult patron a written request to the service provider, a credit card number, or an adult identification code or PIN before the provider can provide the service.

Rapidly changing names and addresses work against accurate accounting of dial-a-porn revenues. Although many porn stars now operate their own telephone services, the economic consolidation common to all media industries is visible in dial-a-porn ads included on hard-core videotapes; these are operated by video companies themselves. Altogether, dial-a-porn services generated between $750 million and $1 billion in 1996.[17] In 1995, Ohio State University students in Columbus made $16 an hour plus commissions on lingerie, videos, and calendars they sold over the phone.[18] In large markets with surplus labor, operators make less. The Florida labor department recently awarded workers' compensation to a Fort Lauderdale telephone sex worker forced to quit. She developed carpal tunnel syndrome because she had to hold the telephone with one hand while using the other to masturbate as she helped clients create fantasies around their specified fetishes. She had asked for $267 a week to offset lost earnings of $400 a week.[19]

The Internet

Some analysts believe that about a third of the current commercial activity on the Internet is pornographic (although that will change as more non–sex-oriented companies develop direct transactions). *Time* says that adult Web sites collectively bring in nearly $1 billion a year, or about a tenth of the entire sex industry, and predicts that the share will increase.[20] The chief industry source also reports that pornography (loosely defined) accounts for 69 percent (or roughly $1 billion worth) of total Internet content sales. The same source maintains that about 84 percent of that 69 percent of content comes from American sources and sites.[21] Large, hot sites can generate revenues of $1 million a month.[22] Porn stars Asia Carrera, Jenteal, Mimi Miyagi, and Vanessa Del Rio have opened Web sites that can bring in up to $.5 million a year, in some cases five times what they made from porn videos (some complain about debugging programs and carpal tunnel syndrome). Obviously these are rough figures, since if every site pulled in $.5 million consistently then the aggregate numbers would be astronomical.[23] Strippers at Virtual Dreams, a Las Vegas–based interactive site, are paid $40,000 a year plus benefits, and they work in a safe, comfortable environment (subscribers pay $5.99 a minute).[24] Internet sales of vibrators have increased the sales of San Francisco's Good Vibrations store, a cooperative enterprise run by women, to $5 million a year.[25] Pornographic Internet companies have not gone public because of the difficulty of getting reputable underwriters to handle the initial public offerings (IPOs). Internet Entertainment Group (IEG), which operates websites, plans to go public when it can find an investment bank to broker a public offering. According to company president Seth Warshavsky, IEG generated profits of $15 million on total revenues of $50 million in 1998; he thinks the company is worth somewhere between $200 million and $500 million.[26] IEG's lead derives from its successful introduction in 1995 of "transaction technologies." The company launched the first effective and secure method for using credit cards to purchase products and services. Major corporations rapidly copied the technology. IEG was also out in front with the "streaming" of audio and video content.[27]

Performance

In 1967, one authority counted 7,000 stripteasers in the United States.[28] By 1991, 62,000 women were dancing topless, and some 750,000 had been dancers at one time or another. The estimated annual income of the industry, including tips given to performers, approached $2 billion.[29] By 1998, the number had risen to 250,000 dancers employed in some 2,500 clubs.[30] No one seems able to count the money, though best estimates put revenues per club in the range of $500,000 to the rare $5 million, which means that Americans now drop more money in strip clubs annually than they spend on the theater, opera, ballet, and classical and jazz concerts combined.[31] The Internal Revenue Service (IRS) is no more precise, despite a reclassification of strippers as employees instead of independent contractors so that clubowners became liable for back Social Security payments, a move that forced many clubs into bankruptcy.[32] The IRS taxes dancers' estimated tips and wages. It has also gone after many porn movie performers on similar grounds, a story that indicates the degree to which sex industries have been coopted by some government agencies. The most reasoned estimate of the annual income (1995) of dancers—"independent contractors"—is $70,000, mostly in cash, mostly from table or lap dancing.[33]

By most reliable estimates, Americans in 1999 consumed roughly nine to ten billion dollars worth of sexual representations, from the distinctly erotic to the graphically pornographic. That is somewhat more than the seven billion they spent in 1998 on spices, sauces, and condiments for a different kind of diet.[34]

Notes

1. William Brigman, "Politics and the Pornography Wars," *Wide Angle* 19, 3 (1997): 152.

2. "The Sex Industry," *Economist* 346 (14–20 February 1998): 21–23.

3. Michael Kaplan, "The Resurrection of Larry Flynt, Owner of Larry Flynt Publications, Inc.," *Folio: The Magazine for Magazine Management* (15 June 1993): 36–38, 89–90.

4. Philippa Kennedy, "A Marriage Made in Sleaze," *Bangkok Post*, 1 November 1994, p. 37; reprinted from the *London Express*.

5. Attorney General's Commission on Pornography, *Final Report*, II, pp. 1039–1238).

6. "Ticker," *Brill's Content* 2, 1 (February 1999): 128.

7. "Words of Love," *New York Times Magazine*, 7 February 1999, p. 21.

8. "Numbers," *Time* (27 December 1999): 49.

9. Updated information can be found on *Adult Video News's* Web site (http://www.avn.com).

10. Jeffrey Gettleman, "L. A. Economy's Dirty Secret: Porn Is Thriving," *Los Angeles Times*, 1 September 1999, pp. A1, A20.

11. Joel Stein, "Porn Goes Mainstream," *Time* (7 September 1998): 54–55.

12. Gettleman, "L. A. Economy's Dirty Secret," pp. A1, A20.

13. Kim Mitchell and Eric Glick, "MSOs Scrambling after Court Ruling," *Cable World* 9(13) (31 March 1997): 1, 98.

14. Debbie Narrod, "Fighting Over the Adult Brand," *Cable World* (8 May 2000): 88–90.

15. "Playboy Weathers 505 Storm," *Cable World* (Pay Per View Special Report) (December 6, 1999): 38A–39A.

16. Linda Greenhouse, "Court Overrules Law Restricting Cable Sex Shows," *New York Times* (23 May 2000): A1, A20.

17. Eric Schlosser, "The Business of Pornography," *U.S. News and World Report* (10 February 1997): 49.

18. Hollie Landfried, "1-900-Phone-Sex," *Ohio State University Independent*, October 1995, p. 6.

19. James Ridgeway, "Mondo Washington," *Village Voice*, 30 November 1999, p. 42.

20. Julian Dibbell, "The Body Electric," *Time Digital* (12 April 1999): 24–27.

21. Ernest Moore, "Adult Content Grabs Lion's Share of Revenue," *Adult Video News Online* (May 1999).

22. John Simons, "The Web's Dirty Secret: Sex Sites Make Lots of Money," *U.S. News and World Report* (19 August 1996): 39–40.

23. David Kushner, "Debbie Does HTML," *Village Voice*, 6 October 1998, p. 47.

24. Daniel Eisenberg, "Sex, Bytes, and Video Dates," *Time Digital* (12 May 1997): 23–24.

25. David Kushner, "Joystick Nation," *Village Voice*, 30 March 1999, p. 34.

26. James Collins, "Wall Street Follies: Where Are All the Paper Billionaires in the On-Line Porn Business?" *New Yorker* (16 August 1999): 23.

27. Frank Rose, "Sex Sells—Young Ambitious Seth Warshavsky Is the Bob Guccione of the 1990s," *Wired* (12 December 1997): 5.

28. Libby Jones, *Striptease* (New York: Simon and Schuster, 1967), p. 5.

29. D. Keith Mano, "Playboy after Hours," *Playboy* 38, 12 (December 1991): 27.

30. *Strippers: The Naked Stages, HBO America Undercover Series*. Produced by Anthony Radziwill (New York: HBO, 1998).

31. Eric Schlosser, "The Business of Pornography," *U.S. News and World Report* (10 February 1997): 44, 48.

32. See the chapter on clubs in Eurydice, *Satyricon USA: A Journey across the New Sexual Frontier* (New York: Scribner's, 1999).

33. Bob Zeigler, "Dancers: They're Not Here to Fall in Love," *Sales and Marketing Management* 147, 7 (July 1995): 56.

34. Joseph A. Harriss, "For the Love of Mustard," *Smithsonian* 31(3) (June 2000): 102–106, 107–110.

Directory of Organizations 6

Protesting sexual expression is an American tradition. Since the nineteenth century, Americans have created hundreds of groups to combat sexual expression and fewer to defend free speech. Today dozens of advocacy groups adopt various moral, religious, and political stances. The most conservative define pornography broadly to include sex education, material on AIDS, or sexual references on television, whereas others object only to what they define as extreme speech or images. Some focus on a single medium, such as music recordings or films. Some censorship organizations respect constitutional safeguards and advocate legal procedures to suppress speech they think dangerous or offensive; others employ economic boycotts and harassment as a way to suppress constitutionally protected speech. Opposing censorship are more liberal groups, most of whom do not specifically approve of any particular form of expression but insist that Americans have a right to hear or see whatever ideas, opinions, and images their fellow citizens may choose to transmit. Producers of pornographic and erotic materials sometimes establish trade organizations or lobbying groups themselves.

Following are addresses and telephone numbers for readers wanting further information from any of these groups. Also included are current web sites for groups who maintain an on-line presence. Web addresses change more rapidly than street addresses, however, so it may be necessary to enter key words into web browsers.

Adult Video Association
270 North Canon Drive, Suite 1370
Beverly Hills, CA 90210
(213) 650-7121

Like other advocacy groups, the Adult Video Association serves as a clearinghouse for educational information, operates a speakers' bureau, publishes occasional newsletters, and lobbies state and federal agencies on behalf of citizens' rights to view sexual materials. It offers some legal assistance and referrals to those fighting censorship.

Adult Video News (AVN)
6700 Valjean Avenue
Van Nuys, CA 91406
(310) 842-7450
Fax: (310) 842-7454
Web site: www.avn.com

Adult Video News, a trade journal, is the source of virtually all the statistics on the pornographic video industry that are quoted by journalists. It is indispensable to an understanding of the industry, its conventions, its skirmishes with legislation (often broken down state by state) and, most significantly, its economics, the latter replete with graphs, charts, and reports. *AVN* routinely reviews videos but also publishes numerous supplements and guides on changing tastes and markets.

American Booksellers Foundation for Free Expression
825 South Broadway
Tarrytown, NY 10591
(914) 591-2665
E-mail: info@bookweb.org
Web site: www.amb00k.org/aba

This organization helps publishers, booksellers, and distributors ensure freedom of expression.

American Civil Liberties Union (ACLU)
132 West 43rd Street
New York, NY 10036
(212) 549-2500
Web site: www.aclu.org/index.html

Established in 1920, the ACLU is a nonprofit, nonpartisan 250,000-member public interest organization devoted exclusively to protecting the basic civil liberties of all Americans. Many of its efforts are directed at equality for those sometimes denied it, especially women, minorities, and the poor, but the mission of the ACLU is to guarantee all individuals their rights as specified by the Bill of Rights. The ACLU opposes all forms of censorship and defends the individual's right to express an opinion (however controversial or extreme), not necessarily the opinion itself. Publications: *Civil Liberties* (quarterly), *Civil Liberties Alert* (monthly), and *Arts Censorship Project Newsletter* (occasional).

American Family Association, Inc. (AFA)
P.O. Drawer 2440
107 Parkgate
Tupelo, MS 38803
(601) 844-5036
Fax: (601) 842-7798
E-mail: afw@afa.net
Web site: www.afa.net

Reverend Donald Wildmon founded this Christian organization formerly known as the National Federation for Decency. The AFA advocates censorship and/or the boycotting of all media products considered "anti-Christian." Its antipornography movement is supplemented by OutReach, a program that "offers help for pornography and other sex addicts." Publication: *American Family Association Journal.*

American Society of Newspaper Editors
P.O. Box 4090
Reston, VA 22090-1700
(703) 648-1144
Fax: (703) 620-4557
E-mail: abosley@asne.org
Web site: www.asne.org

The society is made up of editors of newspapers from around the country, each of which faces daily decisions on what to publish.

The society takes positions on the publication of many types of information, including the sexually explicit, and offers guidance to newspapers and editors on dealing with censorship. Publication: *American Society of Newspaper Editors Bulletin* (nine times a year).

Association of American Publishers
1718 Connecticut Avenue NW, 7th Floor
Washington, DC 20009
(202) 232-3335
Fax: (202) 745-0694
E-mail: jplatt@publishers.org
Web site: www.publishers.org

The Association of American Publishers is the national trade organization of the U.S. book publishing industry and represents nearly 200 members. Its primary concerns are freedom of expression, freedom of publishing, copyright protections, management of new technologies, and protecting publishing markets.

Authors Guild
330 West 42nd Street, 9th Floor
New York, NY 10036
(212) 563-5904
Fax: (212) 564-5363
E-mail: staff@authorguild.org
Web site: www.authorguild.com

A lobbying organization for some 6,500 professional writers, the Authors Guild advocates freedom of expression and works to ensure it on both the local and national levels.

Banned Books Online
E-mail: spok+books@cs.cmu.edu
Web site: www.cs.cmu.edu/Web/People/spok/

Banned Books Online, an electronic exhibit/gallery of books that censors have tried to suppress, is regularly updated on the Web. Its categories include books censored by governments, school boards, and pressure groups. Links to other censorship archives are also useful.

Citizens Against Pornography
P.O. Box 220190
Chantilly, VA 22022
(703) 437-7863

Citizens Against Pornography seeks to block the opening of adult bookstores, halt the production and circulation of adult videos, and curtail the sale of adult magazines (e.g., *Playboy* and *Penthouse*) on newsstands and in other stores. It will provide information to those seeking advice on fighting pornography. Publication: *Update Letter* (occasional).

Comic Book Legal Defense Fund
P.O. Box 693
Northampton, MA 01061
(800) 992-2533
Fax: (413) 582-9046
E-mail: cbldf@compuserve.com
Web site: www.edgeglobal.com/cbldf

This fund was set up to provide legal aid for cartoonists prosecuted for obscenity. It provides information on the latest cases.

Eagle Forum
P.O. Box 618
Alton, IL 62002
(618) 462-5415
Fax: (618) 462-8909
E-mail: eagle@eagleforum.org
Web site: www.eagleforum.org

The Eagle Forum seeks to "enable conservative and pro-family men and women to participate in the process of self-government and public policy." It has an extensive political platform that includes opposing "violence, pornography and attacks on traditional family values by the entertainment industry." Publications: *Phyllis Schlafly Report, Education Reporter.*

Electronic Frontier Foundation (EFF)
1550 Bryant Street, Suite 725
San Francisco, CA 94103
(415) 436-9333
Fax: (415) 436-9993
E-mail: info@eff.org
Web site: www.eff.org/

Established by Mitch Kapor, the inventor of Lotus, and John Perry Barlow, a songwriter for the Grateful Dead, EFF has become one of the leading defenders of freedom on the Internet. Its representatives debate government officials, and the organization lobbies for legislative assurances of civil rights for those on-line. Publications: *EFF Newsletter, Protecting Yourself Online.*

Electronic Privacy Information Center
666 Pennsylvania Avenue SE, Suite 301
Washington, DC 20003
(202) 544-9240
Fax: (202) 547-5482
E-mail: info@epic.org
Web site: www.epic.org

The Electronic Privacy Information Center, financed by the Fund for Constitutional Government, seeks to ensure privacy and individual freedom on the Internet by educating the public and legislators. Publication: *The 1999 Privacy Law Sourcebook.*

Enough Is Enough
P.O. Box 888
Fairfax, VA 22039
(714) 435-9056
E-mail: dj@enough.org
Web site: www.enough.org

Begun in 1992, Enough Is Enough strives to prevent children from accessing pornographic material, to restrict pornography in all markets, and to encourage communities to oppose pornography and to treat its victims with compassion. Publications: *The Internet Safety Kit, Library Action Manual.*

Family Research Council
801 6th Street NW
Washington, DC 20001
(202) 393-2100
Fax: (202) 393-2134
E-mail: corrdept@frc.org
Web site: www.frc.orgresearch models

The Family Research Council believes that pornography is injurious to families and to minors. It promotes "traditional family values" across a variety of social and political issues. Publication: *Washington Watch* (monthly).

Federal Communications Commission (FCC)
445 12th Street SW
Washington, DC 20554

(202) 418-0190 or (800) 225-5322
Fax: (202) 418-0232
E-mail: fccinfo@fcc.gov
Web site: www.fcc.gov

The FCC regulates the nation's airwaves and can provide information about indecency rules and their violations, V-chips and
program ratings, and protecting children from exposure to inappropriate materials.

Feminists Fighting Pornography
Box 6731, Yorkville Station
New York, NY 10128
(212) 410-5182

Speakers sponsored by Feminists Fighting Pornography conduct
workshops and presentations, especially in the Northeast. The
organization advocates new laws regulating pornography, which
it regards as demeaning to women. Publication: *Backlash Times*
(annual).

Feminists for Free Expression (FFE)
2525 Times Square Station
New York, NY 10108-2525
(212) 702-6292
Fax: (212) 702-6277
E-mail: freedom@well.com
Web site: www.well.com/user/freedom

A nonprofit organization established in 1992, FFE is "a group of
diverse feminist women working to preserve the individual's
right and responsibility to read, listen, view and produce materials of her choice without intervention of the State 'for her own
good.'" The organization provides legal services to prevent censorship from silencing the voices of women. Publications: general brochure and FFE series on assorted topics, including
pornography; annual report.

Focus on the Family
P.O. Box 35500
Colorado Springs, CO 80995
(719) 531-5181
Web site: www.family.com

Originally founded by James Dobson, Focus on the Family, an
organization almost twice as large as the Christian Coalition, as-

serts that "permissiveness" is the cause of various social ills and generally espouses a Christian fundamentalist doctrine. Focus on the Family attacks sexual expression in comic books, movies, recordings, television programming, and textbooks. It opposes homosexuality, abortion, the teaching of evolution, and information on the Holocaust, but advocates school prayer. Dobson himself was a member of the Attorney General's Commission on Pornography. Publication: *Focus on the Family Citizen*.

Free Expression Clearinghouse
Web site: www.freeexpression.org

This site, operated by the Free Expression Network and founded in 1991, makes available the materials provided by the following groups, all of them opposed to censorship: Alliance for Community Media, American Arts Alliance, American Society of Newspaper Editors, American Association of University Professors, American Booksellers Foundation for Free Expression, American Civil Liberties Union, American Library Association, Americans United for the Separation of Church and State, Association of Alternative News Weeklies, Association of American Publishers, Association of American University Presses, Association of Independent Video & Filmmakers, Authors Guild, Baptist Joint Committee, Benton Foundation, Center for Media Education, College Art Association, Creative Coalition, Electronic Privacy Information Center, Feminists for Free Expression, Freedom to Read Foundation, Gay & Lesbian Alliance Against Defamation, Human Rights Watch Free Expression Project, Institute for First Amendment Studies, Interfaith Alliance, Lambda Legal Defense and Education Fund, Media Coalition, MeDIA Consortium, Motion Picture Association of America, Mystery Writers of America, Nation Institute, National Alliance for Media Arts & Culture, National Assembly of Local Arts Agencies, National Assembly of State Arts Agencies, National Association of Artists' Organizations, National Association of Recording Merchandisers, National Campaign for Freedom of Expression, National Coalition Against Censorship, National Council of Churches, National Federation of Community Broadcasters, National Gay and Lesbian Task Force, National Humanities Alliance, National PEARL, National Writers Union, PEN American Center, People for the American Way, Playboy Foundation, Pro-Choice Resource Center, Recording Industry Association of America, Rock the Vote, Student Press Law Center, Theatre Communications Group, Thomas Jefferson Center for the Protection of Free Expression, Video Software Dealers Association, and Volunteer Lawyers for the Arts.

Free Speech Coalition
22968 Victory Boulevard, Suite 248
Woodland Hills, CA 91367
(818) 348-9373
Fax: (703) 356-5085
E-mail: contactfsc@freespeechcoalition.org
Web site: www.freespeechcoalition.org/index.htm

The coalition represents various adult entertainment industries and opposes censorship as violating the rights of Americans to see, read, or use sexual products as they wish. It promotes pornography as educational and pleasurable. Publications: brochures and sourcebooks.

Institute for Advanced Study of Sexuality
1523 Franklin Street
San Francisco, CA 94109-4592
(415) 928-1133
Web site: www.iashs.edu

The Institute for Advanced Study of Sexuality has granted graduate degrees in the study of sexology, or sexual behavior in all its aspects, since 1976. The institute grew out of the National Sex Forum, which was originally funded by the Methodist Church but is now operated by the Exodus Trust, a nonprofit educational foundation. Its media catalogs list video, film, and slide packages on sexual topics ranging from masturbation, homosexuality, lovemaking for the disabled and the elderly, erotica, massage, AIDS, vasectomies, patterns of sexual behavior, abortion, women's health issues, and sex therapy. Its Archives of Erotology house one of the largest collections of sexual materials in the world, and librarians respond to letters asking specific questions. Publication: *Multi-Focus Incorporated Media Catalog.*

Institute for First Amendment Studies
P.O. Box 589
Great Barrington, MA 01230
(413) 274-0012
Fax: (413) 274-0245
E-mail: ifas@berkshire.net
Web site: www.berkshire.net/~ifas/fw

This institute focuses its research on the Religious Right with the intent of guaranteeing free expression and upholding the separation of church and state.

Institute for Media Education
P.O. Box 1136
Crestwood, KY 40014
(800) 837-0544
Fax: (502) 241-1552
E-mail: fpp@iglou.com
Web site: www.iglou.com/first~principles/reisman.html

The institute publicizes the efforts of Judith Reisman to combat pornography. Publications: *Kinsey, Sex, and Fraud; "Soft Porn" Plays Hardball; Images of Children; Crime and Violence in Playboy, Penthouse and Hustler,* all by Reisman.

Henry J. Kaiser Family Foundation
2400 Sand Hill Road
Menlo Park, CA 94025
(650) 854-9400
Fax: (650) 854-4800
Web site: www.kff.org

The Kaiser Family Foundation, which is concerned chiefly with health programs, monitors sexual information on television programming such as news shows, soap operas, and prime-time shows. It commissions academic studies to report on the way television disseminates—or fails to disseminate—messages on family planning and warnings about AIDS and the consequences of sexual activity. Its several studies indicate that despite a rise in sexual content on television over the past decade, television productions do not often address issues of responsibility and are especially remiss about the dangers of AIDS and careless reproduction. The foundation will mail or E-mail materials to interested scholars. Publications: Reports such as "Soap Operas and Sexual Activity" (1994), *The Content of Television Talk Shows: Topics, Guests and Interactions* (1995).

Kinsey Institute for Research in Sex, Gender, and Reproduction
Information Services
Morrison Hall 313
Indiana University
Bloomington, IN 47405

(812) 855-7686
E-mail: kinsey@indiana.edu
Web site: www.indiana.edu/~kinsey/

The Institute (founded by sex researcher Alfred Kinsey) archives works on every aspect of sexuality (including material considered pornographic), conducts research, issues publications, mounts exhibits, and hosts visiting scholars in the fields of sex, gender, and reproduction. Publications: Bibliographies on all aspects of sexuality and pornography, *Kinsey Institute Studies in Sex and Society* (a series of books), *Kinsey Institute Monograph Series, Kinsey Institute Data and Codebooks.*

Media Coalition
139 Fulton Street, Suite 302
New York, NY 10038
(212) 587-4025
Fax: (212) 587-2436
E-mail: mediacoalition@mediacoalition.org
Web site: www.mediacoalition.org/

Created in 1973, the coalition is composed of various publishing organizations, including the American Booksellers Association, the Association of American Publishers, and the Magazine Publishers of America. It defends the First Amendment right to sell and publish any materials containing sexual content that cannot be defined as legally obscene. Publications: *The Rev. Donald E. Wildmon's Crusade for Censorship, 1977–1992* and *Catharine A. MacKinnon: The Rise of a Feminist Censor, 1983–1993.*

Media Studies Center (funded by the Freedom Forum)
580 Madison Avenue
New York, NY 10022
(212) 317-6500
E-mail: media@ffnyc.mhs.compuserve.com
Web site: www.mediastudies.org

The Media Studies Center calls itself "the nation's premier media think tank devoted to improving understanding of media issues by the press and the public." The center hosts forums, seminars, and roundtable discussions and sponsors research for media professionals and scholars. The center is interested in exploring issues regarding the effects of media on society. Publications: bimonthly newsletter, working papers ("Radio: The Forgotten Medium"), and *Media Studies Journal.*

Morality in Media (MIM) and National Obscenity Law Center
475 Riverside Drive, Suite 239
New York, NY 10115
(212) 870-3222
E-mail: mimnyc@ix.netcom.com
Web sites: pw1.netcom.com/~nolc/brochure.html; pw2.netcom.com/mimnyc/MAINPAGE HTM

Founded in 1962, MIM defines itself as a "national, interfaith nonprofit organization" that addresses "the exploitation of obscenity in the marketplace and the erosion of decency standards in the media." MIM sponsors a WRAP (White Ribbon Against Pornography) campaign during Pornography Awareness Week, and a "Turn Off TV Day" to protest offensive broadcasting. It maintains that pornography is not a protected form of speech and urges rigorous enforcement of obscenity laws. MIM also houses the National Obscenity Law Center, a clearinghouse of legal information for lawyers, libraries, and the general public. The center collects, abstracts, and files all obscenity decisions in the United States and furnishes them to prosecutors, agencies, and individuals who wish to fairly enforce obscenity laws. Publications: *Morality in Media Newsletter* (monthly), *TV: The World's Greatest Mind-Bender, Obscenity Law Reporter* (3 vols.), and *Obscenity Law Bulletin.*

Motion Picture Association of America (MPAA)
1600 Eye Street
Washington, DC 20006
(202) 293-1966
Fax: (202) 293-1299
E-mail: pegge@mpaa.org
Web site: www.smpte.org/sustain/MPAA.html

The Motion Picture Association of America can trace its history back to the Motion Picture Producers and Distributors of America (MPPDA), a self-policing organization begun in 1922 and generally called the Hays Office after its first head. Under pressure from Catholic censorship groups, the MPPDA created its Production Code in 1930 to eliminate from movies virtually all explicit references to sex and reproduction. In 1945, the major studios formed the Motion Picture Producers' Association (MPPA). In 1966, under Jack Valenti, the MPPA began rating movies as G, M, R, and X. In 1984 the MPPA added a PG-13 (Parental Guidance) rating. By 1990, the renamed Motion Picture

Association of America (MPAA) replaced the "X" rating with "NC-17" (No Children). The MPAA does not provide rationales for its ratings. It opposes censorship, promotes copyright protection, advises parents, and generally lobbies its members for responsible expression.

National Association of Artists' Organizations
918 F Street NW, Suite 611
Washington, DC 20004
(202) 347-6350
E-mail: naao2@naao.org
Web site: www.artswire.org/naao

The National Association of Artists' Organizations is a loose federation that advises groups of artists who encounter censorship or interdictions of their civil liberties and assists them through education, advocacy, litigation (where necessary), and lobbying. Publications: *NAAO Bulletin, Organizing Artists: A Document and Directory of the National Association of Artists' Organizations.*

National Association of Recording Merchandisers
9 Eves Drive, Suite 120
Marlton, NJ 08053
(609) 596-2221
Fax: (609) 596-3268
E-mail: 7272010@compuserve.com
Web site: www.nacm@tampa.com

This trade organization promotes many types of recording merchandise but concentrates on music. It assists record producers with censorship problems.

National Campaign for Freedom of Expression (NCFE)
1429 6th Street NW, PMB 416
Washington, DC 20005-2009
(202) 393-2787
E-mail: ncfe@ncfe.net
Web site: www.artswire.org/ncfe

The NCFE calls itself "an educational and advocacy network of artists, arts organizations, audience members and concerned citizens formed to protect and extend freedom of artistic expression and fight censorship throughout the United States." It identifies itself as the only national organization committed to defending the arts against First Amendment infringements. It offers technical and legal assistance to those fighting censorship and holds educational workshops and programs. Publication: *NCFE Quarterly Bulletin*.

National Campaign to Combat Internet Pornography (NCCIP)
5900 Mosteller Drive, Suite 1221
Oklahoma City, OK 73112
E-mail: nccip@nccip.org
Web site: www.nccip.org

The NCCIP "is a coalition of individuals, businesses, health care professionals and nonprofit organizations committed to ending the importation, storage, distribution and/or display of child pornography and obscenity on the Internet and restricting access on the Internet to minors of sexually explicit material that is harmful to minors." It seeks to accomplish these aims by educating the public about the harmful effects of pornography as well as issues pertaining to obscenity law.

National Coalition Against Censorship (NCAC)
275 7th Avenue
New York, NY 10001
(212) 807-6222
Fax: (212) 807-6245
E-mail: ncac@ncac.org
Web site: www.ncac.org/about.html

Established in 1974, the NCAC is "an alliance of over 40 national nonprofit organizations, including literary, artistic, religious, educational, professional, labor and civil liberties groups," committed to defending First Amendment rights and freedoms as well as educating the public about the dangers of censorship. It includes the NCAC Working Group on Women, Censorship and Pornography. Publications: *Censorship News* (newsletter), *Freedom Is Not a Dirty Word* (pamphlet), *The Sex Panic: Women, Censorship, and "Pornography."*

National Coalition for the Protection of Children and Families (NCPCF)
800 Compton Road, Suite 9224
Cincinnati, OH 45231
(513) 522-0011
E-mail: info@eos.net
Web site: www2.nationalcoalition.org

The former National Coalition Against Pornography, NCPCF aims "to significantly reduce sexual exploitation and violence in America by increasing public awareness of the availability and harm of exploitative and abusive pornography, particularly in the lives of children, supporting the enactment and enforcement, within the Constitution, of limitations on pornography, and offering assistance to people whose lives pornography has harmed." It inspired the creation of other antipornography groups such as Enough Is Enough and the Religious Alliance Against Pornography. The coalition maintains the National Law Center for Children and Families to distribute literature on illegal expression. Publication: *Children, Pornography, and Cyberspace* (brochure).

National Family Legal Foundation
11000 North Scottsdale Road, Suite 144
Scottsdale, AZ 85254
(480) 922-9731
Fax: (480) 922-7240
E-mail: nflf@nflf.com
Web site: www.nflf.com/

Since 1990 the National Family Legal Foundation has provided free legal counsel and other resources to citizens who wish to take action against the harmful effects of sexually oriented businesses. It offers a manual of case law to prosecutors and officials trying to regulate, license, or zone adult enterprises. Publication: *Protecting Communities from Sexually Oriented Businesses.*

National Organization for Women (NOW)
733 15th Street NW, 2nd Floor
Washington, DC 20005
(202) 628-8669
E-mail: now@now.org
Web site: www.now.org/

The National Organization for Women lobbies for the rights of women. Opposing only pornography that degrades women, NOW recognizes that many forms of sexual expression are not degrading to women and holds that women are entitled to explore their own fantasies. Its position is that current laws governing obscenity are generally sufficient.

Office for Intellectual Freedom
American Library Association (ALA)
50 East Huron Street
Chicago, IL 60611
(312) 280-4223 or (800) 545-2433
E-mail: u24803@uicvm.uic.edu
Web site: www.ala.org/

Although intended primarily to advise and assist librarians who encounter censorship problems, the ALA's Office for Intellectual Freedom attempts also to educate the public on its belief that un-fettered access to information and expression is a necessity. Its newsletter circulates lists of books that have come under fire in the nation's libraries. The office sponsors Banned Books Week every year to remind patrons of their freedoms. Publications: *Newsletter on Intellectual Freedom* (periodical), *Banned Books Week Resource Book* (annual).

Parents' Music Resource Center (PMRC)
1500 Arlington Boulevard
Arlington, VA 22304
(703) 527-9466
Fax: (703) 527-9468

The nonprofit Parents' Music Resource Center was founded in 1984 by Tipper Gore and other wives of politicians in Washing-ton. It lobbies for consumer information about messages in music aimed at children and adolescents and functions as a clearing-house for such information. The center promotes parental aware-ness of music videos and stage performances that emphasize drugs and alcohol, and of lyrics that may contain references to the occult, Satanism, sex, suicide, abuse of women, aggression, racism, and violence. The center received the backing of the U.S. Senate in pressuring the music industry to adopt labels indicat-ing that records contain lyrics with references to sexuality, vio-lence, or drugs. Many stores, especially chains, will not carry records or CDs with labels designating explicit content. Publica-tion: *Rising to the Challenge.*

PEN American Center Freedom to Write Committee
568 Broadway, Suite 401
New York, NY 10012
(212) 334-1660
Fax: (212) 334-2181

E-mail: pen@echonyc.com
Web site: www.pen.org/

A worldwide group affiliated with the United Nations, this organization promotes intellectual and artistic freedom, lobbies Congress, defends writers, and alerts the public when writers are suppressed or imprisoned. Committee members write letters to institutions, agencies, and organizations that have abridged freedom of expression; the organization also files lawsuits and submits amicus curiae briefs in court cases.

People for the American Way
2000 M Street NW, Suite 400
Washington, DC 20036
(202) 467-4999
E-mail: pfaw@pfaw.org
Web site: www.pfaw.org/

Among other political activities designed to guarantee rights to all Americans, People for the American Way defends the First Amendment. It advises and assists educators, parents, and professionals threatened by censors.

Rock the Vote!
1460 4th Street, Suite 200
Santa Monica, CA 90401
(310) 656-2464
Fax: (310) 656-2474
E-mail: rocthevote@aol.com
Web site: www.rockthevote.org

Rock the Vote! is a political action group sponsored by members of the music industry alarmed by efforts to censor rock, rap, and other forms of music. It encourages audiences to vote their preferences by electing politicians opposed to censorship and provides information on the industry.

Sex Information and Education Council
of the United States (SIECUS)
32 Washington Place
New York, NY 10003
Web site: www.siecus.org

Incorporated in 1964, SIECUS promotes the idea that sexuality is a natural and healthy aspect of life. It collects, develops, and publishes information, promotes education, and distributes annotated bibliographies on many facets of sexuality, including sexual representation and its uses.

Theater Communications Group
355 Lexington Avenue
New York, NY 10017
(212) 697-5230
Fax: (212) 983-4857
E-mail: custserv@tcg.org

Although designed to assist theater managers, the Theater Communications Group offers information on topics of interest to theater professionals, including how to combat censorship and deal with drama involving sensitive subjects.

Women Against Pornography
358 West 47th Street
New York, NY 10036
(212) 307-5055

Women Against Pornography first came to attention in the 1980s, when it held marches and conducted tours through adult businesses in Times Square. It lobbies Congress and state legislatures for more effective laws to censor pornography, attempts to educate Americans to the harm that pornography causes, and distributes information explaining its cause. Publications: *Where We Stand on the First Amendment: Women Against Pornography Position Paper.*

Print and Nonprint Reference Materials

7

The following sources are selected from an outpouring of criticism on sexual representation, the sheer vastness of which attests to the significance of pornography for U.S. culture at large.

Books

Abel, Richard L. *Speaking Respect, Respecting Speech.* Chicago: University of Chicago Press, 1998.

Abel suggests that we argue continuously about the limits of speech in contemporary culture because issues of identity overshadow many others. He explores gender, racial, and religious divisions and tries to steer a course between civil libertarians and "regulatory enthusiasts" by proposing a climate of discourse that amplifies silenced voices and soothes the injuries caused by extreme speech (such as pornography) through ceremonies of apology constructed by various communities.

Adelman, Bob, ed. *Tijuana Bibles: Art and Wit in America's Forbidden Funnies, 1930s–1950s.* New York: Simon and Schuster, 1997.

This compilation of examples of the demotic art form called Tijuana bibles includes commentary by Adelman and cartoonist Art Spiegelman, an essay on styles of "bibles" by the artist Richard Merkin, and two essays (and a bibliography) on the language and sensibilities of "eight-pagers" by Madeline Kripke.

Allen, Robert C. *Horrible Prettiness: Burlesque and American Culture.* Chapel Hill: University of North Carolina Press, 1991.

The raucous comedy of burlesque nurtured what eventually came to be known as striptease. In some respects, burlesque is the classic example of vulgarity spiraling toward the center of a culture's regard, having produced a generation of Bert Lahrs, Red Buttons, Ann Corios, and Fanny Brices to transform theater, nightclubs, and film. Allen's analytical history, in addition to providing an excellent survey through the 1930s, covers posters, magazines, and stereographs on burlesque; includes a fine discussion of "cooch" dancing; and appends an excellent bibliography of sources and collections.

Allison, Dorothy. *Skin: Talking about Sex, Class and Literature.* Ithaca, N.Y.: Firebrand Books, 1994.

Allison speaks primarily about the difficulties of writing lesbian erotica, some of which include the necessity of getting past stereotypes invented by males. She believes that writing such pornography is important, however, as a way of making sense of lesbian sexuality.

Assiter, Alison, and Avedon Carol, eds. *Bad Girls and Dirty Pictures: The Challenge to Reclaim Feminism.* Boulder, Colo.: Pluto Press, 1993.

This volume contains several important essays, the most notable of which are Alison King's review of the inconclusive research on pornography, "Mystery and Imagination: The Case of Pornography Effects Studies"; Avedon Carol's exposé of the Snuff hoax, "Snuff: Believing the Worst"; and Gayle Rubin's vigorous dissection of the antiporn feminist position, "Misguided, Dangerous and Wrong: An Analysis of Anti-Pornography Politics." All of the essays in the volume are prosex, and most advocate that women create or appropriate a sexual discourse with feminist aims in mind.

Arcand, Bernard. *The Jaguar and the Anteater: Pornography Degree Zero,* Wayne Grady, trans. New York: Verso, 1993.

Part of this volume is a brief history of pornography between 1500 and 1900, including a comparison of Western artifacts with some from India. Arcand traces many disputes to problems with defining pornography, and he reviews the commentary on sexual expression by various postmodern theorists. Pornography symbolizes freedom, Arcand suggests, because its fantasies can be enjoyed privately by individuals but at the risk of alienation, loneliness, and a dependence on the artificial. He notes that more and more specialized technologies deal with erotic expression in a paradoxical dialectic; eroticism drives technology, which then becomes more erotic in order to be more appealing to humans.

Bataille, Georges. *Eroticism.* Paris: Editions de Minuit, 1957. *Death and Sensuality: A Study of Eroticism and the Taboo.* New York: Ballantine Books, 1962. *Eroticism: Death and Sensuality,* Mary Dalwood, trans. San Francisco: City Light Books, 1986.

Bataille's thesis is that pornography derives its power from shock: It creates an eroticism that divorces sex from its natural context. Because Western civilization itself is an artificial construct, it locates eroticism in representations that distance themselves from reproduction. Those attracted to sexual representations are not seeking realism, he postulates, but fantasy. Pornography is thus not a "natural" response to sexuality but is nonetheless a quintessentially human attempt to break moral and esthetic taboos.

Bayles, Martha. *Hole in Our Soul: The Loss of Beauty and Meaning in American Popular Music.* Chicago: University of Chicago Press, 1994.

Bayles does not think that the influx of marginal voices into mainstream music has been esthetic. Graphing the decline of American popular music into perversity, decadence, and obscenity, she maintains that the industry should market better stuff more aggressively, not censor the trash that can be driven out by competition. Bayles believes that the essential vitality of American forms such as jazz (though she acknowledges the sexual origins of jazz) will eventually reshape music and move it beyond travesty.

Burger, John R. *One-Handed Histories: The Eroto-Politics of Gay Male Video Pornography.* New York: Harrington Park Press/Haworth Press, 1995.

Leaving aside its value as entertainment and sexual stimulation, gay pornographic video helps establish cohesiveness among gays who have traditionally been denied a sense of community. So writes Burger, who believes that gay porn video serves "popular memory" in two ways: in the first place, both gays and non-gays can study it as a "cultural document"; in the second, it can function politically to help reshape gay subcultures and their place in the larger culture. At the very least, gay porn makes homosexuals "visible" and impossible to ignore. Burger provides a solid history of the medium as well, with references to directors and actors of various degrees of celebrity.

Buss, David M. *The Evolution of Desire: Strategies of Human Mating.* New York: Basic Books, 1994.

In contrast to social constructionists, who hold that culture shapes desire, evolutionary psychologists and sociobiologists assert that the primary determinants of gender and sexuality are genetics, hormones, and evolution. Like other scientists, Buss thinks that genetic strategies compel males to spread sperm as widely as possible so as to produce offspring. Pornography aimed at men reinforces these strategies by depicting men in congress with a variety of willing females. Survival strategies for females lead them to search for males with desirable genes—manifest as personal attractiveness, physical strength, or financial resources sufficient to protect mates and children. Pornography aimed at women prizes those characteristics. Buss and Neil M. Malamuth, a well-known pornography researcher, have edited *Sex, Power and Conflict: Evolutionary and Feminist Perspectives* (New York: Oxford University Press, 1996) to explore some of those ideas further.

Caldwell, Mark. *A Short History of Rudeness: Manners, Morals, and Misbehavior in Modern America.* New York: Picador, 1999.

Caldwell uses many pornographic examples of the nineteenth and twentieth centuries to illustrate his thesis that what Americans often assume to be the decline of morality is often better characterized as lapses of taste. The book is a witty exploration of shifts in manners, the social conventions that a society creates and maintains in order to reduce friction among its members but also to defend against embarrassment and inappropriate behavior.

Carter, Angela. *The Sadeian Woman and the Ideology of Pornography: An Exercise in Cultural History.* New York: Pantheon, 1979.

Carter analyzes pornography in terms of class, politics, and gender, taking as her starting point the work of the Marquis de Sade. Although de Sade's fantasies clearly subordinated women to stereotypes, Carter maintains, they also undermined an established authoritarian social and political order and thus held out possibilities for women. If they have the courage, writes Carter, women can also find in sexual fantasy a psychic and social liberation. Such an approach is not without danger, she admits, but the benefits might well outweigh risks.

Chapple, Steve, and David Talbot. *Burning Desires: Sex in America, a Report from the Field.* New York: Signet, 1990.

This is perhaps the most informative of several narrative sexual surveys of the United States in recent years, primarily because the authors include their conversations with a wide sampling of people who produce sexual materials and those who oppose them. Among the interviewed are Erica Jong, Tipper Gore, Germaine Greer, Candida Royalle, Annie Sprinkle, Anne Rice, Susie Bright, and Missy Florez. They reflect on the social roles of pornography and their own roles in a debate over expression that still continues.

Chaucer, Lynn S. *Reconcilable Differences: Confronting Beauty, Pornography, and the Future of Feminism.* Berkeley: University of California Press, 1998.

Chaucer argues that confusing sex and sexism—as she believes antiporn feminists do—is one major reason for our culture's inability to find esthetic principles in erotic expression. Western culture has refined its appreciation for bodies over centuries, and esthetic principles enable us to sort through eroticism, find the beautiful even in ugly depictions and degrading postures, and generally reconcile the different imperatives of art and pornography.

Christensen, F. M. *Pornography: The Other Side.* New York: Praeger, 1990.

The author, a Canadian philosopher, exposes myths and misinformation about pornography. He suggests that anger directed against pornography has to do with persistent shame regarding bodily functions rather than concern with violence, especially since there is so little evidence of connections between eroticism and aggression. The real culprits may be false modesty, sexual ignorance, and the lack of education in the United States. Christensen believes that pornography has positive value for a culture hamstrung by sexual repression, dehumanized by technology, oppressed with sterile theories of power, roiled by special interest groups, and divided by suspicion and bickering. According to him, Americans can choose to enjoy pornography or not, and take from it what they will.

de Grazia, Edward. *Girls Lean Back Everywhere: The Law of Obscenity and the Assault on Genius.* New York: Random House, 1992.

The author traces the slow liberalization of American obscenity law in terms of its cost to people and society. He maintains that because censorship stifles the gifted, the novel, and the radical, champions of free speech have had to learn to combat the tactics of authoritarians. Defense attorneys such as Morris Ernst had to learn to use the censors' own tactics; Ernst kept asking for postponements until he got Judge John Woolsey to preside over the *Ulysses* trial. De Grazia's point is that deception is common to both sides because the law does not deal with right and wrong— only with speech itself, which must be protected. *Girls Lean Back* (the title is borrowed from Jane Heap's defense of her publishing parts of James Joyce's *Ulysses* in *The Little Review*) begins with the case of Ida Craddock, imprisoned in 1902 for sending a sex guide, *The Wedding Night,* through the mails; it also deals with celebrated cases of suppressed literature and art in the 1940s and 1950s and includes more recent attacks on Lenny Bruce, Anne Rice, Holly Hughes, Karen Finley, and 2 Live Crew.

Dines, Gail, Robert Jensen, and Ann Russo. *Pornography: The Production and Consumption of Inequality.* New York: Routledge, 1998.

The authors deconstruct various examples of pornography as discourses of oppression that cannot be separated from institutional abuses of power and social and political sources of injustice. They attempt to distinguish feminist antipornography arguments from right-wing and fundamentalist critiques by way of validating the former, and suggest that feminists who have rejected antiporn positions are no longer concerned with violence against women or that they are taking a narrow view of individual rights as opposed to the harm done women as a class.

Dworkin, Andrea. *Pornography: Men Possessing Women.* New York: Putnam's, 1980.

This volume, the chief text of the feminist antiporn movement, asserts that discriminatory sexual expression constitutes the environment in which women live. The author's thesis is that misogyny drives pornography and that pornography in turn feeds misogyny. Pornography enshrines misogyny, Dworkin maintains, by socializing all of society's members, male and female, to accept the subordinate role of women. Defined as a wholly male form of discourse, pornography legitimizes male dominance by insisting on the inequality of men and women. Worse, writes Dworkin, it is the principal instrument for degrading and victimizing all women to gratify a universal male lust animated entirely and solely by hatred. Pornography is thus the sexual reality of America; it is the root of male discrimination against women, a plan for abuse and also its cause, not merely its expression. She believes that sexual representation inevitably reduces women to the status of objects that exist for the gratification of masculine pleasure, and therefore pornography should be subject to legal suppression in the interests of justice.

Elias, James, Veronica Diehl Elias, Vern L. Bullough, Gwen Brewer, Jeffrey J. Douglas, and Will Jarvis, eds. *Porn 101: Eroticism, Pornography, and the First Amendment.* Amherst, N.Y.: Prometheus Books, 1999.

A collection of papers delivered at the August 1998 California conference called World Pornography: Eroticism and the First Amendment, organized by the Center for Sex Research of California State University at Northridge and other groups, to bring together academics, attorneys, critics, and sex workers. The diversity of views on so many topics is unusual for a single volume, and though some are slight, all are informative. Especially noteworthy are David F. Austin's "(Sexual) Quotation Without (Sexual) Harassment? Educational Use of Pornography in the Classroom" and Russell Wilcox's "Cross-Gender Identification in Commercial Pornographic Films."

Estren, Mark. *A History of Underground Comics.* 3rd. ed. Berkeley: Ronin, 1993.

The most authoritative study of sexually graphic American cartoons, Estren's history is indispensable for information on leading exponents of the form such as R. Crumb; an appendix provides a checklist of major underground titles compiled by Clay Geerdes.

Faust, Bernice. *Women, Sex and Pornography: A Controversial Study.* New York: Macmillan, 1980.

Faust maintains that women are more sexually responsive to tactile than visual stimulation and for that reason are not so attracted to the kinds of pornography preferred by men. She admits to understanding why male ejaculation, for example, is exciting, but she also understands why few women are turned on by the sight. Faust applies logic to the study of erotic materials, believes that it is shallow to assume that all porn is an expression of male power, and asserts that men and women should strive for better communication through sexual expression, pornographic or not.

Flowers, Amy. *The Fantasy Factory: An Insider's View of the Phone Sex Industry.* Philadelphia: University of Pennsylvania Press, 1998.

An ethnographic study of operators and, to a lesser extent, of clients, by a scholar who worked in the industry. Dial-a-porn services have evolved from prerecorded messages to exchanges of fantasies between operator and caller. The workers in these enterprises usually come from lower-class backgrounds, drawn to the business because of the money and the flexible hours; they constitute a particular subculture of the sex industry. Some operators work from scripts and others improvise, drawing on experience with previous clients to construct stimulating narratives. Operators learn how to assess a caller's character and requirements, the protocols for dealing with different genders, how to keep callers on the line for maximum credit card charges, and how to construct titillating stories that build toward climax.

Gamson, Joshua. *Freaks Talk Back: Tabloid Talk Shows and Sexual Nonconformity.* Chicago: University of Chicago Press, 1998.

Gamson thinks that scandalous talk shows function as engines of change in social attitudes toward deviant or alternative sexual lifestyles. Preposterous—and even pornographic—as the shows and their guests seem, Americans listen and participate in these fora for marginal voices.

Garber, Marjorie. *Vice Versa: Bisexuality and the Erotics of Everyday Life.* New York: Simon and Schuster, 1995.

Garber addresses current fascination with gender instability by locating bisexuality not on some median between homosexuality and heterosexuality but beyond both. To some degree, she thinks, gender is a matter of fashion, clothing, and lifestyle, a way of renegotiating identities and revamping bodies. Pornography both reflects such trends and influences them by providing signs and cues.

Gerdts, William H. *The Great American Nude: A History in Art.* New York: Praeger, 1974.

Gerdts's book is the best single survey of American representations of the nude, the views of critics, and the reactions of the public, all sketched historically through biographies of painters and sculptors. Noting that American artists like Benjamin West, Gilbert Stuart, and John Singleton Copley had to leave America to learn to draw the nude in Europe, Gerdts praises realist Thomas Eakins with insisting on life drawing for his students in this country in the face of public outcry, then charts the growing tolerance that encouraged George Luks, George Bellows, William Glackens, and Robert Henri. Gerdts covers marginal forms such as pictures of bathing beauties and barroom cuties and includes a chronology of important exhibitions. Freeing depictions of the nude from the taint of obscenity, he says, required artistic determination, increased education, and more tolerant legislation.

Gertzman, Jay. *Bookleggers and Smuthounds: The Trade in Erotica, 1920–1940.* Philadelphia: University of Pennsylvania Press, 1999.

This richly conceived volume explores the American trade in erotica during the period before and after the Depression, when the book industry was lurching toward greater candor. Pornography, says Gertzman, flourishes in periods of economic hardship, as unemployed workers move into the business and consumers who cannot afford other kinds of entertainment purchase books, magazines, and movies that offer more stimulation for the money. New ideas also emerge. Gertzman develops Georg Simmel's concept of the stranger or the outsider—a kind of social scapegoat—into a vision of pornographers as "pariah capitalists" who are condemned for carrying out exactly the sorts of functions, for example, producing or distributing pornography, that society needs. Gertzman notes that East Europeans played that role by publishing works that pushed the limits of candor. Battling against the pornographers were the New York Society for the Suppression of Vice, the U.S. Post Office, and the

FBI, which tried to halt "booklegging," or the practice of clandestine or pirated printing, raided printing shops, and interdicted distribution from bookstores, lending libraries, drugstores, cigar stores, newsstands, and storefronts. Gertzman categorizes erotica across a spectrum from borderline to obscene. These include light erotic fiction, expurgated classics, ballads, jestbooks, and treatises on women and love; potboiling romances and mysteries; anthropological and sociological texts on subjects ranging from hygiene, deviance, marriage, and birth control to prostitution, nudism, and bizarre sexual customs and practices; pamphlets filled with confessions, anecdotes, and graphic stories of seduction or conquest, or Tijuana Bibles, a term applied to explicit comic books or stapled collections of poorly printed stories; and officially forbidden works such as *Lady Chatterley's Lover* and *Tropic of Cancer.*

Gever, Martha, Pratibha Parmar, and John Greyson, eds. *Queer Looks: Perspectives on Lesbian and Gay Film and Video.* New York: Routledge, 1993.

The editors have collected fine essays on what might be called "serious" gay and lesbian erotic experiments in film and video, including comment on avant-garde filmmaker George Kuchar, on independent gay and lesbian filmmakers (e. g., Jerry Tartaglia, Barbara Hammer, Abigail Child, Cecilia Dougherty, Yvonne Rainer, Su Friedrich, and activist video collectives), on the educational aspects of pornographic films, on documentaries such as *Paris Is Burning* and on images of black gay men generally, and on semiotic and narrative differences in films and videos made for gays and lesbians.

Gilfoyle, Timothy J. *City of Eros: New York City, Prostitution, and the Commercialization of Sex, 1790–1920.* New York: Norton, 1992.

Gilfoyle's history of a formative period covers sex industries in America's major city. According to the author, pornographic genres grew out the "sporting world" that included bars, bordellos, prize fights, carnivals, indecent performances in dance and music halls, and other seedy enterprises that provided a context for vulgar expression. The author draws on court records, pornographic magazines and books, and period accounts to explore the class divisions that he views as essential to concepts of the forbidden.

Goldin, Nan. *I'll Be Your Mirror.* New York: Whitney Museum of Art, 1996.

This book showcases Goldin's photographs from an exhibit held from 30 October 1996 to 5 January 1997. The photographer assembled the images as a "diary" of experience. A great observer of erotic states, Goldin has recorded cultural and sexual transformations in people she has known intimately. Few artists are so able to reveal the mysteries of psyches and their relationships through photographs of bodies.

Griffin, Susan. *Pornography and Silence: Culture's Revenge against Nature.* New York: Harper and Row, 1981.

According to Griffin, pornography, defined very loosely as male discourse, is an attack on nature, of which women are the true symbol, and thus an attack on motherhood as well. The masculine dichotomies of pornography separate "soul" and "body," promote artifice, distance males from "nature," and encourage self-hatred, aggression, and deviance. She contrasts pornography's objectification of women with tales of ideal love such as *Tristan and Iseult.*

Hebditch, David, and Nick Anning. *Porn Gold: Inside the Pornography Business.* London: Faber and Faber, 1988.

Although somewhat dated, this work remains one of the best popular investigations of the industry because it deals with entrepreneurs shaking off connections to organized crime and striving for quasi-respectability. The authors interviewed a wide range of people involved in producing books, magazines, videotapes, and ancillary genres. More accurately than anyone else at the time (1987), they estimated the annual worldwide revenues of sexually explicit materials at somewhere in excess of $5 billion, of which the lion's share came from consumer demand for videotapes.

Heidenry, John. *What Wild Ecstasy: The Rise and Fall of the Sexual Revolution.* New York: Simon and Schuster, 1997.

This is a broad, humane, and anecdotal but well-researched account of the sexual revolution of the 1960s, which the author traces back to the 1930s and then carries forward to its loss of energy in the 1980s and 1990s. Heidenry devotes considerable space to the exploits of pornographers, sex performers, and critics of sexual candor.

Hoffmann, Frank. *Analytical Survey of Anglo-American Traditional Erotica.* Bowling Green, Ohio: Popular Press, 1973.
Hoffmann identifies erotic elements as found in various media, then arranges some 400 erotic folklore types keyed to standard folktale and folk literature classification schemes and motif indexes. He demonstrates that narratives, motifs, jokes, and characters from oral tradition recur in modern pornographic genres in print and visual forms.

Horn, Maurice. *Sex in the Comics.* New York: Chelsea House, 1985.
This volume traces sexual themes and images in comic strips and books from many countries, but it devotes most attention to American examples. Horn's history begins with Tijuana bibles, eight-page pornographic booklets, and ranges through the underground comix of the 1960s and 1970s to the alternative, genderbending comics of today.

Hubner, John. *Bottom Feeders: From Free Love to Hard Core—The Rise and Fall of Counterculture Heroes Jim and Artie Mitchell.* New York: Doubleday, 1993.
Hubner explores the social changes behind a counterculture that idolized Jim and Artie Mitchell, advocates of sexual libertarianism and makers of one of the most famous of all porn films, *Behind the Green Door* (1972). Self-consciously subversive, *Behind the Green Door* transformed the Ivory Snow Girl (Marilyn Chambers) into a different sort of American icon, attracting massive audiences in the United States and abroad. Their O'Farrell Theater, located in San Francisco and notorious for graphic acts, nurtured the most prominent porn performers of the 1970s and 1980s, and their fight to liberalize sexual expression attracted many allies. Their nonetheless dark saga ended in a falling out that led to Jim Mitchell killing his brother Artie.

Hunt, Lynn, ed. *The Invention of Pornography: Obscenity and the Origins of Modernity, 1500–1800.* Cambridge, Mass.: MIT Zone, 1993.
Essays by various historians deal with pornographic artifacts from classical Greece and Rome but concentrate on sixteenth-century Italy, eighteenth-century Holland, and seventeenth- and eighteenth-century France and England. They maintain that a pornography fully emergent in the sixteenth century be-

comes inextricably linked with the rise of democracy, the swelling of the middle class, the shifting of population to urban centers, the decline of religious authority, the advent of science and materialism, the codification of law, the development of technology, the evolution of literary realism, the separation of genders, and the concept of modernity itself. Hunt believes that pornography functioned to subvert established order and authority until commercialization blunted its political connotations at the end of the eighteenth century. She also notes that the eighteenth century signaled a shift in pornography's depiction of women. Prior to the 1790s, Hunt says, pornography depicted women as both sexual and autonomous. Afterward, pornography reduced the desire for women's bodies to a component of male bonding.

Jay, Timothy. *Cursing in America: A Psycholinguistic Study of Dirty Language in the Courts, in the Movies, in the Schoolyards, and on the Streets.* Philadelphia: John Benjamins, 1992.

Jay examines obscene language in the streets and as conveyed by various media, including the electronic; speculates on gender differences in the use of obscenity; and discusses what makes words offensive. He believes that factors such as settings, speakers, audiences, and circumstances influence obscene messages, and that some function therapeutically while others are designed to make a good narrative, and still others express aggression and outrage.

Juffer, Jane. *At Home with Pornography: Women, Sex, and Everyday Life.* New York: New York University Press, 1998.

Juffer has studied the home consumption of pornography and erotica by American women as well as the patterns by which they "domesticate" such expression. She believes that such consumption can actually "empower" women by allowing them to explore their own sexualities in private, by informing them about sexual impulses and the pleasure they can bring, and by teaching them how to masturbate and to achieve greater degrees of satisfaction from partners. Improved media and easy access permit women to select from many representations, reject those they find demeaning or alien, and embrace those that are meaningful and erotic. Adult cable channels, lingerie catalogs, cyberporn, sex toys, erotic stories, and other representations of sex thus provide secret but safe sources of pleasure and psychic energy. Juffer's thesis is straightforward: Women (and men) need sexual stimulation in order to live physical and cultural lives, and they take what they need personally and collectively from margins that are continuously replenished by human ingenuity.

Juno, Andrea, and V. Vale, eds. *Angry Women*. San Francisco: RE/Search, 1992.

This volume contains interviews with and personal accounts by sixteen performance artists (Kathy Acker, Susie Bright, Wanda Coleman, Valie Export, Karen Finley, Diamanda Galás, bell hooks, Holly Hughes, Lydia Lunch, Suzie Kerr and Dianne Malley, Linda Montano, Avital Ronell, Sapphire, Carolee Schneemann, and Annie Sprinkle). The artists discuss the rationale behind art on masturbation, sadomasochism, menstruation, gender, violence, age, beauty, and other radical stagings. Extensive bibliographies are appended to each section.

Juno, Andrea, and V. Vale, eds. *Incredibly Strange Films*. San Francisco: RE/Search, 1986.

This volume, perhaps the most comprehensive single survey of exploitation films, is divided into categories: Biker, Juvenile Delinquency, Beach Party, LSD, Women in Prison, Mondo, Industrial Jeopardy, and so on. Chapters deal with such filmmakers as Herschell Gordon Lewis, Ted V. Mikels, Russ Meyer, Irving Klaw, Joe Sarno, David F. Friedman, and Doris Wishman. Analytical commentary and extensive filmographies capture the often bizarre histories of some of these films.

Kappeler, Susanne. *The Pornography of Representation*. Minneapolis: University of Minnesota Press, 1986.

An extreme version of the "male gaze" thesis, this volume argues that patriarchal oppression of women is based on a male esthetic; therefore any and all representations are sexist. As Kappeler presents it, the "male gaze" is a feminist version of original sin: Masculine bias has irrevocably tainted human vision, language, and thought. For that reason women will forever be victims in the most primal sense and can never develop their own ideas, let alone a sexuality unequivocally female, and still less a sexual discourse that speaks to them unless they destroy Western art in the name of justice to women. Kappeler believes women cannot work for equality through art, only through political action, and they must be prepared to junk centuries of representation and start over.

Kendrick, Walter. *The Secret Museum: Pornography in Modern Culture.* New York: Viking, 1987.

Kendrick's history of explicit literature locates the "invention" of pornography at the intersection of two phenomena that came together at the cusp of the eighteenth and nineteenth centuries. The first was the assembling of clandestine archives, or "secret museums," in which collectors hid erotica from the lower classes and from women, an impulse that institutionalized the concept of the forbidden. The second impulse, similar to the first, was a fearful response to the technological acceleration of information about prostitution and other sexual subjects. Because literacy was spreading to the masses, the upper classes urged prohibition, expurgation, and regulation as checks on a rampant democracy that could submerge privacy by making sexual behavior and expression public. In Kendrick's view, pornography is a zone of contest whose skirmish lines are constantly redrawn.

Kimmel, Michael S., ed. *Men Confront Pornography.* New York: Crown, 1990.

Thirty-five essays by males confess to guilty pleasures, recall useful sexual information learned from pornography, or admit to misdirecting their sexual desire toward politically incorrect or socially inappropriate goals as a result of exposure to pornography. Notable among the essays are David Steinberg's "The Roots of Pornography," which suggests that men and women can learn from each other's erotic expression; Fred Small's "Pornography and Censorship," which suggests that gender perception can be changed by education; Douglas Campbell's "One Man's Pleasures," which condemns pornography "as a pernicious socializing agency"; Robert Staples's "Blacks and Pornography," which reports that pornography seems less important in black communities than overt injustice; and Kimmel's "'Insult' or 'Injury': Sex, Pornography, and Sexism," which urges men to join forces with women against "a repressive culture."

Kinsey Institute for Research in Sex, Reproduction, and Gender. *The Art of Desire: Erotic Treasures from the Kinsey Institute.* School of Fine Arts Gallery: Indiana University Press, 1997.

This is a catalog of an exhibit held at the Sofia Gallery of Indiana University in fall 1997. Text and commentary fix the provenance of various objets d'art, paintings, drawings, photographs, and other curiosities from the Kinsey Institute, whose history as a research center and archive is also recounted. Various curators discuss the role of such materials in constructing and fixing objects of desire.

Kipnis, Laura. *Bound and Gagged: Pornography and the Politics of Fantasy in America.* New York: Grove Press, 1996.

Kipnis's thesis is that class is at the heart of controversies over sexual expression. One essay recounts the disturbing case of a poorly educated man entrapped by overzealous investigators who sought him out, encouraged him to discuss his fantasies of sex and violence, and then arrested and imprisoned him for sharing the fantasies that the officers had helped him construct. Other essays analyze the text and pictures of *Hustler* magazine as manifestations of a lower-class sensibility (though Kipnis characterizes that sensibility as extremely vulgar) inveighing against corrupt middle and upper classes. Pornography, Kipnis believes, can embody revolutionary purpose by bridging the gaps between sexuality and gender. She maintains that heterosexual pornography depicts a world that has "two sexes but one gender," as if men and women had been collapsed into a common sexuality.

Lederer, Laura, ed. *Take Back the Night: Women on Pornography.* New York: William Morrow, 1980.

The thirty essays in this volume include contributions by Kathleen Barry, Pauline Bart, Judith Bat-Ada (a.k.a. Judith Reisman), Megan Boler, Charlotte Bunch, Phyllis Chesler, Irene Diamond, Andrea Dworkin, Martha Geve, Wendy Kaminer, Helen Longino, Audre Lorde, Susan Lurie, Marge Piercy, Florence Rush, Alice Walker, and Gloria Steinem. They range from doctrinaire condemnations to thoughtful assessments of representations of gender and sexuality.

Lederer, Laura, and Richard Delgado, eds. *The Price We Pay: The Case against Racist Speech, Hate Propaganda, and Pornography.* New York: Hill and Wang, 1995.

These essays define pornography as the source of discrimination against women, who are subordinated and degraded by sexual representations. Put bluntly, pornography is hate speech. Several contributors contend that the harm to women caused by pornography is self-evident, that such arguments require no empirical verification, and that people whose speech hurts other people should not be protected by concepts of free expression. In sum, they propose that the demands of justice and equality should take precedence over the First Amendment.

Legman, Gershon. *Love and Death: A Study in Censorship.* New York: Breaking Point, 1949.

In this classic study of censorship, Legman attacks the American fondness for violence as perverse. He posits that whenever a society suppresses representations of sexuality, the imagery of violence increases. According to Legman, violence serves as surrogate for sex, and the degree of violence serves as an index to the culture's sexual pathologies. Images of people making love are healthy, he says, whereas images of aggression indicate a fear of sexuality. Nonetheless, sex is still taboo, whereas violence has become acceptable. Legman surveys comic books, literature, and movies and finds that they all exhibit this syndrome. Because pornography generally is free of violence, he maintains, its depictions of raw sex are preferable to mainstream representations that blend extravagant mayhem with sexual reticence.

Lucie-Smith, Edward. *Ars Erotica: An Arousing History of Erotic Art.* New York: Rizzoli, 1997.

Lucie-Smith says that representing sexuality has been an irresistible force in Western art from Botticelli through Mapplethorpe and Cindy Sherman. This volume covers works and artists from all periods and nationalities, arranged thematically. Lucie-Smith believes that distinctions between pornographic and erotic works of art are mostly spurious, having to do with issues of whether penetration and/or deviance are involved, and that time revises judgments.

MacKinnon, Catharine. *Only Words.* Cambridge: Harvard University Press, 1994.

MacKinnon characterizes pornography as a form of hate speech designed not only to discriminate against women but to terrorize them as well. She believes that speech cannot be separated from action: Language has the force of deed, so that a sexual representation is virtually equivalent to sex itself. Pornography—the expression of males—thus actually rapes women. MacKinnon asserts that law in the United States has given primacy to the First Amendment, which ensures freedom of speech for the individual, instead of endorsing the Fourteenth Amendment, which

278 Print and Nonprint Reference Materials

protects groups such as women. She believes that modern American society recognizes only male expression, causing women's voices and hence their freedom to be savagely repressed.

Maines, Rachel. *The Technology of Orgasm: "Hysteria," the Vibrator, and Women's Sexual Satisfaction.* Baltimore: Johns Hopkins University Press, 1998.

Historically speaking, the sexual uses of electric vibrators have usually been camouflaged. The author writes that during the nineteenth century, doctors treated women suffering from "hysteria" by digitally masturbating them to "therapeutic" orgasm. Vibrators, she asserts, evolved as bulky labor-saving devices so that physicians could treat, that is, masturbate, more women. When marketers began to sell vibrators to consumers by mail order, usually through carefully coded magazine advertisements, patients could learn to stimulate themselves, thus to a degree regaining control over their own bodies. Making the vibrator compact and battery-operated domesticated it into one of the most ubiquitous sexual aids in the bedrooms of Americans of every gender. Contemporary manufacturers borrowed the modern phallic shape of vibrators from the dildo, a staple of pornography, in order to make its use obvious through sexual representation.

Martignette, C. G., and L. K. Meisel. *The Great American Pin-Up.* Berlin: Benedikt Taschen, 1995.

This comprehensive volume on the pinup contains 900 illustrations from calendars, magazine covers, centerfolds, playing cards, and other formats, but only from World War II until the mid-1970s. The text is slight, though Martignette and Meisel identify the artists; the volume's value is that it outlines the dimensions of the form.

Michelson, Peter. *Speaking the Unspeakable: Poetics of Obscenity.* Albany, N.Y.: State University of New York Press, 1993; revision of *The Aesthetics of Pornography.* New York: Herder & Herder, 1971.

Michelson believes that literary and esthetic criticism can illuminate pornographic genres, whose chief value is that they force humans to confront their sexual natures. In his view, to suppress pornography is to deny humanity. In discussing pornographic art, literature, and cinema, Michelson posits that high and low forms of expression treat "subversive" material differently and that the principal difference lies in the degree of control. He writes that low forms—those that verge toward the obscene—have an "unpredictable detonation point," whereas high forms—those more acceptable as erotic—exercise more control over obscene energies though a tighter "ecology" of imagery, language, situations, and nuances.

Mielke, Arthur J. *Christians, Feminists, and the Culture of Pornography.* Lanham, Md.: University Press of America, 1995.

The author follows psychologist Robert J. Stoller in ascribing a theological Christian basis to objections to pornography and argues that a more relevant reading is that of Jungian psychology. Mielke insists that pornography should be "spiritually redemptive" to feminists, even in a social system with fixed ideas of marriage and monogamy, because it offers hope for women and men who long for sexual satisfaction. In legitimizing passion and investing desire with excitement, pornography revitalizes a spirituality that has been diminished by the institutionalization of religion; at the very least, writes Mielke, pornography restores the erotic power of ancient theologies. On a less abstract and more personal level, pornography fosters masturbation, candid expression, and ideal fantasies, all of which he views as essential to a healthy sexuality.

Miller, William Ian. *The Anatomy of Disgust.* Cambridge, Mass.: Harvard University Press, 1997.

Although somewhat marginally related to pornography, this work reflects on why certain sexual acts are exciting to some people and repellent to others. Miller discusses fluids, orifices, and postures. For some people disgust is essential to eroticism: "Sex is perceived as dirty, bestial, smelly, messy, sticky, slimy, oozy, and that is precisely, for many, its attraction," he writes.

Mumford, Laura Stempel. *Love and Ideology in the Afternoon: Soap Opera, Women and Television Genre.* Bloomington: Indiana University Press, 1995.

Mumford's book concerns the handful of themes that powerfully shape television soap operas. An obsession with paternity—a common plot device is the discovery that a child was actually fathered by a surprise dad—suggests the subversive nature of televised fantasies. Such surprises destabilize sexuality, writes Mumford, in a way that implicitly underscores the power of women to control reproduction. Even so, she believes that the agendas of most soap operas reinforce cultural patterns of male dominance, racism, classism, and heterosexism, and in doing so offer considerable pleasure even to feminists who decry the patterns.

Nagle, Jill, ed. *Whores and Other Feminists.* New York: Routledge, 1997.

The essays collected here are by sex workers, some of whom are writers, strippers, pornographic performers, performance artists, prostitutes, and labor organizers of workers in sex industries. Annie Sprinkle and Nina Hartley, for instance, argue that pornography has positive aspects, including empowerment for women through the subversion of gender and conventional concepts of identity, a process they think of not so much as transgressive as responsive to historical factors. Other contributors are highly critical of what they and others do for a living, and not all of them can find positive aspects of the business, but every essay brings the enormous insight of experience.

Nead, Lynda. *The Female Nude.* London: Routledge, 1992.

In discussing the history and theories of female nudes in art and pornography, Nead concludes that such pictures must be understood as attempts to define female and male sexuality in a larger context of debate about cultural values and the place of representation in civilization. Nead characterizes that debate as a struggle over ambiguities; artists and critics assert the value of beautiful images while antiporn feminists assert the deleterious effects of male dominance. She writes that the customs and institutions of society shape the meaning of such terms as eroticism and obscenity, sensuality and sexuality, art and pornography, and those meanings change over time. Suspicion about technology and prejudices rooted in class are also factors, Nead asserts, in awarding higher status to paintings than to photographs.

Nestle, Joan. *A Restricted Country.* Ithaca, N.Y.: Firebrand Books, 1987.

In a very real sense, says the author, we know sexuality in the final analysis as pornography: Our experience if not our understanding of sex is at base inevitably and unavoidably pornographic—because fantasy, the upwelling of our erotic imaginations, is always present. A pornographic work is someone's fantasy and is therefore an attempt to communicate, writes Nestle; she argues that the proper response is to find fantasies to share, not to censor. Our own erotic templates, constructed from cultural and personal fetishes, will inevitably resist the fantasies of those in different educational, political, and social categories. Nestle praises the erotic writing of lesbians as a "gift to the world." Knowing that society has always marginalized lesbians and prostitutes, she worries that feminists who attack pornography will unintentionally silence these members of society.

O'Toole, Laurence. *Pornocopia: Porn, Sex, Technology and Desire.* London: Serpent's Tail, 1998.

O'Toole sketches the history and revenues of American porn production houses such as Vivid Video. For the author, pornographic industries illustrate "capitalism in the raw" as they capitalize, compete, and strive for global domination. O'Toole interviews performers and producers in the video industry.

Paglia, Camille. *Sexual Personae: Art and Decadence from Nefertiti to Emily Dickinson.* New York: Vintage, 1991.

Paglia's discussion ranges across the "decadence" of Edgar Allan Poe, Nathaniel Hawthorne, Herman Melville, Ralph Waldo Emerson, Walt Whitman, Henry James, and Emily Dickinson but also suggests that modern American rock musicians employ similar sexual energies. When Paglia ventures into media such as painting and sculpture, she chooses classical or European illustrations. Some of these energies are gendered, the author contends; males in general sublimate sexual energy to build civilizations, while women remain passive because they partake of nature. Paglia believes that feminists who charge pornographers with promoting misogyny and male supremacy do not understand the value of sexual excess. Pornography and art, she claims, are inextricably connected both morally and esthetically. As a vital element in romantic paganism, pornography's role is to stimulate art through outrageous fantasy centered on the body and its sexuality. According to Paglia, pornography and art constantly tap wellsprings of obscenity for creative inspiration.

Payton, Leland, and Crystal Payton. *Girlie Collectibles: Politically Incorrect Objets d'Art.* New York: St. Martin's, 1996.

This is probably the best of several books on sexist kitsch. The Paytons provide witty running commentary and up-to-date price lists for objects ranging from pinup calendars, magazines, and playing cards to the amazing range of artifacts in the shape of (mostly) naked female bodies: mugs, dolls, pipes, salt and pepper shakers, bottles, cigar tins, glasses, coasters, toothbrushes, steins, pens, knives, clocks, ashtrays, can openers, glasses, lamps, and so on. These icons of bad taste attest to the depths of obsession but also extend the realm of sexual folklore.

Perkins, Michael. *The Secret Record: Modern Erotic Literature.* New York: William Morrow, 1977.

After a quick chronological survey of erotic literature beginning with the ancient Greeks, Perkins focuses on American publishers of the 1960s and 1970s, a period in which American pornographic writers professionalized their trade. These included Richard Amory, Diane di Prima, Mary Sativa, Akbar Del Piombo, Barry Malzberg, Marco Vassi, Perkins himself, Harriet Daimler, Marcus Van Heller, Alexander Trocchi, and many others writing for publishers such as Brandon House, Olympia Press (after its move from Paris to New York), Collectors' Publications, and Essex House. Because so many erotic stories were imported to America for so long, says Perkins, modern writers lacked domestic traditions and thus had to invent their own models.

Phillips, Donna-Lee, and Lew Thomas, eds. *Eros and Photography: An Exploration of Sexual Imagery and Photographic Practice.* San Francisco: Camerawork/NFS Press, 1977.

Contributors to this volume deal principally with "erotic" rather than "pornographic" photography; they comment on works by Robert Heinecken, Chris Enos, Joel-Peter Witkin, Arthur Ollman, and others historically important by way of analyzing what makes frames erotic. Especially notable is Hal Fischer's "Toward a Gay Semiotic," which attempts to understand the ways in which photographs code an image for homosexual audiences.

Plummer, Ken. *Telling Sexual Stories: Power, Change and Social Worlds.* New York: Routledge, 1995.

According to Plummer, telling sexual stories is a way of building a sexual self, a form of autobiography and empowerment. He uses as examples rape stories, coming out stories, and recovery stories but covers sexual surveys and focus groups as well. He analyzes the ways in which such stories are constructed, the tropes they employ, the identities they assume, and the role that such stories play in creating a participatory and democratic culture. He is particularly interested in the creation of a new genre of stories of "women liking pornography," noting that our society gives primacy to narratives that denigrate sexual expression and present pornography as invariably "bad." Sexual stories carry their own imperatives, says Plummer. They have proliferated in all cultures as ways of processing experience, as a means of constructing intimacy, as strategies for finding sexual elements to serve as keys to personal identity and one's place in society. Not least, they function as a form of therapy for those marginalized by culture.

Posner, Richard A. *Sex and Reason.* Cambridge, Mass.: Harvard University Press, 1992.

The author, a Justice of the U.S. Court of Appeals for the Seventh District, identifies and discusses five goals of erotic representation: (1) formal, an esthetic achieved through metaphoric and figurative imagery; (2) informational, a purpose achieved through didacticism; (3) ideological, an intent that aims to reinforce, undermine, or change the audience's thinking; (4) aphrodisiac, an attempt to stimulate sexual desire; (5) magical, a construct that exalts fantasy. Having examined the sometimes illogical laws and attitudes governing sexual behavior and expression, Posner calls for greater rationality in the legal arena. For example, if the antiporn feminist argument that pornography is the ideological expression of patriarchy and misogyny is valid, then pornographic messages would be doubly protected as both sexual and political discourse. One discussion explores what Posner sees as contradictions inherent in the alliance between antiporn feminists and political conservatives: Antiporn feminists condemn pornography because they think it causes rape, and conservatives condemn pornography because they think it leads to masturbation instead of intercourse. Because rape is a form of intercourse, then logically conservatives would have to acknowledge that pornography diminishes rape, and feminists would have to acknowledge that pornography diminishes masturbation.

Price, Monroe E., ed. *The V-Chip Debate: Content Filtering from Television to the Internet.* Mahwah, N.J.: Lawrence Erlbaum, 1999.

This volume contains essays by various authorities on the rationale and difficulties of using technology to block objectionable programming and materials in electronic media, and to do so in ways that prevent valuable information from being lost along with the dross.

Radway, Janice A. *Reading the Romance: Women, Patriarchy, and Popular Literature.* Chapel Hill: University of North Carolina Press, 1984.

Radway's volume is one of several critical approaches to the romance, sometimes called "porn for women." Radway agrees with other critics that romance writers create stereotypical men objectified into sexual objects, and she writes that the feminine fantasies are just as infantile as those to be found in male-oriented pornography because they both avoid responsibility. She notes that the romance asserts the value of love in arenas structured by wealth and power.

Reynolds, Simon, and Joy Press. *The Sex Revolts: Gender, Rebellion, and Rock 'n' Roll.* Cambridge, Mass.: Harvard University Press, 1995.

Reynolds and Press apply a Freudian and Lacanian analysis of rock music's evocation of an infantile "oceanic bliss." According to the authors, rock began in rebellious misogyny but has mutated into less phallic obsessions, thanks chiefly to female rockers and genderbenders playing disco, metal and rap, college rock, Brazilian funk, and so on.

Russell, Diana E. H. *Dangerous Relationships: Pornography, Misogyny, and Rape.* Thousand Oaks, Calif.: Sage Publications, 1998.

This book is a revision of Russell's 1994 self-published *Against Pornography: The Evidence of Harm,* which included 100 extremely cruel and ugly photographs (the revision merely describes them) that she believes are the kind that male audiences prefer, but she stresses that even nonviolent pornography leads directly to rape. She distinguishes between pornography and erotica by describing two examples of the latter, one involving the peeling of an orange, the other the copulating of snails, though she does acknowledge that some women think that it might be possible to depict actual humans in representations that are not misogynistic and despicable. Her "pornography causes rape" thesis cites studies purporting to establish such connections. Russell excoriates the National Organization for Women for refusing to con-

demn all forms of sexual expression and writes that such feminists are "irrational."

Schaefer, Eric. *Bold! Daring! Shocking! True!: A History of Exploitation Films, 1919–1959.* Durham, N.C.: Duke University
Press, 1999.

Schaefer deals with various genres (sexual hygiene, miscegenation, drug, nudist, burlesque, white slavery) of the exploitation
film, which usually promised to titillate but almost never delivered much in the way of explicitness. He studies the marketing
strategies of entrepreneurs such as Louis Sonney, Kroger Babb,
Herschel Gordon Lewis, and David Friedman as they constructed the soft-core feature from prurient homilies, middle-
class curiosity, and glimpses of flesh. The key to the success of
exploitation films, he writes, was a carefully orchestrated dynamic of local censorship, clever advertising, precisely targeted
distribution, and skillful exhibition ("adults only") that made audiences think they were going to see something they would not.

Schwartz, Kit. *The Female Member: Being a Compendium of
Facts, Figures, Foibles, and Anecdotes about the Loving Organ.*
New York: St. Martin's, 1988; *The Male Member; Being a Com-
pendium of Fact, Fiction, Foibles and Anecdotes about the Male
Sexual Organ in Man and Beast.* New York: St. Martin's, 1985.

These two volumes gather folklore on human genitalia in amusing but solid narratives. Schwartz supplements the legends with
statistics: how long? how short? how thick? how much and how
often does the male ejaculate? how deep are vaginas? how sensitive are clitorises? He occasionally traces myths and misconceptions to pornographic sources.

Scott, David A. *Behind the G-String: An Exploration of the Stripper's Image, Her Person, and Her Meaning.* Jefferson, N.C.: Mac-
Farland, 1996.

Scott explores the significance of stripping in a society that appears to value the sight of nudity as a counter to economic and
technological pressures. Because striptease is so often regarded
as sexist, he interviews strippers, some of whom regard the profession as demeaning, others as empowering. They speak of motivation, costumes, pay, drawbacks, benefits, standards of beauty
and sexuality, working conditions, and relationships with patrons, bar owners, and each other.

Simpson, Milton. *Folk Erotica: Celebrating Centuries of Erotic Americana.* New York: HarperCollins, 1994.

Simpson surveys and comments on three centuries of erotic folk art, including examples such as Navajo kachina dolls, nineteenth-century carved canes and walking sticks, carved female figures, paintings, constructions, mechanical toys, drawings, sculptures, and other demotic artifacts, some comic, some beautiful, some crude in the extreme.

Steele, Valerie. *Fetish: Fashion, Sex, and Power.* New York: Oxford University Press, 1995.

This volume covers virtually all the identifiable clothing fetishes, even including male underwear. According to Steele, fetishes—and the fantasies that engender and depend on them—bridge sexual realms of the normal and the perverse. Text and illustrations draw specifically on pornographic examples in order to demonstrate how fetishes shared by significant numbers of Americans manifest themselves as sexual expression in mainstream fashion, art, literature, cinema, and politics. She notes, for example, the influence of Irving Klaw's bondage and discipline costumes on contemporary designers and the impact of Tom of Finland's pornographic drawings on fashions now sold in Bloomingdale's. Studying fetishes helps to explain personal relationships, social hierarchies of power and authority, the popularity of certain genres of pornography, and the seemingly irrational desires that grip humans. Steele understands fashion (a term that can be applied to both clothing and pornography) as a discourse or language, a symbolic system created in part to express the many facets of sexuality from gender identification to erotic attraction and specific behaviors.

Steiner, Wendy. *The Scandal of Pleasure: Art in an Age of Fundamentalism.* Chicago: University of Chicago Press, 1995.

Steiner reflects on the ironies of defending an esthetics of the body against the politics of the present. She concentrates on "body" artists such as Robert Mapplethorpe, Andres Serrano, Sally Mann, and Andy Warhol and examines the fundamentalist, feminist, fascist, and liberal factions of political correctness, urging that no work of art be reduced to a single meaning. Like many others, Steiner notes that erotic art is and is not a political agent, precisely because it is rooted in contradiction, and insists on tolerance. Ultimately, says Steiner, only pleasure can justify art. Those who find beauty in sexuality must confront a cultural bias: Most Americans are deeply suspicious of the very notion that one might gaze at a nude figure, standing still or engaged in congress with another, in order to be enraptured by beauty. That prejudice still dogs a magazine such as *Playboy*, whose "Playmates" are far more "beautiful" than "sexy" but whose appeal is tainted in popular consciousness by what is best described as cultural pathology.

Stoller, Robert J. *Porn: Myths for the Twentieth Century*. New Haven, Conn.: Yale University Press, 1991.

In this, one of the last books by Stoller, a psychologist who wrote extensively on pornography, the author interviews performers such as Bill Margold, Nina Hartley, Sharon Kane, Porsche Lynn, and Jim Holliday (a film historian and director) in the hope of confirming his belief that anger, cruelty, humiliation, and the desire for revenge make for a hostility that drives eroticism. The evidence he finds seems equivocal, and he concludes that while the hostility may be there, porn is "pathetic." Pornography is mostly theater, it is full of mistaken notions about sexuality, and it can express a "malignant" sensibility, but he doubts that it causes males to commit rape.

Stone, Allucqère Roseanne. *The War of Desire and Technology at the Close of the Machine Age*. Cambridge, Mass.: MIT Press, 1995.

Stone speculates on the status of the body present in "technosocial space," that is, in an electronic environment that is everywhere and nowhere. If the body is not physically present at an Internet site, what sort of eroticism is available? Stone says that communication technologies have become so sophisticated that they are literally reshaping erotic sensibilities.

Wagner, Peter. *Eros Revived: Erotica of the Enlightenment in England and America*. London: Secker and Warburg, 1988.

Wagner's history draws on records left by publishers, importers, librarians, and collectors of colonial America. Colonists imported erotic works such as John Cleland's *Fanny Hill* (Benjamin Franklin owned a copy, as did Samuel Tilden, governor of New York) and only later began producing their own, taking their cues from continental texts. Obscene expression even in colonial America was commonplace. To argue that the framers of the

Constitution were unacquainted with pornography when they fashioned that document, or that the First Amendment was never intended to cover sexual expression, is to adopt a naive position: Jefferson, Madison, Franklin, and Adams were familiar with scatological and sexually charged political attacks common to the chaos of early democracy. Even so, Wagner is careful to distinguish between an all-purpose term *erotica*, which could encompass bawdy stories, scurrilous jokes, quasimedical treatises, serious satire, and anticlerical expression, and the more specialized term *pornography*, which took on the connotations of vile or dirty only with the rise of bourgeois classes in Victorian times.

Watney, Simon. *Policing Desire: Pornography, AIDS, and the Media.* Minneapolis: University of Minnesota Press, 1987; London: Metheun, 1987.

This book, centered on the ways in which socially constructed attitudes toward sexuality affect responses to AIDS, rejects the cultural assumption that sexuality by itself leads to AIDS and argues in favor of pornography whose message is that sex by itself is wonderful. The author believes that attacks on pornography are often predicated on political assumptions about the nature of democracy, family values, and gender preferences and thus can discriminate against those who reject the constraints of polite discourse, the rigid models of the family, the heterosexual bias of the majority, or simply the linkage between sex and reproduction. Gay sexuality is not structured in the same ways that heterosexuals configure theirs, and therefore gays do not respond in the same ways to ordinary pornography. Watney believes feminist antiporn critiques merely reinforce the rationales for "policing" the expression of both heterosexuals and gays. He claims that pornography's rationale is precisely to represent extremes. To be opposed to porn, he implies, is to be opposed to sex.

Waugh, Tom. *Hard to Imagine: Gay Male Eroticism in Photography and Film from Their Beginnings to Stonewall.* New York: Columbia University Press, 1997.

Waugh's history of erotic gay images applies various visual theories to the presentation of homosexuality to gay and mainstream audiences. He analyzes hundreds of photographs and films as historical markers of power, identity, and desire, determined to recapture a heritage in danger of being lost. Waugh believes that these images were crucial to the formation and maintenance of a gay community and to the development of a gay political consciousness. Gritty, explicit, and far more honest than more circumspect histories, the volume is the principal record of documents that were largely invisible to Americans but that still speak eloquently of the past.

Weatherford, Jack. *Porn Row.* New York: Arbor House, 1986.

Although zoning laws are making adult bookstores rare, Weatherford's ethnographic field study of patrons is still authoritative. Weatherford discounts the myth that pornography is monolithic by arguing that patrons differ markedly in their attractions to various media, their fascination with narrow ranges of fetishes, and the isolation in which they pursue their particular fantasies. The man in search of magazines or films featuring blonde-haired women with large breasts, for example, cannot be deflected by examples in which brunettes or redheads figure prominently. The author, who worked for some months in an adult store in a large urban area to gather his data, believes that the men who haunt such places are responding to social messages that ideal sex brings happiness as much as to biological imperatives.

Webb, Peter. *The Erotic Arts.* Boston: New York Graphic Society, 1975; rev. ed. New York: Farrar, Straus, Giroux, 1983.

Although not up-to-date, Webb's comprehensive volume covers every form of art. He insists that pornography is closely associated with obscenity and believes as well that erotic art is superior because of its emphasis on love and emotion rather than the mechanical aspects of sex. Sex is vital, he admits, but love is more important yet. The book contains an excellent bibliography.

Williams, Linda. *Hard Core: Power, Pleasure, and the Frenzy of the Visible.* Berkeley: University of California Press, 1989.

Film scholar Linda Williams devotes the first part of her book to refuting attacks on pornography by antiporn feminists. She posits that pornographic films are really more about pleasure than they are about power, a factor that helps explain why 50 percent of American women watch porn and why women as a group watch 40 percent of all such videos. Although Williams offers a quick survey of pornographic films, finding the primal erotic moment in Eadweard Muybridge's chronographic motion studies of the "sexuality already encoded in the woman's body," she only analyzes modern pornographic examples. Noting the prevalence of the "money shot," a.k.a. the "cum shot," Williams borrows from Steven Marcus *(The Other Victorians: A Study of Sexuality and Pornography in Mid-Nineteenth Century England* [1965]) the notion that pornographers have long chosen capitalist metaphors for orgasm. Williams advances the theory that such ejaculations are similar to the motifs that punctuate musical comedy, a genre she thinks resembles the hard-core film. Although Williams's thesis tends to reduce porn films to a single heterosexual genre, *Hard Core* is remarkable because the author actually studies the films and because she insists that women can learn from them.

Williams, Tom M. *See No Evil: Christian Attitudes toward Sex in Art and Entertainment.* Grand Rapids, Mich.: Zondervan, 1976.

Although somewhat dated now, this book remains a statement of moderate Christian attitudes toward explicit sexual expression. Williams condemns the immorality of pornography but acknowledges that not all Americans share his views. He does not advocate censorship, and specifically rejects religious interference in secular affairs, but suggests that Christians can legitimately support strategies such as ratings systems for movies and ordinances prohibiting public display of explicit materials. Fairness should rule public life, he writes, so that those who recoil from pornography should not be exposed to it.

Yalom, Marilyn. *A History of the Breast.* New York: Knopf, 1997.

Of the many books on the subject, this is the most informative and authoritative because it studies breasts as they are represented in religion, medicine, politics, literature, photography, and film, often with specific reference to pornographic images. Yalom's history covers styles of shaping, spreading, compressing, uplifting, and augmenting breasts so that their display conforms to standards of beauty and eroticism over the ages.

Bibliographies

Amey, Lawrence, Timothy Hall, Carl Jansen, Charles May, and Richard Wilson, eds. *Censorship.* 3 vols. Pasadena, Calif.: Salem Press, 1997.

These three volumes on all types of censorship are quick reference sources of information on specific legal cases both major and minor. Organized in multiple entries, they cross-reference plaintiffs, defendants, and precedents. Most useful are biographies of individuals, essays on specific types of censorship, and comments on events and consequences.

Burt, Eugene C. *Erotic Art: An Annotated Bibliography with Essays.* Boston: G. K. Hall, 1989.

This volume covers criticism dealing with the subject of erotic art in many countries and periods. The citations are not always complete, and the bibliographic essays are modest. General background categories precede sections arranged chronologically, beginning with ancient art and running through the present, and geographically, beginning with the Near East and continuing through the Mediterranean, Asia, Africa, Oceania, North and South America, and Europe. The volume also breaks out criticism on individual American erotic artists.

Clapp, Jane. *Art Censorship.* Metuchen, N.J.: Scarecrow Press, 1972.

The author annotates hundreds of images that have offended someone in the Western hemisphere and cross-references critical, biographical, and historical data. This reference is easy to use, with more than 600 entries arranged chronologically and also indexed. The drawback is that the volume was published in 1972 and is hard to find, but it is still the principal information source on works of art that have engendered controversy over the years.

Kinsey Institute for Sex, Gender, and Reproduction. *Subject Bibliographies.* Information Services, 416 Morrison Hall, Indiana University, Bloomington, IN 47405.

The Kinsey Institute will photocopy authoritative bibliographies on virtually every pornographic genre, theme, subject, and taste and will provide a list of those available on request. Because the bibliographies are continually revised, however, scholars should inquire as to dates before ordering.

Legman, Gershon. **"Erotic Folksongs and Ballads: An International Bibliography."** *Journal of American Folklore* 103 (October/December 1990): 417–501.

This annotated bibliography outlines the dimensions of erotic folklore of dozens of countries. It cites every major collection of obscene or bawdy drinking, campfire, music hall, military, cowboy, sailor, college and fraternity, and working songs as well as sea chanteys, folk songs, ballads, verses, stories, salty puns, and erotic miscellany. Legman died before he could publish a discography supplement.

Osanka, Franklin Mark, and Sara Lee Johann. *Sourcebook on Pornography*. Lexington, Mass.: Lexington Books, 1989.
Somewhat dated essays and annotated lists of material that vary widely in accuracy and relevance, marshalled to build a case against pornography. Chapter headings include "Defining Pornography"; "Images of Pornography"; "The Nature of the Pornography Industry"; "Pornography's Victims and Perpetrators"; "Scientific Research Studies on Pornography's Influence on Behavior"; "The Morality Perspective"; "The Feminist Perspective"; "Private Enterprise Interests and the Civil Libertarian Perspective"; "Obscenity Law: Its Prosecution and Defense"; "The Civil Rights Antipornography Law"; "Other Ways of Regulating Pornography Through Law"; "Model Pornography Law"; "The National Studies"; "Child Pornography"; and Appendices.

Sellen, Betty-Carol, and Patricia A. Young. *Feminists, Pornography, and the Law: An Annotated Bibliography of Conflict, 1970–1986*. Hamden, Conn.: Shoe String Press/Library Professional Publications, 1987.
A chronology of newspaper notices (1976–1986) provides information on the alliance of antiporn feminists, religious fundamentalists, and political conservatives in a campaign to curtail pornography. Entries also help sort out disputes among feminists of various ideological persuasions.

Slade, Joseph W. *Reference Guide to Pornography and Sexual Representation*. 3 vols. Westport, Conn.: Greenwood Press, 2000.
In addition to providing a history of American pornography, this comprehensive set contains twenty annotated essays on bibliographies and reference tools as well as chapters such as "Histories of Sexuality and Its Representation," "Theoretical Works on Erotica and Pornography," and "Research on Pornography in the Medical and Social Sciences." It also covers major research collections, child pornography, performance art, erotic and pornographic art and photography, motion pictures and videotapes, electronic media, folklore and oral genres, erotic literature, comics, newspapers, magazines, advertising, pornography and law in the United States, and the economics of pornography. The author argues that pornography enriches culture over time by furnishing new ideas; that erotic

representations drive new media technologies and an information economy; and that sexual expression explores basic concepts of the self and society, adds to aesthetic sensibility, and constantly refreshes spoken, written, visual, and electronic languages.

Trager, Oliver, ed. *The Arts and Media in America: Freedom or Censorship.* New York: Facts on File, 1991.

Trager's book is a collection of editorials from around the nation divided into categories: television, movies, and radio; art, performance, flag burning and censorship; publishing and pornography; and music in America. The book contains information on sex in television programming, shock jocks, movie ratings, the National Endowment for the Arts controversy, books and magazines, and record hearings and labels, among other issues.

Essays in Edited Volumes

Brail, Stephanie. "The Price of Admission: Harassment and Free Speech in the Wild, Wild West." In *Wired Women: Gender and New Realities in Cyberspace,* Lynn Cherny and Elizabeth Reba Weise, eds. Seattle: Bay Press, 1996, pp. 141–157.

Brail offers advice to women on how to safely explore erotic sites, and she argues that pornography is not harassment. Because the Net is a rough and vulgar forum, Brail insists that common sense be a woman's guide.

Davis, Angela Y. "I Used to Be Your Sweet Mama: Ideology, Sexuality and Domesticity in the Blues of Gertrude 'Ma' Rainey and Bessie Smith." In *Sexy Bodies: The Strange Carnalities of Feminism,* Elizabeth Grosz and Elspeth Probyn, eds. New York: Routledge, 1995, pp. 231–265.

Although their lyrics were often called pornographic, Ma Rainey and Bessie Smith sang songs that articulated black female sexuality. According to Davis, they looked at sexual relationships realistically, refusing either to sentimentalize love or to exploit either partner. In so doing, they endowed the blues with an eroticism that still defines this popular musical genre.

Mercer, Kobena. "Just Looking for Trouble: Robert Mapplethorpe and Fantasies of Race." In *Sex Exposed: Sexuality and the Pornography Debate,* Lynne Segal and Mary McIntosh, eds. New Brunswick, N.J.: Rutgers University Press, 1993, pp. 92–110.

Mercer tries to decide whether Robert Mapplethorpe's notorious photographs of large black penises "reinforce or undermine racist myths about black sexuality." At first glance the pictures do seem to endorse the racial stereotypes of sniggering folklore, but Mapplethorpe reminds his viewers that "anatomy is [not] truth," says Mercer. What makes the photos so powerful is Mapplethorpe's determination to deconstruct clichés. The subtext here is that photographers who choose to work in explicit images take enormous risks of being misunderstood.

Penley, Constance. **"Feminism, Psychoanalysis, and the Study of Popular Culture."** In *Cultural Studies,* Lawrence Grossberg, Cary Nelson, and Paula A. Treichler, eds. New York: Routledge, 1992, pp. 479–500.

Penley examines what are variously called "fanzines," "slash/zines," or "K/S," a sort of American variation on the Russian samizdat. Here chiefly female fans deliberately subvert the artifacts of popular culture, such as the television program *Star Trek,* by resexualizing them in erotic texts and pictures. Re-gendering in order to undermine cultural assumptions and assert others is a common strategy: For example, the character Spock might be described engaged in oral sex with Captain Kirk. Penley studies many examples of fan-generated erotic encounters, including some based on prime-time programs or films.

Polsky, Ned. **"On the Sociology of Pornography."** In *Hustlers, Beats, and Others.* Garden City, N.J.: Doubleday Anchor, 1969, pp. 183–200; reprinted 1985, Chicago: University of Chicago Press.

In this pioneering study of pornography and class, Polsky observes that pornography provides individuals with fantasies of "impersonal, nonmarital sex" to which they can masturbate. Pornography, he believes, thus discharges urges that might be considered perverse or deviant; this is its real value. Polsky asserts that pornography nonetheless offers more "social" benefits than solitary masturbation to one's own inner pictures by conjuring for the masturbator "erotic imagery that is external to himself, a quasi-real 'other' to whom he can more 'realistically' respond." Polsky writes that the meaning of the term *pornography* has more to do with class than we can imagine; our culture condemns low forms of graphic vulgarity at the same time that it tolerates upper-class erotica and corporate crime.

Ross, Andrew. **"The Popularity of Pornography."** In *No Respect: Intellectuals and Popular Culture.* New York: Routledge, 1989, pp. 171–208.

Ross reviews conservative, feminist, and liberal critiques of pornography. These generally charge pornography with deliberate vulgarity, with undermining love and spirituality, with discrimination against women, or with narrative incoherence. Even those theorists who believe that sex is a legitimate component of art and literature argue that pornography should be esthetically improved or recast to emphasize social responsibility. The problem, writes Ross, is that pornography evokes pleasure as its prime reason for being, and no one can combat or change it without a recognition of this fact.

Steiner, George. **"Night Words: Human Privacy and High Pornography."** In *Language and Silence: Essays on Language, Literature, and the Inhuman.* New York: Atheneum, 1967, pp. 71–86; reprinted in *The Pornography Controversy,* Ray C. Rist, ed. New Brunswick, N.J.: Transaction, 1975, pp. 203–213; reprinted in *The New Eroticism,* Philip Nobile, ed. New York: Random House, 1970, pp. 120–132.

Steiner condemns sexual representation for invading the public arena under the guise of thoughtful reflections on sexuality, a genre he calls "high pornography." Steiner thinks that by revealing what should be kept intimate, pornography undermines personal dignity, erodes a fragile domain of privacy, coarsens public discourse, and generally destroys the sense of what it means to be human. He believes the effects of commercializing sexuality are thus generally damaging to the culture at large.

Weaver, Mary Jo. **"Pornography and the Religious Imagination."** In *For Adult Users Only,* Susan Gubar and Joan Hoff, eds. Bloomington, Ind.: Indiana University Press, 1989, pp. 68–86.

Weaver deplores alliances between conservative Christian fundamentalists and antiporn feminists to combat pornography on the grounds that their attitudes toward sexuality are incompatible. Fundamentalist teachings are themselves inherently masculine and pornographic, she writes, because they assume that women are inferior. By contrast, antiporn feminists are, or should be, open to new concepts of eros in a more progressive theological vision.

Willis, Ellen. **"Feminism, Moralism, and Pornography."** In *Powers of Desire: The Politics of Sexuality*, Ann Snitow, Christine Stansell, and Sharon Thompson, eds. New York: Monthly Review Press, 1983, pp. 460–467.

Willis believes that attacks on pornography usually ignore the issue of how audiences actually use it. One cannot blame pornography for appealing to the sexual feelings that actually drive humans rather than the feelings that a particular group thinks humans ought to have, she writes. Pornography deals in contradictions: On the one hand, pornography endorses the status quo of male dominance and thus seems reactionary; on the other, it rejects a sexual hypocrisy that has harmed women more than men, and may thus seem radical. Moreover, Willis believes, pornography deals in fantasies about the forbidden; some women who rightly condemn actual rape seem to enjoy fantasies of being ravished. Because most pornography is clearly sexual rather than violent, calling pornography violent by definition is dishonest, she attests.

Magazine and Journal Articles

Altimore, Michael. **"The Social Construction of a Scientific Myth: Pornography and Violence."** *Journal of Communication Inquiry* 15, 1 (Winter 1991): 117–133.

The author argues that the assertion of a causal connection between pornography and violence is a socially constructed attempt to avoid confronting issues of social class and race, which have far more to do with crimes of aggression. According to Altimore, studies purporting to demonstrate links are unscientific and largely invalid, but they are comforting because they are so simplistic. Because neither feminists nor other hostile groups are able to articulate a "normal" sexuality, writes Altimore, their critiques of sexual representations merely reflect their own ideologies.

Dyer, Richard. **"Male Gay Porn."** *Jump Cut* 30 (March 1985): 227–229; reprinted as "Coming to Terms" in *Out There: Marginalization and Contemporary Culture*, Russell Ferguson et al., eds. Cambridge, Mass.: MIT Press, 1990, pp. 289–298; reprinted in *Only Entertainment* by Richard Dyer. New York: Routledge, 1992, pp. 121–134.

For Dyer, pornography is joyless and uninspired. He deplores the visual conventions of gay pornographic films, especially the prominence given to ejaculation, an emphasis he thinks skews story narratives. He believes that pornography reinforces the desire for self-gratification rather than mutual satisfaction, that it seems always to endorse the taking of pleasure rather than the giving of it, and in that respect gay pornography sometimes resembles the heterosexual variety. Even so, Dyer says, pornography justifies itself by embodying contradictions: on the one hand, it is a capitalist commodity; on the other hand, it carries messages disruptive to the dominant politics of a culture.

Faludi, Susan. **"The Money Shot."** *New Yorker* (30 October 1995): 64–70, 72–76, 78–82, 84–87; reprinted in Susan Faludi, *Stiffed: The Betrayal of the American Man*. New York: Morrow, 1999.

Reporting on the suicide of Cal Jammer, a veteran male performer in pornographic movies, Faludi discovers that the business of triple-X video pornography negatively affects male performers more than females. Women stars tend to make far more money than their counterparts, who are valued only for their ability to acquire and maintain erections and, whether they are true victims or not, are subject to anomie and despair. Faludi believes that both popular stereotypes and academic theories of pornography distort the human dimensions of sex industries and modern American life.

Findlay, Heather. **"Freud's 'Fetishism' and the Lesbian Dildo Debates."** *Feminist Studies* 18, 3 (Fall 1992): 563–580.

This essay, part of a growing body of work on dildo theory, reviews the scholarly literature on female fetishism (itself a matter of intense debate among psychologists). At issue is whether lesbians, members of a gendered subculture seeking a distinct identity, should use phallic instrumentation to achieve pleasure. Heterosexual pornography has often depicted dildos as staples of lesbian sex, but increasingly porn videos made by and for lesbians incorporate dildos into fantasy scenarios as well.

Gill, Brendan. **"Blue Notes."** *Film Comment* 9, 1 (January–February 1973): 6–11.

Gill, a drama critic for the *New Yorker*, began to analyze hard-core films as soon as they appeared in theaters. In response to criticism that filmed sex wasn't "real," Gill discusses the dramatic elements of onscreen intercourse. He decides that some of the obvious gender inequities are the result of the camera's fondness for action: performed properly, cunnilingus remains largely invisible to an audience, whereas fellatio is both visible and kinetic. Gill thinks that visible male ejaculation is primarily a dramatic if somewhat artificial device for signaling closure to each act of sex and that theatricality is the real test of a given example's appeal.

Gittler, Ian. **"Porn Star: A Diary of Six Years in the Life."** *Rolling Stone* (14 October 1999): 65–66, 69–73.

This article is a disillusioned look at the industry by a photographer who spent some years documenting the "parallel universe" of pornography. As he photographed men and women performers for a book, Gittler discovered that the "terrain" of the industry is one of exploitation and emotional poverty, that the performers often have been warped by abuse as children, and that their lives are obsessive and sad.

Johnson, Eithne, and Eric Schaefer. **"Soft Core/Hard Core: Snuff as a Crisis in Meaning."** *Journal of Film and Video* 45, 2–3 (Summer–Fall 1993): 40–59.

The authors examine the evolution of snuff-film myth by treating it as a cultural progression that began with Laura Mulvey's essay, "Visual Pleasure and Narrative Cinema." In 1975, Mulvey claimed that the very way that Western audiences see films is male, and that male oppression of women thus rests on metaphysical ground. In 1976, a producer recut a movie called *The Slaughter* (1970), shot by Roberta and Michael Findlay in Argentina, retitled it *Snuff*, and hinted in the advertising that one of the actresses had actually been killed during the making of a sex scene in the film. Despite immediate charges of cheap hoax, feminist groups in major cities picketed theaters showing the incoherent footage. According to Johnson and Schaefer, *Snuff* and the myths it engendered (to the effect that deadly films routinely circulated underground) were important because they reinforced the feminist contention that the male gaze is lethal. The process reveals a good deal about the social construction of ideas and urban myths.

Levine, Judith. **"Perils of Desire."** *Village Voice Literary Supplement*, March 1985, pp. 1, 12–15.

In this review of Carol Vance's *Pleasure and Danger*, an anthology of essays that dispute claims of antiporn feminists, Levine agrees with the prosex essayists that antiporn radicals are often mistaken about pornography and callous toward sexual minorities, but she reminds her readers that sexuality does hold dangers for women. Levine believes that despite all its mindless abstractions, antiporn theory does try to uncover linkages between misogyny and antifemale erotica, and even its attempt to equate rape with consensual sexual intercourse has just enough validity to make it plausible to many women who have suffered in their sexual relationships. In short, like many extreme theories, antiporn helps to force reexamination of conventional ideas.

Patton, Cindy. **"Hegemony and Orgasm—Or the Instability of Heterosexual Pornography."** *Screen* 30, 1/2 (Winter/Spring 1989): 100–112.

Patton identifies different genres of pornography by distancing them from forms in which male climax is central. She discusses the difficulties of demonstrating female orgasm visually, for example, but her intent is to persuade critics to study the meanings of pornographic genres, especially in video form.

Rosenfield, Lawrence W. **"Politics and Pornography."** *Quarterly Journal of Speech* 59, 4 (December 1973): 413–422.

Rosenfield's essay asserts that pornography is a response to citizens' sense of political impotence. He believes that humans turn to pornography for gratification when corporate structures destroy older bonds of community, intimacy, and exchange. Pornography thus acts "as a surrogate for freedom." The more poorly a political system serves its citizens, the colder its institutions, the more ineffective its social structures, and the more inhuman its technologies, the greater the appeal of fantasized intimacy.

Schlosser, Eric. **"The Business of Pornography."** *U.S. News and World Report* (10 February 1997): 42–50.

In this comprehensive article, Schlosser estimates that Americans in 1996 spent $8 billion "on hard-core videos, peep shows, live sex acts, adult cable programming, sexual devices, computer porn, and sex magazines." About half the amount came from the 8,000 pornographic videocassettes produced each year (Schlosser quotes trade figures). This number does not include revenues from "women's porn" such as soap operas and romance novels, but does estimate dial-a-porn services at generating $750 million to $1 billion per year.

Slade, Joseph W. **"Violence in the Hard-Core Pornographic Film: A Historical Survey."** *Journal of Communication* 34, 3 (Summer 1984): 148–63.

This analysis of more than a thousand stag films indicates that violence in them is rare. Rape is not a common theme, and levels of any kind of violence in hard-core porn—even today—are far below those in legitimate, mainstream films. The author asks the question, Because stag films were secret and illegal, why did they not include aggression, since doing so would not have increased penalties? His answers: Sex itself is far more taboo than violence and more than satisfying in itself; second, Americans distinguish between sex and violence and decline to conflate them.

Sontag, Susan. **"The Pornographic Imagination."** *Partisan Review* 34, 2 (Spring 1967): 181–212; reprinted in her *Styles of Radical Will.* New York: Delta Books, 1969, pp. 35–73.

Sontag admires pornographic works such as *Story of O* and *The Image* because they embrace the danger that is inherent in all art. At its best, she writes, pornography can thus fulfill the mission of art by confronting chaos, delving deeply into the wellsprings of creativity, and unbridling the imagination. Characters in pornography surrender to the voluptuousness of desire, test the limits of will, and learn truths about themselves. Sontag believes that like other works in the literary tradition, superior pornographic novels do not represent triumphs of experience but sober assessments of the human place in the world; the only real issue is the quality of the work. Civilization arises in part, she believes, from the conflict between our consciousness and our sexuality, and pornography can help mediate.

Stein, Joel. **"Porn Goes Mainstream."** *Time* (7 September 1998): 54–55.

This article, as important for where it appears (in a magazine of general interest) as for what it says, points out that pornography has crossed over into popular acceptance. Stein quotes a slightly conservative $4 billion estimate (1998) for sex video sales and rentals; this and some of his other figures differ from those of other observers and attest to the difficulty of reliable reporting (see the "Economics of Pornography" section of Chapter 5). Stein notes that porn videos account for 14 percent of all rentals and almost 50 percent of the entire rental industry. He suggests that the porn industry replicates Hollywood patterns of monopoly: the

"Big Four" video companies (Metro, Vivid, VCA, Wicked) dominate distribution. Vivid markets its products through increasingly upscale outlets and mail-order, co-owns with Playboy the AdulTVision cable channel, and is working on virtual reality and interactive systems. Metro Video already trades on Wall Street on the NASDAQ exchange. Of more interest is Stein's chronicling of the popularity of porn stars who appear in advertisements and other "legitimate" venues.

Suggs, Donald. **"Hard Corps: A New Generation of People of Color Penetrates Porn's Mainstream."** *Village Voice,* 21 October 1997, pp. 39–40.

This is a report on trends by blacks, Hispanics, and Asians to make hard-core videos, on the assumption that pornography is a legitimate form of communication. Although such groups wish to profit financially, they also want to use pornography—which some think legitimizes desire—to advance the sexuality of minorities toward a central social consciousness.

Tierney, John. **"Porn, the Low-Slung Engine of Progress."** *New York Times,* 9 January 1994, sec. 2, pp. 1, 18.

Tierney advances the thesis that sexual representation helps to drive successive waves of media innovations, from cave drawings and Sumerian pictographs and classic canvasses and printing presses to VCRs and the Internet. For example, he cites statistics in support of the contention that pornography was crucial to the development of Beta and VHS VCRs, and that pornographic videos still account for more than 20 percent of the industry's rentals. He makes similar cases for other communication technologies, especially the Internet.

Periodicals

Adult Video News
AVN Publications, Inc.
6700 Valjean Avenue
Van Nuys, CA 91406
(800) 521-2474 or (310) 842-7450
Fax: (310) 842-7454

This trade journal is the source of virtually all the statistics on the pornographic video industry that are quoted by journalists. It is indispensable to an understanding of the industry, its conventions, its skirmishes with legislators and prosecutors (often broken down state by state), and, most significantly, its economics, the latter replete with graphs, charts, and reports. A typical issue will highlight a successful video rental business in a particular state. *AVN* routinely reviews videos, primarily for video merchandisers rather than consumers, and advises retailers on promotions, packaging, marketing strategies, specialty items, and dealing with the public. Originally oriented toward heterosexual markets, it now routinely provides information on gay and lesbian audiences and products. During any given year, *AVN* publishes several supplements and guides on changing tastes and trends.

Factsheet Five
Box 170099
San Francisco, CA 94117
E-mail: jerod23@well.sf.ca.us

Indispensable monthly information on "'zines," the magazines—often just stapled sheets—put out by Americans of all persuasions on a variety of subjects, many of them sexual.

Good Vibes Gazette
1210 Valencia Street
San Francisco, CA 94110

A quarterly published by the women's collective that runs the Good Vibrations Company, an enterprise that markets vibrators, videos, books, and magazines primarily for women.

Scholarly magazines with frequent articles on pornography include:
Archives of Sexual Behavior. New York, 1971–.
Journal of the History of Sexuality. Chicago, 1990–.
Journal of Sex Research. New York, 1965–.

Videotapes and Films

Dreamworlds II: Desire/Sex/Power in Rock Video
Length: 55 min.
Cost: $195/rental $125
Date: 1995

Distributor: Media Education Foundation
26 Center Street
Northampton, MA 01060
(800) 897-0089
Produced by Sut Jhally

This videotape excerpts images and video clips from MTV to expose the sexism in their portrayal of women. The video contends that the male gaze pervades music videos, which are aimed primarily at the sensibilities of adolescent males and which gratify male expectations by objectifying women. (Not recommended is the first version, *Dreamworlds* [1990], which is doctrinaire, pompous, and unintentionally funny.)

Lenny Bruce: Swear to Tell the Truth
Length: 80 min.
Cost: not yet released in video
Date: 1998
Distributor: Home Box Office Documentary Films
1100 Avenue of the Americas
New York, NY 10036
(212) 512-1000
Produced and directed by Robert B. Weide (Whyaduck Films)

This is a documentary study of the destruction of comedian Lenny Bruce by police and censors intent on prosecuting him for obscenity. It is a tale of the failure of the American judicial system to protect free speech.

Not a Love Story
Length: 69 min.
Cost: $295/rental $80
Date: 1982
Distributor: National Film Board of Canada Library
22-D Hollywood Avenue
Ho-Ho-Kus, NJ 07423
(800) 542-2184
Directed by Bonnie Sherr Klein

This film follows a stripper as she discusses her craft with various antiporn feminists. The film narrows the hunt for sources of gender inequity to pornographers such as Suze Randall, the reigning female pinup photographer; entrepreneurs in the sex industries who exploit women; and those who justify sexual expression on the grounds of free speech or redress of sexual ignorance. Few films on the subject have engendered so much debate.

Patently Offensive: Porn under Siege
Length: 58 min.
Cost: $350/rental $125
Date: 1992
Distributor: Filmmakers Library
               124 East 40th St.
               New York, NY 10016
               (212) 808-4980
Produced by Harriet Koskoff

This videotape interviews Barry Lynn, P. E. Dietz, A. Nichols Groth, Ralph Ginzburg, Carole Vance, Al Goldstein, Frederick Schauer, Andrea Dworkin, and representatives of Women Against Pornography, the National Organization for Women, and the National Christian Association for comment on legal, economic, social, and moral issues. Discussion ranges over individual rights, censorship, feminist theory, artistic freedom, family values, and the role of pornography in redefining the image culture of America.

Ratings, Morals, and Sex on TV
Length: 58 min.
Cost: $29
Date: 1998
Distributor: Showtime Video
               1813 Westchester Ave.
               Bronx, NY 10472
               (718) 931-0817

Documentary on conflicts over control of the nation's airwaves featuring interviews with a variety of television producers, critics, and advocates and opponents of candor. Included are Tim Doyle, producer of *Ellen;* Stuart Elliott, advertising columnist for the *New York Times;* Ted Harbert, former president of ABC Entertainment; Marta Kauffman, cocreator of *Friends;* David Milch, executive producer of *NYPD Blue;* Robert Peters, president of Morality in Media; and Frank Rich, op-ed columnist for the *New York Times.*

Sex: The Annabel Chong Story
Length: 86 min.

Cost: not yet released on video
Date: 1998
Distributor: will be available on video in 2001 from
www.reel.com
Directed by Gough Lewis; A Coffee House Film
Production/Omni International/Greycat Releasing

This documentary scrutinizes the life and career of porn starlet Annabel Chong (real name Grace Quek), a University of Southern California student from Singapore. After achieving instant notoriety because of her publicized preference for anal sex, Chong attempted to become the world's most famous performer by engaging in videotaped intercourse with 251 men in ten hours in January 1995. Her fame lasted for only a few months, when Jasmine St. Clair broke Chong's record. (The video made of Chong's event remains the best-selling porn cassette of all time.) Although Chong considers herself a crusader for women's rights to sexual fulfillment and justifies her behavior in terms of romantic if self-destructive experience ("At least I've lived," she says, and claims to be happy "in the heart of Armageddon"), she has encountered exploitation by filmmakers, suffered through the anxieties of AIDS tests, and been shamed by her family and friends in Singapore.

Sphinxes without Secrets: Women Performance Artists Speak Out

Length: 90 min.
Cost: $95
Date: 1991
Distributor: San Francisco Art Commission
25 Van Ness Avenue
San Francisco, CA 94102
(415) 252-2590
Directed by Maria Beatty

Lenora Champagne, Ellie Covan, Diane Torr, Robbie McCauley, Arlene Raven, Rachel Rosenthal, Martha Wilson, Carolee Schneeman, Laurie Anderson, Holly Hughes, Diamanda Galas, and many others voice their determination to undermine cultural phobias about women's bodies; to combat racism, sexism, and homophobia; to break the male gaze by returning control of women's bodies to themselves; and to subvert convention generally. Although performance art may be explicit, say the artists, it does not cater to erotic fantasies. As Hughes puts it, such performances permit women to "excavate themselves."

The Story of X: 100 Years of Adult Film and Its Stars
Length: 58 min.
Cost: $19.99
Date: 1998
Distributor: Playboy
                 P.O. Box 809
                 Itasca, IL 60143-0809
                 (800) 423-9494
Produced by Playboy Entertainment/Calliope Films

This videotape offers discreet clips from historically important films. The documentary approach highlights commentary from producers, historians, and critics such as David Friedman, Andrea Dworkin, Donald Wildmon, and Russ Meyer. Discussions cover the evolution of candor, affronts to taste, the role of women, and issues of free speech.

Strippers: The Naked Stages
Length: 58 min.
Cost: not yet released on video
Date: 1998
Distributor: Home Box Office Documentary Films
                 1100 Avenue of the Americas
                 New York, NY 10036
                 (212) 512-1000
Produced by Anthony Radziwill

This documentary follows two novice dancers as one flourishes and the other leaves the profession. Strippers and club owners discuss working conditions, the longevity of performers, and the marketplace. More than 2,500 men's clubs now employ more than 250,000 women as strippers. The producers point out that "good" strippers—those skilled at eye contact and lap dancing—can make thousands of dollars a night, but that the costs in emotions, status, and short careers can be brutal.

Where the Heart Roams
Length: 87 min.
Cost: $39.95
Date: 1991
Distributor: New Video Group
                 126 5th Avenue, 15th Floor
                 New York, NY 10011
                 (212) 206-8600
Directed by George Csicsery

This Point of View documentary from PBS focuses on the journey of the "Love Train" taking romance authors and fans from Los Angeles to New York for an awards ceremony. Barbara Cartland, author of 360-plus romances, laments on camera that the genre she helped invent is now clearly pornographic, and another writer admits that the intent in such fiction is to "turn men into sex objects," a goal that has been accelerated by a women's movement that fosters such fantasies. Others detail the important aspects of male characters in romances: strong but sensitive, courageous but intelligent, dangerous but rich, good-looking and stylish but not "sweet" or "vulnerable." Various authors tell the filmmaker that women's pornography, like their own writings, pays close attention to feeling and setting.

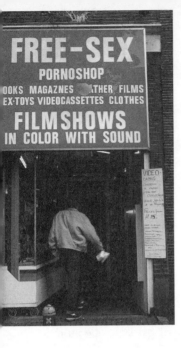

Glossary

Although jurists and social scientists have invented some terms in order to discuss pornography, other terms come from folklore and popular culture. Some are more colorful than precise.

adult arcade A store that sells pornographic books, photos, magazines, and appliances; it may provide private booths in which patrons can watch pornographic movies or live performers.

advisory labels Warnings of explicit lyrics affixed to record, disc, and cassette jackets. The stickers alert consumers (some read "Parental Advisory") to content that may include references to sexuality, alcohol, racism, violence, drugs, and Satanism.

antidisplay ordinances Statutes by which municipalities can prohibit the display of graphic material visible to passersby in public spaces.

antiporn feminists Term adopted by some feminists to describe those who believe that sex itself is the fountainhead of inequity between men and women and that sexual expression perpetuates discrimination because it depicts or encourages intercourse. It is of course possible to be an antiporn feminist without being antisex.

blasphemy Speaking impiously of a supreme being or sacred things, or holding religion up to ridicule or denigration. Early American definitions of obscenity often explicitly referred to blasphemy, a concept that survives in prohibitions against "profane" speech.

box cover   The cardboard jacket of a pornographic videotape. The text and pictures describe the plot and action of the tape, often inventing language for that purpose.

burlesque   Vaudeville theater originally devoted to comedy, song, and novelty acts but which added striptease to attract customers drawn away by movies.

catharsis theory   The theory that reading or watching sexual materials actually discharges tension—thus diminishing aggressive responses—by providing relief through masturbation to those inclined to violence. The theory is not popular among researchers because no one can figure out a way to test it.

censorship societies   Groups that attained quasilegal status because they avoided ostensible religious ties. Boston's New England Watch and Ward Society, New York's Society for the Suppression of Vice, Chicago's Illinois Vigilance League, and Washington's International Reform Federation were the largest.

chat rooms   Electronic on-line "sites" at which people can discuss topics of mutual interests; some of these are devoted to sexual subjects.

child pornography   Sexual representations involving children. Illegal by federal and state statute and relentlessly prosecuted, child pornography is quite distinct from sexual expression by and for adults. The latest (1995) ruling, *United States v. Knox*, 977 F.2d 815 (3d Cir.), criminalizes even digitally constructed images of fully clothed children if they can be said to sexually appeal to someone.

commodification   The practice of commercializing sex through representations to be bought and sold. As used by some critics, the term has a Marxist connotation, but other media theorists note that all ideas and images are commodified in an information economy.

community standards   A term central to tests for obscenity. The Supreme Court's decision in *Miller v. California* (1973) speaks of local rather than national standards, but jurists still argue over whether "community" refers to a small town, a state, or a region. Critics charge that community standards are impossible to determine quantitatively or qualitatively no matter what the size of the population.

Comstock Codes   1873 revisions to Title 18 of the U.S. Code. The so-called Comstock Codes include Section 1461, which prohibited materials dealing not simply with lewd expression or articles and devices used for immoral purposes but also birth control articles "advertised or described in a manner calculated to lead another to use or apply it for preventing conception or producing abortion, or for any indecent or immoral use"; Section 1462, which prohibited the importation of obscene matter and its interstate transportation; and Section 1463, which was aimed at advertising, especially obscene language on "wrappers deposited for mailing." Later, Section 1464 would be added to cover indecent radio communication.

cybersex Term applied to digitalized sexual representations ranging from E-mail discussions to erotic computer programs and Internet sex sites.

Deep Throat Title of the 1972 pornographic film directed by Gerard Damiano (who borrowed $25,000 from the mob to shoot it) that became so popular (the appeal was called "porn chic") that it opened the way to public showings of other hard-core features. *Deep Throat* starred Linda Lovelace, who suppressed her gag reflex in order to orally engulf a penis. The term thus also applies to her fellatio technique, now standard throughout the heterosexual and gay porn industries.

desensitization Theory that exposure to pornography will render a person less concerned with deviant or antisocial behavior. Some studies indicate that males watching films that justify male characters' rape of women characters on the grounds that the latter "really want it" become desensitized to the violence inherent in rape, at least for the short term. Some researchers use the term "disinhibited" instead.

deviance Behavior that departs from the norm. Some opponents of pornography believe that sexual materials encourage deviance. Psychiatrists recognize only specific forms of behavior as deviant (see DSM IV), and these may differ from public perceptions.

dial-a-porn Prerecorded or interactive sexual messages marketed by telephone since the late 1970s. "Watts-line" (prefix 900) dial-a-porn services generate substantial traffic and income from callers interested in specific fetishes or acts.

dildo theories Debate as to whether dildos, given their obvious phallic symbolism, are appropriate tools of satisfaction for politically aware women. Some believe that they are acceptable if shaped differently (like a dolphin, say), while others argue that only fingers or tongues should be used.

effects research Study of the consequences of exposure to sexual materials. Most studies of effects are quantitative and require manipulation of subjects in controlled laboratory experiments.

ejaculation The "money shot" or "cum shot" that brings a sexual encounter to dramatic closure in hard-core films, when the male visibly ejaculates semen. The obvious male bias offends some women, who point out that visible signs of female pleasure are mostly absent. In the interests of gender equity, some women performers have trained themselves to ejaculate fluids, but the movement has not caught on in the industry.

electronic filters Blocking technologies that can screen out objectionable material from electronic media. V-chips block television programming with adult ratings; net filters (SurfWatch, Surf Nanny) prevent children from accessing explicit materials on Web sites; and blocking circuits provided by telephone companies prevent minors from using dial-a-porn services.

erotic Term used to refer to sexual representation, connoting elegance and an upper-class quality that makes it socially acceptable. The term implies that pornographic (i.e., lower-class or vulgar) elements have been purged or sanitized, perhaps by emphasizing affection, romance, or spirituality through polite language or discreet images instead of concentrating on the physical aspects of sex rendered in offensive words and graphic pictures. Erotic materials have high deniability; one can claim that he or she is not aroused by them.

ethnographic studies Ethnographers study sexual behavior and communication directly as it takes place in different contexts and subcultures. Scholars take jobs in adult bookstores or pornographic theaters, for example, in order to observe and interpret the experience of patrons.

exploitation films An enormous genre of soft-core pornographic movies that originated in white slavery exposés and pseudomedical "documentaries" on marriage techniques and venereal disease in the early 1900s. Modern exploitation films are sometimes broken out into subcategories such as women-in-gangs, women-in-prison, topless adventure, biker chick, juvenile delinquent, beach party, drug saga, and so on, all of which provide occasions for sensationalism, violence, and nudity.

family values Term for opposition to depictions of sex, which are assumed to be destructive to properly constituted families.

fantasy The chief content of pornography and also an essential component of sexual arousal for humans of any gender. According to some psychologists, fantasy "enables" sexuality by creating a psychic setting for arousal.

fetish For psychiatrists, a nonliving object (e.g., female undergarments) that triggers sexual fantasies, urges, or behaviors. Freud believed that only males were subject to fetishes, which he construed as penis substitutes, but some modern feminists insist that fetishes affect women too. For most Americans, a fetish refers simply to a well-developed sexual preference or taste, as for large breasts, narrow male buttocks, leather garments, blonde hair, and so on.

Forty Thieves A group of pre–World War II exploitation film producers who shot grubby films on miscegenation, birth control, unwed mothers, venereal disease, and other taboo subjects for gullible audiences.

forum shopping Practice of Justice Department prosecutors who "shop" around for a court in a conservative area. They then entice dealers to mail or E-mail materials to someone in the community so that they can indict the dealer, impanel a jury that will find the materials obscene, and obtain convictions of expressions that are legal elsewhere in the country.

gender There is debate about whether gender is derived from nature or nurture. According to some scholars and laypersons, gender is mutable; sexuality lies between the legs, gender between the ears. Others claim that orientation toward males or females as sexual partners is at least partly fixed by genetic or biological programming.

Gresham's Law Economic theory advanced by financier Sir Thomas Gresham (1519?–1579) that bad coinage drives out good; as applied to culture, the belief that vulgarity will cheapen all other expression.

hard-core pornography Representations that explicitly illustrate sex by depicting penetration or genital contact.

hate speech Expression that degrades or denigrates someone. Though usually the term refers to verbal hostility directed against minorities, antiporn feminists maintain that pornography, which they define as the discourse of males, is a form of hate speech directed at women.

indecency A term applied principally to expression on radio and television, which courts have held are more invasive of the home than other media. The closest the Federal Communications Commission has come to defining indecency is to say that although such material may not be obscene or pornographic, it depicts "sexual or excretory activities or organs" in terms that "are patently offensive as measured by contemporary community standards for the broadcast medium."

libel Written or pictorial messages that cause injury by unjustly holding a private person (rather than one in public life) up to ridicule or damaging his or her character. Libel laws have evolved over centuries to balance the rights of individuals against the rights of the press and public. Early conceptions of obscenity defined it as a species of libel.

loop A strip of hard-core 8-millimeter film with its ends joined so that it runs continuously, usually found in a coin-operated projector booth for private viewing.

male gaze A concept originally associated with visual theorist Laura Mulvey, it asserts that a masculine way of seeing is so pervasive that humans cannot visualize reality in any other way. The male gaze thus inevitably and forever subordinates women.

marginal On the edge; sexual expression is often called marginal to indicate its distance from mainstream expression. Over time, marginal expression can move to the center of a culture's consciousness.

masturbation Every day millions of Americans masturbate, an activity that depends on the conversion of sexual fantasy into kinetic energy.

How many of these fantasies are shaped or triggered by pornographic materials no one knows, but such a figure would doubtless be high.

National Endowment for the Arts   Government agency originally created to fund public art, more recently a political battlefield commanded by conservatives who wish to deny the agency's much-reduced funds to artists who refuse to pledge not to create indecent works.

objectification   What pornography is alleged to do to humans. All representations objectify humans, i.e., reduce them to particular qualities or attributes, but sexual representations are less sanctioned than others.

obscenity   To be legally obscene, a representation, taken as a whole, (1) has to include material that depicts or details in an obviously offensive way acts that a state legislature has defined as objectionable; (2) has to appeal to the prurient interest (a lustful fascination with the lewdly disgusting) of an average citizen, applying contemporary community standards; and (3) has to lack serious artistic, literary, political, or scientific merit.

peep-show cubicle   Arcade fixture invented by Reuben Sturman in the 1970s. Patrons enter the booth, drop a quarter in a slot, and watch either a pornographic movie or a person disrobing.

penile plethysmograph   A volumetric device for detecting erections, originally designed by Karl Freund in order to keep homosexuals out of the Czech army. If the strain-gauge plethysmograph (basically an elastic ring fitted around the penis and electronically attached to a recorder) sensed an erection when the inductee was shown homosexual porn, he was rejected. The plethysmograph has become a favorite tool of the porn researcher, who wires subjects to test arousal as they read books, look at photos, or watch movies.

performance art   A kinetic, dramatic, experimental, and increasingly feminist form of expression that sometimes makes use of explicit representation to "deconstruct" attitudes toward gender, nudity, or morality. According to some observers, sex industries are more important sources of funding for performance art than the National Endowment for the Arts because the former provide a living for serious artists. Like formally trained artists, strippers and actresses in pornographic films sometimes take up performance art to validate their experiences and to express a female sexuality struggling against male conventions.

photo sets   Suites of small photographs depicting sexual scenes, sometimes on a single theme or sexual act, circulated in loose or stapled form so that they can fit in a pocket and be passed secretly from hand to hand.

physique photos   Pictures of nude or nearly nude males aimed at homosexual viewers.

pinup   Pinup can refer to photographs, as in the centerfolds that can be taken from magazines to affix to walls, but historically has meant a "cheesecake" drawing or painting of a woman in suggestive pose. Major artists included Alberto Vargas, Rolf Armstrong, Billy DeVorss, Gil Elvgren, Zöe Mozert, Harry Aikman, Earl MacPherson, Peter Driben, Fritz Willis, and Bill Randall. Their hyperbolic images, which parodied rather than set standards of feminine pulchritude and sensuality, have been reproduced for calendars, cigarette lighters, playing cards, aircraft fuselages, and so on.

pornography   A term defined largely by legal efforts to regulate sexual expression. Unlike obscenity, pornography is legal in America, but the difference between pornography and obscenity lies largely in the mind of the beholder. The term was invented in the mid-nineteenth century, and etymologically means "writing about prostitutes." Antiporn feminists tried to redefine it in the 1970s as the discriminatory discourse of males, and conservatives also invest the word with unpleasant connotations.

pornography commissions   There have been two major American commissions, the President's Commission on Obscenity and Pornography (1970) and the Attorney General's Commission on Pornography (1986), also known as the Meese Commission. The first recommended that pornography for adults be decriminalized; the second recommended that visual and electronic forms of sexual expression be recriminalized.

pressure groups   Organizations devoted to forcing media to censor expression, usually by boycotting advertisers who sponsor messages or programs the organizations do not like. The organizations (to be distinguished from censorship societies) are often religious in nature, ranging from the Catholic Legion of Decency to the Protestant American Family Association.

prior restraint   In obscenity law, a legal term indicating that a form of expression has been prohibited before it has been judicially determined to be obscene.

prurience   Lustful or lascivious thoughts, with undertones of disgust, shame, and degradation. The term has long been part of the definition of obscenity precisely because it lacks precision.

pulp fiction   Early term for stories that seemed sensational and salacious, usually printed on cheap pulp paper.

qualitative research   Humanistic research that uses theoretical models to focus on the content, cultural context, and presumed effects of pornography.

quantitative research   Social-scientific research that uses laboratory experiments and mathematical methods to test assumptions about pornography and its effects.

research models   The cluster of theoretical assumptions that determines the direction of research into pornography. Examples are the ther-

316 Glossary

apeutic/educational model (pornography's effects are beneficial and didactic); the psychoanalytic model (pornography encapsulates fantasies representing childhood conflicts); the Marxist model (pornography is a tool of the ruling class for subordinating workers); the feminist model (pornography represents and causes male oppression of women); and the sociological model (pornography is an agent of social change).

RICO legislation   RICO stands for Racketeer Influenced and Corrupt Organizations statute (1970); it is a legal tactic used to seize all of a defendant's assets even if only a small fraction of his or her products are judged obscene.

sadomasochism (S/M or S & M)   A subcategory of pornography that cuts across gender divisions, sadomasochism involves the derivation of pleasure from the infliction of pain—mental or physical—on oneself or others. Critics charge that sadomasochistic representations merely exploit cruelty and violence and that people who enjoy them are psychologically flawed. Adherents insist that such representations use fetishistic scenarios to dramatize and demystify personal and social power relationships and that the ritualistic elements replicate religious (and even specifically Christian) patterns of degradation and exaltation.

safe harbors   Late-evening broadcast hours during which adults can see and hear messages inappropriate for children. A federal court ruled in 1991 that radio and television indecency could be forbidden between 6 A.M. and 10 P.M. but that a 24-hour prohibition is unconstitutional because it denies adults access to mature entertainment or information.

samizdat   Russian word for handwritten or typewritten manuscripts that can be secretly passed from hand to hand rather than being published. Early pornographic fiction circulated in this form in the United States.

Section 2257   A legal provision to the United States Code that producers of photographic, motion picture, and video materials with sexual content are required to keep records of the ages of all performers on file at a specific location and in charge of a specific individual, and that the records be available for inspection.

Seven Dirty Words   The popular name of the Pacifica radio case (1973) in which George Carlin (in a monologue called "Seven Words You Can't Say on Television") discussed on air the reasons that seven dirty words should be regarded as obscene. The program was judged indecent, and WBAI, the broadcaster, was sanctioned by the FCC.

sexist   Expression biased on the basis of assumptions about gender; not to be equated or confused with sexuality.

sexology   The study of human sexuality, a field that draws on many disciplines in the sciences and the humanities.

sexual appliances   (a.k.a. sex toys) Devices or compounds to enhance pleasure, some (e.g., dildos) of which are designed as representations of body parts. Some states (e.g., Georgia) prohibit such appliances as obscene.

sexual revolution   The alleged liberalization of attitudes toward sex that took place in America during the 1960s and 1970s, especially among the youthful counterculture.

sexual scripts   Carefully wrought fantasies that individuals build from memories, experiences, traumas, myths, and beliefs. Certain pornographic narratives or sequences of images may appeal because they seem to follow the same scripts.

shock jock   Term originally applied to radio disk jockeys and announcers who pushed the limits of sexual candor on the air; now applied to television program hosts (e.g., Howard Stern) as well.

slash/zines, especially "Kirk/Spock" or K/S zines   A category of small magazines, usually pages stapled together, produced almost exclusively by and for women, who extract the sexual meanings and stimulation they want from programs and stories that are otherwise aimed at men. These are anthologies of fan-authored and fan-drawn sexual stories about the captain and first officer of the starship *Enterprise*. They range from soft- to hard-core narratives; some estimates set their number in the tens of thousands. Other zines in this category eroticize primetime programming and movies for different genders.

snuff films   Alleged films in which people are killed during sexual intercourse. This urban myth was created by the publicity surrounding a 1976 mainstream movie entitled *Snuff*, a scruffy effort that was effectively merchandised by its producer and inadvertently promoted by feminist protesters. Extensive searches by the FBI and other agencies have never turned up an authentic snuff film.

soap operas   Long-running afternoon television series (named for sponsorship by soap companies) that some broadcasters call "pornography for women," though males have always constituted part of the audience. The programs' seamy, sentimental plots dramatize sexual transgression and pornographic themes but seem to be losing popularity because of greater numbers of women entering the workforce and competition from "real-life" soap operas such as presidential scandals and tabloid television shows. Soap-operas are a "crossover" genre; hard-core movie actors have found new careers on afternoon TV.

social construction   A qualitative theory that reality is "constructed" by social, political, and economic forces as they act on language and thought to make humans accept certain assumptions. Pornographic materials as sites of social construction can provide information about how notions of beauty, gender, and other attributes are shaped. So can pornography research, which is constructed out of particular assumptions about sexuality and gender.

sociobiology   A discipline premised on the conviction that biology and genetic programming manifest themselves in human behavior, sexual and otherwise. Sociobiologists generally think that pornography mimics sexual stimulation found in nature. A pornographic video, for example, highlights female sexual cues—large breasts, say, or well-developed pelvises—associated with ease of child-bearing and therefore attractive to males biologically driven to reproduce; romance novels directed at women emphasize the wealth, good looks, and aggression mixed with tenderness that females associate with alpha males capable of protecting them and their offspring. Some sociobiologists now prefer the term *evolutionary psychologists.*

sodomy   An omnibus legal term that indicates a "crime against nature." Depending on the specific state, sodomy in obscenity statutes may refer to homosexual intercourse, oral sex, or mutual masturbation, but also to heterosexual anal intercourse, oral sex, penetration by objects, or even bestiality.

soft-core pornography   Representations in which sex is merely alluded to or, at most, simulated. Because it is so often used to symbolize actual sex, violence is far more likely to be associated with soft-core than with hard-core genres that boldly depict intercourse.

stag films (a.k.a. blue movies)   Hardcore sexual movies clandestinely made and circulated from about 1905 to 1968, when they became quasi-legal. Shown at the all-male gatherings that gave them their name, stag films were silent, black and white, deliberately crude shorts about twelve minutes in length. They depicted explicit intercourse in plots drawn mostly from folklore.

statistical correlations   Numerical comparisons of the circulation of pornographic materials and rates of sexual crime in specific areas. Some studies have indicated that an increase in one is matched by an increase in the other; other studies discount this relationship.

striptease   Sometimes called "pornography set to music." Stripteasers include topless dancers, lap dancers, and showgirls who dance naked for men, men who dance naked for women, men who dance naked for gay men, and women who dance naked for lesbian audiences in more than 2,500 clubs in the United States.

taboo   Polynesian word that originally referred to menstruation. When used in reference to pornography, as in "breaking a taboo," the word indicates that representation has depicted some prohibited sexual practice.

Tijuana bibles   Term first applied to manuscripts of sexual stories stapled together and distributed clandestinely but now associated with explicitly drawn eight-page comics popular from the 1920s to the 1940s.

These usually debunked celebrities by depicting them in sexual acts. According to some critics, the eight-page comic is the only original American pornographic form.

vaginal photoplethysmograph Feminine version of the plethysmograph for recording sexual arousal while subjects are exposed to sexual representations. The tampon-shaped photoplethysmograph is inserted into a subject's vagina to measure secretions and to photograph changes in tissue color and erectility.

V-chip Mandated under Section 551 of the Communications Act of 1996; see electronic filters.

virtual sex The ultimate representation, a still-being-invented technology that will simulate actual sex. Participants wire parts of their bodies in order to experience the sensations of intercourse through computer programming or remote electronic contact.

volunteer bias Skewing that may result when subjects volunteer for experiments to determine the effects of pornography. Evidence suggests that the attitudes, experience, and values of volunteers differ from those of other experimental populations.

women's romances A pornographic print genre aimed primarily at women. Categories of romances range from soft- to hard-core novels, and some (e.g., Regency Romances) focus on particular periods, but all foreground fantasies involving stereotypically masculine sex objects feminized by love. Romances are a $1-billion-a-year industry in the United States.

X-rated A label indicating strong sexual content. By 1990, the Motion Picture Association of America (MPAA) was forced to replace the "X" rating with "NC-17" (No Children; no one under 17) because it had failed to trademark the X, which was then appropriated by adult movie makers to signify strong content in their ads. The intent of the NC-17 designation was to permit serious treatment of sexuality without burdening a film with the onus of an X, since many newspapers would not carry advertising for movies bearing the older label. Pornography producers still use the term and sometimes multiply the number of Xs.

zoning ordinances Statutes by which municipalities can segregate adult businesses from those who find them inappropriate to specific areas. Such ordinances prohibit adult businesses in close proximity to residences, schools, and churches, provided that such enterprises are permitted in spaces whose location does not place undue hardship on those who would like to travel to them.

Index

Acconi, Vito: *Seedbed* and, 155
Acker, Kathy, 72, 274
Adam & Eve, 237
Adams, John, 288
Adler, Polly, 105
Adlow, Elijah, 28, 148–49
Adult Entertainment District, 155
Adult Film Association, 103
Adult Video Association, 244
Adult Video News (AVN), 236, 244, 301–2
AdulTVision, 236, 237, 301
Adventures of Anna P., or The Belle of New York, 67–68
Adventures of Lucinda Hartley, The, 66
Adventures of Sweet Gwendolyn, The, 77
Advertising, 292; middle-class, 14
African Americans: popular culture and, 53; redress for, 18; romances and, 72–73; stereotypes about, 6–7, 76
Afternoon of a Faun (Stravinsky), satirization of, 15
Aggression: eroticism and, 265; pornography and, 87; representations of, 24–25
Aggressive Gals, 63
Aguerra, Susan, 76
AIDS, 109; impact of, 88–89; information on, 162; pornography and, 288
Aikman, Harry, 77
Aladdin, 70
Aldrich, Ann, 71
Alexandar, Tara, 157

Alexander v. United States (1993), 163, 226–27
Alien and Sedition Acts (1798), 56, 142
All in the Family, 111, 154
Allen, Woody: on sex, 30
Ally McBeal, 115
Alpert, Merry, 99
Alternative lifestyles, 113, 268
Amateur Action Bulletin Board, 117, 163
American Booksellers Association, 160
American Booksellers Association, Inc., v. William H. Hudnut III, Mayor, City of Indianapolis (1985), 222–23
American Booksellers Foundation for Free Expression, 244
American Booksellers, Inc., v. Commonwealth of Virginia (1986), 223–24
American Civil Liberties Union (ACLU), 28, 160, 245; censorship movements and, 30
American Civil Liberties Union v. Janet Reno, Attorney General of the United States (1996), 227–28
American Council of the Blind, 160
American Erotica, 62
American Encyclopedia of Sex (Niemoller), 51
American Family Association, Inc. (AFA), 245

321

International Reform Federation, 27

Internet, 163, 301; children and, 40; indecency on, 164; pornography and, 115–19, 238–29; restrictions on, 118; sex sites on, 117, 164, 165; speech issues on, 35; videostreaming on, 18. *See also* Web sites

Internet Entertainment Group (IEG), 116; profits for, 239

interView, Warhol and, 62

Irigaray, Luce: on gender/language, 52

Ivy League Stripper (Mattson), 89

Jackson, Andrew, 56

Jackson v. United States (1992), 162

Jacobellis v. Ohio (1964), 151, 213

Jacobson v. United States (1991), 226

James, Henry, 75, 281

Jameson, Jenna, 108, 237

Jammer, Cal: suicide of, 297

"Jane of the Bouncing Bottom" (Sewall), 70

Janet Reno v. ACLU (1997), 228

Jazz Age, 55, 58, 84

Jazza-Ka-Jazza, 59

Jefferson, Thomas, 56, 288

Jeffries, B. G., 68

Jenkins v. Georgia (1974), 156, 218–19

Jenteal, 237, 238

Jerome, Ivan: arrest of, 38

Jerry Springer Show, 2, 112

"Jim," 77

Joffrey Ballet, 85

John Baumgarth Company, pinup calendar by, 94

Johnson, Lyndon, 152

Johnson, Virginia E., 152

Jokes: circulation of, 54; dirty, 53, 54. *See also* Sexual humor

Jong, Erica, 72, 265

Joseph Burnstyn, Inc., v. Wilson, Commissioner of Education of New York (1952), 149, 208–9

Journal of Sex Research, 302

Journal of the History of Sexuality, 302

Joy, Bill: on GNR, 118–19

Joyce, James, 33, 59, 70, 148, 266; Random House and, 71

Judson Dance Troupe, 84–85

Juggs, 63

Jurgen (Cabell), 69

Juvenile delinquency, moral panic over, 76

JVC, VHS and, 157

Kahane, Jack: Obelisk Press and, 71

Kaish, Morton, 79

Kaminer, Wendy, 276

Kane, Sharon, 287

Kaprow, Allan, 90

Keating, Charles H., Jr., 27, 161

Kefauver Commission, 94, 98; moral panic and, 29, 76

Kefauver, Estes, 150

Kelley, John, 149

Kelley, Tom: shots by, 94

Kellogg, John Harvey, 68

Kelly, Valerie, 64

Kendrick, Walter: on pornography, 5

Kennedy, John F., 85

Kennedy, Monica, 86

Kennedy School of Political Science, 118

Kerouac, Jack, 71

Keyhole Detective Cases, 59

Khomeni, Ayatollah, 34

Kids (Clark), 99

King, Alexander, 59, 75

Kingsley Int'l Pictures Corp. v. Regents of the University of the State of New York (1959), 211

Kinnard, Rupert, 78

Kinsey, Alfred, 149

Kinsey Institute, 32, 92, 252–53, 275, 291; photo archive of, 98

Kirk, Captain: oral sex with, 294; Spock and, 65

Kirk/Spock, 65, 317

Kiss, 62

Kiss Me Deadly (Spillane), 71

Kitsch, 73, 281–82

Klaw, Irving, 63, 98, 150, 274; biographical sketch of, 186–88; costumes by, 286; photographs by, 77, 94

J oseph W. Slade (Ph.D., New York University, 1971), Professor of Telecommunications at Ohio University, has lectured at universities or advised communication agencies in Russia, Estonia, Latvia, Lithuania, Thailand, Korea, and Fiji. In 1986–1987, he was Bicentennial Professor of American Studies at the University of Helsinki, Finland. He has held several fellowships, including the National Endowment for the Humanities Institute for Humanities and Technology at the University of Chicago (1976–1977). The author of several dozen articles and essays on literature, film, technology, and culture, Slade has coedited (with Judith Yaross Lee) *Beyond the Two Cultures: Essays on Science, Technology, and Literature* and written *Thomas Lake Harris and the Brotherhood of the New Life; Thomas Pynchon;* and *Pornography and Sexual Representation: A Reference Guide.* He is currently writing a book on the Maxim family of inventors.